Welcome

English Heritage is proud to look after the national collection of historic sites and monuments. Every year we invest millions of pounds in conservation and improvements and this year will be no exception. In order to do this we increasingly rely on the loyalty and generosity of our members and of the public at large. So my first duty is to thank everyone who supported us over the last year either by membership or by simply visiting one of our sites. We hope to grow the number of people who support English Heritage in the important work we do to pass on these historic places for future generations. Please encourage your friends to join us and benefit from a full year of exploration and discovery at some of the most historic places in the country.

There is certainly much to discover in 2011. Summer sees the opening of further wartime exhibitions at Dover Castle, and at Witley Court, in Worcestershire, the restoration moves into another phase with the East Parterre returned to its original layout. I also hope you will visit Wrest Park, in Bedfordshire, where, after a £3.8m makeover, it will once more take its place as one of the great eighteenth century landscapes.

I am confident that this year's handbook will be an inspiration and help you and your family appreciate the wider work of English Heritage. Thank you again for your support.

SIMON THURLEY

Chief Executive of English Heritage

2011 will be a wonderful year of exploration and discovery for our members.

© Hugo Burnand

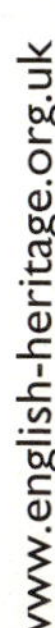

How to use this book

Opening Times

All dates are listed in chronological order, and are valid from

1 Apr 2011.

All information is correct at the time of going to press. Due to unforeseen circumstances, some opening times may change. Please call Customer Services or check our website before you travel to any of our properties.

At some of our properties, visitors cannot be admitted less than one hour before closing time. Please call in advance to confirm individual policies.

Where properties have a **keykeeper**, please contact them before setting off. For those open at **'any reasonable time'**, please visit during daylight hours for safety reasons and to avoid causing a disturbance.

Properties showing this symbol may be closed at certain times for private events, please call in advance to check.

Some of our smaller staffed properties may close between 1pm and 2pm. Please call Customer Services for more information.

This handbook gives details of all English Heritage properties and other properties to which English Heritage members receive free or discounted entry.

Property entries are colour-coded by region (see map opposite for breakdown), and are listed alphabetically within these regions.

Website details are on all property pages, should you prefer to look electronically for property details. **We recommend that you check www.english-heritage.org.uk before you visit for the latest events information and last-minute property updates.**

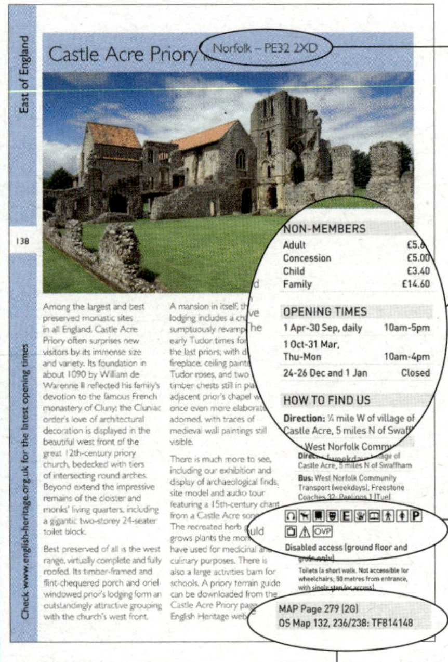

East of England

Castle Acre Priory

Norfolk – PE32 2XD

138

Among the largest and best preserved monastic sites in all England, Castle Acre Priory often surprises new visitors by its immense size and variety. Its foundation in about 1090 by William de Warenne II reflected his family's devotion to the famous French monastery of Cluny: the Cluniac order's love of architectural decoration is displayed in the beautiful west front of the great 12th-century priory church, bedecked with tiers of intersecting round arches. Beyond extend the impressive remains of the cloister and monks' living quarters, including a gigantic two-storey 24-seater toilet block.

Best preserved of all is the west range, virtually complete and fully roofed. Its timber-framed and flint-chequered porch and oriel-windowed prior's lodging form an outstandingly attractive grouping with the church's west front.

A mansion in itself, th... lodging includes a ch... sumptuously revamp... early Tudor times fo... the last priors; with d... fireplace, ceiling paint... Tudor roses, and two... timber chests still in pla... adjacent prior's chapel w... once even more elaborat... adorned, with traces of medieval wall paintings still visible.

There is much more to see, including our exhibition and display of archaeological finds, site model and audio tour featuring a 15th-century chant from a Castle Acre son... The recreated herb g... grows plants the mon... have used for medicinal a... culinary purposes. There is also a large activities barn for schools. A priory terrain guide can be downloaded from the Castle Acre Priory page... English Heritage web...

NON-MEMBERS

Adult	£5.6
Concession	£5.00
Child	£3.40
Family	£14.60

OPENING TIMES

1 Apr-30 Sep, daily	10am-5pm
1 Oct-31 Mar, Thu-Mon	10am-4pm
24-26 Dec and 1 Jan	Closed

HOW TO FIND US

Direction: ¼ mile W of village of Castle Acre, 5 miles N of Swaff...

Bus: West Norfolk Community Transport (weekdays), Freestone Coaches 32; Peelings 1 (Tue)

OVP

Disabled access (ground floor and grounds only)

Toilets (a short walk. Not accessible for wheelchairs; 50 metres from entrance, with single step for access).

MAP Page 279 (2G)
OS Map 132, 236/238: TF814148

Check www.english-heritage.org.uk for the latest opening times

Where possible, we have included postcodes to assist with digital route-planning.

Essential information such as opening times, admission prices for non-members, contact details and travel directions are included for each property.

Symbols show the facilities which are available, from catering and toilet facilities to whether a property is available for corporate or private hire. The key is on the inside front cover.

Details of OS LandRanger and Explorer map references are provided for easy location of each property, with specific map numbers (LandRanger; Explorer) followed by the grid reference.

NB. All maps in this handbook are created using Ordnance Survey mapping. Unless otherwise credited, they are © Crown Copyright and database right 2011. Ordnance Survey Licence number 100019088.

Contents

CONTACTS

CUSTOMER SERVICES

WEBSITE
www.english-heritage.org.uk

EMAIL
customers@english-heritage.org.uk

TELEPHONE
0870 333 1181
(geographic call rates apply)

ADDRESS
English Heritage
PO Box 569
Swindon SN2 2YP England

FACSIMILE
01793 414926

Minicom text telephone for the deaf or hard of hearing 0800 015 0516

PAPER

TEXT: Ultra Lux Semi Gloss 100% recycled.
COVER: Revive Pure 100% recycled.

recycle
When you have finished with this handbook please recycle it

Membership

English Heritage looks after over **400 properties**, ranging from prehistoric sites, Roman towns, deserted medieval villages and historic battlefields to castles, abbeys, forts, historic houses, gardens and palaces. And your membership entitles you to free, unlimited entry to all of them… plus free entry for up to six accompanied children (under 19) per member, within your family group. Unaccompanied children aged 16-19 can also use their parents' membership card to gain free entry.

You are also entitled to free or reduced-price entry to a wide range of events (see page 22). Please note that some properties may charge a small supplementary fee when an event is being held.

More places to visit…

…in England

You are entitled to free or discounted entry to many other properties throughout England upon production of your membership card. See the back pages within each region of this handbook for details of participating attractions. (Please note discounts may not apply on event days at these properties, as they are not owned or managed by English Heritage).

…in Britain

During your first year of membership, you get half-price entry to properties in Wales and Scotland and on the Isle of Man. During subsequent years of membership, your entry will be free. See pages 266-270 for details.

Heritage Today

Our exclusive members-only magazine contains all the news and behind-the-scenes information from our properties, as well as a full seasonal events guide and in-depth and expert articles including historical biographies, social history and architectural features.

Contact us

If you have comments or views to share, contact the Membership Department on 0870 333 1182.

English Heritage
Customer Services
PO Box 570
Swindon SN2 2YR

members@english-heritage.org.uk

2011 highlights

New projects and old places: **an editor's choice for 2011**

Already hailed for its fabulous evocation of a medieval royal palace – and if you haven't seen this yet, you really should – 1 **Dover Castle** (p.58) also unveils another attraction this year. From June 2011 a vivid new display within the Secret Wartime Tunnels, *Operation Dynamo: Rescue from Dunkirk*, will recreate the crucial evacuation of British and allied troops from the Dunkirk beaches on the actual site where this operation was planned. The new *Wartime Tunnels Uncovered* exhibition, meanwhile, explores how the 'Dunkirk Spirit' helped snatch victory from the jaws of defeat.

For something completely different, visit 2 **Wroxeter Roman City** (p.194) to see the recreated Roman town villa, featuring during 2011 in a Channel 4 television show – predicted to be a cross between 'Big Brother' and 'Time Team'!

Fittingly for Queen Victoria's seaside retreat, 3 **Royal Osborne** (p.83) hosts a more peaceful recreation for 2011 – the Palm Terrace overlooking the Solent, as designed by Prince Albert. And don't miss the restored garden bench carved from coal, originally for Albert's beloved Great Exhibition of 1851.

2011 is a great year for English Heritage's gardens. From August the 'Sleeping Beauty' gardens of 4 **Wrest Park** (p.152) will be far more extensively opened up, with the Walled Garden, a new café and other features available for the first time. London's 5 **Chiswick House and Gardens** (p.35) – including the 19th-century conservatory with its famous camellia collection – have enjoyed a £12m restoration, and new downloadable plays will help bring them to life. And, at 6 **Witley Court and Gardens** (p.192), where major work on the East Parterre is now complete, there is a new play area in the Wilderness Garden, complete with a tree house.

Planning your visit

We are committed to ensuring that our properties are enjoyed by and accessible to all.

ACCESS

In this handbook, the ♿ symbol indicates that at least some areas of the property are accessible to disabled people.

Access Guide

For a thorough guide to accessibility and the special facilities at many of our properties, please refer to our free Access Guide. This offers an honest assessment of which of the landscapes and buildings in our care have the most to offer disabled visitors, including those with alternative routes for wheelchair users, or with features like scented gardens, tactile objects/displays and specially, created audio tours. Information on parking and drop-off points is also included, with an indication of some of the obstacles you may encounter, such as steep steps, or grounds which may become waterlogged in wet weather.

Some of these features and facilities will also be of interest to families and carers with young children, or those who like to include both children and grandparents in their days out.

Please also remember that if you are disabled, your carer is admitted free.

How to order

Please call 0870 333 1181, minicom 0800 015 0516 or email **customers@english-heritage.org.uk**. Alternatively, go to **www.english-heritage.org.uk/accessguide** to download your free copy. Information on our properties is also available by fax on 01793 414926. For individual property fax numbers, please telephone or email Customer Services.

The Access Guide is also available in large type, in Braille, on tape or disk by region. You will also find the most up-to-date information on the English Heritage website **www.english-heritage.org.uk/daysout**

ADMISSIONS

There are three levels of charges for non-members shown in this handbook (adult/concession/child). Children under five are admitted free to all our properties. Family tickets are available at some of our larger properties, and this is indicated where applicable. In most cases, family tickets admit two adults and three children. This may vary at properties not managed by us.

For example:

Adult	£2.50
Concession	£1.90*
Child (under 16 years)	£1.30

*The concessions apply to senior citizens, jobseekers and students with relevant ID. Prices may vary from the example shown above.

Entry to all our properties is free to all members on presentation of a valid membership card.

Groups and Parties

Discounts of 15% (10% at Stonehenge) are available for groups of 11 or more visitors paying together. Call Customer Services on 0870 333 1181 for a copy of our *Group Visits Guide*. We recommend that groups book in advance.

Overseas Visitor Pass OVP

An Overseas Visitor Pass (OVP) allows unlimited free access to over 100 of our properties for one or two weeks.

With your OVP you enjoy free entry to all English Heritage properties listed in this handbook marked with the OVP symbol, plus free or reduced entry to hundreds of exciting events.

There may be a charge for some events at our properties (same rate as English Heritage members). Check on our website for details of events. The OVP does not entitle you to free admission at properties not managed by English Heritage and not marked with the OVP symbol.

For more information please call 0870 333 1181 or visit www.english-heritage.org.uk/ovp

CAR PARKING P

At a small number of properties where car parking is limited and at a premium, we have to charge a small fee for parking to ensure that our members and visitors have priority. Members and paying visitors visiting these properties will be given a refund on admission (except at Battle Abbey, Kenwood and Marble Hill House). We have indicated the properties where a charge applies within the individual listings in the handbook. Any revenue raised from car parking will be re-invested in the care and maintenance of our properties. Please note that we reserve the right to vary this policy from time to time for operational reasons. We have disabled parking spaces at many of our sites.

Look out for special displays, exhibitions and visitor centres at many of our properties.

CATERING AND PICNICS

Refreshments are available at restaurants and tearooms at some properties, many located within historic buildings. Visitors are also welcome to picnic in the grounds of many properties. Please check individual listings for details.

DOGS

Dogs on leads are welcome where possible. Please see individual listings for details. Assistance dogs welcome everywhere.

EDUCATIONAL VISITS

Visiting historic properties is an important way of inspiring school children and adult learners about history. We actively encourage these visits by providing free entry to our properties for pre-booked educational groups. We also provide a range of resources to enable teachers and students to get the most out of their visit.

We follow the Department for Children, Schools and Families' guidelines on health and safety on educational visits, and require a ratio of one adult to every six children for groups containing pupils from years 1 to 3, one adult to every 10-15 pupils for groups containing pupils from years 4 to 6 and one adult to every 15 pupils for groups with pupils from year 7 and above.

FAMILIES AND CHILDREN

We welcome families with children of all ages. Many of our properties include special features, exhibitions or educational facilities suitable for children. Some offer baby-changing facilities. For safety reasons, babies cannot be carried in back carriers at certain properties. You are responsible for the children's supervision and safety at all times: please ensure a sensible number of adults in relation to the number of children.

FAMILY LEARNING

Look out for the exciting range of resources we are developing at many of our properties. Already featured at over 50 properties, these range from free children's activity sheets and back packs to book boxes, and 'Very Big Books' for younger children – as well as interactive Discovery Centres.

GUIDES AND TOURS

Audio guides are available at over 50 of our properties. Some sites have special audio guides for children or people with learning difficulties (see Access Guide for more details). In exceptional circumstances, for instance when an event is taking place or for larger groups of visitors, audio guides may not be available. To check for events see the Events section of *Heritage Today* magazine, visit **www.english-heritage.org.uk/events** or call Customer Services. Guidebooks are also on sale at staffed properties or through our postal service – call 01761 452966.

Guided tours for pre-booked groups of 11 or more are available at an extra charge at many sites. Call the site or visit our website **www.english-heritage.org.uk/daysout**

OPENING TIMES

Please see page 4 for information on opening times.

PHOTOGRAPHY

Non-commercial photography is welcome in all our grounds. For conservation reasons, it is not permitted inside some properties.

PUBLIC TRANSPORT AND CYCLING

Public transport details are correct at the time of going to press. However, we advise you to check all services before travelling. We are grateful to the Confederation of Passenger Transport (www.cpt-uk.org), the UK trade association for the bus, coach and light rail industry, for providing this information. If you notice any errors, please email them to johnb@cpt-uk.org

Call Sustrans on 0845 113 00 65 or visit the website www.sustrans.org.uk for cycle route information.

SAFETY 

Due to their historic nature, some of our properties have features which could be hazardous – steep slopes, sheer drops, slippery or uneven surfaces, steep/uneven steps and deep/fast-flowing water. Please pay attention to all safety notices.

These properties are marked ⚠ in this handbook, but if you are in any doubt about hazards, please call the property in advance. Please take care when you visit, and remember to wear suitable footwear. Always prevent fires and do not climb on the monuments at any of our properties.

Please be aware that in areas of woodland or deer pasture there is a slight risk of tick bites which may lead to Lyme Disease. In order to avoid such bites, it is advisable to keep vulnerable parts of the body covered, and/ or to use insect repellent.

We encourage children to have fun, but please ensure they are supervised at all times. Our staff are always willing to advise on safety issues.

SATELLITE NAVIGATION

A free download of our properties is available at **www.english-heritage.org.uk/satnav**

SMOKING

Smoking is not permitted inside any of our properties.

TOILETS 

Toilets are available at or near many of our properties. Please check individual listings.

Details of all bus travel in England is available from Traveline on 0871 200 2233 or online at www.traveline.org.uk

Call Sustrans on 0845 113 00 65 or visit the website www.sustrans.org.uk for cycle route information.

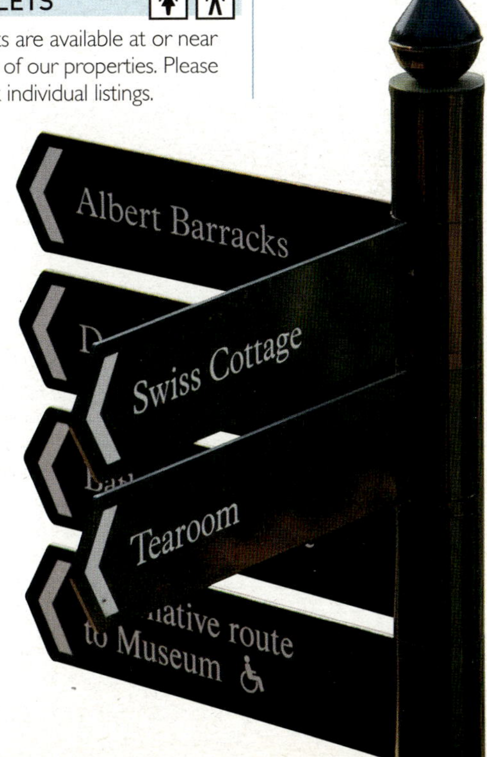

About us

Everywhere we look, history surrounds us. English Heritage champions our historic places and advises Government and others on how to help today's generation get the best out of our heritage, and ensure that it is protected for future generations.

If you share our passion for England's historic environment and want to help us make the past part of our future, view our current vacancies or register for our job alerts at **www.english-heritage.org.uk/jobs**

Who are we?

English Heritage was established in 1983 as the Historic Buildings and Monuments Commission for England. We are the Government's principal adviser on the historic environment, and are partly funded by the Department for Culture, Media & Sport (DCMS). We also work with other Government departments, including the Department for Communities & Local Government (CLG) and the Department for the Environment, Food & Rural Affairs (Defra).

The work of English Heritage is overseen by a Chair and a board of up to 16 Commissioners appointed by the Secretary of State. On a day-to-day basis the organisation is run by the Chief Executive, Simon Thurley, supported by an Executive Board of four Directors. You can find out more at **www.english-heritage.org.uk/about**

What do we do?

English Heritage is the Government's principal adviser on heritage. We advise on what should be protected, and on how changes to our most important buildings and sites should be managed. We offer grants, provide training, education services and advice, as well as maintaining the national archive and looking after over 400 sites that form the national collection of our built and archaeological heritage. People often ask how we differ from the National Trust. What distinguishes English Heritage is our role in advising Government, including about which buildings and places to protect and our responsibility for advising local authorities on planning proposals affecting places that are already protected.

How are we funded?

We are partly funded by Government, and partly by revenue earned from our properties. We rely on membership, donations,

fundraising and the National Lottery for more than a third of our funding, so your membership really does make a difference.

Why is our work important?

Heritage is all around us. It helps us understand how the past has shaped who we are. It makes places more interesting and characterful, and is a powerful driver of tourism and prosperity in this country. From stately homes to modest terraced houses, and from industrial buildings to shops and offices, most heritage is in private hands, but benefits everyone by enriching the environment we live in. We help promote and protect our heritage because of the benefits it can bring to communities all around the country, and because we believe that future generations should have the opportunity to enjoy England's historic environment in the same way we do today.

If you have any queries about any aspect of your membership or English Heritage, your first point of contact should be Customer Services. Our promise to you is that we will:

- aim to answer your query quickly and proactively in a friendly and helpful manner. Where we are unable to provide an immediate answer we will investigate your query and respond within a timescale agreed with you
- endeavour to answer calls within 15 seconds and emails and letters within 5 working days
- protect your personal information and take all reasonable precautions to ensure its safety
- accept and review any feedback or comments you make to us about our services or properties, and pass these comments on for consideration in the future

Contact us

Website
www.english-heritage.org.uk

Email
customers@english-heritage.org.uk

Telephone
0870 333 1181
Lines open:
8.30am-5pm Mon-Fri (6.30pm in summer), and 9am-5pm Sat

Address
English Heritage
PO Box 569
Swindon SN2 2YP
England

Facsimile
01793 414926

Minicom text telephone for the deaf or hard of hearing
0800 015 0516

At work

How your membership helps

English Heritage is a non-profit-making organisation, so every penny of members' subscriptions contributes towards the maintenance and enhancement of the historic properties in our care and assists us with our tasks of protecting the historic environment and making the past a part of our future. We aim to do this by creating a cycle of **understanding, valuing, caring for** and **enjoying** our historic environment. These are some of the ways in which your membership helps us to do this…

ENGLISH HERITAGE JOHN LENNON 1940-1980 Musician and Songwriter lived here in 1968

Enjoying and valuing

Our properties

We currently look after over 400 historic properties that are open to the public. All are listed in this members' handbook.

Apart from maintaining all and staffing many of these properties, we also pursue a policy of continuous property enhancement, to which membership fees contribute. This includes the opening up of previously inaccessible areas of castles and abbeys; the re-creation or re-presentation of gardens and landscapes; and many other improvements to increase visitors' enjoyment and understanding. Each year sees new enhancement projects, marked as 'New for 2011' in the relevant property listing.

Interpretation

At many of our properties we provide visitor centres, exhibitions and educational and family learning resources. On-site interpretation of individual properties ranges from state-of-the-art multi-media presentations and free audio tours to informative interpretation panels. Our new web resource, **Portico**, to be launched in April 2011, offers a wealth of research material on each English Heritage property. All our interpretation is founded on meticulous and continuing research, and is updated as funds permit.

Publications

We publish guidebooks to many of our properties and every year sees additions to the large-format Red Guides series. Written by leading experts, these feature specially-commissioned photography, reconstruction drawings and fascinating eye-witness accounts. Each includes a tour of the site and a history of the property and the people who lived and worked there. A series of regional guides to our free sites now covers the whole country.

Guidebooks are only a small proportion of our vast publishing programme on an immense variety of subjects. These range from academic works on archaeology, architecture and building conservation to wider interest illustrated books on general history and sporting heritage. We also produce over 50 free conservation leaflets offering practical advice on such matters as Looking After Places of Worship and Conservation Areas.

A printed catalogue of our priced publications is available from our Customer Services team on 0870 333 1181 and a full search facility for all publications is available at **www.english-heritage.org.uk/publications**

Promoting our heritage doesn't stop with our own properties. Here are some of the other ways your membership helps us with this task.

Blue Plaques

Blue plaques mark the houses where great men and women have lived, worked and helped to shape today's world. English Heritage operates the London-wide blue plaques scheme, and provides advice and guidance to others interested in putting up commemorative plaques.

All suggestions for English Heritage plaques come from members of the public. To qualify, a person must have been dead for 20 years, or the centenary of their birth must have passed, and a building associated with them must survive. To nominate someone for a blue plaque in London, or for general advice about commemorative plaques, visit **www.english-heritage.org.uk/blueplaques**

Heritage Open Days

English Heritage now also provides national co-ordination for Heritage Open Days, which annually celebrate England's rich architecture, heritage and culture. For four days in September, buildings of every age and function open their doors for free; ranging from castles to factories, town halls to tithe barns, parish churches to Buddhist temples. Many are normally closed to the public, while others usually charge for admission. Organised and run by hundreds of local organisations and thousands of volunteers, this is a once-a-year chance to discover hidden treasures and enjoy tours and activities bringing to life the stories and traditions of individual places and communities. For more info, visit **www.heritageopendays org.uk**

Your membership assists us in the crucial task of...

Caring

Grants

English Heritage is a vital source of grants to individuals, local authorities and voluntary organisations to undertake urgent repairs, and to conserve and enhance the historic environment. More than half of England's Grade I listed buildings are Places of Worship, which benefit greatly from these grants. We also advise the Heritage Lottery Fund on grants to worthwhile schemes which do not fit our grant criteria. Visit **www.english-heritage.org.uk/grants**

Archaeology

As the national archaeology service for England, we set standards and provide detailed archaeological knowledge. We also implement the statutory protection of England's 183,000 Scheduled Monuments. Visit **www.english-heritage.org.uk/archaeology**

We are likewise responsible for all English maritime archaeological sites, from low water to a 12-nautical mile territorial limit. Designated Wrecks range from Bronze Age cargoes to early submarines, while sites range from sandy beaches to rocky seabeds. Offshore installation or extraction works can affect submerged properties and wrecks, so we advise government on their implications. For more information, visit **www.english-heritage.org.uk/interactivewreckmap**

Conservation

Listed Buildings

We understand that buildings need to change to thrive. We work proactively with homeowners and local authorities on the designation of listed buildings and the best system for their protection, ensuring that any changes made to their structure recognise their historic potential. Most listed buildings date from before 1840, but we also designate some later buildings. Grade I and Grade II* buildings are of outstanding architectural or historic interest and particular importance to England's built heritage. Visit **www.english-heritage.org.uk/listing**. To view details and images of listed buildings, visit **www.imagesofengland.org.uk**

We also designate for protection monuments and landscapes, such as ruins and earthworks. We work with local authorities on designating Conservation Areas, characterised by architectural and historic features worth preserving or enhancing.

Battlefields are important sources of archaeological and historic interest, and over 40 are on our Register of Historic Battlefields. We keep a similar Register of Parks and Gardens, including the country's most important green spaces. Visit **www.english-heritage.org.uk/conservation**

Statutory advice

We publish an annual Heritage at Risk Register of listed buildings and scheduled monuments at risk from neglect and decay, and award grants to local authorities to undertake urgent repairs to these buildings.

Policies

Among our key responsibilities is to develop robust policies that protect and promote the historic environment: we publish the evidence to support these policies annually as *Heritage Counts* (**www.heritagecounts.org.uk**).

We also play an important role in international conservation, working with UNESCO and advising on the designation and management of World Heritage Sites in England and campaigning in Brussels and Strasbourg on behalf of the historic environment.

Funding from membership also helps with…

Understanding

Research

Our research and training programmes increase understanding of the historic environment, helping us to guide its management in an informed and sustainable way. We concentrate on poorly-understood building types as well as on specific properties and areas. For more information email **buildingshistory@english-heritage.org.uk**

Training: crafts and skills

Traditional skills are at risk of dying out in England. Of the workforce of 97,000 who work on traditional buildings, it is estimated that fewer than 30,000 have the appropriate craft skills. English Heritage supports training in these essential skills, ensuring there will be a continuing source of craftspeople to preserve England's half a million listed historic buildings and Buildings at Risk.

Education and Volunteering

Our learning programmes encourage people of all ages and abilities to understand, value, care for and enjoy their historic environment. Each year, we stage a variety of activities for schools, families, adult learners and hard-to-reach communities. These help to inspire current and future generations with a lifetime's passion for their heritage.

Education – learners go free

At English Heritage we believe that experiencing the local historic environment should be central to the curriculum of every school in England: and that every child should have the opportunity to visit the English Heritage property closest to them. We know that working in the outdoor classroom setting of an historic property develops new skills, deepens understanding and expands knowledge for young people, so we welcome schools and other learning groups to our properties completely free of charge. We are also providing more on-site learning resources, such as book bags, handling collections, costumes and activities.

Group leaders can download free resources and safety information from our website, arrange free preparatory visits, and book 'Discovery Visits'. Featuring hands-on activities led by specialist educators, trained staff and volunteers, Discovery Visits truly bring history to life for children: they have won 19 Sandford awards for their quality. We also publish *Heritage Learning* magazine, packed with teaching ideas and delivered free to schools, plus quarterly e-newsletters, and regional guides for learning groups.

English Heritage Education is a lead partner in 'Engaging Places', which encourages teachers and young people to work creatively with their built environment. See **www.engagingplaces.org.uk** for inspiring case studies and ideas.

Volunteering

Volunteering is an important feature at many English Heritage properties. Volunteer activities include room stewarding, gardening, curatorial cleaning and delivering education workshops through the national Education Volunteering Programme. Benefits for volunteers include learning new skills, meeting like-minded people and helping to ensure that our heritage is understood and enjoyed by all. To find out more, or to register interest in becoming a volunteer, visit our website **www.english-heritage.org.uk/volunteering**

This is only a summary of how your membership fee helps us to promote, understand and protect England's historic heritage.

For more information about our work and who we are, visit **www.english-heritage.org.uk**

Please donate

Donations and legacies contribute to projects that benefit our visitors and that could not happen without your support. The following are just some of the notable projects we completed last year. In these testing economic times we are particularly grateful for your help.

To find out more contact our Fundraising Department at fundraising@english-heritage.org.uk (tel: 020 7973 3538), visit **www.english-heritage.org.uk/supportus** or call Customer Services on 0870 333 1181.

The Portuguese Service of tableware was made for the first Duke of Wellington, to honour his leadership in the Peninsular War. Its magnificent silver Centrepiece is 8.03m long, so cleaning and conserving it has been a painstaking task. The Centrepiece is now in pride of place in the Dining Room at **Apsley House** in London.

At **Mount Grace Priory** in North Yorkshire, we were excited to discover a large section of almost pristine Morris & Co. wallpaper behind a cupboard. Two rooms there have now been refurbished in the Arts and Crafts style, decorated with wallpaper reproduced from the original wood blocks.

The 70th anniversary of the Dunkirk evacuation – 'Operation Dynamo' – was commemorated widely across the country. English Heritage remembered the astonishing events of 1940 at **Dover Castle**, the HQ for Operation Dynamo. Thousands of visitors took part in our WWII events and we also asked the public to record their memories of wartime Dover for the Dunkirk Memory Box. These moving first-hand accounts of lives affected by Operation Dynamo are included in the new permanent displays for the Secret Wartime Tunnels, opening in 2011.

Fundraising is vitally important to English Heritage and the contributions we receive from Lottery funders, charitable foundations and companies are also crucial to the success of our projects. We hope that your travels in England this year will take you to some of the many sites where your donations have helped us accomplish something memorable.

There are many ways to help; from making a donation to leaving a gift in your Will for the future. And if you haven't yet signed up to the Gift Aid scheme, please consider doing so now. You can make a donation when you renew your membership at any of our properties or online at **www.english-heritage.org.uk/supportus**

With your help we raised £54.4 million last year for England's precious heritage. Thank you.

The Centrepiece of the Portuguese Service at Apsley House.

National Monuments Record

The archive of English Heritage, the National Monuments Record (NMR), holds over 10 million photographs, plans, drawings, reports, records and publications covering England's archaeology, architecture and social and local history.

VISIT US ONLINE

www.english-heritage.org.uk/nmr

- **1 million** descriptions of historical photographs and documents.
- **80,000** historic photographs of England from the 1850s to the present day.
- Over **400,000** records relating to England's archaeological sites (including maritime sites) and architecture.
- More than **320,000** contemporary colour photographs of England's listed buildings.
- National and local records for England's historic sites and buildings.
- Buy our finest images as prints, framed prints or on canvas.
- Images for learning – resources for teachers.

VISIT US IN SWINDON

For access to our wider archive, you can call, email, write or visit us at our offices in Swindon. There we handle individual enquiries and carry out searches of our collections on your behalf – our standard service is ***free of charge***. Alternatively you can pop in and do your own research. Let us know when you're coming to get the most from your visit.

Contact us

NMR Enquiry & Research Services:
National Monuments Record
English Heritage, Kemble Drive
Swindon SN2 2GZ

Telephone: 01793 414600

Fax: 01793 414606

Email:
nmrinfo@english-heritage.org.uk

Opening times

Public Search Room
Tue-Fri: 9.30am-5pm

Hiring a property

Celebrations can now be arranged at selected English Heritage properties. Experienced staff are on hand to help fine-tune arrangements and ensure your event will provide lasting memories for years to come.

Properties available for hire are marked with a [hire symbol] throughout the handbook. Those also licensed for civil ceremonies are marked with a [bell symbol].

For more information on exclusive hire, please contact the Hospitality Managers on the property telephone numbers below, or visit **www.english-heritage.org.uk/hospitality**

PROPERTIES FOR HIRE

London

Eltham Palace [bell symbol]
Tel: 020 8294 2577

Kenwood
Tel: 020 7973 3416

Marble Hill House [bell symbol]
Tel: 020 7973 3416

Ranger's House [bell symbol]
Tel: 020 8294 2577

Wellington Arch
Tel: 020 7973 3416

South East

Royal Osborne, Isle of Wight
Tel: 01983 203055

East

Bolsover Castle, Derbyshire Tel: 01246 856456 [bell symbol]

Wrest Park, Bedfordshire [bell symbol]
Tel: 01525 863704

South West

Old Wardour Castle, Wiltshire Tel: 01305 820868 [bell symbol]

Pendennis Castle, Cornwall [bell symbol]
Tel: 01326 310106

Portland Castle, Dorset [bell symbol]
Tel: 01305 820868

St Mawes Castle, Cornwall [bell symbol]
Tel: 01326 310106

West

Kenilworth Castle and Elizabethan Garden, Warwickshire [bell symbol]
Tel: 01926 857 482

What could be a more stunning setting for a wedding, civil partnership ceremony, birthday celebration, anniversary dinner or corporate event than an historic English Heritage property?

Events

From family fun days, craft fairs and exhibitions to spectacular battle displays, our events offer something for everyone to enjoy. With the largest historical events programme in Europe, you'll have hundreds of activities to choose from throughout the year.

Sign up for events updates
Get regular updates of news and events direct to your inbox. Simply visit **www.english-heritage.org.uk/newsletter** to register. Alternatively, keep up to date with our events programme at **www.english-heritage.org.uk/events** or check your latest copy of *Heritage Today*.

Festival of History
The Festival of History is the highlight of our events calendar. With more than 50 different shows each day, it's an action-packed weekend for all the family. Experience over 2000 years of history, and watch as over 1000 re-enactors make this the ultimate historical adventure. The Festival will be held at Kelmarsh Hall, Northamptonshire, on 16 & 17 July.

Performing Arts
We've got a great variety of music and theatre events throughout the year – both indoors and out. From seasonal concerts to historical plays, you're bound to find a production for all ages and tastes.

Big Battle Spectaculars
If you enjoy huge historical re-enactments then our 'tour de force' events could be just for you. Including the St George's Festival on 23-25 April and the Battle of Hastings on 15-16 October.

Design, Interiors and Craft Fairs
If you fancy a change from the high street, these events offer a different kind of retail therapy. You'll be able to buy unusual gifts for all the family and also explore the beautiful surroundings at our properties.

Hobbies and Special Interests
Improve your gardening skills with a hands-on lecture or tour, walk one of our trails or admire a display of classic cars. We've got lots of special events for all kinds of interest throughout the year.

Tours, Talks and Exhibitions
From cookery demonstrations to curator's tours and art exhibitions, you'll find a wide choice to suit everyone.

Time Travellers Go…

Get ready for the return of our Time Travellers! Children of all ages enjoyed taking part in our historical events last year, from trying on medieval armour and hands-on spy training to sailing a ship in a mock sea battle.

Armed with their very own passport, children can learn centuries-old skills and earn prizes by completing tasks and collecting stickers at our properties.

Our Time Travellers Go… events get bigger every year, with an exciting range to choose from in 2011 from training to be a Roman fighter to knot-tying or going on Ugly Bug Safaris!

Visit www.english-heritage.org.uk/timetravellersgo

Exclusive Members' Events

Go behind the scenes, learn a new skill and discover the secrets concealed by some of the most intriguing properties in England.

We hold over 75 events throughout the year, which are available exclusively to members.

See *Heritage Today* for details.

Books and gifts

Many of our historic properties feature visitor centres packed with a range of gifts and books to enhance your visit. You can also order most of these items over the phone on 01761 452966, by post or online at **www.english-heritageshop.org.uk**

Gifts & Souvenirs

Every year we introduce new products to our shops. Whether it be specially selected books, jewellery, toiletries, toys, gifts or souvenirs, the ranges reflect the style, history and location of each property. From national monuments to country houses, magnificent gardens to castle ruins, you will find something in our gift shops to suit.

Exclusive Products

We also work with individual properties to develop gifts for particular events and projects: many are developed exclusively for English Heritage. Last year we introduced a range of exclusive and contemporary designer products specifically for the *Extraordinary Measures* event, a highly successful contemporary art exhibition at **Belsay Hall**.

At **Audley End House**, the old Coach House was converted into a second shop, offering a wider selection of gifts and organic produce from the garden.

From June 2011 visit the transformed Secret Wartime Tunnels at **Dover Castle**, where new re-interpretation and a new shop promise to deliver a unique and memorable experience.

Food & Drink

We are continually enhancing our range of food and drink, and a number of properties also now stock a locally-sourced range. With tastings available in most sites, this has proved so popular that we have extended local produce ranges to additional properties for 2011.

Partner Products

We work closely with a range of carefully selected companies to bring our members, supporters and the wider public a range of distinctive products and services, all bearing the English Heritage brand. These ranges are developed to provide value and inspiration to our members and supporters. Each company makes a valuable contribution to us, helping us to continue to protect the historic environment. To find out more, look for features in *Heritage Today* magazine, or go to **www.english-heritage.org.uk**

Books

We publish books on a wide range of subjects including archaeology, architectural history, sporting heritage, general and illustrated history. Our forthcoming publishing programme promises exciting additions to our successful *Played in Britain* series – a hugely popular series of books on Britain's sporting and recreational heritage. We are also looking forward to new titles in our flagship *Informed Conservation* series – lavishly illustrated books which contain detailed accounts of an area's buildings and their importance in both physical and historical contexts. You can buy selected titles at our gift shops, or view the full range on our website **www.english-heritageshop.org.uk**

Guidebooks

We also publish guidebooks to many of our properties. These contain more historical information, combined with the most up-to-date research and a tour of the properties.

Properties which have a guidebook are marked with a 🕮 symbol throughout this handbook.

Many of the gifts in our shops are available to purchase online. You can shop by category, from jewellery to tapestries, or by theme, from Celtic to Art Deco.

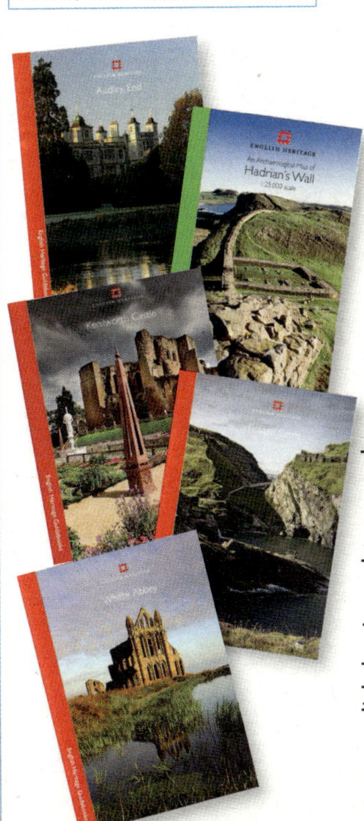

Please note: all products are subject to availability.

Visit our online shop at **www.english-heritageshop.org.uk** and sign up to our shop newsletter to keep up to date with special offers and events. Alternatively, call our mail order line on 01761 452966 to order over the phone.

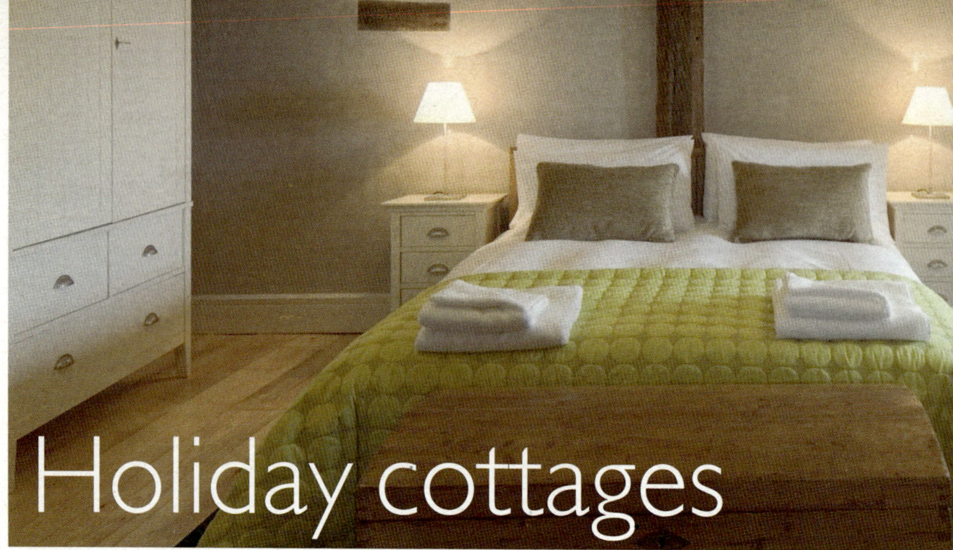

Holiday cottages

Location is one of the key principles behind the development of our holiday cottages, which are all positioned at the heart of an historic property – where history, discovery and enjoyment are just on the doorstep.

Not only are the locations unsurpassed, they also offer the unique opportunity to experience a very special place in peace and privacy. At most of our cottages and apartments, when the property closes for the day and the public go home, you will have the joy of knowing that the major part of the gardens and grounds are there just for you to enjoy.

Our cottages and apartments are located within easy reach of the best of England's countryside, bustling market towns, historic houses, cathedrals, churches and glorious gardens. Many also have well-marked walking and cycling trails close by.

Sensitively combining contemporary design with historic interiors, each cottage is unique, but always a 5-Star experience. We'll even treat you to a sumptuous welcome hamper on arrival. Visit our website or call us, and we'll show you the best holidays England has to offer. Reservations 0870 333 1187 or visit **www.english-heritage.org.uk/book-and-buy/holiday-cottages**

Walmer Castle

Holiday Cottages

Audley End House	Cambridge Lodge
Battle Abbey	South Lodge
Carisbrooke Castle	The Bowling Green Apartment
Dover Castle	The Sergeant Major's House and Peverell's Tower
Hardwick Old Hall	East Lodge
Kirby Hall	Peacock Cottage
Mount Grace Priory	Prior's Lodge
Royal Osborne	Pavilion Cottage
Pendennis Castle	The Custodian's House and Callie's Cottage NEW FOR 2011
Rievaulx Abbey	Refectory Cottage
St Mawes Castle	Fort House
Walmer Castle	The Garden Cottage and The Greenhouse Apartment
Witley Court	Pool House Cottage

For a brochure or to make a booking call reservations on 0870 333 1187.

Audley End House

Images:

1. Sergeant Major's House, Dover Castle
2. The Garden Cottage, Walmer Castle
3. Sergeant Major's House, Dover Castle
4. East Lodge, Hardwick Old Hall
5. Custodian's House, Pendennis Castle

Chiswick House – see page 35

London

Enfield
Barnet
Harrow
Haringey
Waltham Forest
Redbridge
Havering
Hillingdon
Brent
Camden
Hackney
Islington
Barking
Tower Hamlets
Newham
Ealing
Kensington
Hammersmith
Westminster
The City
Southwark
Greenwich
Hounslow
Lambeth
Bexley
Wandsworth
Richmond
Lewisham
Merton
Kingston
Bromley
Sutton
Croydon

Introducing London

Remember to check opening times before you visit any of our properties.

Details of all bus travel in England are available from Traveline on 0871 200 2233 or visit www.traveline.org.uk

For travel information in London call Transport for London on 020 7222 1234 or visit www.tfl.gov.uk

Camden

Kenwood

Greenwich

Eltham Palace and Gardens

Ranger's House – the Wernher Collection

Hounslow

Chiswick House and Gardens

Kingston-upon-Thames

Coombe Conduit

Richmond-upon-Thames

Marble Hill House

Southwark

Winchester Palace

Tower Hamlets

London Wall

Westminster

Apsley House

Chapter House and Pyx Chamber

Jewel Tower

Wellington Arch

Capital Days Out

London's English Heritage members and visitors are almost uniquely blessed with opportunities for ready-made 'days out', most of them easily achievable by public transport. Indeed, many of our London properties cry out for a whole day's visit in themselves. In the west, **Chiswick House and Gardens** have much new to admire this year – the splendidly restored 300-feet-long conservatory with its famous camellia collection are particularly worth seeing – while **Marble Hill House** in its Richmond riverside parkland is a tempting target on summer weekends. To the north, a bus will take you to the gates of **Kenwood**, with its opportunities for long walks through woods rich in wildlife – including the loved or loathed 'London parks parakeets' – and its really excellent café: the house itself offers wonderful paintings, and changing winter exhibitions in the Orangery. Many English Heritage London properties in fact host special events, so it is always worth checking their websites while planning a trip.

To the south, **Eltham Palace and Gardens** – Art Deco extravaganza, medieval palace and fine gardens – makes a varied whole day out, while Dulwich Picture Gallery offers two-for-one entry to English Heritage members. Nearer to Eltham Palace are the wonders of Greenwich's **Ranger's House – The Wernher Collection**, which could be combined (by the energetic) with visits to the nearby Royal Observatory and the National Maritime Museum. And central London walks in Hyde Park, past the Serpentine and the Round Pond, naturally lead – especially in uncertain weather – to **Wellington Arch** and the dazzling delights of **Apsley House**, an indoor day out par excellence.

Make the most of your membership and keep up to date with upcoming events, the latest news and special offers by subscribing to our e-newsletter. Register online at **www.english-heritage.org.uk/newsletter** and we'll deliver the latest from English Heritage straight to your inbox.

Images:
(left) Chiswick House and Gardens
(top centre) Marble Hill House
(top right) Eltham Palace and Gardens
(bottom centre) Ranger's House – The Wernher Collection (Image: © The Wernher Foundation)
(bottom right) Kenwood

Check www.english-heritage.org.uk for the latest opening times

Apsley House

Hyde Park – W1J 7NT

Apsley House, home of the first Duke of Wellington and his descendants, stands right in the heart of London at Hyde Park Corner. For over 200 years, this great metropolitan mansion has been known colloquially as 'Number 1 London', because it was the first house encountered after passing the tollgates at the top of Knightsbridge.

The Waterloo Gallery

Piccadilly Drawing Room

Statue of Napoleon by Canova

Wellington enthusiasts may also be interested in visiting the spectacular Wellington Arch opposite Apsley House (see p.43), and elegant Walmer Castle (p.74), the duke's residence when he was Lord Warden of the Cinque Ports.

Apsley House was originally designed and built by Robert Adam between 1771 and 1778 for Baron Apsley – from whom it takes its name. It passed to the Wellesley family in 1807, being first owned by Richard and then his younger brother Arthur Wellesley – the Duke of Wellington.

Wellington is most famous for defeating Napoleon at the Battle of Waterloo in 1815, but this was only the culmination of a brilliant military career. He was also a major politician, rising from representing a small Irish constituency in 1790 to Prime Minister in 1828.

Redesigned to reflect the Duke of Wellington's rising status, Apsley House's dazzling interiors are magnificent examples of the Regency style. They provided the perfect backdrop for entertaining, particularly at the annual Waterloo Banquets which commemorated the great victory.

Inside Apsley House you will see many aspects of the first Duke's life and work, including his outstanding art collection. Paintings by many famous artists are hung throughout the first floor, many of them part of the Spanish Royal Collection which came into Wellington's possession after the Battle of Vitoria in 1813. A colossal nude statue of Napoleon by Canova dominates the stairwell at the centre of the house.

Throughout his military career, the Duke was presented with a vast collection of silver plate and unique porcelain as trophies from grateful nations. Many of these can be seen in the Plate and China Room. Wellington's victories are celebrated in the

Above: Recently conserved silver-gilt centrepiece.

fine British craftsmanship of the magnificent Wellington Shield, designed by Thomas Stothard, and the impressive candelabra presented by the Merchants and Bankers of the City of London.

When the seventh Duke of Wellington gave the house to the nation in 1947, the family retained the private rooms, which they still use today. This makes Apsley House not only the last surviving great London town house open to the public, but also the only property managed by English Heritage in which the original owner's family still live.

Don't miss our 15-minute Walk and Talk Gallery Tours which take place twice daily throughout the year.

www.english-heritage.org.uk/apsleyhouse

NEW FOR 2011

The Dining Room and its splendid ceiling has been redecorated and restored, with a new carpet. Admire the magnificent and recently conserved silver-gilt centrepiece.

NON-MEMBERS

Apsley House	
Adult	£6.30
Concession	£5.70
Child	£3.80
Joint ticket with Wellington Arch	
Adult	£7.90
Concession	£7.10
Child	£4.70
Family	£20.50

OPENING TIMES

1 Apr-31 Oct, Wed-Sun & Bank Hols	11am-5pm
1 Nov-31 Mar, Wed-Sun	11am-4pm
24-26 Dec and 1 Jan	Closed

HOW TO FIND US

Direction: 149 Piccadilly, Hyde Park Corner

Train: Victoria ½ mile

Bus: From surrounding areas

Tube: Hyde Park Corner, adjacent

Tel: 020 7499 5676

OVP

Disabled access (limited).

MAP Page 276 (4E)
OS Map 176, 161/173: TQ284799

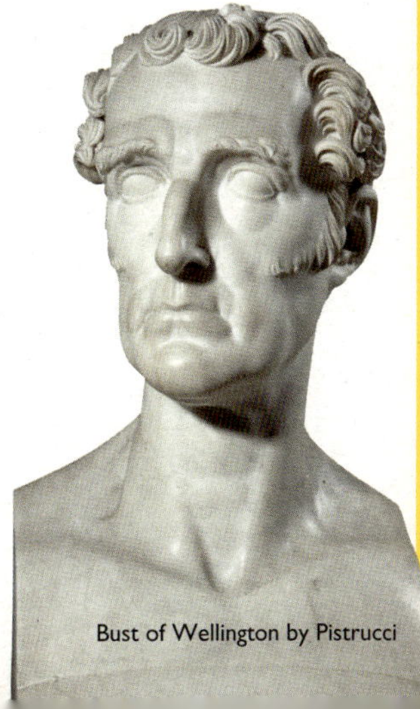

Bust of Wellington by Pistrucci

Chapter House and Pyx Chamber
Westminster Abbey – SW1P 3PA

Built by the royal masons in 1250, the Chapter House of Westminster Abbey was used from the 13th to the 16th century by Benedictine monks for their daily meetings. It was also sometimes used as a meeting place of the King's Great Council and the Commons, predecessors of today's Parliament.

A beautiful octagonal building with a vaulted ceiling and delicate central column, it offers rarely seen examples of medieval sculpture, an original floor of glazed tiles and spectacular wall paintings. The 11th-century Pyx Chamber also has a medieval tiled floor, and was used as a monastic and royal treasury. It contains a 13th-century stone altar which survived the Reformation.

During 2009/10, English Heritage funded a major programme of conservation repairs to the external historic fabric of the Chapter House. This included repairs to the roof, gutters, stonework on the elevations and flying buttresses, and repairs to the lead light glazing – thus preserving this highly important building for future generations.

Chapter House free to EH members. Under the care and management of the Dean and Chapter of Westminster. www.westminster-abbey.org

OPENING TIMES

Throughout the year, Mon-Sun	10am-4pm
Good Fri, 24-26 Dec and 1 Jan	Closed
May be closed at short notice on state and religious occasions	

HOW TO FIND US

Direction: Through the cloister from Dean's Yard if you only want to visit the Chapter House. Turn into Dean's Yard off Broad Sanctuary. Turn left along the square and go through the entrance-way into the cloister

Please show your EH membership card to the Marshal at the gate

Train: Victoria and Charing Cross both ¾ mile, Waterloo 1 mile

Bus: From surrounding areas

Tube: Westminster and St James' Park stations both ¼ mile

Tel: 020 7654 4900

MAP Page 277 (4F)
OS Map 176/177, 161/173: TQ299795

Chiswick House and Gardens
See feature opposite

Coombe Conduit
Kingston-upon-Thames KT2 7HE

These two brick-walled chambers, connected by an underground passage, were once part of a system which collected water from nearby springs and channelled it to Hampton Court Palace.

Managed by the Kingston-upon-Thames Society.

OPENING TIMES

Apr-Sep, every 2nd Sun	2pm-4pm

HOW TO FIND US

Direction: Coombe Lane on the corner of Lord Chancellor's Walk

Train: Norbiton ¾ mile or Raynes Park 1 mile then bus 57

Bus: Tfl 57 Kingston – Streatham

Tube: Wimbledon then bus 57

Tel: 020 8541 3108/020 8942 7387

www.kingstonuponthamessociety.co.uk

MAP Page 276 (4E)
OS Map 176, 161: TQ204698

The Home of Charles Darwin, Down House
See feature – Page 62

Eltham Palace and Gardens
See feature – Page 36

Chiswick House and Gardens Chiswick – W4 2RP

Chiswick House Gardens are a site of international importance, both as the birthplace of the English Landscape Movement, and as the setting for one of the most beautiful houses in London.

Chiswick House is among the most glorious examples of 18th-century British architecture. The third Earl of Burlington, who designed this noble Roman-style Palladian villa, drew inspiration from his 'grand tours' of Italy. The sumptuous interiors, created by William Kent, include a rich collection of paintings which complements the beautiful painted and gilded ceilings. Old Master paintings which show the diversity of Burlington's collections are displayed in the Red and Green Velvet rooms.

Chiswick House Gardens, spreading over 65 acres, have inspired countless designed landscapes, from Blenheim Palace to Central Park in New York. Highlights of a £12m restoration unveiled in 2010 include the planting of over 1600 trees, including trees propagated from the original 18th-century cedars of Lebanon; the opening up of historic views from the Classic Bridge; and the complete refurbishment of the 19th-century conservatory, housing an internationally important collection of camellias – possibly the oldest collection outside China and Japan.

Complete your day by visiting the acclaimed modern airy café. For more information including events and activities, visit www.chgt.org.uk

Managed by Chiswick House and Gardens Trust in partnership with English Heritage.

The Golden Compass.

www.english-heritage.org.uk/chiswickhouse

NEW FOR 2011

Listen to Chiswick

Ten 3-minute plays by exciting new playwrights bring the story of this outstanding garden to life. From late spring, download them from the English Heritage or CHGT website in advance of your visit.

Available for corporate and private hire – contact Chiswick House and Gardens Trust 020 8742 2762

Licensed for civil wedding ceremonies

NON-MEMBERS

Adult	£5.50
Concession	£5.00
Child	£3.30
Family	£14.30

OPENING TIMES

1 Apr-31 Oct
Sun-Wed & Bank Hols 10am-5pm

1 Nov-31 Mar Available for group tours – please call for details

HOW TO FIND US

Direction: Burlington Lane, W4

Train: Chiswick ½ mile

Bus: TfL 190, E3

Tube: Turnham Green ¾ mile

Tel: 020 8995 0508

OVP

Disabled access (ground floor; wheelchair stair-climber to first floor, please call to confirm use prior to visit).

Dogs on leads (restricted areas only).

Parking (charged – off westbound A4).

MAP Page 276 (4E)
OS Map 176, 161: TQ210775

Eltham Palace and Gardens

Greenwich – SE9 5QE

When millionaires Stephen and Virginia Courtauld built their 1930s Art Deco mansion by the Great Hall of medieval Eltham Palace, they created a masterpiece of 20th-century design.

Virginia Courtauld's bathroom

Colonnaded main entrance

The inclusive audio tour at Eltham Palace features the voice of actor David Suchet, best known for his role as Agatha Christie's Poirot.

Dining room door detail

Completed in 1936, the red brick exterior of the house was built in sympathy with the older building. But the interior remains a glamorous 1930s showpiece, an eclectic mix of Art Deco, ultra-smart ocean-liner style and cutting-edge Swedish design.

The dining room is a tour de force, with pink leather upholstered chairs, bird's-eye maple veneered walls, a shimmering aluminium-leaf ceiling, and black-and-silver doors portraying animals and birds.

Even more exotic is Virginia Courtauld's vaulted bathroom, complete with onyx bath and sink and gold-plated bath taps. Luxury also emanates from the centrally-heated sleeping quarters of the Courtaulds' pet ring-tailed lemur, Mah-Jongg. Equipped with all the latest modern conveniences, the house featured underfloor heating, a centralised vacuum cleaner and a built-in audio system.

Upstairs is a display of discoveries from the Courtauld era, including original furniture and family photographs. Visitors can also enjoy a restored original 10-minute Courtauld home movie, giving an intimate glimpse of their family life. A display celebrating the Royal Army Education Corps' (RAEC) post-World War II association with Eltham Palace highlights a further chapter in its fascinating history. It includes a recreation of an officer's bedroom of the 1960s, together with exhibition panels and a photograph album telling the story of the RAEC's time here.

The medieval palace presents a striking contrast to the opulent 1930s house. The Great Hall, with its stunning hammerbeam roof, was built for Edward IV in the 1470s, and Henry VIII spent much of his childhood here.

The palace's 19 acres of beautiful gardens feature both 20th-century and medieval elements. These include a rock garden sloping down to the moat, a medieval bridge, a stunning herbaceous border, and plenty of picnic areas. Striking at any time of year, garden highlights include the spring bulbs and the wisteria cascading over the classical pergola in summer.

Eltham Palace hosts the popular Art Deco Fair in May and September, and a large historical event over a weekend in June. Look out for details in *Heritage Today* or on our website.

The Gathering Storm; Bright Young Things; Brideshead Revisited; Shanghai; Revolver.

www.english-heritage.org.uk/elthampalace

Available for corporate and private hire

Licensed for civil wedding ceremonies

NON-MEMBERS

House and Garden	
Adult	£9.30
Concession	£8.40
Child	£5.60
Family	£24.20
Garden only	
Adult	£5.80
Concession	£5.20
Child	£3.50

OPENING TIMES

1 Apr-31 Oct, Sun-Wed	10am-5pm
1 Nov-31 Dec, Sun-Wed	11am-4pm
24-26 Dec and 1-31 Jan	Closed
1 Feb-31 Mar, Sun-Wed	11am-4pm

Also open on Sat 7 May, 18 Jun and 10 Sep

The property may close at short notice, please ring in advance for details

HOW TO FIND US

Direction: Off Court Rd SE9, Jct 3 on the M25, then A20 to Eltham

Train: Eltham and Mottingham, both ½ mile

Bus: TfL bus services 124,126 or 161 and then a short walk

Tel: 020 8294 2548

Disabled access (and parking via Court Yard entrance).

Parking (signed off Court Rd).

Pushchairs and large rucksacks need to be left at reception.

No photography allowed inside the house.

New guidebook.

MAP Page 277 (4F)
OS Map 177, 162: TQ424740

Check www.english-heritage.org.uk for the latest opening times

Kenwood Hampstead – NW3 7JR

In a wonderfully picturesque setting overlooking Hampstead Heath, this outstanding house was remodelled by Robert Adam between 1764 and 1779 into a majestic villa for the great judge, Lord Mansfield. Its interior is packed with treasures and its richly decorated library is one of Adam's great masterpieces, a feast for the eyes.

Library sofa and mirrored recess

Lady Mary Leslie by Reynolds

The Brew House Restaurant and Café is a great place to stop for home-made food or a cup of tea throughout the day.

Adam Library

Brewing magnate Edward Cecil Guinness, first Earl of Iveagh, bought Kenwood House and estate in 1925, and bequeathed them to the nation in 1927, along with part of his collection of pictures. The Iveagh Bequest includes important paintings by many great artists, including Rembrandt, Vermeer, Turner, Reynolds and Gainsborough, joined by Constable's oil sketch *Hampstead Heath*. The paintings beautifully complement Kenwood's dignified yet intimate interiors.

The first floor displays an equally beautiful but very different array of paintings. The Suffolk Collection consists of 41 paintings, predominantly family portraits, and was passed down through the Suffolk and Berkshire families from the 1580s. Particularly rich in sumptuous costume and textile detail, it includes an astounding set of full-length portraits of extravagantly dressed Jacobean ladies and noblemen, painted by William Larkin in 1614 to celebrate a family wedding, as well as paintings by Van Dyck and Lely and portraits of Kings Charles I and James II. Visitors can also view fascinating collections of jewellery, cameos and buckles, along with purchases from a sale of objects from Scone Palace, the Mansfields' Scottish home. Mansfield family items and furnishings thus returned to Kenwood include silver tableware, four chairs in the Chinese Chippendale style and a family portrait by Sir Peter Lely.

The splendid facilities of the Service Wing – which displays a restored 18th-century bath house – include the imaginatively-decorated Brew House café, with its paved refreshment terraces.

The leafy parkland surrounding Kenwood, abounding in fine mature trees, was particularly influenced by the great English landscape gardener, Humphry Repton. Set high on a hill, the views of London from these tranquil grounds are amazing. Visitors can also enjoy the lakeside walks and meandering wildlife-rich woodland paths.

Most of the grounds are accessible by gravel path and grass, but there are slopes to manage.

A variety of guided tours are available for a small charge: please call the house for details.

Look on our website, or ring the house, for details of our popular winter exhibitions in the Orangery.

Notting Hill; Mansfield Park; Scenes of a Sexual Nature; Venus

www.english-heritage.org.uk/kenwoodhouse

Available for corporate and private hire

OPENING TIMES

1 Apr-31 Mar, daily	11.30am-4pm
24-26 Dec and 1 Jan	Closed

The Park opens earlier and stays open later

House and grounds free; donations welcome (£3). Pre-booked group tours available

HOW TO FIND US

Direction: Hampstead Lane, NW3

Train: Gospel Oak or Hampstead Heath

Bus: Tfl 210 Finsbury Park – Golders Green

Tube: Golders Green or Archway then bus 210

Tel: 020 8348 1286

Disabled access (ground floor only; toilets).

Dogs on leads (restricted areas only).

Garden shop and house shop.

Parking (Charge applies. Disabled bays. Mobility service available on request).

Please note: Kenwood hosts regular events and acclaimed summer concerts.

MAP Page 276 (3E)
OS Map 176, 173: TQ271874

Jewel Tower
Westminster – SW1P 3JX

The Jewel Tower, or 'King's Privy Wardrobe', was built c. 1365 to house Edward III's treasures. One of only two buildings from the medieval Palace of Westminster to survive the fire of 1834, the tower features a 14th-century ribbed vault. It displays *Parliament Past and Present*, a fascinating exhibition about the history of Parliament, and the second floor includes panels telling the story of this small but important building.

The remains of a moat and medieval quay are still visible outside.

NON-MEMBERS

Adult	£3.20
Concession	£2.90
Child	£1.90

OPENING TIMES

1 Apr-31 Oct, daily	10am-5pm
1 Nov-31 Mar, daily	10am-4pm
24-26 Dec and 1 Jan	Closed

Last admission ½ hour before closing

HOW TO FIND US

Direction: Located on Abingdon Street, opposite the southern end of the Houses of Parliament (Victoria Tower)

Jewel Tower

Train: Victoria and Charing Cross ¾ mile, Waterloo 1 mile

Bus: From surrounding areas

Tube: St James's Park and Westminster ¼ mile

Tel: 020 7222 2219

OVP

Light refreshents available.

Disabled access (limited).

MAP Page 277 (4F)
OS Map 176/177, 161/173: TQ301793

Kenwood
See feature – Page 38

London Wall
Tower Hill

This is the best-preserved remnant of the Roman wall which once formed part of the eastern defences of Roman Londinium. Built c. AD 200, the wall defined the shape and size of London for over a millennium.

OPENING TIMES

Free access

HOW TO FIND US

Direction: Located outside Tower Hill Underground station, EC3

London Wall

Train: Fenchurch Street or London Bridge

Bus: From surrounding areas

Tube: Tower Hill or Tower Gateway

MAP Page 277 (3F)
OS Map 176/177, 173: TQ336807

Marble Hill House
See feature opposite

Ranger's House – The Wernher Collection
See feature – Page 42

Wellington Arch
See feature – Page 43

Winchester Palace
Southwark

Part of the great hall of Winchester Palace, built in the early 13th century as the London house of the Bishops of Winchester, including the striking rose window which adorns the west gable. Most of the palace was destroyed by fire in 1814.

OPENING TIMES

Free access

HOW TO FIND US

Direction: Next to Southwark Cathedral and the Golden Hinde replica ship; corner of Clink St and Storey St, SE1

Train/Tube: London Bridge ¼ mile

Bus: From surrounding areas

MAP Page 277 (4F)
OS Map 176/177, 173: TQ325803

Marble Hill House Richmond – TW1 2NL

Marble Hill House is the last complete survivor of the elegant villas and gardens which bordered the Thames between Richmond and Hampton Court in the 18th century. It was begun in 1724 for the remarkable Henrietta Howard, mistress of King George II when he was Prince of Wales, and friend of some of the cleverest men in England. The house and gardens were planned by a coterie of fashionable connoisseurs, including Mrs Howard's neighbour, the poet Alexander Pope.

A lovely Palladian villa still set in 66 acres of riverside parkland, Marble Hill was intended as an Arcadian retreat from crowded 18th-century London. Today the beautiful grounds are the perfect place to relax. The interiors of the house have been exquisitely restored and recreated, and some of its dispersed original contents have been re-assembled from as far afield as Philadelphia and Melbourne, Australia. There is also a fine collection of early Georgian paintings, including portraits of Mrs Howard and her circle. There can be few places in England that better recall the atmosphere of Georgian fashionable life. A display recreates the Chinese wallpaper Henrietta Howard hung in the dining room. A unique paper has been designed to fit the room, each sheet different and hand painted by Chinese artists.

Nanny MacPhee 2 The Big Bang

www.english-heritage.org.uk/marblehill

Available for corporate and private hire

Licensed for civil wedding ceremonies

NON-MEMBERS

Adult	£5.30
Concession	£4.80
Child	£3.20
Family	£13.80

OPENING TIMES

1 Apr-31 Oct
Sat: Entry by guided tours only at 10.30am and 12pm
Sun: Entry by guided tours only at 10.30am, 12pm, 2.15pm and 3.30pm

Tours last around 1½ hours

1 Nov-31 Mar – available for group tours – please call for details

HOW TO FIND US

Direction: Richmond Rd, Twickenham

Train: St Margaret's or Twickenham

Bus: Tfl 33, 490, H22, R68, R70

Tube: Richmond 1 mile

Tel: 020 8892 5115

P OVP

Café (Coach House Café, open all year).

Disabled access (exterior & ground floor only; toilets).

Parking charge.

MAP Page 276 (4E)
OS Map 176, 161: TQ173736

Check www.english-heritage.org.uk for the latest opening times

Ranger's House – The Wernher Collection

Greenwich Park – SE10 8QX

© Jon Wyand

Ranger's House is an elegant Georgian villa built in 1723, which became the official residence of the 'Ranger of Greenwich Park'. From 1815 this post was held by Princess Sophia Matilda, niece of George III. It remained an aristocratic and then royal home until 1902.

The house stands on the borders of Greenwich Park, and the Meridian Line passes through its grounds. Today it houses the Wernher Collection – an astounding display of medieval and Renaissance works of art, all purchased by the diamond magnate Sir Julius Wernher (1850-1912).

Arranged within the panelled interiors of this graceful mansion, the Wernher Collection presents a glittering spectacle – a sumptuous arrangement of silver and jewels, paintings and porcelain.

Nearly 700 works of art are on display, including early religious paintings and Dutch Old Masters, minute carved Gothic ivories, fine Renaissance bronzes and silver treasures. Together these pieces reveal the genius of medieval craftsmen, and the unparalleled quality of Renaissance decorative arts.

Entrance is by guided tour only (included in the entrance fee), providing a detailed insight into the history of the Collection.

With Greenwich and Blackheath nearby, Ranger's House makes a great day out.

Please note: No photography in the house.

www.english-heritage.org.uk/rangershouse

© The Wernher Foundation

Available for corporate and private hire

Licensed for civil wedding ceremonies

NON-MEMBERS

Adult	£6.30
Concession	£5.70
Child	£3.80

OPENING TIMES

1 Apr-30 Sep, Sun-Wed, Entry by guided tours only at 11.30am and 2.30pm. Tours last around 1½ hours

1 Oct-31 Mar Available for group tours – please call for details

The property may close at short notice, please ring in advance for details

HOW TO FIND US

Direction: Ranger's House is on Chesterfield Walk and overlooks the junction of General Wolfe Road and Shooters Hill Road

DLR: Deptford Bridge then bus 53

Train: Blackheath ¾ mile

Bus: TfL 53, 386

River: Greenwich Pier

Tel: 020 8853 0035

P OVP

Toilets (including disabled).

MAP Page 277 (4F)
OS Map 177, 161/162: TQ388769

Wellington Arch Hyde Park – W1J 7JZ

Set in the heart of Royal London at Hyde Park Corner, Wellington Arch is a landmark for Londoners and visitors alike. Originally commissioned as a grand outer entrance to Buckingham Palace, this massive monument was moved to its present site in 1882.

For glorious panoramas over London's Royal Parks and the Houses of Parliament, take the lift to the balconies just below the spectacular bronze sculpture surmounting the arch. The largest bronze sculpture in Europe, this depicts the angel of peace descending on the chariot of war. The balconies also offer unique views of the Household Cavalry, passing beneath to and from the Changing of the Guard at Horse Guards Parade.

Inside the Arch, three floors of exhibits tell its fascinating history.

Apsley House (see p.32), opposite Wellington Arch, was the London home of the Duke of Wellington.

www.english-heritage.org.uk/wellingtonarch

Available for corporate and private hire

NON-MEMBERS

Adult	£3.90
Concession	£3.50
Child	£2.30
Joint ticket with Apsley House	
Adult	£7.90
Concession	£7.10
Child	£4.70
Family	£20.50

OPENING TIMES

1 Apr-31 Oct, Wed-Sun & Bank Hols	10am-5pm
1 Nov-31 Mar, Wed-Sun	10am-4pm
24-26 Dec and 1 Jan	Closed

Last admission ½ hour before closing

The property may close at short notice, please ring in advance for details

HOW TO FIND US

Direction: Hyde Park Corner, W1J

Train: Victoria ¾ mile

Bus: From surrounding areas

Tube: Hyde Park Corner, adjacent

Tel: 020 7930 2726

E OVP

Please note: Exclusive group tours are available every Mon, with illustrated talk and refreshments on request (small charge).

MAP Page 276 (4E)
OS Map 176, 161/173: TQ284798

Associated attractions in London

These visitor attractions, all independent of EH, offer discounts to our members. Please call before you visit to confirm details. A valid EH membership card must be produced for each member.

The Albert Memorial
Kensington SW7

A professional Blue Badge guide explains the statues and mosaics of the Albert Memorial, bringing to life this iconic Victorian monument, erected in memory of Queen Victoria's husband.

Tours at 2pm/3pm 1st Sun of month from Mar to Dec.

Tel: 020 7495 5504

www.tourguides.co.uk

£5 discount tour price

1

Churchill War Rooms
London SW1A 2AQ

Learn more about the man who inspired Britain's finest hour at the interactive museum, then step back in time to view Churchill's underground headquarters, the nerve centre of Britain's war effort, which remain as they were in 1945.

5 mins from Jewel Tower

Tel: 020 7930 6961

www.iwm.org.uk

2 for 1 adult entry

Danson House
Kent – DA6 8HL

The most significant building at risk in London in 1995, one of Sir Robert Taylor's finest villas. Now restored for the nation by English Heritage and open to the public.

10 mins from J2 M25

Tel: 020 8303 6699

www.dansonhouse.org.uk

Adults: £4.50 plus 2 for 1 entry

6

Dulwich Picture Gallery
London SE21 7AD

Dulwich Picture Gallery, England's first public gallery, will celebrate its Bicentenary in 2011 and will welcome its visitors with a series of international loan masterpieces and special events all year.

Tel: 020 8693 5254

www.dulwichpicturegallery.org.uk

2 for 1 entry (permanent collection)

HMS Belfast
London SE1 2JH

Visit the largest surviving example of Britain's 20th century naval power and explore over nine decks of history. Moored on the Thames between London Bridge and Tower Bridge.

5 mins from Winchester Palace

Tel: 020 7940 6300

www.iwm.org.uk

2 for 1 adult entry

Kensal Green Cemetery
Kensal Green W10

First London cemetery, established to cope with the population explosion of the Industrial Revolution. Spectacular Victorian Gothic mausoleums. Tours (2pm Sunday) include visit to catacombs twice a month.

Tel: 07904 495012

www.kensalgreen.co.uk

£4.00 discount tour price

EH Members

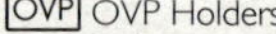
OVP Holders

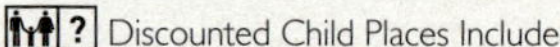
Discounted Child Places Included

London Canal Museum
London N1 9RT

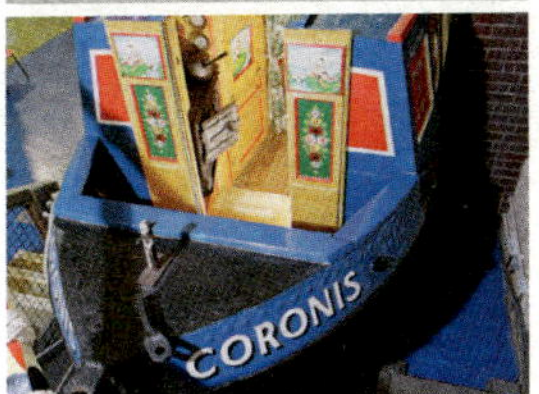

The museum tells the story of London's fascinating canals: the people and their horses and trades. The building is a unique piece of London's heritage – a former ice warehouse where visitors can peer into a giant Victorian ice well.

Winchester Palace 2 miles

Tel: 020 7713 0836

www.canalmuseum.org.uk

2 for 1 entry
OVP 1

London Transport Museum
London WC2E 7BB

Lively galleries depict transport and how it shaped the lives of people living and working in London. Featuring iconic transport posters, the Routemaster bus and the world's first underground steam train.

Close to Chapter House and Wellington Arch

Tel: 020 7565 7298

www.ltmuseum.co.uk

2 for 1 entry
OVP

London Statues

In 1999 English Heritage assumed responsibility for the maintenance of 47 statues and monuments within central London, including the Wellington Arch, which you are invited to explore (see p.43).

Statues provide a fascinating insight into the preoccupations of the period. Many of them are associated with wars and military campaigns, such as the Napoleonic Wars, the Boer War and the two World Wars, whilst others represent Royal figures such as Charles I (1633) and Edward VII (1921).

A leaflet giving more information about the intriguing history of 20th-century war memorials in London is available from Customer Services (tel 0870 333 1181).

The Capital's Monuments

Viscount Alanbrooke Whitehall, SW1
Queen Anne Queen Anne's Gate, SW1
Belgian War Memorial Victoria Embankment
Simon Bolivar Belgrave Square, SW1
Duke of Cambridge Whitehall, SW1
Colin Campbell Waterloo Place, SW1
Carabiniers Memorial Chelsea Embankment, SW3
Edith Cavell St Martin's Place, WC2
Cenotaph Whitehall, SW1
King Charles I Whitehall, SW1
Queen Charlotte Queen Square, WC1
Clive of India King Charles St, SW1
Christopher Columbus Belgrave Square, SW1
Crimea Memorial Waterloo Place, SW1
Thomas Cubitt St George's Drive, Pimlico, SW1
Lord Curzon Carlton House Terrace, SW1
Duke of Devonshire Whitehall, SW1
Edward VII Waterloo Place, SW1
General Eisenhower Grosvenor Square, W1
Sir John Franklin Waterloo Place, SW1
General de Gaulle Carlton Gardens, SW1
King George II Golden Square, W1
King George III Cockspur St, SW1
General Gordon Victoria Embankment
Earl Haig Whitehall, SW1
Sir Arthur Harris St Clement Danes, WC2
Lord Herbert Waterloo Place, SW1
King James II National Gallery, Trafalgar Square, WC2
Duke of Kent Crescent Gardens (locked), Portland Place, W1
Baron Lawrence Waterloo Place, SW1
Machine Gun Corps Apsley Way, W1
Montgomery Whitehall, SW1
Lord Napier of Magdala Queen's Gate, SW7
Marble Arch W1
Florence Nightingale Waterloo Place, SW1
Samuel Plimsoll Victoria Embankment
Lord Portal Victoria Embankment
Sir Walter Raleigh Old Royal Naval College, Greenwich, SE10
Royal Artillery Memorial Apsley Way, W1
General de San Martin Belgrave Square, SW1
Captain Scott Waterloo Place, SW1
Viscount Slim Whitehall, SW1
Lord Trenchard Victoria Embankment
George Washington Trafalgar Square, WC2
Duke of Wellington Apsley Way, W1
Wellington Arch and Quadriga Apsley Way, W1
King William III St James's Square, SW1

Dover Castle – see page 58

South East

www.english-heritage.org.uk/southeast

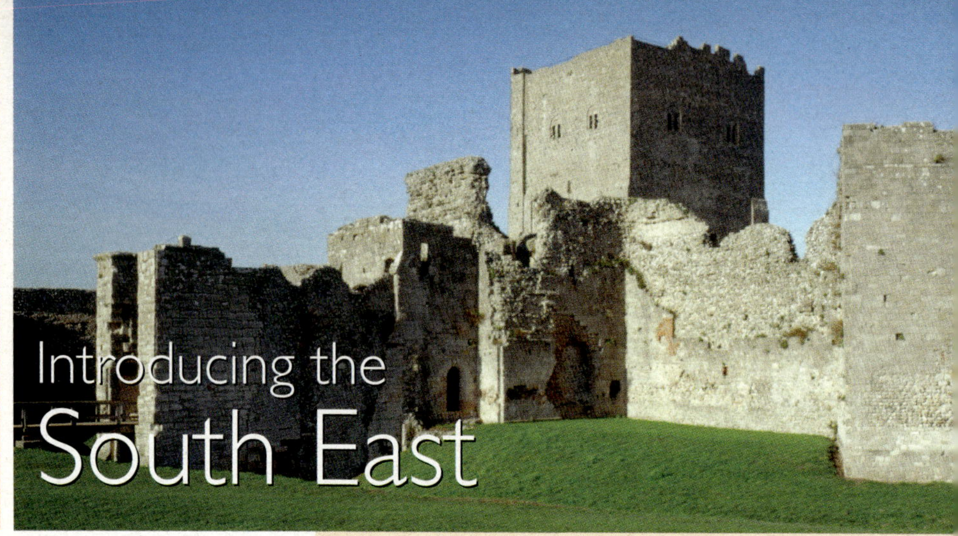
Introducing the
South East

Remember to check opening times before you visit any of our properties.

Details of all bus travel in England are available from Traveline on 0871 200 2233 or visit www.traveline.org.uk

Make the most of your membership and keep up to date with upcoming events, the latest news and special offers by subscribing to our e-newsletter. Register online at **www.english-heritage.org.uk/newsletter** and we'll deliver the latest from English Heritage straight to your inbox.

Berkshire

Donnington Castle

Hampshire

Bishop's Waltham Palace
Calshot Castle
Flowerdown Barrows
Fort Brockhurst
Fort Cumberland
The Grange at Northington
Hurst Castle
King James's and Landport Gates
Medieval Merchant's House
Netley Abbey
Portchester Castle
Royal Garrison Church
Silchester Roman City Walls and Amphitheatre
Southwick Priory
Titchfield Abbey
Wolvesey Castle (Old Bishop's Palace)

Kent

Bayham Old Abbey
Deal Castle
Dover Castle
Dymchurch Martello Tower
Eynsford Castle
Faversham Stone Chapel
The Home of Charles Darwin, Down House
Horne's Place Chapel
Kit's Coty House and Little Kit's Coty House
Knights Templar Church
Lullingstone Roman Villa
Maison Dieu
Milton Chantry
Old Soar Manor
Reculver Towers and Roman Fort
Richborough Roman Amphitheatre
Richborough Roman Fort
Rochester Castle
St Augustine's Abbey and Conduit House
St Augustine's Cross
St John's Commandery
St Leonard's Tower
Sutton Valence Castle
Temple Manor
Upnor Castle
Walmer Castle and Gardens
Western Heights

Oxfordshire

Abingdon County Hall Museum
Deddington Castle
Minster Lovell Hall and Dovecote
North Hinksey Conduit House
North Leigh Roman Villa
Rollright Stones
Uffington Castle, White Horse and Dragon Hill
Wayland's Smithy

Images:
(left) Portchester Castle
(top centre) Royal Garrison Church
(top right) Netley Abbey
(bottom centre) Fort Brockhurst
(bottom right) Titchfield Abbey

Hampshire Holidays

Everyone wants to get the best value both from English Heritage membership and from a day out: and for 'best value' in the South East, it is hard to match the closely-set English Heritage sites around Portsmouth and Southampton. A good starting point might be **Portchester Castle**, surely the most impressive Roman fortress in southern Britain: amazingly, its massive multi-towered walls date substantially from the 3rd century AD. Updated with a strong new keep in medieval times, the castle was the first of the long succession of fortifications which eventually made Portsmouth – the Royal Navy's principal base and dockyard – the most heavily defended port in Europe.

King James's and Landport Gates and the **Royal Garrison Church** still bear witness to the great dockyard's history, as do its famous ships – Henry VIII's *Mary Rose*; Nelson's *Victory*; and the pioneering 1860s iron warship *HMS Warrior*. The *Warrior* belongs to the period of intense Anglo-French rivalry which also saw Portsmouth protected by a ring of state-of-the-art Victorian fortresses, including **Fort Brockhurst**. This now houses rarely-seen treasures from English Heritage's archaeological collections, so it is well worth timing a day out to coincide with its opening days. Not all the area's English Heritage sites, indeed, relate to the defence of the realm. A visit to Southampton's **Medieval Merchant's House**, for example, could easily be combined with a trip to well-preserved **Netley Abbey**, or **Titchfield Abbey**, strikingly converted into a Tudor mansion. For both these last two you can download audio tours in advance of your visit, helping you to get even more from a day out.

Check www.english-heritage.org.uk for the latest opening times

Abingdon County Hall Museum
Oxfordshire – OX14 3HG

This splendid 17th-century Baroque building housed a courtroom for Assizes, raised on arches over a market space. It now houses the Abingdon Museum.

Managed by Abingdon Town Council, maintained by English Heritage.

www.abingdonmuseum.org.uk

OPENING TIMES

Closed for renovation in 2011, re-opening in May 2012

HOW TO FIND US

Direction: In Abingdon, 7 miles south of Oxford; in Market Place

Train: Radley 2½ miles

Bus: Oxford Bus Co X2, X3, 4, X13, 35, Stagecoach 31, 34, Thames Travel 32, 32B, 32C, RH Transport 32A, Grayline 43, 44, 46, 48, 49A, Heyfordian 114 & 116

Tel: 01235 523703

MAP Page 276 (3C)
OS Map 164, 170: SU498971

Appuldurcombe House
See Isle of Wight – Page 79

1066 Battle of Hastings, Abbey and Battlefield
See feature – Page 52

Bayham Old Abbey
Kent – TN3 8BE

The impressive ruins of an abbey of Premonstratensian 'white canons', on the Kent-Sussex border. They include much of the 13th to 15th-century church, the chapter house and a picturesque 14th-century gatehouse. Now set in a landscape designed by Humphry Repton, the famous landscape gardener, who also planned the grounds of Kenwood House in London. Rooms in the 'Georgian Gothick' dower house are also open to visitors.

NON-MEMBERS

Adult	£4.20
Concession	£3.80
Child	£2.50

OPENING TIMES

1 Apr-30 Sep, daily	11am-5pm
1 Oct-31 Mar	Closed

HOW TO FIND US

Direction: 1¾ miles W of Lamberhurst, off B2169

Train: Frant 4 miles then bus

Bus: Autocar 256 (Tunbridge Wells – Wadhurst)

Tel: 01892 890381

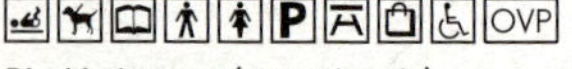

Disabled access (grounds only).

MAP Page 277 (5G)
OS Map 188, 136: TQ650365

Bishop's Waltham Palace
Hampshire – SO32 1DH

The ruins of a medieval palace (and its later additions) used by the bishops and senior clergy of Winchester as they travelled through their diocese. Winchester was the richest diocese in England, and its properties were grandiose and extravagantly appointed. Much of what can be seen today is the work of William Wykeham, who was bishop from 1367. The ground floor of the farmhouse is occupied by the Bishop's Waltham Town Museum, which exhibits local artefacts.

Other palaces of the bishops of Winchester include Farnham Castle Keep (p.56) and Wolvesey Castle (Old Bishop's Palace) (p.78).

OPENING TIMES

Grounds
1 May-30 Sep, Sun-Fri 10am-5pm
(Grounds may be open on Sat please ring before visiting)

Farmhouse Museum
1 May-30 Sep, Sat-Sun 2pm-4pm

HOW TO FIND US

Direction: In Bishop's Waltham

Train: Botley 3½ miles

Bus: Brijan bus 7, 8, 17, Stagecoach bus 63 & 69, Blue Star F

Tel: 01489 892460

Disabled access (grounds only).

Dogs on leads (restricted areas only).

MAP Page 276 (6C)
OS Map 185, 119: SU552174

Check www.english-heritage.org.uk for the latest opening times

Boxgrove Priory
West Sussex

The guest house and other remains of a Benedictine priory: much of the fine 12th to 14th-century monastic church survives as the parish church.

OPENING TIMES

Any reasonable time in daylight hours

HOW TO FIND US

Direction: N of Boxgrove; 4 miles E of Chichester, on minor road off A27

Train: Chichester 4 miles

Bus: Stagecoach in the South Downs 55 from Chichester

Parking

MAP Page 276 (6D)
OS Map 197, 121: SU908076

Bramber Castle
West Sussex

The remains of a Norman castle on the banks of the River Adur, founded by William de Braose c. 1073. The earthworks are dominated by a towering wall of the keep-gatehouse.

NEW FOR 2011

New graphic panels describe the castle.

OPENING TIMES

Any reasonable time in daylight hours

HOW TO FIND US

Direction: On W side of Bramber village, off A283

Bramber Castle

Train: Shoreham-by-Sea 4½ miles

Bus: Brighton & Hove 2, 20 & Compass Bus 100 & 106

Parking (limited).

MAP Page 276 (6E)
OS Map 198, 122: TQ185107

Calshot Castle
Hampshire – SO45 1BR

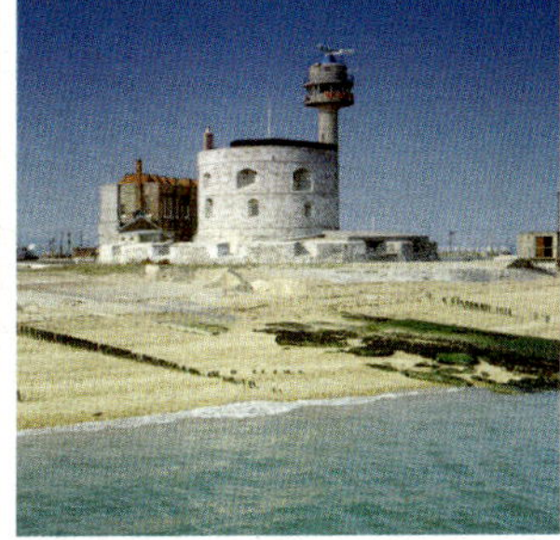

This artillery fort, built by Henry VIII to defend the sea passage to Southampton, later saw service in both World Wars.

Managed by Hampshire County Council.

NON-MEMBERS

Adult	£3.00
Concession	£2.10
Child	£2.10
Family	£7.60

OPENING TIMES

1 Apr-30 Sep, daily	10.30am-4.30pm

HOW TO FIND US

Direction: On spit, 2 miles SE of Fawley, off B3053

Bus: Solent Blue Line Bluestar 9 & H3 pass within 1 mile

Tel: 02380 892023; when castle is closed, please call 02380 892077

Disabled access (Keep: ground floor only; toilets).

MAP Page 276 (6C)
OS Map 196, OL22/OL29/119: SU489025

Camber Castle
East Sussex

The ruins of an unusually unaltered artillery fort, built by Henry VIII to guard the port of Rye. There are limited opening times, but regular guided walks round Rye Harbour Nature Reserve include the castle.

Contact the Reserve Manager for further details.

Managed by Rye Harbour Nature Reserve.

www.wildrye.info/reserve/cambercastle

NON-MEMBERS

Adult	£3.00
Concession	£1.50
(Subject to change)	

Accompanied children free

OPENING TIMES

1 Jul-30 Sep, Sat-Sun (plus Bank Holiday weekends Apr-Sep)	2pm-5pm

Last entry 4.30pm

HOW TO FIND US

Direction: 1 mile walk across fields, off the A259; 1 mile S of Rye, off Harbour Road. No vehicle access. Follow the public footpath from Brede Lock

Train: Rye 1¼ miles

Bus: From surrounding areas to Winchelsea or Rye, then 1½ mile walk; or Coastal Coaches 344 Hastings – Northiam then ¾ mile walk

Tel: 01797 223862

MAP Page 277 (6H)
OS Map 189, 125: TQ922185

Carisbrooke Castle
See Isle of Wight – Page 80

1066 Battle of Hastings, Abbey and Battlefield

East Sussex – TN33 0AD

Perhaps the most famous date in English history – 1066 is the year the Normans defeated the English at the Battle of Hastings. William the Conqueror founded 'Battle' Abbey as penance for the bloodshed and as a memorial to the dead. Here, on the site of its high altar, you can stand at the very spot where King Harold of England fell.

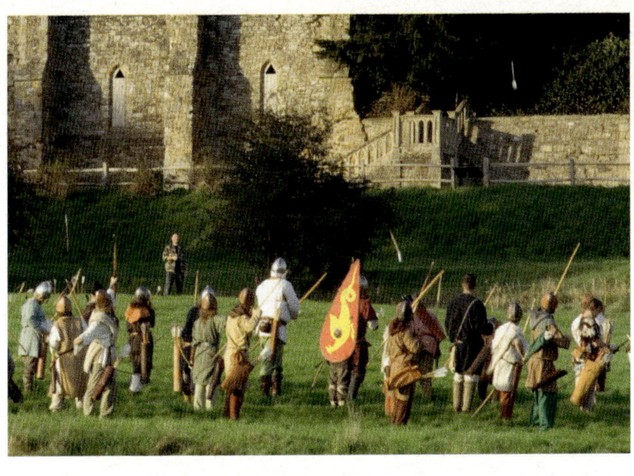

Don't miss the spectacular re-enactment of the Battle of Hastings, which takes place on 15 and 16 October.

An imaginative exhibition, *1066: The Battle for England*, brings the background and impact of this renowned conflict vividly to life. Up-to-date technology and interactive displays draw a striking picture, from both English and Norman viewpoints, of the years which led up to the conflict. They also illustrate the impact this pivotal battle had on shaping English history. Listening points, graphic presentations, hands-on exhibits and touch-screen displays explore how life was for the opposing sides. Central to the exhibition is a short film, narrated by David Starkey, which dramatically recounts the events preceding the bloody struggle, culminating on 14 October 1066 when 'the fields were covered in corpses, and all around the only colour to meet the gaze was blood-red'. *[The Chronicle of Battle Abbey]*.

The audio tour vividly describes and re-creates the sounds of the battle on the very site where it took place. From their ridge-top 'shield wall' the English watched the Normans advancing towards them. Early in the battle, part of the Norman army panicked and retreated, but William rallied his soldiers and successfully counterattacked. Several 'pretended retreats' followed, in which the English were lured into breaking ranks in pursuit, only to be cut down. After some ten hours of fighting, the Normans launched an assault which finally broke the fatally-weakened English shield wall. At this stage King Harold was killed, perhaps struck in the eye by an arrow as depicted in the famous Bayeux Tapestry. By nightfall the Norman victory was complete. The audio tour uses 'interviews' with soldiers, monks and key figures of the time to retell the story of this fateful event, and there also is a version especially created for children.

Battle Abbey enjoyed great wealth and special privileges as the symbol of Norman triumph. Though little of its original Norman structure survives, you can still see many later monastic buildings, including the dormitory range with its fine vaulted novices' chamber. The west range, incorporating the abbots' Great Hall, was converted into a

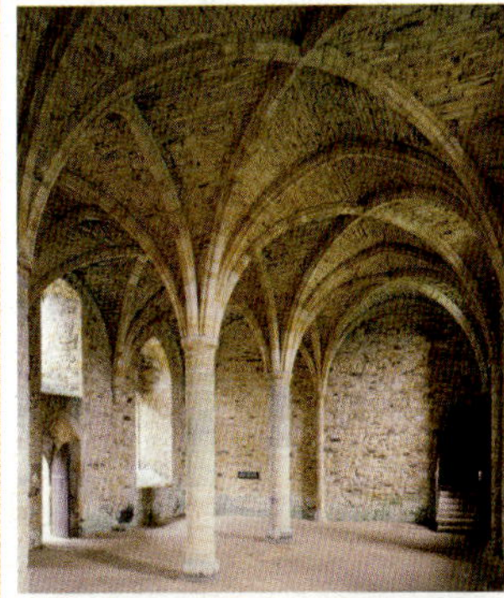

1066 Battle of Hastings, Abbey and Battlefield | continued

From Battle you can take the 1066 Walk to Pevensey Castle (one of Britain's oldest strongholds) where William first landed before moving to Hastings (see p.70).

mansion after Henry VIII's Dissolution of the Monasteries, and is now a school (Abbots Hall tours in school holidays). Best preserved and most impressive of all is the Great Gatehouse, rebuilt in about 1338 and among the finest surviving monastic entrances in Britain. The battlefield – later part of the abbey's Great Park – and abbey were purchased for the nation in 1976.

Visit the abbey museum, which explores the history of the abbey and includes artefacts found on-site during excavations. Children will also enjoy the Discovery Centre which is open every weekend and throughout the school holidays, when family-focused guided tours of the site also run. Look out, too, for our programme of family-friendly events, including the Battle of Hastings re-enactment, 15 & 16 October.

Take a break in the stylish café, serving light lunches and all-day refreshments. Contemporary in design, it has both indoor and outdoor seating and wonderful views of the historic gatehouse.

Following your visit, why not spend a pleasant afternoon in Battle town: it has a Town Trail, museum, plenty of antique shops and hosts events and farmers' markets. From Battle you can take the '1066 Walk' to Pevensey Castle (one of Britain's oldest strongholds) where William first landed before moving to Hastings.

Find out about other places in the area by visiting the Tourist Information Centre in the site shop, which is accessible from Battle High Street.

www.english-heritage.org.uk/1066

Holiday cottage available to let

NON-MEMBERS

Adult	£7.30
Concession	£6.60
Child	£4.40
Family	£19.00

OPENING TIMES

1 Apr-30 Sep, daily	10am-6pm
1 Oct-31 Mar, daily	10am-4pm
24-26 Dec and 1 Jan	Closed

HOW TO FIND US

Direction: In Battle, at south end of High St. Take the A2100 off the A21

Train: Battle ½ mile

Bus: Renown Coaches 95, Countryliner 304 & 355, Battle Community Transport B71, B73, B75, B79, B80 & B8

Tel: 01424 775705/776787 (shop)

Local Tourist Information: Battle and Bexhill Tourist information 01424 776789/776790

E OVP

Audio tours (suitable for families, the visually impaired and for those in wheelchairs or with learning difficulties. Also available in Dutch, French, German, Japanese and Spanish; braille guides in English only). Audio tours are complimentary but will not be issued on special events days.

Café – winter opening may be limited. Please call for details.

Disabled access (grounds and visitor centre).

Dogs on leads (restricted areas only).

Parking (charge payable for members and non-members).

MAP Page 277 (6G)
OS Map 199, 124: TQ749157

Deal Castle Kent – CT14 7BA

© Skyscan Balloon Photography

Deal Castle is one of the finest Tudor artillery castles in England. It is among the earliest and most elaborate of a chain of coastal forts, which also includes Calshot, Camber, Walmer and Pendennis Castles. Most were built 'with all speed, and without sparing any cost' between 1539 and 1542 by order of King Henry VIII, who feared an invasion by European Catholic powers. Its squat, rounded bastions were designed to deflect incoming cannon balls, and acted as platforms from which to fire increasingly sophisticated artillery pieces. Deal is also equipped for close-quarter defence, with no less than 145 embrasures for firearms. The fort guarded the sheltered anchorage of 'the Downs' – the stretch of water between the shore and the hazardous Goodwin Sands, a graveyard of ships.

The foreign invasion never materialised, but Deal Castle saw hard fighting during the Second Civil War (1648). Taken by forces from the rebel Royalist fleet, it was twice besieged by Parliamentarians, and finally surrendered after the bloody repulse of a relief attempt.

Today, it is a fascinating castle to explore, with long, dark passages, battlements and a massive basement in which an absorbing exhibition is housed. A pleasant cycle path links Deal and Walmer Castles along the beachfront.

NON-MEMBERS

Adult	£4.80
Concession	£4.30
Child	£2.90
Family	£12.50

OPENING TIMES

1 Apr-30 Sep, daily	10am-6pm
1 Oct-31 Mar	Closed

HOW TO FIND US

Direction: SW of Deal town centre

Train: Deal ½ mile

Bus: Stagecoach East Kent services 13, 13A, 84, 84A, Kent Top Temps Travel 541, 542, 544 & 593

Tel: 01304 372762

Audio tours (also available in Dutch, French and German).

Disabled access (courtyards and ground floor only, parking available).

MAP Page 277 (5J)
OS Map 179, 150: TR378522

Deddington Castle
Oxfordshire

These extensive earthworks are the remains of an 11th-century motte and bailey castle.

Managed by Deddington Parish Council.

OPENING TIMES

Any reasonable time in daylight hours

HOW TO FIND US

Direction: S of B4031 on E side of Deddington; 17 miles N of Oxford

Train: King's Sutton 5 miles

Bus: Stagecoach in Oxfordshire 59/A/B Oxford – Banbury, to within ½ mile

MAP Page 276 (2C)
OS Map 151, 191: SP472316

Donnington Castle
West Berkshire

The striking, twin-towered, 14th-century gatehouse of this castle, later the focus of a Civil War siege and battle, survives amid impressive earthworks.

OPENING TIMES

Any reasonable time in daylight hours; exterior viewing only

HOW TO FIND US

Direction: 1 mile N of Newbury, off B4494

Train: Newbury 1¼ miles

Bus: Newbury Buses 6, 6A & 107

Disabled access (steep slopes within grounds).

MAP Page 276 (4C)
OS Map 174, 158: SU461692

Dover Castle
See feature – Page 58

Down House – see The Home of Charles Darwin
See feature – Page 62

Dymchurch Martello Tower
Kent – TN29 0NL

One of 103 ingeniously-designed artillery towers built from 1805 at vulnerable points around the south and east coasts to resist threatened Napoleonic invasion. Exterior viewing only.

OPENING TIMES

Viewing by appointment only – please call 01304 211067

HOW TO FIND US

Direction: In Dymchurch, from High St only

Train: Sandling 7 miles; Dymchurch (Romney, Hythe and Dymchurch Railway) adjacent

Bus: Stagecoach in East Kent 101 &102

MAP Page 277 (5H)
OS Map 189, 138: TR102292

Eynsford Castle
Kent – DA4 0AA

The substantial stone walls of a very early Norman 'enclosure castle', begun c. 1085-7 and unusually little-altered by later building works. This rare survival stands in an attractive village setting, not far from Lullingstone Roman Villa (p.67).

OPENING TIMES

1 Apr-30 Sep, daily	10am-6pm
1 Oct-30 Nov, daily	10am-4pm
1 Dec-31 Jan, Wed-Sun	10am-4pm
1 Feb-31 Mar, daily	10am-4pm
24-26 Dec and 1 Jan	Closed

Eynsford Castle

HOW TO FIND US

Direction: In Eynsford, off A225

Train: Eynsford 1 mile

Bus: Griffin Bus 408 & 419 & 420; Go-Coach 421

MAP Page 277 (4F)
OS Map 177, 162: TQ542658

Farnham Castle Keep
Surrey – GU9 0JA

The impressive motte and shell keep of a castle founded in 1138 by Bishop Henry of Blois. Long a residence of the wealthy bishops of Winchester, the accommodation in the keep was updated in the 1520s. The keep was abandoned after Civil War service, but much altered parts of the medieval bishops' residence remain in use in private hands. A viewing platform and stairway now reveal the buried remains of an earlier tower.

Managed by Farnham Castle.

OPENING TIMES

1 Apr-23 Dec, Mon-Fri (or dusk, whichever is earlier)	9am-5pm
Sat-Sun & Bank Hols	10am-4pm
24 Dec-31 Jan	Closed
1 Feb-31 Mar, Mon-Fri (or dusk, whichever is earlier)	9am-5pm
Sat-Sun & Bank Hols	10am-4pm

Last admission 30 minutes before closing time

HOW TO FIND US

Direction: ½ mile N of Farnham town centre, on A287

Farnham Castle Keep

Train: Farnham ¾ mile

Bus: Stagecoach Service 71 passes the castle, but other Stagecoach services stop nearby

Tel: 01252 713393

OVP

MAP Page 276 (5D)
OS Map 186, 145: SU837473

Faversham Stone Chapel (Our Lady of Elverton)
Kent

The ruins of the small Anglo-Saxon and medieval chapel of Stone-next-Faversham – the only Christian building in England to incorporate within its fabric the remains of a 4th-century Romano-British pagan mausoleum. It lay close to the probable site of the small Roman town of Durolevum and its Roman cemetery at Ospringe, finds from which can be seen at Maison Dieu (see p.66).

Managed by The Faversham Society.

www.faversham.org/society

OPENING TIMES

Any reasonable time in daylight hours

HOW TO FIND US

Direction: In field immediately North of A2 just West of Ospringe and opposite Faversham Road

Train: Faversham 1½ miles

Bus: Chalkwell 324, Arriva/ Chalkwell 333, Chalkwell/ Kent Top Travel 335

Faversham Stone Chapel

Tel: 01795 534542

E-mail: ticfaversham@btconnect.com

MAP Page 277 (4H)
OS Map 178, 149: TQ992613

Flowerdown Barrows
Hampshire

Three Bronze Age burial mounds, once part of a much larger 'barrow cemetery', including two bowl barrows, and the largest and finest disc barrow in Hampshire.

OPENING TIMES

Any reasonable time in daylight hours

HOW TO FIND US

Direction: Off B3049, out of Winchester to Littleton; at crossroads in centre of village

Train: Winchester 2 miles

Bus: Stagecoach in Hampshire 7, 7A, 25, 68

MAP Page 276 (5C)
OS Map 185, 132: SU459320

Fort Brockhurst
Hampshire – PO12 4DS

© Skyscan Balloon Photography

Fort Brockhurst

One of a number of forts built in the 1850s and 1860s to protect Portsmouth and its vital harbour against a French invasion. Largely unaltered, the parade ground, gun ramps and moated keep can all be viewed.

The fort currently stores a treasure trove of objects from English Heritage's extensive reserve collections. Objects on display have been excavated from sites in the South East and South West. They include stonework, textiles, jewellery and furniture from many periods, as well as rarely-seen treasures on tour from stores in the North and East. The Collections Access Centre offers pre-booked adult and school groups a hands-on experience of English Heritage's rich and varied collections of artefacts, under the guidance of a curator, conservator or trained educator.

Portchester Castle – which acted as a prison during the Napoleonic Wars – is nearby (see p.72).

OPENING TIMES

The fort is open on the 2nd Sat of every month from 1 Apr-30 Sep, 11am-3pm. The Collections Resource Centre will also be open

HOW TO FIND US

Direction: Off A32, in Gunner's Way, Elson; on N side of Gosport

Train: Fareham 3 miles

Bus: First 81-7 Fareham – Gosport Ferry (passes Fareham; also Gosport Ferry links with Portsmouth & Southsea)

Tel: 02392 581059

Fort Brockhurst

Disabled access (grounds and ground floor only).

Dogs on leads (restricted areas only).

MAP Page 276 (6C)
OS Map 196, OL29/119: SU596021

Fort Cumberland
Hampshire – PO4 9LD

Perhaps England's most impressive piece of 18th-century defensive architecture, Fort Cumberland was reconstructed in pentagonal form by the Duke of Richmond between 1785 and 1810, and designed to protect Langstone Harbour. Southsea beach is nearby. Access is by pre-booked guided tour only.

OPENING TIMES

Open for pre-booked group guided tours and Heritage Open Days

HOW TO FIND US

Direction: In Portsmouth's Eastney district on the estuary approach, via Henderson Rd off Eastney Rd, or from the Esplanade

Train: Fratton 2 miles

Bus: First 15, 16/A Portsmouth Harbour – Hayling Ferry

Tel: 02392 378291

MAP Page 276 (6C)
OS Map 196, 119/120: SZ683993

The Home of Charles Darwin, Down House
See feature – Page 62

Dover Castle Kent – CT16 1HU

'The Key to England' for over nine centuries, the mighty fortress of Dover Castle displays at its core a dazzling evocation of a medieval royal palace. From June 2011 the Secret Wartime Tunnels beneath it will also host an atmospheric new presentation of the 'Miracle of Dunkirk', master-minded here in 1940.

Henry II and his successors reared the mighty stone castle, creating here the first 'concentric' fortress in western Europe.

Check www.english-heritage.org.uk for the latest opening times

© J.Perugia

Commanding the shortest sea crossing between England and the continent, Dover Castle boasts a long and immensely eventful history. Its spectacular site atop the famous 'White Cliffs' was originally an Iron Age hill fort, and still houses a Roman lighthouse. The Anglo-Saxon church beside it was probably part of a Saxon fortified settlement, converted soon after 1066 into a Norman earthwork castle. Thereafter Dover Castle was garrisoned uninterruptedly until 1958, a record equalled only by the Tower of London and Windsor Castle. From 1740 its defences were updated in response to every European war involving Britain, and were crucially tested during the darkest days of World War II.

The Great Tower Re-creation

Dover Castle is above all a great medieval fortress, created by King Henry II and his Plantagenet successors. At its heart stands the mighty Great Tower, the grandest and among the last of the keeps raised by the kings of England during the 11th and 12th centuries. Built between 1180 and 1185, this symbol of kingly power was also a palace designed for royal ceremony. Here, Henry could welcome and impress distinguished visitors to England – particularly noble pilgrims travelling to the new shrine in Canterbury Cathedral of St Thomas Becket.

The entire interior of Henry's Great Tower palace has been breathtakingly recreated as it might have appeared when newly completed. Visitors begin their tour in the exhibition near the foot of the towering keep, where imaginative interactive displays tell the dramatic story of Henry II and his turbulent brood – *A Family at War*. A man of superhuman energy and violent rages, Henry ruled an empire stretching from the Scottish Borders to the Pyrenees, but proved unable to master his own quarrelsome and treacherous family. Children can help European pilgrims reach Becket's shrine at Canterbury and visitors can 'Ask the Experts' about the recreated rooms, of which a virtual tour is provided for those unable to tour the Great Tower itself.

Ascending the stairs into the Great Tower, visitors meet the first of the many lifelike projected figures which help to guide them round the six great recreated rooms and several lesser chambers of the palace. Among the most spectacular is the King's Hall, dominated by its canopied throne and decked with wall hangings and recreations of contemporary furniture, all brilliantly coloured. The vibrant colours of the Great Tower's interiors, reflecting medieval reality, are indeed the most striking aspect of the re-creation.

The tour continues via the Royal Chapel to the King's Chamber, focussed on the royal bed. Next come the Guests' Bedchamber and the Guest Hall, shown ready for a feast. The cavernous ground floor is fascinatingly set as the fully-equipped royal Kitchen, Brewery and Bakehouse, while the Armoury displays replicas of the weapons used by Henry's household knights. On selected days, visitors may also encounter costumed live interpreters – including Henry himself – throughout the Great Tower.

A Mighty Fortress

Visitors can then climb to the Great Tower's roof for panoramic views over the castle's immense complex of fortifications, with busy Dover harbour below. Around his impressive keep, Henry built a powerful inner curtain wall, with beyond that an outer curtain wall. These three mutually-supporting lines of defence made Dover the very first 'concentric' fortress in western Europe. Its defences were severely tested during the epic sieges of 1216-17, when the castle resisted ten months of attack.

Check www.english-heritage.org.uk for the latest opening times

Dover Castle continued

Admiralty Lookout

Intrepid visitors can still descend into the 'Medieval Tunnels', burrowed beneath the castle during and after the 1216-7 siege. To counter the threat of invasion from Napoleonic France, a second and much larger network of tunnels was begun in 1797, housing secure underground barracks for over 2000 soldiers.

The Finest Hour: Dover at War

At the beginning of World War II these tunnels were recommissioned and extended, housing a hospital and becoming a bomb-proof nerve centre for the defence of Dover and the coast. Here Vice Admiral Ramsay directed 'Operation Dynamo', the evacuation of British and Allied troops from the Dunkirk beaches in May and June 1940. Thereafter the castle was a frontline fortress, witnessing the air and sea battles which named this area 'Hellfire Corner'.

The cliff-top Admiralty Lookout also played an important role in both World Wars. Inside, a First World War Fire Command Post has been recreated, with displays on the castle's role as a naval signal station.

The Stone Hut, built in 1912 for the Royal Garrison Artillery, is now used as an archaeological store for the South East. On the first Friday of every month (or by pre-arranged booking), visitors can view changing exhibitions of treasures from across the region, including artefacts from both World War II and the Cold War.

All this, and very much more, makes Dover Castle well worth a whole day's exploration.

The Other Boleyn Girl, starring Natalie Portman and Scarlett Johanssen; Zeffirelli's *Hamlet*, starring Mel Gibson; and *To Kill a King*, starring Dougray Scott.

www.english-heritage.org.uk/dovercastle

NON-MEMBERS

Adult	£16.00
Concession	£14.40
Child	£9.60
Family	£41.60

Price includes Secret Wartime Tunnels tour. Additional charges for members and non-members may apply on event days

OPENING TIMES

1 Apr-31 Jul, daily	10am-6pm
1-31 Aug, daily	9.30am-6pm
1-30 Sep, daily	10am-6pm
1-31 Oct, daily	10am-5pm
1 Nov-31 Jan, Thu-Mon	10am-4pm
1 Feb-31 Mar, daily	10am-4pm
24-26 Dec and 1 Jan	Closed

Last admission and last tour, 1 hour before closing. Secret Wartime Tunnels tour: the Underground Hospital is accessed through timed tour slots which are booked on arrival at the castle. Groups of 11+ are asked to call the site in advance

PLEASE NOTE: The Secret Wartime Tunnels complex will be closed until Saturday 4 June 2011, when *Operation Dynamo: Rescue from Dunkirk* and the new exhibition, shop and catering areas open. During this period tours of the Underground Hospital will continue, and a series of 'Hidden Dover' tours of other areas of the castle, led by our expert guides, will also be available. As availability of these tours may be limited, we advise visitors to check the website or call the site for full details. The Great Tower and other attractions within the castle remain fully open throughout the year

HOW TO FIND US

Direction: E of Dover town centre

Train: Dover Priory 1½ miles

Bus: Stagecoach 15/X & 80

Tel: 01304 211067

Local Tourist Information: Dover 01304 205108

E P OVP

Please refer to the Dover Castle web page or ring the site directly for information on accessibility. Mobility scooters, wheelchair routes and guides are available on site.

Dogs on leads (restricted areas only).

We advise you to wear comfortable shoes.

MAP Page 277 (5J)

OS Map 179, 138: TR325419

NEW FOR 2011 | Dover Castle

Operation Dynamo: Rescue from Dunkirk

At 6:57 on May 26th 1940, in a small room deep beneath Dover Castle in a complex of tunnels cut from the chalk of the White Cliffs, a teleprinter spluttered into life. The words of its brief message – 'Operation Dynamo is to commence' – were meaningless to all but a few.

One of the few was Vice Admiral Bertram Ramsay and this was the bad news he had been expecting. Gathering his staff officers together, with a calmness born of over 40 years of service in the Royal Navy, he set the operation in motion. The British Army and its French allies were trapped at Dunkirk, backs to the sea, fighting for their lives in a shrinking pocket of land. Ramsay and his staff had to bring them back and if anyone thought it impossible, nobody said.

The tunnels of Dover Castle were home to Ramsay's naval headquarters. From the onset of the Second World War in September 1939, the handful of men and women based there had planned the activities of a determined squadron of Royal Navy ships whose task was to keep the enemy out of the Straits of Dover. Operation Dynamo was entirely different, demanding rapid planning and round-the-clock working to assemble and send a huge improvised fleet of ships, naval and civilian, large and small, to Dunkirk, under attack from air, sea and land. Over 300,000 soldiers were depending on Ramsay, his HQ staff and the sailors in his ships.

On June 4th 2011, English Heritage will re-open the tunnels to evoke those dark days of 1940 via dramatic sets that will reveal the countdown to war, the lightning strike of the German army across Western Europe, and the trapping of the British Army on the open beaches and shattered town of Dunkirk. Visitors walking through the tunnels will see, hear, and feel the danger of Operation Dynamo, the role played by Ramsay and his Dover command, and the extraordinary suffering, sacrifice and bravery of all those who enabled the miraculous Rescue from Dunkirk.

© Imperial War Museum

© Imperial War Museum

Check www.english-heritage.org.uk for the latest opening times

The Home of Charles Darwin, Down House

Kent – BR6 7JT

A delightful place to visit in itself, Down House is also a site of outstanding international significance. Here the famous scientist Charles Darwin lived with his family for forty years; here he worked on his revolutionary theories; and here he wrote *On the Origin of Species by Means of Natural Selection* – the book which shook the Victorian world and has influenced our thinking ever since.

Visitors are guided round Darwin's family rooms by a hand-held multimedia tour, narrated by Sir David Attenborough and Andrew Marr. The tour also includes the extensive gardens – Darwin's 'outdoor laboratory' and the place where he made many of his discoveries.

Stop off at the tearoom, situated in Darwin's kitchen area, for a refreshing break before exploring the grounds.

Darwin's work and personality are vividly reflected throughout the house and gardens. The ground floor rooms have been recreated as they appeared when he lived here with his indefatigably supportive wife Emma – a member of the renowned Wedgwood family – and their many children. They include the 'Old Study' where Darwin wrote his books, following a rigid routine despite chronic illness and frequent good-natured interruptions by his children. It still displays his chair, writing desk and many personal items. The family's Drawing Room – with Emma's grand piano – Billiard Room and Dining Room are also on show, likewise mainly furnished with items original to the house. Visitors are guided round Darwin's family rooms by a hand-held multimedia tour, narrated by Sir David Attenborough and Andrew Marr. The tour now also includes the extensive gardens – Darwin's 'outdoor laboratory' and the place where he made many of his discoveries.

The video guide includes commentaries by experts, animations, film footage and games for all the family. It is one of many exciting interactive developments at the Home of Charles Darwin introduced to celebrate the 200th anniversary of Darwin's birth and the 150th anniversary of the publication of *On the Origin of Species* in 2009.

'Uncovering Origin' Exhibition

An exciting exhibition on the house's first floor covers Darwin's life, his scientific work, and the controversy which it provoked. It includes many previously unseen objects, with highlights including manuscript pages from the *Origin of Species*; Darwin's hat, microscope and notebooks; and a copy of *Das Kapital* inscribed to him by Karl Marx.

Beginning with an introduction to Darwin, his place in Victorian science, and the impact of his theories, the displays continue with his famous five-year voyage aboard the *Beagle* in 1831-6, including a full-scale recreation of his ship's cabin. The notebooks and journals compiled on this round-the-world voyage have been digitised and annotated, allowing visitors to explore them page by page. Further displays highlight the *Origin of Species*, a book which sold out its first edition immediately and gave Darwin wealth, as well as international recognition and notoriety. They also examine how his theories were publicised and defended, principally via

The Home of Charles Darwin – Down House | continued

letter-writing. Visitors can explore some of his key ideas (including his investigations into the expression of emotions in humans and animals) through hands-on interactives and installations. The Darwin children's schoolroom celebrates family life at Down.

There is also an education room, available for family learning at weekends, and a research room for those interested in delving deeper.

Experiments in the Gardens

By no means the stereotypically stern Victorian father, Darwin involved his children in his practical experiments in the extensive grounds of Down House. Visitors too can now follow these via the video guide, beginning with Darwin's 'weed garden' illustrating the struggle for existence in nature.

The sundial amid pretty flowerbeds highlights Emma Darwin's role as a gardener; an iconic mulberry tree recalls family traditions; and a 'lawn experiment' investigates proliferation of plant species. Further afield are the 'worm stone', which Darwin used to measure undermining by earthworms, and a 'fungi field'.

The nearby hot-house features some of Darwin's most fascinating experiments, involving carnivorous plants, exotic orchids and climbing species. The curiously-shaped tennis court evokes his family and social life, and there is a working beehive in the laboratory. After a tour of the extensive kitchen gardens, visitors finally reach what is for many a place of pilgrimage: the wooded Sandwalk, Darwin's famous 'thinking path', which he paced five times a day while working out his theories.

Virtual Access

Gain virtual access to Darwin's world through the Home of Charles Darwin pages on the English Heritage website. Features include interactive digital highlights from one of the rarest Darwin manuscript collections in the world, including his *Beagle* notebooks and diary, plus a virtual tour of parts of the house and grounds.

No photography is allowed inside the house.

Unfortunately picnics are not allowed in the grounds, as they are part of a 'Site of Importance for Nature Conservation.' A tearoom with outdoor seating space is available.

www.english-heritage.org.uk/darwin

NON-MEMBERS	
Adult	£9.90
Concession	£8.90
Child	£5.90
Family	£25.70

OPENING TIMES	
1 Apr-30 Jun, Wed-Sun & Bank Hols	11am-5pm
1 Jul-31 Aug, daily	11am-5pm
1 Sept-31 Oct, Wed-Sun	11am-5pm
1 Nov-18 Dec, Wed-Sun	11am-4pm
19 Dec-31 Jan	Closed
1 Feb-31 Mar, Wed-Sun	11am-4pm

Please note: on open days, gardens can be accessed from 10am

HOW TO FIND US

Direction: Luxted Rd, Downe; off A21or A233

Train: Orpington 3¾ miles

Bus: TfL bus R8 from Orpington passes; TfL bus 146 from Bromley North & South terminates in Downe village ½ mile from property

Tel: 01689 859119

E P OVP

Audio tour is the multimedia tour.

Parking (plus space for one coach).

MAP Page 277 (4F)
OS Map 177/187,147: TQ431611

The Grange at Northington
Hampshire

Set like a lakeside temple in a landscaped park, the Grange at Northington is the foremost example of the Greek Revival style in England. Created between 1804 and 1809 when William Wilkins encased an earlier house in Classical facades, most striking is the temple front supported on eight gigantic columns. It provides a stunning backdrop for the opera evenings which take place here in the summer; call 01962 868600 for details.

The 1999 film, *Onegin*, with Ralph Fiennes.

OPENING TIMES

Exterior only:

1 Apr-31 May, daily	10am-6pm
1 Jun-31 Jul, daily	9am-12pm
1 Aug-30 Sep, daily	10am-6pm
1 Oct-31 Mar, daily	10am-4pm

Closes 12pm June and July for opera evenings

24-26 Dec and 1 Jan	Closed

HOW TO FIND US

Direction: Located 4 miles N of New Alresford, off B3046 along a farm track – 450 metres (493 yards)

Train: Winchester 8 miles

Bus: Nearest bus service is Stagecoach Hampshire 64 to Itchen Abbas or Mervyns Coaches 95, 96 to Lunways then 3 mile walk

Tel: 01424 775705

Disabled access (with assistance, steep steps to terrace).

MAP Page 276 (5C)
OS Map 185, 132: SU562362

Horne's Place Chapel
Kent

A rare survival of a fine domestic chapel, built for William Horne in 1366 and attached to his timber-framed manor house, which was attacked during the Peasants' Revolt of 1381. The house and chapel are privately owned.

OPENING TIMES

By prior arrangement; please call 01304 211067

HOW TO FIND US

Direction: 1½ miles N of Appledore

Train: Appledore 2½ miles

Bus: Stagecoach East Kent service 11B (one return weekday journey) & Kent Top Temps service 293 (Mon, Wed, Thu, Fri only)

Parking (nearby).

MAP Page 277 (5H)
OS Map 189, 125: TQ958309

Hurst Castle
Hampshire – SO41 0TP

One of the most advanced of the artillery fortresses built by Henry VIII: used as a prison for eminent 17th-century captives, including King Charles I, and later strengthened during the 19th and 20th centuries.

Hurst Castle

It commands the narrow entrance to the Solent.

Managed by Hurst Castle Services.

NON-MEMBERS

Adult	£4.00
Concession	£3.50
Child	£2.50

OPENING TIMES

1 Apr-30 Sep, daily	10.30am-5.30pm
1-31 Oct, daily	10.30am-4pm

Occasional opening winter weekends – please ring 01590 642500 to confirm

HOW TO FIND US

Direction: 1½ mile walk on shingle spit from Milford-on-Sea. Best approached by ferry from Keyhaven – call 01590 642500 for ferry details and fares

Train: Lymington Town 6½ miles

Bus: Wilts & Dorset X12 to Milford-On-Sea to within 2½ miles, or 1 mile to ferry

Tel: 01590 642344

Dogs on leads (restricted areas only).

Tearoom/restaurant (Castle Café, not managed by EH. Open Apr-May weekends only, Jun-Sep daily).

Parking (charge payable, at Milford seafront or Keyhaven).

MAP Page 276 (7B)
OS Map 196, OL22/OL29: SZ318897

King James's and Landport Gates, Portsmouth

Hampshire – PO1 2EJ

Two ornamental gateways, once part of Portsmouth's defences, King James's Gate (of 1687) has been moved, but Landport Gate (1760), once the principal entrance to Portsmouth and possibly based on a design by Nicholas Hawksmoor, remains in its original position.

OPENING TIMES

Any reasonable time in daylight hours; exterior viewing only

HOW TO FIND US

Direction: King James's Gate forms the entrance to United Services Recreation Ground (officers), Burnaby Rd; Landport Gate as above, men's entrance on St George's Road

Train: Portsmouth Harbour ¼ mile

Bus: First services 5, 5A, 6, 6A, 15, 16A and Stagecoach service 700 pass Landport Gate. First services 15, 19 and Stagecoach 23 passes within a short walk of King James Gate

MAP Page 276 (6C)
OS Map 196, OL29/119
King James's Gate: SZ636999
Landport Gate: SZ634998

Kit's Coty House and Little Kit's Coty House

Kent

The remains of two megalithic 'dolmen' burial chambers, Impressive Kit's Coty has three uprights and a massive capstone; Little Kit's Coty, alias the Countless Stones, is now a jumble of sarsens.

Kit's Coty House and Little Kit's Coty House

OPENING TIMES

Any reasonable time in daylight hours

HOW TO FIND US

Direction: W of A229 2 miles N of Maidstone

Train: Aylesford 2½ miles

Bus: Arriva 101 & 142. Kent Top Temps 150

MAP Page 277 (4G)
OS Map 178/188, 148
Kit Coty's House: TQ745608
Little Kit Coty's House: TQ744604

Knights Templar Church, Dover

Kent

The foundations of a small medieval church, traditionally the site of King John's submission to the Papal Legate in 1213.

OPENING TIMES

Any reasonable time in daylight hours

HOW TO FIND US

Direction: On the Western Heights above Dover

Train: Dover Priory ¾ mile

Bus: Kent Passenger Services 593 from Dover town centre

Tel: 01304 211067

Dogs on leads (restricted areas only).

MAP Page 277 (5J)
OS Map 179, 138: TR313407

Lullingstone Roman Villa

See feature opposite

Maison Dieu

Kent – ME13 8NS

This 13th and 16th-century flint and timber-framed building is virtually all that survives of a much larger complex. It included a 'hospital' for the overnight lodging of pilgrims to Canterbury; a royal suite where many crowned heads stayed on their way to or from the continent; and a school. In layout and appearance it was much like a small monastery. The present building now known as the Maison Dieu is thought to have been a chantry-priest's house. It houses a museum focussing on the Maison Dieu foundation itself and its immediate neighbourhood, and on the extensive finds made during excavations at the main complex and an important Roman cemetery nearby.

Managed by The Faversham Society.

www.faversham.org/society

NON-MEMBERS

Adult	£2.00
Concession	£1.00
Accompanied Children	Free

OPENING TIMES

22 Apr-31 Oct, Sat-Sun, & Bank Hols	2pm-5pm

Group visits at other times by appointment

HOW TO FIND US

Direction: On main A2 on W corner of Water Lane in village of Ospringe. Public car park 300yds W

Train: Faversham ¾ mile

Bus: Chalkwell 324, Arriva/ Chalkwell 333, Chalkwell/ Kent Top Travel 335

Tel: 01795 534542

E-mail: ticfaversham@btconnect.com

E

MAP Page 277 (4H)
OS Map 178, 149: TR003609

Lullingstone Roman Villa

Kent – DA4 0JA

Among the most outstanding Roman villa survivals in Britain, Lullingstone Roman Villa has been vividly re-displayed, providing a unique – and all-weather – opportunity to trace Roman domestic life over three centuries.

Set in the attractive surroundings of the Darent Valley, the villa was begun in about AD 100, and developed to suit the tastes and beliefs of successive wealthy owners. These may have included the family of Pertinax, Governor of Britain and later Roman Emperor for just 87 days in AD 193. Additions included a heated bath-suite and a remarkable underground pagan 'cult-room', including a rare painting of three water-nymphs, by far the oldest wall-painting in English Heritage care.

The villa reached its peak of luxury in the mid-4th century, when a big new dining room was added. This still displays spectacular mosaics, including *Europa and the Bull* and *Bellerophon Killing the Chimera*. By now Christians, the owners also created a 'house-church' above the pagan cult-room: the wall-paintings discovered here are among the earliest surviving evidence for Christianity in Britain. Pagan worship may, however, have continued, suggesting a relaxed relationship between the old and new faiths.

All this is appealingly interpreted in the galleries overlooking the fully excavated remains. These display Lullingstone Roman Villa's fascinating and recently-returned collection of Roman artefacts, enlivened by paintings by the award-winning children's illustrator, Jane Ray. Children and other visitors can also play Roman board games, handle original building materials and try on Roman costumes. A specially-commissioned film and light show brings the villa to life, lighting up areas of the remains as the film reveals how they were once used.

NON-MEMBERS

Adult	£5.90
Concession	£5.30
Child	£3.50
Family	£15.30

OPENING TIMES

1 Apr-30 Sep, daily	10am-6pm
1 Oct-30 Nov, daily	10am-4pm
1 Dec-31 Jan, Wed-Sun	10am-4pm
1 Feb-31 Mar, daily	10am-4pm
24-26 Dec and 1 Jan	Closed

HOW TO FIND US

Direction: ½ mile SW of Eynsford; off A225; off junction 3 of M25

Bus: Griffin Bus 408, 419 & 420; Go Coach 421 to Eynsford village then 1 mile walk

Train: Eynsford 2 miles

Tel: 01322 863467

Parking charge £2.50 to non-members.

MAP Page 277 (4F)

OS Map 177/188, 147/162: TQ530651

Check www.english-heritage.org.uk for the latest opening times

Medieval Merchant's House
Hampshire – SO1 0AT

John Fortin, a merchant who traded with Bordeaux, started building this house c. 1290. A residence and place of business, it stood on one of the busiest streets in medieval Southampton. Now restored to its mid-14th-century appearance by the removal of later additions, it is equipped with replica period furnishings. It stands near the medieval town wall, built to defend Southampton against seaborne attacks. Netley Abbey (p.69), Calshot Castle (p.51) and Hurst Castle (p.65) are all within reasonable travelling distance.

NON-MEMBERS

Adult	£4.00
Concession	£3.60
Child	£2.40

OPENING TIMES

1 Apr-30 Sep, Sun only 12pm-5pm

HOW TO FIND US

Direction: 58 French St, ¼ mile S of city centre, just off Castle Way (between High St and Bugle St)

Train: Southampton ¾ mile

Bus: Unilink U1, U6; First 11A, 12A, 16, 16A

Tel: 02380 221503

OVP

Disabled access (one step).

MAP Page 276 (6B)
OS Map 196, OL22: SU419112

Milton Chantry
Kent – DA12 2BH

Mainly encased in brick but still retaining its 14th-century timber roof, this was in turn part of a hospital, a chantry chapel, a public house and a Georgian barracks before its basement became a World War II gas decontamination chamber. The building is within Gravesham's Heritage Quarter and currently exhibits a fascinating insight into the borough's heritage.

Managed by Gravesham Borough Council.

OPENING TIMES

2 Apr-25 Sep, Sat, Sun & Bank Hols 12pm-5pm

Admission outside these times by appointment

HOW TO FIND US

Direction: In New Tavern Fort Gardens; E of central Gravesend, off A226

Train: Gravesend ¾ mile

Bus: Arriva and Red Route services pass within a short distance

Tel: 01474 321520

MAP Page 277 (4G)
OS Map 177/178, 162/163: TQ653743

Minster Lovell Hall and Dovecote
Oxfordshire

© Skyscan Balloon Photography

The extensive and picturesque ruins of a 15th-century riverside manor house, including a fine hall, south-west tower and complete nearby dovecote. The home of Richard III's henchman Lord Lovell.

OPENING TIMES

Any reasonable time in daylight hours. Dovecote – exterior only

HOW TO FIND US

Direction: Adjacent to Minster Lovell church; 3 miles W of Witney, off A40

Train: Charlbury 7 miles

Bus: Stagecoach in Oxford S2, 233. Bakers 6. Swanbrook 853. Also Villager Community Bus. Then short walk

MAP Page 276 (2B)
OS Map 164, 180: SP325113

Netley Abbey
Hampshire

The most complete surviving Cistercian monastery in

Netley Abbey

southern England, with almost all the walls of its 13th-century church still standing, along with many monastic buildings. After the Dissolution, the buildings were converted into the mansion house of Sir William Paulet. Even in ruins, the abbey continued to be influential, inspiring Romantic writers and poets. A free downloadable audio tour is available from the English Heritage website.

OPENING TIMES

1 Apr-30 Sep, daily	10am-6pm
1 Oct-31 Mar, Sat-Sun	10am-4pm
24-26 Dec and 1 Jan	Closed

HOW TO FIND US

Direction: In Netley; 4 miles SE of Southampton, facing Southampton Water

Train: Netley 1 mile

Bus: First 16/16A

Tel: 02392 378291

Toilets (nearby, across the road near the estuary).

Gravel car park, limited spaces.

MAP Page 276 (6C)
OS Map 196, OL22: SU453090

North Hinksey Conduit House
Oxfordshire

Roofed conduit for Oxford's first water mains, constructed during the early 17th century.

North Hinksey Conduit House

OPENING TIMES

Exterior viewing only
1 Apr-30 Sep, Thu-Sun & Bank Hols 10am-4pm

HOW TO FIND US

Direction: In North Hinksey off A34; 1½ miles W of Oxford. Located off track leading from Harcourt Hill; use the footpath from Ferry Hinksey Lane (near railway station)

Train: Oxford 1½ mile

Bus: Heyfordian service 44. Also Stagecoach Brookes Bus service U1 passes within ¾ mile

MAP Page 276 (3C)
OS Map 164, 180: SP495050

North Leigh Roman Villa
Oxfordshire

The remains of a large, well-built Roman courtyard villa. The most important feature is a nearly complete mosaic tile floor, patterned in reds and browns.

OPENING TIMES

Grounds – any reasonable time in daylight hours. There is a viewing window for the mosaic tile floor.

HOW TO FIND US

Direction: 2 miles N of North Leigh; 10 miles W of Oxford, off A4095

Train: Hanborough 3½ miles

Bus: Stagecoach in Oxford 11 & 242 to within 2 miles

Pedestrian access only from main road – 550 metres (600 yards).

Parking (lay-by, not in access lane).

MAP Page 276 (2B)
OS Map 164, 180: SP397154

Northington Grange
See The Grange at Northington – Page 65

Old Soar Manor
Kent – TN15 0QX

A small but complete portion of a stone manor house built c. 1290. The first floor 'solar' private chamber, with attendant chapel and garderobe, stands over a vaulted undercroft.

Managed by the National Trust on behalf of English Heritage.

OPENING TIMES

2 Apr-29 Sep, Sat-Thu 10am-6pm

HOW TO FIND US

Direction: 1 mile E of Plaxtol

Train: Borough Green and Wrotham 2½ miles

Bus: Autocar 222 Tonbridge – Borough Green; New Enterprise 404 from Sevenoaks. On both, alight at the E end of Plaxtol, then ¾ mile by footpath

Tel: 01732 810378

Parking (limited).

MAP Page 277 (5G)
OS Map 188, 147/148: TQ619541

Royal Osborne
See Isle of Wight – Page 83

Pevensey Castle
East Sussex – BN24 5LE

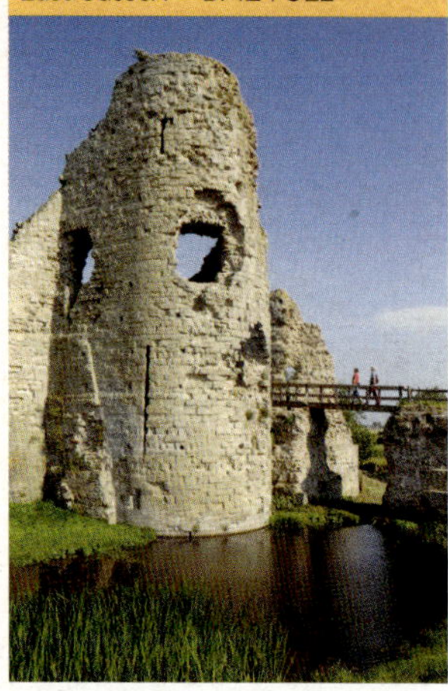

With a history stretching back over 16 centuries, Pevensey Castle chronicles more graphically than any other fortress the story of Britain's south coast defences.

Beginning in the 4th century as one of the last and strongest of the Roman 'Saxon Shore' forts – two-thirds of whose towered walls still stand – it was the landing place of William the Conqueror's army in 1066.

During the century after the Conquest a full-scale Norman castle, with a great square keep and a powerful gatehouse, was built within one corner of the fort. In the 1250s the towered bailey wall was constructed, and soon put to the test during the great siege of 1264. Later still the castle was strengthened to face the threat of the Spanish Armada in 1588. This was not Pevensey's last military service: during World War II, pillboxes and machine-gun posts were cunningly camouflaged among its ancient walls.

An exhibition with artefacts found on site and an audio tour tell the story of the castle.

Pevensey Castle

NON-MEMBERS

Adult	£4.80
Concession	£4.30
Child	£2.90
Family	£12.50

OPENING TIMES

1 Apr-30 Sep, daily	10am-6pm
1-31 Oct, daily	10am-4pm
1 Nov-31 Mar, Sat-Sun	10am-4pm
24-26 Dec and 1 Jan	Closed

HOW TO FIND US

Direction: In Pevensey off A259

Train: Pevensey & Westham or Pevensey Bay, both ½ mile

Bus: Stagecoach 10 or 99

Tel: 01323 762604

OVP

Dogs on leads (restricted areas only).

Parking (charge payable). Car park managed by Pevensey Town Trust.

Toilets (nearby).

MAP Page 277 (6G)
OS Map 199, 123/124: TQ645048

Portchester Castle
See feature – Page 72

Reculver Towers and Roman Fort
Kent – CT6 6SS

An imposing landmark, the twin 12th-century towers of the ruined church stand amid the remains of an important Roman 'Saxon Shore' fort and a Saxon monastery. Richborough Roman Fort is within easy travelling distance.

NEW FOR 2011

New graphic panels guide you around the site.

OPENING TIMES

Any reasonable time in daylight hours; external viewing only

Reculver Towers and Roman Fort

HOW TO FIND US

Direction: At Reculver; 3 miles E of Herne Bay

Train: Herne Bay 4 miles

Bus: Stagecoach in East Kent 7, 7A and Kent Top Temps 36

Tel: 01227 740676

Disabled access (grounds only – long slope up from car park).

MAP Page 277 (4J)
OS Map 179, 150: TR228693

Richborough Roman Fort and Amphitheatre
See opposite

Rochester Castle
Kent – ME1 1SW

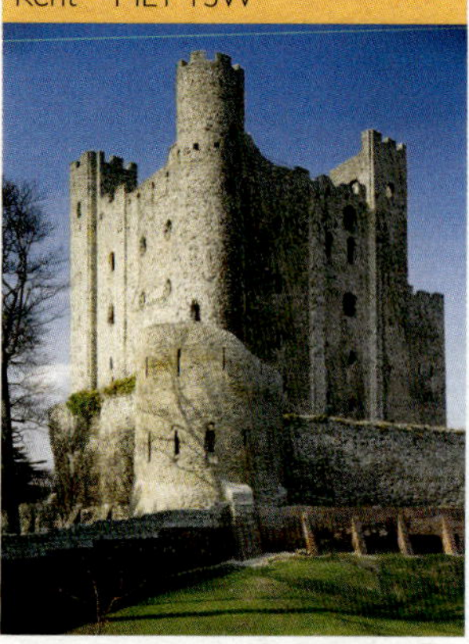

Strategically placed astride the London Road, guarding an important crossing of the River Medway, this imposing fortress has a complex history of destruction and rebuilding. Its mighty Norman tower-keep of Kentish ragstone was built c. 1127 by William of Corbeil, Archbishop of Canterbury, with the encouragement of Henry I. Consisting of three floors above a basement, it still stands 113 feet high. Attached is a tall protruding forebuilding, with its own set of defences to pass through before the keep

Rochester Castle

itself could be entered at first floor level.

In 1215, garrisoned by rebel barons, the castle endured an epic siege by King John. Having first undermined the outer wall, John used the fat of 40 pigs to fire a mine under the keep, bringing its southern corner crashing down. Even then the defenders held out within the building, until they were eventually starved out after a resistance of nearly two months.

Rebuilt under Henry III and Edward I, the castle remained a viable fortress in the 15th century, but a century later it was decaying. Today it stands as a proud reminder of the history of Rochester, along with the nearby cathedral and Dickensian cobbled streets.

Managed by Medway Council. www.medway.gov.uk

NON-MEMBERS

Adult	£5.50
Concession	£3.50
Child	£3.50
Family	£14.50

OPENING TIMES

1 Apr-30 Sep, daily	10am-6pm
1 Oct-31 Mar, daily	10am-4pm
Last admission 45 mins before closing	
24-26 Dec and 1 Jan	Closed

HOW TO FIND US

Direction: By Rochester Bridge (A2); junction 1 of M2 and junction 2 of M25

Train: Rochester ½ mile

Bus: From surrounding areas

Tel: 01634 335882

OVP

Audio tours (small charge).

Toilets (in castle grounds).

New guidebook.

MAP Page 277 (4G)
OS Map 178, 148/163: TQ741686

Richborough Roman Fort and Amphitheatre

Kent – CT13 9JW

© Skyscan Balloon Photography

Evocatively sited amid the East Kent marshes, Richborough Roman Fort is the most symbolically important of all Roman sites in Britain, witnessing both the beginning and almost the end of Roman rule here. Now landlocked, in AD 43 it overlooked a sheltered channel where the invading Roman forces first came ashore: the line of the Roman foreshore, now two miles inland from the sea, was discovered in 2008 by English Heritage archaeologists digging just outside the fort wall.

The landing was commemorated by a mighty triumphal arch, whose foundations still survive: the arch also provided an impressive gateway for arrivals at what became the port of 'Rutupiae', the province's main point of entry.

By the mid-3rd century, however, Roman Britain was threatened by sea-borne raiders. A fort was therefore hastily created within the port. At first defended by the triple ditches still visible, but soon after by stone walls, this became one of the most important of the 'Saxon Shore' forts. It was also among the last to be regularly occupied: there was still a large Roman population here in the early 5th century.

You can choose to reach the fort as the Romans would have done, by boat. Boats sail from Sandwich, but not every day: please contact the site for more information.

NON-MEMBERS

Adult	£4.80
Concession	£4.30
Child	£2.90
Family	£12.50

OPENING TIMES

Fort:

1 Apr-30 Sep, daily	10am-6pm
1 Oct-31 Mar	Closed

Amphitheatre: Any reasonable time in daylight hours, access across grazed land from footpath; please call 01304 612013 for details

HOW TO FIND US

Direction: At the A256/A257 roundabout, take the road for Sandwich and then turn left at the fire station

Train: Sandwich 2 miles

Bus: Stagecoach East Kent 13A, 14, 88/A then walk using Stour Valley Walk/Saxon Shore Way

Tel: 01304 612013

OVP

Dogs on leads (restricted areas only).

MAP Page 277 (4J) OS Map 179, 150
Fort: TR324602
Ampitheatre: TR321598

Portchester Castle Hampshire – PO16 9QW

© Skyscan Balloon Photography

Portchester Castle's commanding location has made it a major factor in the Solent's defences for hundreds of years.

The most impressive and best-preserved of the Roman 'Saxon Shore' forts, Portchester Castle was originally built in the late 3rd century. Covering an area of nearly ten acres, it is the only Roman stronghold in northern Europe whose walls still mainly stand to their full 6 metre height, complete with most of their originally twenty towers. Subsequently housing a Saxon settlement, the huge waterside fortress became a Norman castle in the 12th century, when a formidable tower-keep was built in one corner.

Portchester Castle was in the front line throughout the Hundred Years War, serving as a staging-post for expeditions to France and repelling cross-Channel raids. Richard II transformed part of the castle into a palace in 1396, and Henry V used it as an embarkation point for the Agincourt campaign in 1415. Thereafter it saw little action, but was used to house troops in the Civil War, and prisoners of war during the Dutch and Napoleonic Wars and the Anglo-American War of 1812-14.

An exhibition in the keep interprets the history of the castle and Portchester village, and displays finds excavated on site. The inclusive audio tour explains life in the castle over the centuries, from the point of view of some of the people who worked or were incarcerated there.

www.english-heritage.org.uk/portchestercastle

NON-MEMBERS

Adult	£4.80
Concession	£4.30
Child	£2.90
Family	£12.50

OPENING TIMES

1 Apr-30 Sep, daily	10am-6pm
1 Oct-31 Mar, daily	10am-4pm
24-26 Dec and 1 Jan	Closed

HOW TO FIND US

Direction: On the S side of Portchester off A27; Junction 11 on M27

Train: Portchester 1 mile

Bus: First 1A, 5, 5A Fareham – Southsea to within ¼ mile

Tel: 02392 378291

E P OVP

Disabled access (grounds and lower levels only).

Dogs on leads (outer grounds only).

Toilets (facilities are in the car park, operated by Fareham District Council).

MAP Page 276 (6C)
OS Map 196, OL29/119: SU625046

Rollright Stones
Oxfordshire

Traditionally a monarch and his courtiers petrified by a witch, the Rollright Stones consist of three groups: the King's Men stone circle; the Whispering Knights burial chamber; and the single King Stone. These funerary and ceremonial monuments span nearly 2000 years of Neolithic and Bronze Age development.

Managed and owned by The Rollright Trust. Refreshments, toilet, guidebook and postcards available at Wyatts Farm Shop: c. 1 mile east towards Great Rollright.

NON-MEMBERS

Adult	£1.00
Child (over 7 years)	50p

OPENING TIMES

Entry between sunrise and sunset all year by permission of the Rollright Trust

HOW TO FIND US

Direction: Off unclassified road between A44 and A3400; 3 miles NW of Chipping Norton, near villages of Little Rollright and Long Compton

Train: Moreton-in-Marsh 6½ miles

Bus: Stagecoach 50 (Chipping Norton – Stratford Upon Avon) passes within ½ mile

Contact: sitemanager@rollrightstones.co.uk

Parking (in lay-by).

MAP Page 276 (2B)
OS Map 151, OL45/191: SP297309

Royal Garrison Church, Portsmouth
Hampshire – PO1 2NJ

Royal Garrison Church was constructed c. 1212 as part of a hospital complex. Although the nave was badly damaged in a 1941 fire-bomb raid on Portsmouth, the chancel remains roofed and furnished.

Managed by the Friends of the Royal Garrison.

OPENING TIMES

1 Apr-30 Sep, Mon-Sat	11am-4pm

(contact the keykeeper at other times, tel 02392 378291)

HOW TO FIND US

Direction: In Portsmouth; on Grand Parade S of High St

Train: Portsmouth Harbour ¾ mile

Bus: First services 6, 6A, 16A, 19 and Stagecoach 700 pass within a short walk

Tel: 02392 378291

Parking (nearby).

MAP Page 276 (6C)
OS Map 196, OL29/119: SZ633992

St Augustine's Abbey
Kent – CT1 1PF

This great abbey, marking the rebirth of Christianity in southern England, was founded shortly after AD 597 by St Augustine. Originally created as a burial place for the Anglo-Saxon kings of Kent, it is part of the Canterbury World Heritage Site, along with the cathedral and St Martin's Church.

The impressive and historically important abbey is situated outside the city walls, but should not be missed by visitors. You can also enjoy the museum and free audio tour.

St Augustine's Abbey

NON-MEMBERS

Adult	£4.80
Concession	£4.30
Child	£2.90
Family	£12.50

OPENING TIMES

1 Apr-30 Jun, Wed-Sun & Bank Hols	10am-5pm
1 Jul-31 Aug, daily	10am-6pm
1 Sep-31 Oct, Sat-Sun	10am-5pm
1 Nov-31 Mar, Sat-Sun	10am-4pm
24-26 Dec and 1 Jan	Closed

HOW TO FIND US

Direction: In Canterbury, ¼ mile E of Cathedral Close

Train: Canterbury East and West, both ¾ mile

Bus: From surrounding areas

Tel: 01227 767345

Local Tourist Information: Canterbury 01227 766567

Audio tours (interactive).

Disabled access (all site can be viewed, but some steps).

Parking (nearby).

MAP Page 277 (4J)
OS Map 179, 150: TR155578

St Augustine's Abbey Conduit House
Kent

The Conduit House is part of the monastic waterworks which supplied nearby St Augustine's Abbey.

OPENING TIMES

Any reasonable time in daylight hours; exterior viewing only

HOW TO FIND US

Direction: In King's Park. Approx. 5-10 min walk from St Augustine's Abbey. Please call or ask at the abbey for directions

Train: Canterbury East or West, both 1½ miles

MAP Page 277 (4J)
OS Map 179, 150: TR159580

Walmer Castle and Gardens

Kent – CT14 7LJ

Originally built during the reign of Henry VIII as part of a chain of coastal artillery defences against Catholic attack from Europe, Walmer Castle has evolved over time into an elegant residence.

There is a pleasant cycle path along the beach front between Deal and Walmer Castles.

The Dining Room

Walmer Castle is the official residence of the Lord Warden of the Cinque Ports. Once an important military command, supervising the five ('Cinque') south-eastern ports which provided ships for medieval England's defence, the Lord Wardenship was later granted as an honorary distinction. It is easy to imagine why the Duke of Wellington, who held the post for 23 years, enjoyed his time here so much.

Wellington's spirit lives on at Walmer Castle, where the armchair in which he died in 1852 can still be seen. His campaign bed also remains on display as a testament to his spartan tastes, along with a pair of original 'Wellington boots' and many personal effects in the fascinating on-site Wellington museum.

Successive Lords Warden have left their mark on Walmer Castle. Thus Lady Hester Stanhope used local militia to create new landscaping as a surprise for her uncle, Lord Warden William Pitt: while Lord Warden W.H. Smith – member of the famous stationer's family – saved many of the valuable furnishings now on display.

Recent Lords Warden have been provided with private apartments above the gatehouse, and both Sir Robert Menzies (former Australian Prime Minister) and Her Majesty Queen Elizabeth the Queen Mother made regular visits to the castle, as does the current title holder, Admiral the Lord Boyce. Some of the rooms used by the Queen Mother are open to visitors, as is her magnificent garden, given to Her Majesty on her 95th birthday.

The beautiful gardens also include the Broad Walk, with formal borders framed by the famous Cloud Yew Hedge; a commemorative lawn; woodland walk; croquet lawn and a working kitchen garden. The gardens include areas carefully managed to encourage wild flowers and insects. These wild garden areas are also a great place to spot birds.

Home-made lunches and teas are available at the Lord Warden's Tearoom and there is a well-stocked gift shop. An audio tour is available and plants are on sale.

Holiday cottages available to let

www.english-heritage.org.uk/walmercastle

NON-MEMBERS

Adult	£7.30
Concession	£6.60
Child	£4.40
Family	£19.00

OPENING TIMES

1 Apr-30 Sep, daily	10am-6pm
1-31 Oct, Wed-Sun	10am-4pm
1 Nov-29 Feb	Closed
1-31 Mar, Wed-Sun	10am-4pm

Closed 1-3 July when Lord Warden in residence

HOW TO FIND US

Direction: On coast S of Walmer, on A258; Junction 13 of M20 or from M2 to Deal

Train: Walmer 1 mile

Bus: Stagecoach East Kent service 84/84A

Tel: 01304 364288

Local Tourist Information: Deal 01304 369576 and Dover 01304 205108

OVP

Audio tours (also in Dutch, French and German).

Disabled access (courtyard and garden only; parking available).

Parking (near approach to castle).

MAP Page 277 (5J)
OS Map 179, 138: TR378501

St Catherine's Oratory

See Isle of Wight – Page 79

St Augustine's Cross

Kent

This 19th-century cross in Saxon style marks what is traditionally believed to be the site of St Augustine's landing on the shores of England in AD 597. Accompanied by 30 followers, Augustine is said to have held a mass here before moving on.

OPENING TIMES

Any reasonable time in daylight hours

HOW TO FIND US

Direction: 2 miles E of Minster off B29048

Train: Minster 2 miles

Bus: Eastonways 42 from Ramsgate

MAP Page 276 (4J)
OS Map 179, 150: TR340642

St John's Commandery

Kent

The flint-walled 13th-century chapel and hall of a 'Commandery' of Knights Hospitallers, later converted into a farmhouse. It has a remarkable medieval crown post roof and 16th-century ceilings with moulded beams.

St John's Commandery

OPENING TIMES

Any reasonable time in daylight hours for exterior viewing. Internal viewing by appointment only; please call 01304 211067

HOW TO FIND US

Direction: 2 miles NE of Densole, off A260

Train: Kearsney 4 miles

Bus: Stagecoach in East Kent 16/A Folkestone Central – Canterbury, to within 1 mile

MAP Page 277 (5J)
OS Map 179/189, 138: TR232440

St Leonard's Tower

Kent

An early and well-preserved example of a small free-standing Norman tower keep, surviving almost to its original height. It was probably built c. 1080 by Gundulf, Bishop of Rochester, and takes its name from a chapel of St Leonard which once stood nearby.

Managed by West Malling Parish Council.

OPENING TIMES

Any reasonable time in daylight hours for exterior viewing. Internal viewing by appointment only; please call 01732 870872

HOW TO FIND US

Direction: Nr West Malling, on unclassified road W of A228

Train: West Malling 1 mile

Bus: New Venture 53, 88, 123 Arriva 72 & 77. New Venture/ Arriva 70 & 151

Disabled access (grounds only).

MAP Page 277 (4G)
OS Map 178/188, 148: TQ676571

Silchester Roman City Walls and Amphitheatre

Hampshire

Originally a tribal centre of the Iron Age Atrebates, Silchester

Silchester Roman City Walls and Amphitheatre

became the large and important Roman town of Calleva Atrebatum. Unlike most Roman towns, it was never re-occupied or built over after its abandonment in the 5th century, so archaeological investigations give an unusually complete picture of its development. The complete circuit of its 3rd-century walls, among the best-preserved Roman town defences in England and 2½ km (1½ miles) long, can still be traced, although none of the buildings within them survive above ground. Outside them are the remains of a Roman amphitheatre, which provided seating for over 4500 spectators. A free downloadable audio tour is available from the English Heritage website.

OPENING TIMES

Any reasonable time in daylight hours

HOW TO FIND US

Direction: On a minor road, 1 mile E of Silchester

Train: Bramley or Mortimer, both 2¾ miles

Bus: Reading Buses 2A to Mortimer West End (1 mile). Stagecoach Hampshire 14, 15 to Silchester (within ½ mile). Otherwise Stagecoach Jazz2 from Basingstoke to Tadley and then 2½ mile walk

P

MAP Page 276 (4C)
OS Map 175, 159: SU639624

Southwick Priory

Hampshire

Remains of a wealthy Augustinian priory, originally founded at Portchester: once a famous place of pilgrimage. Only part of the refectory wall survives.

Southwick Priory

OPENING TIMES

Any reasonable time in daylight hours

HOW TO FIND US

Direction: Fully accessible through Southwick village, signposted. Please park in car park opposite

Bus: First services 38, 38A, 138 & 139

MAP Page 276 (6C)
OS Map 196, 119: SU629084

Sutton Valence Castle
Kent

The ruins of a small 12th-century Norman keep, with panoramic views over the Weald.

OPENING TIMES

Any reasonable time in daylight hours

HOW TO FIND US

Direction: 5 miles SE of Maidstone; in Sutton Valence village, on A274

Train: Headcorn 4 miles, Hollingbourne 5 miles

Bus: Arriva 12 Maidstone – Tenterden (passes Headcorn)

MAP Page 277 (5G)
OS Map 188, 137: TQ815491

Temple Manor
Kent

Part of a manor house of the Knights Templar, built in about 1240, with a fine first floor hall displaying traces of wall paintings.

Managed by Medway Council.
www.medway.gov.uk

OPENING TIMES

1 Apr-31 Oct, Sat-Sun	11am-4pm
1 Nov-31 Mar	Closed

For group visits please call 01634 402276

HOW TO FIND US

Direction: Located in Strood (Rochester), off A228

Train: Strood ¾ mile

Temple Manor

Bus: Arriva 140, 141 and Arriva and Nu Venture 151 from Chatham, or Arriva 700, 701, 711 from Rochester then short walk

Disabled access (grounds only).

MAP Page 277 (4G)
OS Map 178, 148/163: TQ733685

Titchfield Abbey
Hampshire – PO15 5RA

The ruins of a 13th-century Premonstratensian abbey, later converted into a Tudor mansion. The church was rebuilt as a grand turreted gatehouse. Information panels tell the story of the monastery and its conversion into a mansion. A free downloadable audio tour is available from the English Heritage website.

OPENING TIMES

1 Apr-30 Sep, daily	10am-5pm
1 Oct-31 Mar, daily	10am-4pm
24-26 Dec and 1 Jan	Closed

HOW TO FIND US

Direction: Located ½ mile N of Titchfield, off A27

Train: Fareham 2 miles

Bus: First 26 & 28

Tel: 02392 378291

MAP Page 276 (6C)
OS Map 196, 119: SU542067

Uffington Castle, White Horse and Dragon Hill
Oxfordshire

These atmospheric sites lie along the Ridgeway. Uffington 'Castle' is

Uffington Castle, White Horse and Dragon Hill

a large Iron Age hillfort, Dragon Hill a natural mound associated in legend with St George. The famous and enigmatic White Horse is the oldest chalk-cut hill figure in Britain, and is believed to be more than 3000 years old.

Managed by the National Trust on behalf of English Heritage.

OPENING TIMES

Any reasonable time in daylight hours

HOW TO FIND US

Direction: S of B4507, 7 miles W of Wantage

Bus: RH Transport 67 to Kingston Lisle, then approx 1 mile walk. X47 (Saturdays only) passes closer to the site

Parking (pay and display). Free to EH members.

MAP Page 276 (3B)
OS Map 174, 170: SU301866

Upnor Castle
Kent – ME2 4XG

Set in tranquil grounds adjoining a riverside village, this rare example of an Elizabethan artillery fort was begun in 1559 and redeveloped in 1599-1601 to protect warships moored at Chatham dockyards. Despite a brave attempt, it entirely failed to do so in 1667, when the Dutch sailed past it to burn or capture the English fleet at anchor.

Managed by Medway Council.
www.medway.gov.uk

NON-MEMBERS

Adult	£5.50
Concession	£3.50
Child	£3.50
Family	£14.50

Upnor Castle

OPENING TIMES

1 Apr-31 Oct, daily 10am-6pm

Last admission 45 mins before closing

1 Nov-31 Mar Closed

May close early on Fri and Sat for weddings. Please call in advance to check

HOW TO FIND US

Direction: At Upnor, on unclassified road off A228

Train: Strood 2 miles

Bus: Arriva service 197 from Chatham

Tel: 01634 718742 or 01634 338110 when castle is closed

Audio guide (small charge).

Disabled access (grounds only).

Parking (at a slight distance from castle – park before village).

MAP Page 277 (4G)
OS Map 178, 163: TQ759706

Walmer Castle and Gardens

See feature – Page 74

Waverley Abbey

Surrey

Ruins of the church and monastic buildings of the first Cistercian abbey in England, founded in 1128. A free downloadable audio tour is available from the English Heritage website.

OPENING TIMES

Any reasonable time in daylight hours

HOW TO FIND US

Direction: 2 miles SE of Farnham, off B3001; off Junction 10 of M25

Train: Farnham 2 miles

Bus: Stagecoach in Hants & Surrey 46 Guildford – Aldershot (passing Farnham)

Parking (limited).

MAP Page 276 (5D)
OS Map 186, 145: SU868453

Wayland's Smithy

Oxfordshire

A fine and atmospheric Neolithic chambered long barrow 2km (1¼ miles) along the Ridgeway from the Uffington White Horse: it was once believed to be the habitation of the Saxon smith-god Wayland.

Managed by the National Trust on behalf of English Heritage.

OPENING TIMES

Any reasonable time in daylight hours

HOW TO FIND US

Direction: On the Ridgeway; ¾ mile NE of B4000, Ashbury – Lambourn Road

Bus: Thamesdown Transport service 47 then a short walk along the Ridgeway path; X47 (Saturdays only)

Parking (may be a charge).

MAP Page 276 (3B)
OS Map 174, 170: SU281854

Western Heights, Dover

Kent

A huge fortification begun during the Napoleonic Wars and completed in the 1860s, designed to protect Dover from French invasion.

OPENING TIMES

Any reasonable time in daylight hours

Free to visit the outside and moat. Drop Redoubt fortress open on special occasions and annual open weekend 11-12 June 2011, visit www.doverwesternheights.org

Western Heights, Dover

HOW TO FIND US

Direction: Above Dover town on W side of harbour

Train: Dover Priory ¾ mile

Bus: Kent Passenger Services 593

Tel: 01304 211067

MAP Page 277 (5J)
OS Map 179, 138: TR312408

Wolvesey Castle (Old Bishop's Palace)

Hampshire

Wolvesey has been an important residence of the wealthy and powerful Bishops of Winchester since Anglo-Saxon times. Standing next to Winchester Cathedral, the extensive surviving ruins of the palace date largely from the 12th-century work of Bishop Henry of Blois. The last great occasion here was on 25 July 1554, when Queen Mary and Philip of Spain held their wedding breakfast in the East Hall. A free downloadable audio tour is available from the English Heritage website.

OPENING TIMES

1 Apr-30 Sep, daily 10am-5pm

1 Oct-31 Mar Closed

HOW TO FIND US

Direction: ¾ mile SE of Winchester Cathedral, next to the Bishop's Palace; access from College St

Train: Winchester ¾ mile

Bus: From surrounding areas

Tel: 02392 378291

MAP Page 276 (5C)
OS Map 185, 132: SU484291

Yarmouth Castle

See Isle of Wight – Page 79

The Isle of Wight

Appuldurcombe House
Isle of Wight – PO38 3EW

The shell of Appuldurcombe, once the grandest house on the Isle of Wight and still an important example of English Baroque architecture, the 1701 east front has now been restored. It stands in 'Capability' Brown-designed grounds. An exhibition of photographs and prints depicts the house and its history. You can also visit the Freemantle Gate (part of the 1770s neo-Classical addition to the estate) on the nearby public footpath, and the adjacent Falconry Centre (not under the care of English Heritage – extra charge applies).

Managed by Mr and Mrs Owen.

NON-MEMBERS

Adult	£4.00
Concession	£3.50
Child	£2.75
Family	£13.00

OPENING TIMES

1 Apr-30 Sep, Sun-Fri	10am-4pm
Sat	10am-12pm
1 Oct-31 Mar	Closed

Last entry 1 hour before closing

HOW TO FIND US

Direction: Wroxall ½ mile, off B3327

Train: Shanklin 3½ miles then bus

Bus: Southern Vectis 3 (Ryde – Newport) & Wight Bus 31

Appuldurcombe House

Ferry: Ryde 11 miles (Wightlink 0870 582 7744; Hovercraft 01983 811000); West Cowes 12 miles, East Cowes 12 miles (both Red Funnel – 0844 844 9988)

Tel: 01983 852484

MAP Page 276 (7C)
OS Map 196, OL29: SZ543800

Carisbrooke Castle
See feature – Page 80

St Catherine's Oratory
Isle of Wight

The tall, medieval, octagonal tower, allegedly a lighthouse, was built here in 1328 as penance for stealing church property from a wrecked ship. Affectionately known as the Pepperpot, it stands on one of the highest parts of the Isle of Wight. It is part of the Tennyson Heritage Coast, a series of linked cliff-top monuments. A later lighthouse can be seen nearby.

Managed by the National Trust on behalf of English Heritage.

OPENING TIMES

Any reasonable time in daylight hours

HOW TO FIND US

Direction: E of Blackgang roundabout, off A3055

Train: Shanklin 9 miles

Bus: Southern Vectis service 6 to Blackgang Chine and then ½ mile walk

Ferry: West Cowes 14 miles, East Cowes 14 miles (both Red Funnel – 0844 844 9988); Yarmouth 15 miles (Wightlink – 0870 582 7744)

MAP Page 276 (7C)
OS Map 196, OL29: SZ494773

Royal Osborne
See feature – Page 83

Yarmouth Castle
Isle of Wight – PO41 0PB

This last, and most sophisticated, addition to Henry VIII's coastal defences was completed after his death in 1547, with the first new-style 'arrowhead' artillery bastion built in England. Displays inside the castle include atmospheric recreations of how the rooms were used in the 16th century and an exhibition about the many wrecks which occurred in the treacherous stretch of sea which the castle overlooks. Also a magnificent picnic site, with views over the Solent.

NON-MEMBERS

Adult	£4.00
Concession	£3.60
Child	£2.40

OPENING TIMES

1 Apr-30 Sep, Sun-Thu	11am-4pm

HOW TO FIND US

Direction: In Yarmouth, adjacent to car ferry terminal

Bus: Southern Vectis 7 & Needles Tour & Island Coaster (summer only)

Ferry: Wightlink – 0871 376 1000 (Lymington – Yarmouth)

Tel: 01983 760678

OVP

Disabled access (ground floor only).

Parking (coaches and cars 200 metres (220 yards). Charges payable).

MAP Page 276 (7B)
OS Map 196, OL29: SZ354898

Carisbrooke Castle Isle of Wight – PO30 1XY

A fascinatingly varied site to visit, Carisbrooke Castle has been the key to the Isle of Wight's security for more than nine centuries. This great hilltop-crowning fortress has a keep to climb for panoramic views, a colourful history, and of course the famous Carisbrooke donkeys.

After the Spanish Armada passed alarmingly close in 1588, Carisbrooke was updated as an artillery fortification by surrounding it with 'bastioned' outer earthworks, still impressively visible.

There has been a fortress here since Saxon times, but the present castle was begun in c. 1100, when the Isle of Wight was granted to the de Redvers family. They raised the great stone shell-keep on its towering mound and after 1262 the formidable Countess Isabella de Redvers extensively rebuilt the whole stronghold. Following the addition of its double-towered 14th-century gatehouse, Carisbrooke Castle experienced its only siege in 1377, beating off a French raiding force. After the Spanish Armada passed alarmingly close in 1588, the castle was updated as an artillery fortification by surrounding it with 'bastioned' outer earthworks, still impressively visible.

Most famous among the castle's extensive cast of past residents was Charles I, imprisoned here in 1647-8 after his defeat in the Civil War. At first comfortably accommodated in the Constable's Lodging, he later became a closely guarded captive: an attempt to escape was foiled only when he became wedged in the window bars.

Much later, Princess Beatrice, Queen Victoria's youngest daughter and Governor of the Isle of Wight between 1896-1944, made Carisbrooke Castle her summer home. The Edwardian-style Princess Beatrice garden, designed by TV and radio gardening presenter Chris Beardshaw, was inspired by the Princess, and includes a fountain and plantings in the rich colours of the royal arms. We are grateful to the late Mrs Dorothy Frazer, whose generous bequest and devotion to the island has made the creation of this garden possible. Princess Beatrice also commissioned the altar painting in the tranquil castle chapel in memory of a son killed in action in 1914.

The castle's most beloved modern residents are undoubtedly the renowned Carisbrooke donkeys.

The castle's most beloved modern residents are undoubtedly the renowned Carisbrooke donkeys. These happy, hard-working animals still operate the tread wheel in the Elizabethan wheelhouse, which raises water 49 metres (161 feet) from the castle well.

They give daily demonstrations, and their story is told in a film hosted by Jupiter the cartoon donkey, voiced by locally-raised comedian Phill Jupitus.

The on-site Carisbrooke Museum (managed by the Carisbrooke Museum Trust) provides more historical information about the castle, as well as Charles I memorabilia.

An extensive presentation – including film, hands-on weapons and family interactives and a virtual tour – highlights Carisbrooke Castle's long and often tumultuous history.

www.english-heritage.org.uk/carisbrookecastle

Holiday cottage available to let

NON-MEMBERS	
Adult	£7.30
Concession	£6.60
Child	£4.40
Family	£19.00

OPENING TIMES	
1 Apr-30 Sep, daily	10am-5pm
1 Oct-31 Mar, daily	10am-4pm
24-26 Dec and 1 Jan	Closed

HOW TO FIND US

Direction: 1¼ miles SW of Newport. Follow signs for Carisbrooke village and then the castle

Bus: Southern Vectis 6, 38 & Wightbus 36 pass nearby to within ¼ mile

Ferry: West Cowes 5 miles, East Cowes 6 miles (Red Funnel – 0844 844 9988); Fishbourne 6 miles, Ryde 8 miles, Yarmouth 9 miles (Wightlink 0871 376 1000; Hovercraft Ryde 01983 811000)

Tel: 01983 522107

Local Tourist Information: 01983 813813

Disabled access (grounds and lower levels only).

Tearoom (open Apr-Oct).

MAP Page 276 (7C)
OS Map 196, OL29: SZ486878

Royal Osborne Isle of Wight – PO32 6JX

The Drawing Room

After her marriage to Prince Albert in 1840, Queen Victoria felt the need for a family residence in the country. To use her words, 'a place of one's own – quiet and retired'.

'It is impossible to imagine a prettier spot,' wrote the Queen after a visit to Osborne House.

Royal Osborne continued

Marble sculptures, commissioned by Victoria and Albert, line the classically designed Grand Corridor of the house.

The Durbar Room

Walled Garden Entrance

The Audience Room

Queen Victoria knew and liked the Isle of Wight after visiting as a child, and she and the Prince Consort were both determined to buy a property there.

'It is impossible to imagine a prettier spot,' wrote the Queen after a visit to Osborne House. In 1845 the royal couple purchased the property with an estate of 342 acres, plus the adjacent Barton Manor to house equerries and grooms and to serve as the home farm.

Before the deeds had even changed hands, master builder Thomas Cubitt had been approached – firstly to build a pavilion to house private apartments and then to demolish the old house and add further wings for the royal household. Once all the work was complete, an exquisite pair of Italianate towers dominated the landscape and looked out over passing ships in the nearby Solent.

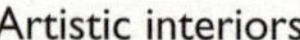

Artistic interiors

The interiors of Osborne House abound with opulence in both architectural design and decoration. Marble sculptures, commissioned by Victoria and Albert, line the classically designed Grand Corridor of the house and recall the royal couple's love of the arts. Portraits and frescos adorn the walls, serving as a reminder of the family's links to the crowned heads of Europe, and of the unrivalled supremacy of the British Empire. Family photographs on the desks of Queen Victoria and Prince Albert offer a further insight into the way they lived.

Queen Victoria's role as Empress of India is celebrated in the richly decorated Durbar Room. Constructed from 1890-91, the room served as an elaborate banqueting hall and every surface, from floor to ceiling, is ornately embellished.

The walls are decorated with symbols from India, including Ganesh – the elephant god of good fortune – and the deeply coffered ceiling is composed of fibrous plaster. The completion of the room coincided with the introduction of electricity,

Visitors can choose to bring a picnic, have a light lunch in the café, or eat in the stylish Terrace Restaurant.

so the Indian-influenced lamp stands were designed to take full advantage of this emerging technology.

Italianate gardens

Prince Albert worked with Cubitt on the Italianate designs for the terraced formal gardens which complement the house. Visitors can now enjoy the Walled Garden much as Victoria and Albert did, since English Heritage restored it as part of the Contemporary Heritage Gardens Scheme.

The grounds also contain a summerhouse, a museum, and a miniature fort and barracks, as well as the Swiss Cottage, originally built as an educational tool where the royal children could learn domestic skills. There is a beautiful wild flower meadow near the Swiss Cottage and rare red squirrels can be seen throughout the gardens. There is a courtesy minibus, with wheelchair access, to Swiss Cottage.

Queen Victoria loved to stroll through the gardens, and the primroses in the woods were her particular favourites. Most of the gardens are accessible on tarmac and compacted gravel paths.

The Terrace Restaurant has wonderful views across the Terrace Gardens down to the Solent. It has waiter-served lunches and afternoon teas. (Please note: for non-members, admission tickets to Royal Osborne must be purchased for access to the Terrace Restaurant.)

The exhibition in the Petty Officers Quarters is the best place to start any visit. It covers various aspects of the sumptuously furnished house and magnificent grounds, as well as the lives and personalities of the Victorian royal family and the servants who cared for them. Here you will also find a café, serving refreshments and light lunches, and a large shop.

A children's play area and picnic tables are located off the visitors' car park.

Christmas at Royal Osborne

On Saturday 19 and Sunday 20 November, Royal Osborne opens the festive season with its popular annual Victorian Christmas event. The ground floor of the house, dressed festively for the season, remains open for guided tours Wednesday to Sundays until Sunday 8 January. Find out how the Victorian Royal Family celebrated Christmas with these fascinating tours led by our expert guides. Visit **www.english-heritage.org.uk/royalosborne** for details.

NEW FOR 2011

The Palm Terrace

A keen horticulturalist, Prince Albert was responsible for the layout of the terraces overlooking the Solent – the view is said to have reminded him of the Bay of Naples – and for the introduction of many fine trees onto the estate. The original palm (Latin name *Trachycarpus fortunei*) was a gift to the Royal couple from King Ferdinand of Portugal. It was one of the first ever to be planted in this country following its introduction in 1849 by Robert Fortune, after whom it is named. It died in 2003 and the current tree – its direct descendent – was planted in 2004 by Queen Elizabeth II. The remainder of the Palm Terrace is planted to recreate its Victorian appearance. It includes beds featuring camellias and pampas grass and a pergola with wisteria and climbing roses for summer colour, and vines producing small grapes in the autumn.

Also to be seen here for the first time is a newly-restored seat made from coal. It was brought to Royal Osborne after display at the Great Exhibition in London, one of Prince Albert's favourite projects.

Royal Osborne continued

The grounds also contain a summerhouse, a museum, and a miniature fort and barracks, as well as the Swiss Cottage, originally built as an educational tool where the royal children could learn domestic skills.

The Swiss Cottage

The Swiss Cottage Interior

Available for corporate and private hire

Holiday cottage available to let

NON-MEMBERS

House and Grounds	
Adult	£11.50
Concession	£10.40
Child	£6.90
Family	£29.90

OPENING TIMES

1 Apr-30 Sep, daily (house closes 5pm)	10am-6pm
1-31 Oct, daily	10am-4pm
2 Nov-31 Mar, Wed-Sun Pre-booked guided tours. Last tour is 2.30pm	10am-4pm
24-26 Dec and 1 Jan	Closed
23 Nov-8 Jan	Xmas themed tours

HOW TO FIND US

Direction: 1 mile SE of East Cowes

Train: Ryde Espalande 7 miles, Wootton (IoW Steam Railway) 3 miles

Bus: Southern Vectis services 4 and 5

Ferry: East Cowes 1½ miles (Red Funnel. Tel: 0844 844 9988); Fishbourne 4 miles; Ryde 7 miles (Wightlink. Tel: 0871 376 1000)

Tel: 01983 200022

Local Tourist Information: Cowes and Newport 01983 813818

Baby carriers are available at the house entrance as pushchairs are not permitted.

Disabled access – access for wheelchairs to the first floor is by an existing lift. Manual wheelchairs are available to borrow on a first come, first served basis. Mobility scooters are not permitted inside the house, but they can be used in the gardens.

MAP Page 276 (7C)
OS Map 196, OL29: SZ516948

Associated attractions in the South East

These visitor attractions, all independent of EH, offer discounts to our members. Please call before you visit to confirm details. A valid EH membership card must be produced for each member.

Anne of Cleves House
Lewes East Sussex BN7 1JA

15th-century timber framed Wealden hall-house, given to Anne as part of her divorce settlement from Henry VIII. Houses displays of period furnishings, Lewes history and Bonfire festivities, Tom Paine, and the Wealden iron industry. Enclosed garden.

Tel: 01273 474610

www.sussexpast.co.uk/anneofcleves

50% discount on entry

Arundel Castle
West Sussex BN18 9AB

Arundel Castle has developed from an 11th-century fortification to a magnificent Stately Home. Explore both a medieval castle and an elegant house with outstanding gardens.

Tel: 01903 882173

www.arundelcastle.org

Discounted castle and gardens, GoldPlus ticket

3

Dover Museum and Bronze Age Boat Gallery
Kent CT16 1PB

This modern interactive museum tells the story of Dover's rich history, and displays the world's oldest prehistoric seagoing boat, discovered nearby.

Managed by Dover District Council.

Close to Dover Castle

Tel: 01304 201066

www.dovermuseum.co.uk

50% discount on entry

Fishbourne Roman Palace
West Sussex PO19 3QR

The remains of a palatial Roman building of the 1st century AD. View unique Roman mosaics and replanted Roman garden. Tours of the palace site or behind the scenes, when artefact handling is possible. Café, picnic area, free parking.

Tel: 01243 785859

www.sussexpast.co.uk/fishbourne

50% discount on entry

Fort Amherst
Chatham, Kent ME4 4UB

Fort Amherst is a fine example of a Napoleonic fortress. Restored areas open to the public include the 2500ft underground tunnel system, gun batteries, and WWII civil defence display.

8 mins from Rochester Castle

Tel: 01634 847747

www.fortamherst.com

20% discount on entry

6

Goodwood House
West Sussex PO18 0PX

The family seat of the Dukes of Richmond and Gordon, set in the heart of the Sussex Downs, houses astonishing treasures, including celebrated paintings by George Stubbs and Canaletto.

5 mins from Boxgrove Priory

Tel: 01243 755048

www.goodwood.com

50% discount on entry

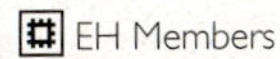

EH Members

OVP Holders

? Discounted Child Places Included

Associated attractions in the South East continued

The Historic Dockyard Chatham
Kent ME4 4TZ

Discover 400 years of maritime history at this fascinating dockyard of the Age of Sail. NEW – No.1. Smithery, a joint project with the National Maritime Museum and Imperial War Museum. An all-round maritime treasure house for the whole family.

15 mins from J1 and J4 of M2

Tel: 01634 823800

www.thedockyard.co.uk

15% discount on entry

Leeds Castle
Kent ME17 1PL

Set in 500 acres of beautiful parkland, there's a lot to discover at Leeds Castle. Attractions include the gardens, aviary, maze and grotto, Knights' Realm playground, dog collar museum and the 'World of Wings' free-flying bird show.

2 miles from J8 of M20

Tel: 01622 765400

www.leeds-castle.com

10% discount on entry

Not valid on event days

Lewes Castle & Barbican House Museum
Lewes East Sussex BN7 1YE

This imposing Norman castle offers magnificent views across the town of Lewes and surrounding downland. The adjacent Barbican House holds an extensive collection of local history and archaeological artefacts.

Tel: 01273 486290

www.sussexpast.co.uk/lewescastle

50% discount on entry

Lullingstone Castle and The World Garden
Kent DA4 0JA

Lullingstone Castle is one of England's oldest family estates. Home of the amazing World Garden, containing nearly 8000 different plant species from across the globe, planted to show their countries of origin.

5 mins from Lullingstone Roman Villa

Tel: 01322 862114

www.lullingstonecastle.co.uk

2 for 1 entry

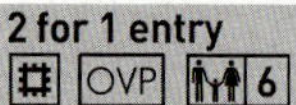

Marlipins Museum
West Sussex BN43 5DA

Once a medieval customs house, Marlipins now holds artefacts from the Shoreham area and its maritime past, plus a collection of local archaeological material. The upstairs gallery has displays on the local silent film industry and transport, plus changing exhibitions. Full disabled access.

Tel: 01273 462994

www.sussexpast.co.uk/marlipins

50% discount on entry

Michelham Priory
East Sussex BN27 3QS

Enter through the 14th-century gatehouse and explore the Tudor mansion which evolved from the former Augustinian Priory. Set on a tranquil island encircled by England's longest water-filled medieval moat. Extensive gardens, artefacts and dramatic Elizabethan Great Barn.

Tel: 01323 844224

www.sussexpast.co.uk/michelham

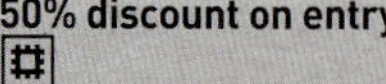

EH Members | OVP OVP Holders | Discounted Child Places Included

Newport Roman Villa
Isle of Wight PO30 1HA

Discover this Romano-British farmhouse with its fine bath suite, in suburban Newport. Hands-on activities: mosaic making and weaving; herb garden and museum display. Open Easter to October.

5 mins from Carisbrooke Castle

Tel: 01983 529720

www.iwight.com/museums

40% discount on entry

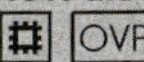

Penshurst Place & Gardens
Kent TN11 8DG

Ancestral home of Viscount De L'Isle, set in the Weald of Kent, with a stunning medieval Baron's Hall and Tudor gardens. The Staterooms contain fine furniture, tapestries, porcelain and portraits.

15 mins from Hildenborough J of A21

Tel: 01892 870307

www.penshurstplace.com

Free admission to house
if grounds ticket purchased

The Priest House
West Sussex RH19 4PP

Standing in the beautiful surroundings of a traditional and fragrant cottage herb garden on the edge of Ashdown Forest, the Priest House is an early 15th-century timber-framed hall-house with a dramatic roof of Horsham stone.

Tel: 01342 810479

www.sussexpast.co.uk/priesthouse

50% discount on entry

The Royal Pavilion
Brighton and Hove BN1 1EE

This Regency palace was the magnificent seaside residence of King George IV. The exterior, which was inspired by Indian architecture, contrasts with interiors decorated in Chinese taste.

Tel: 03000 290900

www.brighton-hove-pavilion.org.uk

20% discount on adult ticket
2

Rycote Chapel
Oxfordshire OX9 2PE

This 15th-century chapel has original furniture, including exquisitely carved and painted woodwork. Owned by Mr and Mrs Bernard Taylor. Managed by the Rycote Buildings Charitable Foundation.

1 Apr-30 Sep, Fri-Sun 2pm-6pm
Groups by appointment only.
No coaches.

3 miles SW of Thame off A329

Tel: 01844 210210

£2.50 entry (subject to change)

Westenhanger Castle and Barns
Kent CT21 4HX

A 14th-century Castle with 16th-century outbuildings. The great barn was built by Thomas 'Customer' Smythe.

Only open on Tuesdays for tourism and guided groups by appointment.

8 miles from Dover Castle

Tel: 01227 738451

www.kentcastle.co.uk

20% discount on entry

Tintagel Castle – see page 122

South West

www.english-heritage.org.uk/southwest

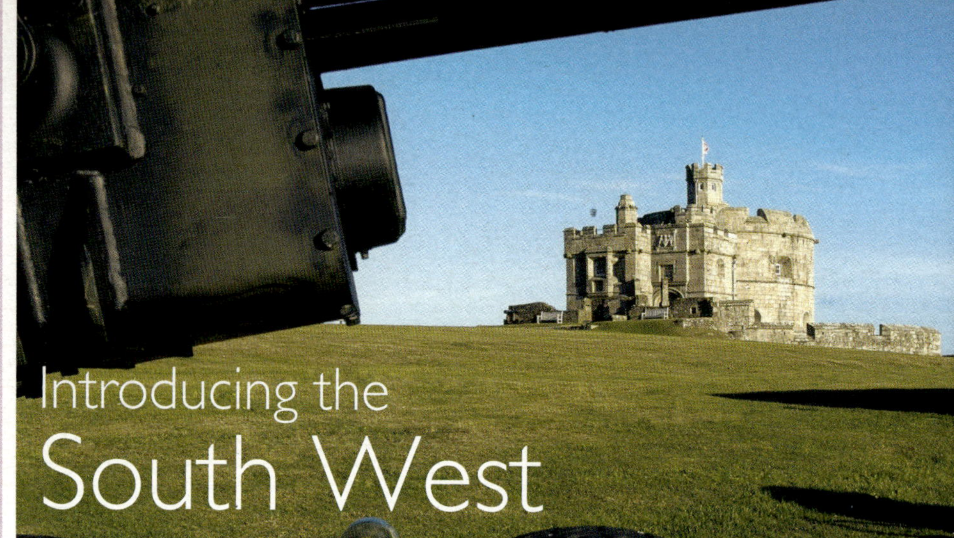

Introducing the South West

Remember to check opening times before you visit any of our properties.

Details of all bus travel in England are available from Traveline on 0871 200 2233 or visit www.traveline.org.uk

Make the most of your membership and keep up to date with upcoming events, the latest news and special offers by subscribing to our e-newsletter. Register online at **www.english-heritage.org.uk/newsletter** and we'll deliver the latest from English Heritage straight to your inbox.

Images:
(Above) Pendennis Castle
(top centre) Dartmouth Castle
(top right) St Mawes Castle
(bottom centre) Kirkham House
(bottom right) Totnes Castle

Bristol & Bath

- Sir Bevil Grenville's Monument
- Stanton Drew Circles and Cove
- Stoney Littleton Long Barrow
- Temple Church

Cornwall

- Ballowall Barrow
- Carn Euny Ancient Village
- Chysauster Ancient Village
- Dupath Well
- Halliggye Fogou
- Hurlers Stone Circles
- King Doniert's Stone
- Launceston Castle
- Pendennis Castle
- Penhallam Manor
- Restormel Castle
- St Breock Downs Monolith
- St Catherine's Castle
- St Mawes Castle
- Tintagel Castle
- Tregiffian Burial Chamber
- Trethevy Quoit

Devon

- Bayard's Cove Fort
- Berry Pomeroy Castle
- Blackbury Camp
- Dartmouth Castle
- Grimspound
- Hound Tor Deserted Medieval Village
- Kirkham House
- Lydford Castle and Saxon Town
- Merrivale Prehistoric Settlement
- Okehampton Castle
- Royal Citadel (Plymouth)
- Totnes Castle
- Upper Plym Valley

Dorset

- Abbotsbury Abbey Remains
- Christchurch Castle and Norman House
- Fiddleford Manor
- Jordan Hill Roman Temple
- Kingston Russell Stone Circle
- Knowlton Church and Earthworks
- Maiden Castle
- The Nine Stones
- Portland Castle
- St Catherine's Chapel
- Sherborne Old Castle
- Winterbourne Poor Lot Barrows

Gloucestershire

- Belas Knap Long Barrow
- Blackfriars
- Cirencester Amphitheatre
- Great Witcombe Roman Villa
- Greyfriars
- Hailes Abbey
- Kingswood Abbey Gatehouse
- Notgrove Long Barrow
- Nympsfield Long Barrow
- Odda's Chapel
- Offa's Dyke
- Over Bridge
- St Briavels Castle
- St Mary's Church
- Uley Long Barrow (Hetty Pegler's Tump)
- Windmill Tump Long Barrow

Isles of Scilly

- Bant's Carn Burial Chamber and Halangy Down Ancient Village

Check www.english-heritage.org.uk for the latest opening times

© Skyscan Balloon Photography

- Cromwell's Castle
- Garrison Walls
- Harry's Walls
- Innisidgen Lower and Upper Burial Chambers
- King Charles's Castle
- Old Blockhouse
- Porth Hellick Down Burial Chamber

Somerset

- Butter Cross
- Cleeve Abbey
- Farleigh Hungerford Castle
- Gallox Bridge
- Glastonbury Tribunal
- Meare Fish House
- Muchelney Abbey
- Nunney Castle
- Yarn Market

Wiltshire

- Alexander Keiller Museum
- Avebury
- Bradford-on-Avon Tithe Barn
- Bratton Camp and White Horse
- Chisbury Chapel
- Hatfield Earthwork (Marden Henge)
- Ludgershall Castle and Cross
- Netheravon Dovecote
- Old Sarum
- Old Wardour Castle
- The Sanctuary
- Silbury Hill
- Stonehenge
- West Kennet Avenue
- West Kennet Long Barrow
- Windmill Hill
- Woodhenge

Boats and Castles

English Heritage's huge South West region offers an immense range of possible single-base days out. In Cornwall, for instance, visits to **Pendennis Castle** and its little sister **St Mawes Castle** can easily be combined with a trip to Falmouth's National Maritime Museum, which offers a 10% discount to English Heritage members. Other tempting trips might begin in the famously attractive South Devon town of Totnes, still commanded by **Totnes Castle**, its classic Norman 'motte and bailey' fortress. Totnes has many other charms – museums, markets, and an amazing array of 'alternative' shops and cafés – and is also the boarding point for summer season boat trips to Dartmouth. An hour and a quarter's voyage, past creekside villages, a heronry and a vineyard, takes you to this busy little port, overlooked by its famous Royal Naval College. From the quay you can take a further short boat trip to **Dartmouth Castle**, in its outstandingly picturesque site guarding the harbour mouth.

Back in the town, you can view **Bayard's Cove Fort**, and perhaps visit the medieval privateer-mayor John Hawley, founder of Dartmouth Castle, magnificently commemorated with his two wives in St Saviour's church, which he also financed. Or you could take another ferry across the Dart to Kingswear, and then in summer the steam train to Paignton, to visit surprising **Kirkham House**. Only a short drive from Paignton or Totnes, moreover, stands **Berry Pomeroy Castle** in its remote wooded setting. Whether or not you believe in its alleged multitudes of ghosts, this medieval fortress unusually combined with a Jacobean mansion is undoubtedly the most perfect of Devon's romantic ruins.

Check www.english-heritage.org.uk for the latest opening times

Avebury Wiltshire

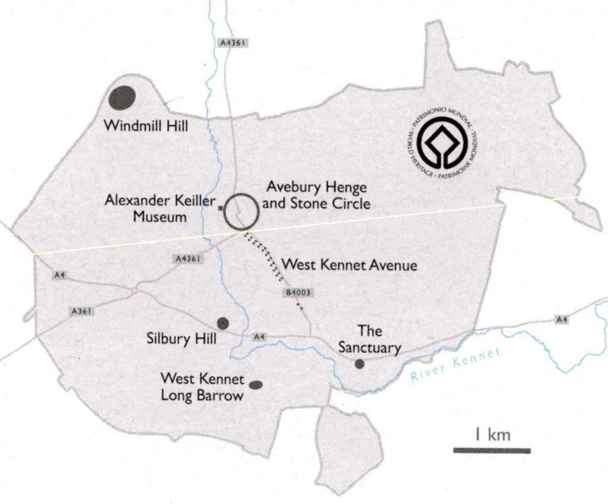

Avebury rivals – some would say exceeds – Stonehenge as the largest, most impressive and complex prehistoric site in Britain. The henge, built and altered over the centuries from about 2600 BC to 2400 BC, now appears as a huge circular bank and ditch, enclosing an area of approximately 25 acres (10 hectares), including part of Avebury village. Within this 'henge' ditch is an inner circle of great standing stones, enclosing two more stone circles, each with a central feature.

The site's present appearance owes much to the marmalade heir Alexander Keiller, who excavated and re-erected many stones during the 1930s, and whose archaeological collections are displayed in the nearby museum. Many stones had been broken or buried in medieval and later times, one crushing its destroyer as it fell.

Avebury is part of a wider complex of Neolithic and Bronze Age monuments, with many other ceremonial and ritual sites in English Heritage care. West Kennet Avenue (p.96) joined it to the Sanctuary (p.95), and another stone avenue connected it with Beckhampton. West Kennet Long Barrow (p.96) and Windmill Hill (p.96) are also nearby, as is the huge and mysterious Silbury Hill (p.95). This extraordinary assemblage of sites seemingly formed a huge 'sacred landscape', whose use and purpose can still only be guessed at. Avebury and its surroundings have, with Stonehenge, achieved international recognition as a World Heritage Site.

Avebury Henge and Stone Circles are in the freehold ownership of the National Trust and in English Heritage guardianship. They are managed by the National Trust on behalf of English Heritage, and the two organisations share the cost of managing and maintaining the property.

OPENING TIMES

Any reasonable time

Usual facilities may not be available around the summer solstice 20-22 June. Please call 01672 539250 before you visit

HOW TO FIND US

See Alexander Keiller Museum

See Alexander Keiller Museum.

MAP Page 275 (3J)
OS Map 173, 157: SU102700

Avebury, Alexander Keiller Museum Wiltshire – SN8 1RF

One of the most important prehistoric archaeological collections in Britain, housed in the Stables Gallery, includes many artefacts from the World Heritage Site (WHS) monuments. The admission fee includes access to both the Stables and Barn Galleries. The Barn Gallery (belonging to the National Trust) tells the story of the WHS, its monuments, and the people associated with it.

The Museum, which sits within the Avebury WHS, is in the freehold ownership of the National Trust and in English Heritage guardianship on behalf of the Secretary of State for the DCMS; the museum collection is on loan from the DCMS.

NON-MEMBERS

Adult	£4.40
Child	£2.20
Family (2+2)	£12.20
Family (1+3)	£7.90

Reduced price when arriving by cycle or public transport

OPENING TIMES

1 Apr-31 Oct, daily	10am-6pm
1 Nov-31 Mar, daily	10am-4pm
24-26 Dec and 1 Jan	Closed

HOW TO FIND US

Direction: In Avebury, 7 miles W of Marlborough

Train: Pewsey 10 miles; Swindon 11 miles

Bus: Stagecoach in Swindon service 49. Connect2 line 43; Wilts & Dorset service 96

Parking (Visitor car park free to EH members. S of Avebury off A4361. Free disabled visitors' parking in village car park).

MAP Page 275 (3J)
OS Map 173, 157: SU099700

Avebury, The Sanctuary Wiltshire

Begun in about 3000 BC, the Sanctuary was originally a complex circular arrangement of timber posts, with the later addition of stone settings. These components are now indicated by concrete slabs and posts. Its function remains a mystery: possibly it enshrined the dwelling place of some revered person, and certainly numbers of human bones were found here, accompanied by food remains suggesting elaborate death rites and ceremonies. Later, the West Kennet Avenue was constructed to connect it with newly-built Avebury, reinforcing the status of this enigmatic but clearly very important site.

The Sanctuary is in DCMS ownership and in English Heritage guardianship. It is managed by the National Trust on behalf of English Heritage, and the two organisations share the cost of managing and maintaining the property.

OPENING TIMES

Any reasonable time

Usual facilities may not apply around the summer solstice 20-22 June. Please call 01672 539250 before you visit

HOW TO FIND US

Train: Pewsey 9 miles, Bedwyn 12 miles

Bus: Wilts & Dorset service 96; A.D.Rains/Bodmans X76

Parking (in lay-by).

MAP Page 275 (3J)
OS Map 173, 157: SU118680

Avebury, Silbury Hill Wiltshire

The largest man-made prehistoric mound in Europe, mysterious Silbury Hill compares in height and volume to the roughly contemporary Egyptian pyramids.

Built in about 100 years around 2400 BC, it apparently contains no burial. Though clearly important in itself, its purpose and significance remain unknown.

There is no access to the Hill itself. This is to prevent erosion of archaeological deposits and rare chalk grassland (the Hill is a Site of Special Scientific Interest).

Find out more about the recent conservation project (2000-2008) at **www.english-heritage.org.uk/silbury**

NEW FOR 2011

New graphic panels tell you about the site.

OPENING TIMES

Viewing area during reasonable daylight hours. Strictly no access to the hill itself

Usual facilities may not apply around the summer solstice 20-22 June. Please call 0870 333 1181 before you visit

HOW TO FIND US

Direction: 1 mile W of West Kennet on A4

Train: Pewsey 9 miles, Swindon 13 miles

Bus: Stagecoach in Swindon service 49; Wilts & Dorset service 96. Both pass within ¾ m of the site. Also A.D.Rains/Bodmans X76

Disabled access (viewing area).

MAP Page 275 (3J)
OS Map 173, 157: SU100685

Avebury, West Kennet Avenue

Wiltshire

An 'avenue', originally of around 100 pairs of prehistoric standing stones, raised to form a winding 1½ mile ritual link between the pre-existing monuments of Avebury and The Sanctuary.

West Kennet Avenue is in the freehold ownership of the National Trust and in English Heritage guardianship. It is managed by the National Trust on behalf of English Heritage, and the two organisations share the cost of managing and maintaining the property.

OPENING TIMES

Any reasonable time

Usual facilities may not apply around the summer solstice 20-22 June. Please call 01672 539250 before you visit

HOW TO FIND US

Direction: Runs alongside B4003

Train: Pewsey 9 miles, Swindon 12 miles

Bus: Stagecoach in Swindon service 49. Connect2 line 43; Wilts & Dorset service 96

Parking (in lay-by).

Disabled access (on roadway).

MAP Page 275 (3J)
OS Map 173, 157: SU105695

Avebury, West Kennet Long Barrow

Wiltshire

One of the largest, most impressive and most accessible Neolithic chambered tombs in Britain. Built in around 3650 BC, it was used for a short time as a burial chamber, nearly 50 people being buried here before the chambers were blocked.

West Kennet Long Barrow is in private ownership and in English Heritage guardianship. It is managed by the National Trust on behalf of English Heritage, and the two organisations share the cost of managing and maintaining the property.

OPENING TIMES

Any reasonable time

Usual facilities may not apply around the summer solstice 20-22 June. Please call 01672 539250 before you visit

HOW TO FIND US

Direction: ¾ mile SW of West Kennet, along footpath off A4

Train: Pewsey 9 miles, Swindon 13 miles

Bus: Stagecoach in Swindon service 49; Wilts & Dorset service 96. Both pass within ¾ mile of the site. Also A.D.Rains/Bodmans X76

Parking (in lay-by).

MAP Page 275 (3J)
OS Map 173, 157: SU105677

Avebury, Windmill Hill

Wiltshire

© Skyscan Balloon Photography

The classic Neolithic 'causewayed enclosure', built around 3600 BC, with three concentric but intermittent ditches covering an area of approximately nine hectares (22 acres). Large quantities of animal bones, cereal crops, stone tools, artefacts and pottery were found here, suggesting the communal gathering of people to feast, trade and carry out ritual activities.

Windmill Hill is in the freehold ownership of the National Trust and in English Heritage guardianship. It is managed by the National Trust on behalf of English Heritage, and the two organisations share the cost of managing and maintaining the property.

OPENING TIMES

Any reasonable time

Usual facilities may not apply around the summer solstice 20-22 June. Please call 01672 539250 before you visit

HOW TO FIND US

Direction: 1¼ miles NW of Avebury

Train: Swindon 11 miles

Bus: Stagecoach in Swindon service 49; Wilts & Dorset service 96. Both pass within ¾ mile of the site. Also A.D.Rains/Bodmans X76

MAP Page 275 (3J)
OS Map 173, 157: SU087714

Abbotsbury Abbey Remains
Dorset

Part of a monastic building, perhaps the abbot's lodging, of the Benedictine Abbey of Abbotsbury. St Catherine's Chapel is within half a mile.

OPENING TIMES
Any reasonable time

HOW TO FIND US
Direction: Located in Abbotsbury, off B3157, near the churchyard

Train: Upwey 7½ miles

Bus: First X53 & 253; South West Coaches 61, 62 (Wed, Fri only)

Parking (charged).

MAP Page 275 (5H)
OS Map 194, OL15: SY578852

Abbotsbury, St Catherine's Chapel
Dorset

Set high on a hilltop overlooking Abbotsbury Abbey, this sturdily buttressed and barrel-vaulted 14th-century chapel was built by the monks as a place of pilgrimage and retreat.

OPENING TIMES
Any reasonable time

HOW TO FIND US
Direction: ½ mile S of Abbotsbury; by path from village, off B3157. Path leads off signposted lane to Swannery

Train: Upwey 7 miles

Bus: First X53 & 253; South West Coaches 61, 62 (Wed, Fri only)

MAP Page 275 (5H)
OS Map 194, OL15: SY573848

Bayard's Cove Fort:
see Dartmouth, Bayard's Cove Fort – Page 100

Ballowall Barrow
Cornwall

In a spectacular cliff-edge position, this unique Bronze Age tomb has a long and complex history as a sacred site. Seen as excavated in 1878 by Cornish antiquarian William Borlase.

Managed by the National Trust.

OPENING TIMES
Any reasonable time

HOW TO FIND US
Direction: 1 mile W of St Just, near Carn Gloose

Train: Penzance 8 miles

Bus: First 10, 300 (summer only); Western Greyhound 504, 507, 509

MAP Page 274 (7A)
OS Map 203, 102: SW355312

Belas Knap Long Barrow
Gloucestershire

A particularly fine example of a Neolithic long barrow of c. 3800 BC, featuring a false entrance and side chambers. Excavated in 1863 and 1865, when the remains of 31 people were found in the chambers. The barrow has since been restored.

Managed by Gloucestershire County Council.

OPENING TIMES
Any reasonable time

HOW TO FIND US
Direction: Near Charlton Abbots; ½ mile on Cotswold Way

Train: Cheltenham 9 miles

Bus: Villager Community Bus service V10 stops within ½ mile of the site. Otherwise Castleways service 606 & 656 to within 1¾ miles or Castleways 559 to Winchcombe village then walk

MAP Page 275 (1J)
OS Map 163, OL45: SP021254

Berry Pomeroy Castle
Devon – TQ9 6LJ

Tucked away in a steep wooded valley, Berry Pomeroy Castle is the perfect romantic ruin. Within the 15th-century defences of the Pomeroy family castle, still displaying a wall painting of the Three Kings in its gatehouse chamber, looms the dramatic ruined shell of its successor, the great mansion of the Seymours. Begun in the 1560s and ambitiously enlarged from c. 1600, their mansion was intended to become the most spectacular house in Devon, a match for Longleat and Audley End.

Never completed, and abandoned by 1700, it became the focus of blood-curdling ghost stories, recounted in the audio tour. Woodland walks from the car park (including steep tracks) provide fine views of the ruins from below.

www.english-heritage.org.uk/berrypomeroy

NON-MEMBERS

Adult	£4.70
Concession	£4.20
Child	£2.80

OPENING TIMES

1 Apr-30 Jun, daily	10am-5pm
1 Jul-31 Aug, daily	10am-6pm
1-30 Sep, daily	10am-5pm
1-31 Oct, daily	10am-4pm
1 Nov-31 Mar	Closed

HOW TO FIND US
Direction: 2½ miles E of Totnes off A385

Check www.english-heritage.org.uk for the latest opening times

Berry Pomeroy Castle

Train: Totnes 3½ miles

Bus: Stagecoach in Devon 111, 112

Tel: 01803 866618

OVP

Disabled access (grounds and ground floor only).

Parking (no coach access), at end of long drive (approx. ¾ mile).

Café (not managed by EH) open Tue-Sun, Thu-Sun in Oct.

New guidebook from summer 2011.

MAP Page 275 (6F)
OS Map 202, OL20/110: SX839623

Blackbury Camp
Devon

An Iron Age hillfort with impressive ramparts, now surrounded by woodland.

OPENING TIMES

Any reasonable time

HOW TO FIND US

Direction: Off B3174/A3052

Train: Honiton 6½ miles

Bus: Stagecoach Devon 52A, First X53 & X54 alight at Three Horseshoes on A3052 between Sidford & Seaton and then public footpath (steep climb c. 1 mile)

MAP Page 275 (5G)
OS Map 192/193, 115: SY187924

Blackfriars, Gloucester:
see Gloucester, Blackfriars – Page 102

Bradford-on-Avon Tithe Barn
Wiltshire

A spectacular 14th-century monastic stone barn, 51 metres (168 ft) long, with a sophisticated timber-cruck roof.

OPENING TIMES

Daily	10.30am-4pm
25 Dec	Closed

HOW TO FIND US

Direction: Located ½ mile S of town centre off B3109

Bradford-on-Avon Tithe Barn

Train: Bradford-on-Avon ¼ mile

Bus: Bodman service 37 & 95 (Tue only), Libra Travel service 96, Frome Minibuses service 98 & X96 to Frome Road canal bridge and then short walk

Parking (adjacent, not managed by EH – charge applies).

MAP Page 275 (3H)
OS Map 173, 156: ST823604

Bratton Camp and White Horse
Wiltshire

Below an Iron Age hillfort, enclosing a much earlier long barrow, stands the Westbury White Horse. Cut into the hillside in 1778, this replaced a slightly older horse, commemorating King Alfred's legendary victory over the Danes nearby.

OPENING TIMES

Any reasonable time

HOW TO FIND US

Direction: 2 miles E of Westbury off B3098, I mile SW of Bratton

Train: Westbury 3 miles

Bus: Bodman 87/8 Trowbridge – Devizes (passes Westbury)

MAP Page 275 (3J)
OS Map 184, 143: ST900516

Butter Cross, Dunster:
see Dunster, Butter Cross – Page 100

Carn Euny Ancient Village
Cornwall

Among the best preserved ancient villages in the South West, occupied from Iron Age until late Roman times. It includes the foundations of stone houses and an intriguing 'fogou' underground passage.

Managed by the Cornwall Heritage Trust.

Carn Euny Ancient Village

OPENING TIMES

Any reasonable time

HOW TO FIND US

Direction: 1¼ miles SW of Sancreed off A30

Train: Penzance 6 miles

Bus: Western Greyhound service 509 to Grumbla

Parking 600 metres (660 yards) away in Brane.

MAP Page 274 (7A)
OS Map 203, 102: SW402288

Chisbury Chapel
Wiltshire

A pretty thatched and flint-walled 13th-century chapel, later used as a barn.

OPENING TIMES

Any reasonable time

HOW TO FIND US

Direction: Off unclassified road, ¼ mile E of Chisbury, off A4; 6 miles E of Marlborough

Train: Bedwyn 1 mile

Bus: Wiltshire Bus services 20 & 22 to Chisbury turn then ½ mile walk

MAP Page 275 (3K)
OS Map 174, 157: SU280660

Christchurch Castle and Norman House
Dorset

The remains of Christchurch Castle include parts of the mound-top keep and, more unusually, the 12th-century riverside chamber block or 'Constable's House'. This very early example of domestic architecture includes a rare Norman chimney. There is an important 12th-century church nearby.

OPENING TIMES

Any reasonable time

Christchurch Castle and Norman House

HOW TO FIND US

Direction: Located in Christchurch, near the Priory

Train: Christchurch ¾ mile

Bus: From surrounding area

MAP Page 275 (5K)
OS Map 195, OL22: SZ160927

Chysauster Ancient Village
Cornwall – TR20 8XA

This Iron Age settlement was originally occupied 2000 years ago. The village consisted of stone-walled homesteads known as 'courtyard houses', found only on the Land's End peninsula and the Isles of Scilly. The houses line a 'village street', and each had an open central courtyard surrounded by a number of thatched rooms. There are also the remains of an enigmatic 'fogou' underground passage.

www.english-heritage.org.uk/chysauster

NON-MEMBERS

Adult	£3.40
Concession	£3.10
Child	£2.00

OPENING TIMES

1 Apr-30 Jun, daily	10am-5pm
1 Jul-31 Aug, daily	10am-6pm
1-30 Sep, daily	10am-5pm
1-31 Oct, daily	10am-4pm
1 Nov-31 Mar	Closed

HOW TO FIND US

Direction: Located 2½ miles NW of Gulval, off B3311

Train: Penzance 3½ miles

Bus: Western Greyhound 508 then 1½ mile walk; Western Greyhound 516 then 1¾ mile walk

Tel: 07831 757934

OVP

MAP Page 274 (7B)
OS Map 203, 102: SW472350

Cirencester Amphitheatre
Gloucestershire

The earthwork remains of one of the largest Roman amphitheatres in Britain, built in the early 2nd century. It served the Roman city of Corinium (now Cirencester), then second only in size and importance to London, and had a capacity of around 8000 spectators. Later fortified against Saxon invaders.

OPENING TIMES

Any reasonable time

HOW TO FIND US

Direction: Located W of Cirencester, next to the bypass. Access from the town, or along Chesterton Lane from the W end of the bypass, on to Cotswold Ave

Train: Kemble 4 miles

Bus: Pulham's 855 (Fosse Link); Stagecoach 59; Stagecoach 51; 51A (Sun only)

MAP Page 275 (2J)
OS Map 163, OL45/169: SP020014

Cleeve Abbey
Somerset – TA23 0PS

The picturesque Cistercian abbey of Cleeve boasts the most impressively complete and unaltered set of monastic cloister buildings in England. Standing roofed and two storeys high, they include the gatehouse; the 15th-century refectory with its glorious angel roof; an unusual 'painted chamber'; and the floor of an earlier refectory, decked from end to end with 13th-century heraldic tiles, the protection of which is the subject of an ongoing high profile English Heritage research project. The great dormitory is one of the finest examples in the country. Beneath it are the newly-vaulted warming room, and the sacristy with more early 13th-century tilework and decoration.

An exhibition and virtual tour tell the story of abbey life, and a story bag, *Brother Cedric and the Missing Sheep*, is a fun way for families to explore the abbey together.

www.english-heritage.org.uk/cleeve

NON-MEMBERS

Adult	£4.20
Concession	£3.80
Child	£2.50

OPENING TIMES

1 Apr-30 Jun, daily	10am-5pm
1 Jul-31 Aug, daily	10am-6pm
1-30 Sep, daily	10am-5pm
1-31 Oct, daily	10am-4pm
1 Nov-31 Mar	Closed

HOW TO FIND US

Direction: Located in Washford, ¼ mile S of A39

Train: Washford ½ mile (West Somerset Railway)

Bus: First 28 & Webber 18

Tel: 01984 640377

OVP

Disabled access (grounds and ground floor only, plus toilet).

Dogs on leads (in grounds only).

Refreshments available.

MAP Page 275 (4F)
OS Map 181, OL9: ST047407

Dartmouth Castle
See feature – page 101

Dartmouth, Bayard's Cove Fort
Devon

Small Tudor artillery fort guarding Dartmouth's inner harbour, picturesquely sited on the quayside.

OPENING TIMES
Any reasonable time

HOW TO FIND US
Direction: Located in Dartmouth, on the riverside

Train: Paignton 8 miles via ferry

Bus: First 93 or Stagecoach 111/112 to Dartmouth Pontoon or Stagecoach 22, 24, 120 to Kingswear Banjo then ferry

MAP Page 275 (6F)
OS Map 202, OL20: SX879509

Dunster, Butter Cross
Somerset

The transplanted stump of a medieval stone cross, once a meeting-place for butter-sellers.

Managed by the National Trust.

OPENING TIMES
Any reasonable time

HOW TO FIND US
Direction: Beside minor road to Alcombe, 350 metres (400 yards) NW of Dunster parish church

Train: Dunster (West Somerset Railway) 1 mile

Bus: First 398, WebberBus 564; Quantock Motor Services (summer) 400; First 28, WebberBus 105/106 to within ½ mile walk

MAP Page 275 (4F)
OS Map 181, OL9: ST823604

Dunster, Gallox Bridge
Somerset

This ancient stone bridge – originally 'gallows bridge'– once carried packhorses bringing fleeces to Dunster market.

Managed by the National Trust.

OPENING TIMES
Any reasonable time

Dunster, Gallox Bridge

HOW TO FIND US
Direction: Located off A396 at the S end of Dunster village

Train: Dunster ¾ mile (West Somerset Railway)

Bus: First 398; WebberBus 107, 564 (Mon/Wed/Fri); Quantock Motor Services 400 (summer). First 28 & WebberBus 18, 106 to Dunster Steep then ½ mile

MAP Page 275 (4F)
OS Map 181, OL9: SS989432

Dunster, Yarn Market
Somerset

This fine 17th-century timber-framed octagonal market hall is a monument to Dunster's once-flourishing cloth trade.

Managed by the National Trust.

OPENING TIMES
Any reasonable time

HOW TO FIND US
Direction: In Dunster High St

Train: Dunster (West Somerset Railway) ½ mile

Bus: First 398; WebberBus 107, 564 (Mon/Wed/Fri); Quantock Motor Services 400 (summer). First 28 & WebberBus 18, 106 to Dunster Steep then ½ mile

MAP Page 275 (4F)
OS Map 181, OL9: SS992438

Dupath Well
Cornwall

This charming well-house of c. 1500 stands over an ancient spring believed to cure whooping cough. Built by the Augustinian canons of nearby St Germans priory, it houses the remains of an immersion pool for cure-seekers.

Managed by the Cornwall Heritage Trust.

Dupath Well

OPENING TIMES
Any reasonable time

HOW TO FIND US
Direction: 1 mile E of Callington off A388

Train: Gunnislake 4½ miles

Bus: Main services to Callington are First 76 or Western Greyhound 576 then ½ mile

MAP Page 274 (6D)
OS Map 201, 108: SX375692

Farleigh Hungerford Castle
See feature – Page 102

Fiddleford Manor
Dorset

The principal parts of a small stone manor house, probably begun c. 1370 for William Latimer, Sheriff of Somerset and Dorset. The hall and solar chamber display outstandingly fine timber roofs.

Please note: The adjoining building is a private residence and is not open to visitors.

NEW FOR 2011
New graphic panels guide you around the house.

OPENING TIMES
1 Apr-30 Sep, daily	10am-6pm
1 Oct-31 Mar, daily	10am-4pm
24-26 Dec and 1 Jan	Closed

HOW TO FIND US
Direction: 1 mile E of Sturminster Newton off A357

Bus: Damory 310 & 368; Wilts & Dorset X8

Disabled access (ground floor only – with 1 step).

Parking (no coach access).

MAP Page 275 (4H)
OS Map 194, 129: ST801136

Dartmouth Castle Devon – TQ6 0JN

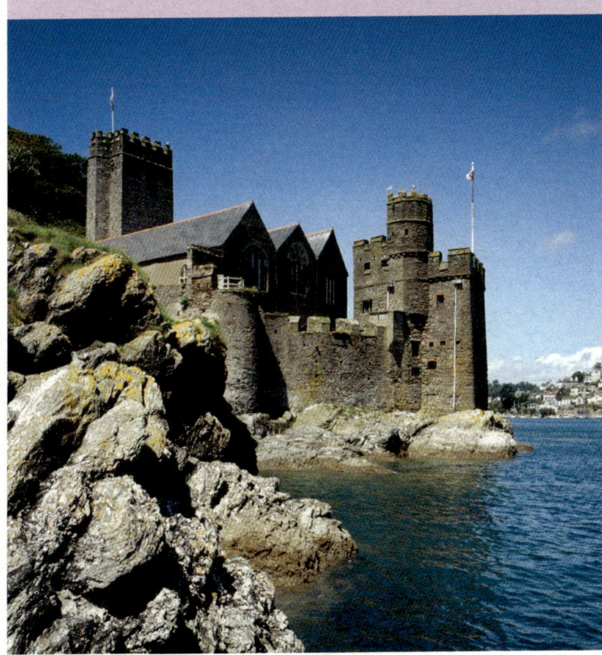

One of the most picturesquely-sited forts in England. For over six hundred years Dartmouth Castle has guarded the narrow entrance to the Dart Estuary and the busy, vibrant port of Dartmouth.

This fascinating complex of defences was begun in 1388 by John Hawley, privateering mayor of Dartmouth and the prototype of the flamboyant 'Shipman' in Chaucer's *Canterbury Tales*. About a century later the townsmen added the imposing and well-preserved 'gun tower', probably the very first fortification in Britain purpose-built to mount 'ship-sinking' heavy cannon. Climb to the top for breathtaking views across the estuary, and see how this could be blocked in wartime by a heavy chain.

Unusually incorporating the fine church of St Petrox, the castle saw action during the Civil War and continued in service right up until World War II. Successive up-dating included the Victorian 'Old Battery' with its remounted heavy guns, guardrooms and maze of passages to explore. Here, a dramatic film-sequence recreates a Victorian gun-firing, and throughout the fortress displays retell the castle's six centuries of history.

Complete your adventure with a boat-trip from picturesque Dartmouth quay, landing you a short walk from the castle.

www.english-heritage.org.uk/dartmouth

NON-MEMBERS

Adult	£4.70
Concession	£4.20
Child	£2.80

OPENING TIMES

1 Apr-30 Jun, daily	10am-5pm
1 Jul-31 Aug, daily	10am-6pm
1-30 Sep, daily	10am-5pm
1-31 Oct, daily	10am-4pm
1 Nov-31 Mar, Sat-Sun	10am-4pm
24-26 Dec and 1 Jan	Closed

HOW TO FIND US

Direction: 1 mile SE of Dartmouth off B3205, narrow approach road. No coach access

Train: Paignton 8 miles via ferry

Bus: Stagecoach in Devon 22, 24 & 120 to Kingswear, then ferry to Dartmouth and 1 mile walk; First 93, Stagecoach 111 or 112 to Dartmouth then 1 mile walk

Tel: 01803 833588

Parking (not owned by EH, charged).

Tearooms (not managed by EH).

Toilets (not managed by EH).

MAP Page 275 (6F)
OS Map 202, OL20: SX887503

Check www.english-heritage.org.uk for the latest opening times

Farleigh Hungerford Castle

Somerset – BA2 7RS

Farleigh Hungerford was begun in the 1370s by Sir Thomas Hungerford, Speaker of the Commons, and extended in the 15th century by his son Walter, Lord Hungerford, distinguished soldier and statesman. The remains of their fortified mansion include two tall corner towers and a complete castle chapel, crowded with family monuments and bedecked with wall-paintings. In the chapel's crypt the coffins of many Hungerfords are still visible, several with attached 'death masks'.

The colourful Hungerford family included two members executed during the Wars of the Roses and another – who imprisoned his wife here for four years – beheaded by Henry VIII. A Tudor Lady Hungerford burnt her murdered husband's body in the castle's oven.

The story of Farleigh and its owners is told in extensive displays in the Priest's House and through an audio tour. There is a touch-screen virtual tour for disabled visitors and family and educational facilities including a 'book box', schools base and historic costumes.

www.english-heritage.org.uk/farleigh

NEW FOR 2011

Learn more about medieval herbs in the newly-labelled Medieval Herb Garden.

NON-MEMBERS

Adult	£4.00
Concession	£3.60
Child	£2.40

OPENING TIMES

1 Apr-30 Jun, daily	10am-5pm
1 Jul-31 Aug, daily	10am-6pm
1-30 Sep, daily	10am-5pm
1-31 Oct, daily	10am-4pm
1 Nov-31 Mar, Sat-Sun	10am-4pm
24-26 Dec and 1 Jan	Closed

HOW TO FIND US

Direction: In Farleigh Hungerford, 9 miles SE of Bath; 3½ miles W of Trowbridge on A366

Train: Avoncliffe 2 miles; Trowbridge 3½ miles

Bus: Libra 96 from Trowbridge (pass close to ≋ Trowbridge) to within 1½ miles

Tel: 01225 754026

Disabled access (Chapel and Priest's House, ground floor only. Disabled toilet).

Refreshments available.

MAP Page 275 (3H)

OS Map 173, 143/156: ST801576

Gallox Bridge, Dunster

See Dunster, Gallox Bridge – Page 100

Glastonbury Tribunal

Somerset – BA6 9DP

A fine, late-15th-century stone town house, with an early Tudor façade and panelled interiors. Now contains a Tourist Information Centre and the Glastonbury Lake Village Museum.

Managed by Glastonbury Tribunal Ltd.

NON-MEMBERS

Museum:

Adult	£2.50
Concession	£2.00
Child	£1.00
Senior	£1.50

OPENING TIMES

Mon-Thu	10am-4pm
Fri-Sat	10am-4.30pm
Sun	Closed
25-26 Dec and 1 Jan	Closed

Opening hours may be varied during peak season

HOW TO FIND US

Direction: In Glastonbury High St

Bus: Bakers-Dolphin service 668 passes site. First 29, 375, 376 & 377 pass within ½ mile

Tel: 01458 832954

Disabled access (ground floor – 2 steps).

Parking (charged).

MAP Page 275 (4H)

OS Map 182/183, 141: ST499389

Gloucester, Blackfriars

Gloucestershire

One of the most complete surviving friaries of Dominican 'black friars' in England, later converted into a Tudor house and cloth factory. Notable features include the church and the fine scissor-braced dormitory roof.

Gloucester, Blackfriars

ENTRY

Non-Member	£3.50
EH Member	£3.00
Child	Free

OPENING TIMES

For opening times please check the website for more details www.english-heritage.org.uk/blackfriars

HOW TO FIND US

Direction: In Blackfriars Lane, off Ladybellegate St, off Southgate St, Gloucester

Train: Gloucester ½ mile

Bus: Short walk from Gloucester Bus Station

Parking (adjacent. Charge applies, not managed by EH).

MAP Page 275 (2J)
OS Map 162, 179: SO829184

Gloucester, Greyfriars
Gloucestershire

Substantial remains of an early Tudor friary church of Franciscan 'grey friars'.

OPENING TIMES

Any reasonable time

HOW TO FIND US

Direction: On Greyfriars Walk

Train: Gloucester ½ mile

Bus: Gloucester Bus Station ½ mile

MAP Page 275 (2J)
OS Map 162, 179: SO832184

Great Witcombe Roman Villa
Gloucestershire

The remains of a large and luxurious villa built c. AD 250, with a bathhouse complex and possibly the shrine of a water spirit.

Great Witcombe Roman Villa

OPENING TIMES

Exterior: Reasonable daylight hours

HOW TO FIND US

Direction: Located 5 miles SE of Gloucester off A46; ½ mile S of reservoir in Witcombe Park; 400 metres (440 yards) from Cotswold Way National Trail

Train: Gloucester 6 miles

Bus: Stagecoach service 46 to Green Street then 1 mile walk. Or Stagecoach 10 to Brockworth and 2 mile walk

Parking (no access for coaches. No parking permitted in the lane to or beyond the car park).

MAP Page 275 (2J)
OS Map 163, 179: SO899142

Greyfriars, Gloucester:
see Gloucester, Greyfriars – left

Grimspound
Devon

The best known of many Dartmoor prehistoric settlements, Grimspound dates from the late Bronze Age. The remains of 24 stone houses survive within a massive boundary wall.

Managed by the Dartmoor National Park Authority.

OPENING TIMES

Any reasonable time

HOW TO FIND US

Direction: 6 miles SW of Moretonhampstead, off B3212

Bus: Country Bus (summer only) Transmoor Link service 82 Exeter St David's–Plymouth. Alight at Challacombe Cross then walk 1¼ mile. There is also a year-round service 98 operated by DAC Coaches between Tavistock and Bellever (Postbridge) which is 5 mile walk from Grimspound

MAP Page 274 (5E)
OS Map 191, OL28: SX701809

Hailes Abbey
Gloucestershire – GL54 5PB

© Andrew Tryner

The Cistercian abbey of Hailes was founded in 1246 by Richard of Cornwall, King Henry III's brother, in thanksgiving for deliverance from shipwreck, and dissolved on Christmas Eve 1539. Though never housing large numbers of monks, it had extensive and elaborate buildings, financed by pilgrims visiting its renowned relic, 'the Holy Blood of Hailes' – allegedly a phial of Christ's own blood.

Eleven interpretation panels guide you around the abbey buildings and an audio tour brings the site to life. Sculptures, stonework and other site finds are displayed in the museum. The adjacent parish church displays notable medieval wall-paintings. Plant sales are available throughout the season.

www.english-heritage.org.uk/hailes

Owned by the National Trust, managed and maintained by English Heritage.

NON-MEMBERS

Adult	£4.20
Concession	£3.80
Child	£2.50

National Trust members admitted free, but charged for audio tour (£1)

Hailes Abbey

OPENING TIMES

1 Apr-30 Jun, daily	10am-5pm
1 Jul-31 Aug, daily	10am-6pm
1-30 Sep, daily	10am-5pm
1-31 Oct, daily	10am-4pm
1 Nov-31 Mar	Closed

HOW TO FIND US

Direction: 2 miles NE of Winchcombe off B4632. On the Cotswold Way National Trail

Train: Cheltenham 10 miles

Bus: Castleways service 606 from Cheltenham to within 1 mile

Tel: 01242 602398

P OVP

Disabled access (ramp to museum, disabled toilet).

Refreshments available.

MAP Page 275 (1J)
OS Map 150/163, OL45: SP050300

Halliggye Fogou
Cornwall

Roofed and walled in stone, this complex of passages is the largest and best-preserved of several mysterious underground tunnels associated with Cornish Iron Age settlements. The purpose of such 'fogous' – a Cornish-language word meaning 'cave' – is unknown. Refuges, storage chambers or ritual shrines have all been suggested.

Free entry to the fogou. Entry to the rest of the Trelowarren Estate is charged.

Managed by the Trelowarren Estate.

OPENING TIMES

Reasonable daylight hours Apr-Sep, but completely blocked Oct-Mar, inclusive

HOW TO FIND US

Direction: 5 miles SE of Helston off B3293. E of Garras on Trelowarren Estate. There is a lay-by at the side of the lane through the Trelowarren Estate. Walk up hill and the entrance to the fogou is signposted through a gate

Halliggye Fogou

Train: Penryn 10 miles

Bus: Western Greyhound 538 or First 32 (Sun) to Garras and then c. 1 mile walk

P

Parking (free to members).

Visitors are advised to bring a torch.

MAP Page 274 (7B)
OS Map 203, 103: SW713239

Hatfield Earthwork (Marden Henge)
Wiltshire

The earthworks of a Neolithic henge and monumental mound, by a loop in the River Avon.

OPENING TIMES

Any reasonable time

HOW TO FIND US

Direction: 5½ miles SE of Devizes, off A342; NE of village of Marden

Train: Pewsey 5 miles

Bus: Tourist Coaches 210 (Thu, Sat), 249; Wiltshire Connect 2 bookable bus L1. Ring 08456 525 255

MAP Page 275 (3J)
OS Map 173, 130: SU092583

Hound Tor Deserted Medieval Village
Devon

The remains of four 13th-century stone farmsteads, on land originally farmed in the Bronze Age. This isolated Dartmoor hamlet was probably abandoned in the early 15th century. A free downloadable audio tour is available from the English Heritage website.

Managed by the Dartmoor National Park Authority.

Hound Tor Deserted Medieval Village

OPENING TIMES

Any reasonable time

HOW TO FIND US

Direction: 1½ miles S of Manaton, ½ mile from the Ashburton road

Bus: Dartmoor Sunday Rover network (summer only). Countrybus/270, Dartline 272 or Carmel/Countrybus 274 to Harefoot Cross then 1½ mile walk

P

Parking (½ mile walk across moor to monument).

MAP Page 274 (5E)
OS Map 191, OL28: SX746788

Hurlers Stone Circles
Cornwall

Three fine late Neolithic or early Bronze Age stone circles arranged in a line, a grouping unique in England. Probably the best examples of ceremonial circles in the South West, they are traditionally reputed to be the remains of men petrified for playing 'hurling' on a Sunday.

Managed by the Cornwall Heritage Trust.

OPENING TIMES

Any reasonable time

HOW TO FIND US

Direction: Located ½ mile NW of Minions, off B3254

Train: Liskeard 7 miles

Bus: Western Greyhound 574 from Liskeard to Minions or 574 to Darite or Upon Cross then 1 mile walk; DAC Coaches 261; Group Travel 236

P

Parking ¼ mile walk.

MAP Page 274 (6D)
OS Map 201, 109: SX258714

Jordan Hill Roman Temple
Dorset

The foundations of a 4th-century Romano-Celtic temple.

OPENING TIMES
Any reasonable time

HOW TO FIND US
Direction: Located 2 miles NE of Weymouth, off A353

Train: Upwey or Weymouth, both 2 miles

Bus: First 4/4B, 31, X53 & Southwest 230

MAP Page 275 (5H)
OS Map 194, OL15: SY699821

King Doniert's Stone
Cornwall

Two richly carved pieces of a 9th-century 'Celtic' cross, with an inscription commemorating Dumgarth, British King of Dumnonia, who drowned in c. AD 875.

Managed by the Cornwall Heritage Trust.

OPENING TIMES
Any reasonable time

HOW TO FIND US
Direction: 1 mile NW of St Cleer, off B3254

Train: Liskeard 7 miles

Bus: DAC 79B & Western Greyhound 574

Parking (in lay-by).

MAP Page 274 (6D)
OS Map 201, 109: SX236688

Kingston Russell Stone Circle
Dorset

A late Neolithic or early Bronze Age circle of 18 fallen stones, on a hilltop overlooking Abbotsbury and the sea.

Kingston Russell Stone Circle

OPENING TIMES
Any reasonable time

HOW TO FIND US
Direction: Located 2 miles N of Abbotsbury; 1 mile along a footpath off minor roads, not signposted, 1¾ miles

Train: Weymouth (10½ miles) or Dorchester South or West (both 8 miles)

Bus: First X53, 253, Southwest 61, 62 (Wed, Fri) then 2 mile walk

Limited parking on road verge at access to farm. Access to Stone Circle on foot only via public footpaths, off minor roads. 1¾ mile. No off-road vehicle access.

MAP Page 275 (5H)
OS Map 194, OL15: SY578878

Kingswood Abbey Gatehouse
Gloucestershire

This 16th-century gatehouse, one of the latest monastic buildings in England, displays a richly sculpted mullioned window. It is the sole survivor of this Cistercian abbey.

OPENING TIMES
Exterior: open any reasonable time

Interior: key available from 3 Wotton Road, Abbey St 10am-3.30pm weekdays only

HOW TO FIND US
Direction: In Kingswood, off B4060; 1 mile SW of Wotton-under-Edge

Train: Yate 8 miles

Bus: First 310 or Wessex Connect 627

Public toilets near to monument.

MAP Page 275 (2H)
OS Map 162/172, 167: ST747920

Kirkham House, Paignton
Devon

This late medieval stone house, afterwards split into three cottages, was restored in the 1960s. Furnished with modern furniture, illustrating traditional craftsmanship and the original use of the rooms.

Managed in association with the Paignton Preservation & Local History Society.

OPENING TIMES
22 & 25 Apr, 2 & 30 May, 29 Aug & every Sun in Jul-Aug	2pm-5pm
Heritage Open Days	11am-4pm

HOW TO FIND US
Direction: Located in Kirkham St, off Cecil Rd, Paignton

Train: Paignton ½ mile

Bus: From surrounding areas

MAP Page 275 (6F)
OS Map 202, OL20/110: SX885610

Knowlton Church and Earthworks
Dorset

The siting of this ruined medieval church at the centre of a Neolithic ritual henge earthwork symbolises the transition from pagan to Christian worship.

OPENING TIMES
Any reasonable time

HOW TO FIND US
Direction: SW of Cranborne on B3078

Bus: Nordcat service, call 0845 602457 for details, Damory 325 (Thu only)

MAP Page 275 (4J)
OS Map 195, 118: SU024103

Launceston Castle
Cornwall – PL15 7DR

© Skyscan Balloon Photography

Set on a large natural mound, Launceston Castle dominates the surrounding landscape. Begun soon after the Norman Conquest, its focus is an unusual keep consisting of a 13th-century round tower built by Richard, Earl of Cornwall, inside an earlier circular shell-keep. The tower top is now reached via a dark internal staircase.

The castle long remained a prison and George Fox, founder of the Quakers, suffered harsh confinement here in 1656. An exhibition traces 1000 years of history, with finds from site excavations.

www.english-heritage.org.uk/launceston

NON-MEMBERS

Adult	£3.40
Concession	£3.10
Child	£2.00

OPENING TIMES

1 Apr-30 Jun, daily	10am-5pm
1 Jul-31 Aug, daily	10am-6pm
1-30 Sep, daily	10am-5pm
1-31 Oct, daily	10am-4pm
1 Nov-31 Mar	Closed

HOW TO FIND US

Direction: In Launceston

Bus: First 76, X85 (Sat); Western Greyhound 510 & 576; Group Travel 220, 223, 225 & 236

Tel: 01566 772365

Disabled access (outer bailey, exhibition and shop).

MAP Page 274 (5D)
OS Map 201, 112: SX331846

Ludgershall Castle and Cross
Wiltshire

The ruins and earthworks of a royal castle dating mainly from the 12th and 13th centuries, frequently used as a hunting lodge. The remains of the medieval cross stand in the centre of the village.

OPENING TIMES

Any reasonable time

HOW TO FIND US

Direction: Located on the N side of Ludgershall, off A342

Train: Andover 7 miles

Bus: Stagecoach 8, 80

Disabled access (part of site only and village cross).

Parking (limited).

MAP Page 275 (3K)
OS Map 184/185, 131: SU264512

Lydford Castle and Saxon Town
Devon

Beautifully sited on the fringe of Dartmoor, Lydford boasts three defensive features. Near the centre is a small-scale Norman keep on a mound, built as a prison. It later became notorious for harsh punishments – 'the most annoyous, contagious and detestable place within this realm'. To the south is an earlier Norman earthwork castle; to the north, Saxon town defences. A free downloadable audio tour is available from the English Heritage website.

OPENING TIMES

Any reasonable time

HOW TO FIND US

Direction: In Lydford off A386; 8½ miles S of Okehampton

Bus: Beacon Bus 118; First 187 (summer only)

MAP Page 274 (5E)
OS Map 191/201, OL28: SX509848

Maiden Castle
Dorset

Among the largest and most complex Iron Age hillforts in Europe, Maiden Castle's huge multiple ramparts enclose an area equivalent to 50 football pitches, protecting several hundred residents. Excavations in the 1930s and 1980s revealed the site's 4000-year history, from a Neolithic causewayed enclosure to a small Roman temple built on the site in the 4th century AD. They also produced evidence of an extensive late Iron Age cemetery, where many of the burials had suffered horrific injuries in attacks or skirmishes. Information panels guide you around the hillfort and illustrate its long history. A free downloadable audio tour is available from the English Heritage website.

OPENING TIMES

Any reasonable time

HOW TO FIND US

Direction: 2 miles S of Dorchester, off A354, N of bypass

Train: Dorchester South or West, both 2 miles

Bus: First 31, then 1 mile walk

MAP Page 275 (5H)
OS Map 194, OL15: SY669884

Meare Fish House
Somerset

The only surviving building of comparable purpose in England, this housed Glastonbury Abbey's official in charge of the (then) adjacent lake fishery. Its design, miniaturising the components of larger medieval houses, is also unique.

NEW FOR 2011

A graphic panel interprets the building.

Meare Fish House

OPENING TIMES

Any reasonable time. Key available from Manor House farm

HOW TO FIND US

Direction: In Meare village, on B3151

Bus: Bakers-Dolphin service 668 Cheddar – Street

MAP Page 275 (4G)
OS Map 182, 141: ST458417

Merrivale Prehistoric Settlement – Devon

The remains of a Bronze Age settlement, side-by-side with several sacred sites, including three stone rows, a stone circle, standing stones and burial cairns, probably constructed over a long period between c. 2500 BC and 1000 BC.

Managed by the Dartmoor National Park Authority.

OPENING TIMES

Any reasonable time

HOW TO FIND US

Direction: 1 mile E of Merrivale

Train: Gunnislake 10 miles

Bus: DAC service 98 Yelverton-Tavistock (with connections from Plymouth); Dartline service 272

MAP Page 274 (6E)
OS Map 191, OL28: SX554748

Muchelney Abbey
Somerset – TA10 0DQ

This atmospheric and once-remote 'great island' amid the Somerset Levels has many rewards for visitors. Beside the clearly laid out foundations of the wealthy medieval Benedictine

Muchelney Abbey

abbey (and its Anglo-Saxon predecessor) stands a complete early Tudor house in miniature. Originally the abbots' lodgings, this charming building includes a magnificent great chamber with ornate fireplace, carved settle and stained glass; two rooms with time-faded walls painted to resemble cloth hangings; and a pair of kitchens with fine timber roof. Parts of the richly decorated cloister walk and refectory are incorporated, and nearby is the thatched two-storey monks' lavatory, unique in Britain.

Exhibitions illustrate monastic life with a fascinating collection of site finds, including decorated tiles and stonework. Much improved facilities for disabled visitors include a touch-screen tour. A 'story bag' is a fun way for families to explore the abbey together.

www.english-heritage.org.uk/muchelney

The adjacent parish church and medieval Priest's House are not managed by English Heritage.

NON-MEMBERS

Adult	£4.20
Concession	£3.80
Child	£2.50

OPENING TIMES

1 Apr-30 Jun, daily	10am-5pm
1 Jul-31 Aug, daily	10am-6pm
1-30 Sep, daily	10am-5pm
1-31 Oct, daily	10am-4pm
1 Nov-31 Mar	Closed

HOW TO FIND US

Direction: In Muchelney, 2 miles S of Langport via Huish Episcopi

Bus: South West Coaches 10 (Wed only); Somerset County 850 (Thu only); First 54 then 1 mile walk from Huish Episcopi

Tel: 01458 250664

OVP

Muchelney Abbey

Dogs on leads (in grounds only).

Disabled access (grounds and most of ground floor, adapted toilet).

Refreshments available.

MAP Page 275 (4G)
OS Map 193, 129: ST429249

Netheravon Dovecote
Wiltshire

A charming 18th-century brick dovecote, still with most of its 700 or more nesting boxes.

OPENING TIMES

Exterior viewing only

HOW TO FIND US

Direction: In Netheravon, 4½ miles N of Amesbury on A345

Train: Pewsey 9 miles, Grateley 11 miles

Bus: Wilts & Dorset 5/6 Salisbury – Swindon (passes close to Salisbury and Swindon)

MAP Page 275 (3J)
OS Map 184, 130: SU147484

The Nine Stones
Dorset

Now in a wooded glade, this small prehistoric circle of nine standing stones was constructed around 4000 years ago. Winterbourne Poor Lot Barrows (p.121) are nearby.

OPENING TIMES

Any reasonable time

HOW TO FIND US

Direction: 1½ miles SW of Winterbourne Abbas, on A35

Train: Weymouth 4½ miles

Bus: First 31 Weymouth – Axminster (passing Dorchester South)

Parking (in small lay-by opposite, next to barn).

Warning: Very busy main road, cross with care.

MAP Page 275 (5H)
OS Map 194, OL15/117: SY611904

Old Sarum Wiltshire – SP1 3SD

© Skyscan Balloon Photography

The great earthwork of Old Sarum stands near Salisbury on the edge of Wiltshire's chalk plains. Its mighty ramparts were raised in about 500 BC by Iron Age peoples, and later occupied by the Romans, the Saxons and, most importantly, the Normans.

William the Conqueror paid off his army here in 1070, and in 1086 summoned all the great landowners of England here to swear an oath of loyalty. A Norman castle was built on the inner mound, and joined soon afterwards by a royal palace. By the middle of the 12th century a new town occupied much of the great earthwork, complete with a noble new Norman cathedral, the mother church of a huge diocese.

But Norman Sarum was not destined to thrive. Soldiers and priests quarrelled and life on the almost waterless hilltop became intolerable. The solution was a move downhill to the new settlement now known as Salisbury, where a new cathedral was founded in 1220. Thereafter Old Sarum went into steep decline. Its cathedral was demolished and its castle was eventually abandoned. But the largely uninhabited site continued to 'elect' two MPs, becoming the most notorious of the 'Rotten Boroughs' swept away by the 1832 Reform Act.

Today, the remains of the prehistoric fortress and of the Norman palace, castle and cathedral evoke memories of thousands of years of history, which are interpreted by graphic panels throughout the site.

Visit the website for details of special events.

Old Sarum was one of the main inspirations behind Ken Follet's international bestseller *The Pillars of the Earth*, adapted as Channel 4's major TV series in 2010.

www.english-heritage.org.uk/oldsarum

NON-MEMBERS

Adult	£3.70
Concession	£3.30
Child	£2.20

OPENING TIMES

1 Apr-30 Jun, daily	10am-5pm
1 Jul-31 Aug, daily	9am-6pm
1-30 Sep, daily	10am-5pm
1-31 Oct, daily	10am-4pm
1 Nov-31 Jan, daily	11am-3pm
1-29 Feb, daily	11am-4pm
1-31 Mar, daily	10am-4pm
24-26 Dec and 1 Jan	Closed

HOW TO FIND US

Direction: 2 miles N of Salisbury, off A345

Train: Salisbury 2 miles

Bus: Wilts & Dorset Stonehenge Tour service. See www.thestonehengetour.info

Tel: 01722 335398

Local Tourist Information Salisbury: 01722 334956

P OVP

Disabled access (outer bailey and grounds only, disabled toilet).

Refreshments available.

MAP Page 275 (4J)
OS Map 184, 130: SU138327

Check www.english-heritage.org.uk for the latest opening times

Old Wardour Castle Wiltshire – SP3 6RR

Beautifully sited beside a lake, Old Wardour Castle was built in the late 14th century by John Lord Lovel as a lightly fortified but showy and luxurious residence. A hexagonal tower house ranged round a central courtyard, its form is very unusual in England.

Substantially updated by the staunchly Roman Catholic Arundell family after c. 1570, the castle saw much fighting during the Civil War. In 1643 the 60-year-old Lady Arundell was forced to surrender it to Parliament. But the new garrison was almost immediately besieged in turn by Royalist forces led by her son. After an eventful 10 months of bombardment and undermining, they finally capitulated in March 1644.

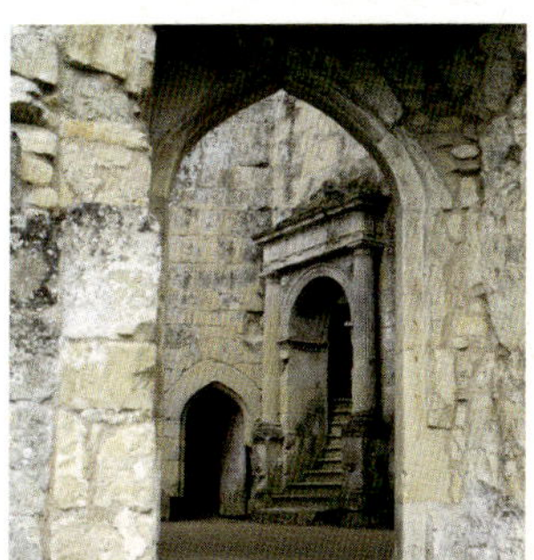

The badly damaged castle became a romantic ruin, and was incorporated in the 18th century into the landscaped grounds of Lord Arundell's New Wardour House (not managed by English Heritage, no public access). The castle's setting in a Registered Landscape enhances the significance of this hidden jewel.

Visit the website for details of special events.

Part of the film *Robin Hood, Prince of Thieves*, was filmed here.

www.english-heritage.org.uk/oldwardour

Licensed for civil wedding ceremonies

NON-MEMBERS

Adult	£4.00
Concession	£3.60
Child	£2.40

OPENING TIMES

1 Apr-30 Jun, daily	10am-5pm
1 Jul-31 Aug, daily	10am-6pm
1-30 Sep, daily	10am-5pm
1-31 Oct, daily	10am-4pm
1 Nov-31 Mar, Sat-Sun	10am-4pm
24-26 Dec and 1 Jan	Closed

HOW TO FIND US

Direction: Located off A30 2 miles SW of Tisbury. Also accessible from A350 (narrow rural roads), coaches approach with care

Train: Tisbury 2½ miles

Bus: Wilts & Dorset service 26 Salisbury – Shaftesbury (passes Tisbury)

Tel: 01747 870487

OVP

Disabled access (grounds and ground floor only), disabled toilet.

Refreshments available.

MAP Page 275 (4J)
OS Map 184, 118: ST939263

Notgrove Long Barrow
Gloucestershire

A grassed-over Neolithic long barrow containing stone-lined burial chambers, on the crest of a high Cotswold ridge.

Managed by Gloucestershire County Council.

OPENING TIMES

Any reasonable time

HOW TO FIND US

Direction: Located 1½ miles NW of Notgrove, on A436

Bus: Pulham's 801 Moreton-in-Marsh – Cheltenham (passes close to Moreton-in-Marsh)

MAP Page 275 (1J)
OS Map 163, OL45: SP096212

Nunney Castle
Somerset

The striking and picturesque moated castle of Nunney was built in the 1370s by Sir John de la Mere, a local knight who was beginning to enjoy royal favour. Extensively modernised in the late 16th century, the castle was held for the King during the Civil War, but quickly fell to Parliamentarian cannon in 1645: not until Christmas Day 1910, however, did the gun-damaged portion of the wall finally collapse.

Nunney Castle

OPENING TIMES

Any reasonable time

HOW TO FIND US

Direction: Located in Nunney, 3½ miles SW of Frome, off A361 (no coach access)

Train: Frome 3½ miles

Bus: First 161/2 Frome – Wells

Disabled access (exterior only).

MAP Page 275 (3H)
OS Map 183, 142: ST737457

Nympsfield Long Barrow
Gloucestershire

A large Neolithic burial mound with spectacular vistas over the Severn Valley. Its internal burial chambers are uncovered for viewing.

Managed by Gloucestershire County Council.

OPENING TIMES

Any reasonable time

HOW TO FIND US

Direction: Located 1 mile NW of Nympsfield on B4066

Train: Stroud 5 miles

Bus: Cotswold Green 35 (weekdays). Stagecoach 264 (Tue & Fri) to ¾ mile from the site

MAP Page 275 (2H)
OS Map 162, 167/168: SO794013

Odda's Chapel
Gloucestershire

One of the most complete surviving Saxon churches in England, this chapel was built in 1056 by Earl Odda, and rediscovered in 1865 subsumed into a farmhouse. Nearby is the equally famous Saxon parish church.

Odda's Chapel

OPENING TIMES

1 Apr-31 Oct, daily	10am-6pm
1 Nov-31 Mar, daily	10am-4pm
24-26 Dec and 1 Jan	Closed

HOW TO FIND US

Direction: Located in Deerhurst off B4213, at Abbots Court; SW of parish church

Train: Cheltenham 8 miles

Bus: Service 652 (Thu only); Veolia (Astons) 351, then 1½ mile walk from Apperley

Parking (not EH, charges apply).

MAP Page 275 (1J)
OS Map 150, 179: SO869298

Offa's Dyke
Gloucestershire

A three-mile section of the great earthwork boundary dyke built along the Anglo-Welsh border by Offa, King of Mercia, probably during the 780s. This especially impressive wooded stretch includes the Devil's Pulpit, with fine views of Tintern Abbey.

OPENING TIMES

Any reasonable time

HOW TO FIND US

Direction: Located 3 miles NE of Chepstow, off B4228. Via Forest Enterprise Tidenham car park, 1 mile walk (waymarked) down to The Devil's Pulpit on Offa's Dyke (access is suitable only for those wearing proper walking shoes and is not suitable for the very young, old or infirm)

Train: Chepstow 7 miles

Bus: Chepstow Classic Bus service 69 to Tintern then 1 mile walk

MAP Page 275 (2H)
OS Map 162, OL14/167
SO546011-ST549975

Portland Castle Dorset – DT5 1AZ

The history of this fort, which overlooks Portland harbour, is diverse and fascinating. Built by Henry VIII to defend the anchorage against possible French and Spanish invasion, its squat appearance is typical of the artillery forts built in the early 1540s.

Unusually for a fort of this period, the castle has seen much interior alteration, though the exterior remains largely unchanged. It first witnessed serious fighting during the Civil War, when it was seized by both Parliamentarians and Royalists.

It became a Seaplane Station during World War I, and was in the forefront of the D-Day preparations which helped to end World War II.

The Governor's Garden, designed by Christopher Bradley-Hole as part of the Contemporary Heritage Garden series, contains an impressive circular amphitheatre made from local Portland stone, with two-level seating for about 200 people. This perfectly sheltered spot is a great place to enjoy the dramatic sea and harbour views.

There is an audio tour and a Touch Tour for the visually impaired. You can even come face-to-face with Henry VIII in the Great Hall.

www.english-heritage.org.uk/portland

Enjoy a refreshing sea journey to Portland Castle from Weymouth aboard *My Girl*, a World War II veteran boat. 10% discount for EH members – valid 2 Apr to 31 Oct 2011. Tel 01305 785000 or visit www.whitemotorboat.freeuk.com

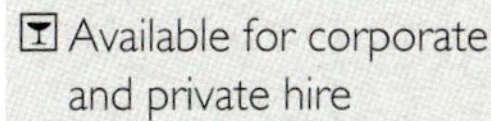

Available for corporate and private hire

Licensed for civil wedding ceremonies

NON-MEMBERS

Adult	£4.30
Concession	£3.90
Child	£2.60
Family	£11.20

OPENING TIMES

1 Apr-30 Jun, daily	10am-5pm
1 Jul-31 Aug, daily	10am-6pm
1-30 Sep, daily	10am-5pm
1-31 Oct, daily	10am-4pm
1 Nov-31 Mar	Closed

Parts of the castle may be unavailable for short periods during private events

HOW TO FIND US

Direction: Overlooking Portland Harbour in Castletown, Isle of Portland

Train: Weymouth 4½ miles

Bus: First summer service 501 serves the castle direct. At other times South West Coaches service 210 & First service 1 pass close by

Ferry: From Weymouth Harbour, Good Fri-end Oct (weather permitting). Call the castle for details

Tel: 01305 820539

OVP

Disabled access – Captain's House, ground floor of castle and Governor's Garden. Disabled toilet.

Captain's House Tearoom (table service for the disabled), variable closing in Oct.

MAP Page 275 (6H)
OS Map 194, OL15: SY685744

Check www.english-heritage.org.uk for the latest opening times

Pendennis Castle Cornwall – TR11 4LP

Constructed between 1540 and 1545, Pendennis and its sister, St Mawes Castle, form the Cornish end of the chain of coastal castles built by Henry VIII to counter a threat from France and Spain. Thereafter, Pendennis was frequently adapted to face new enemies over 400 years, right through until World War II.

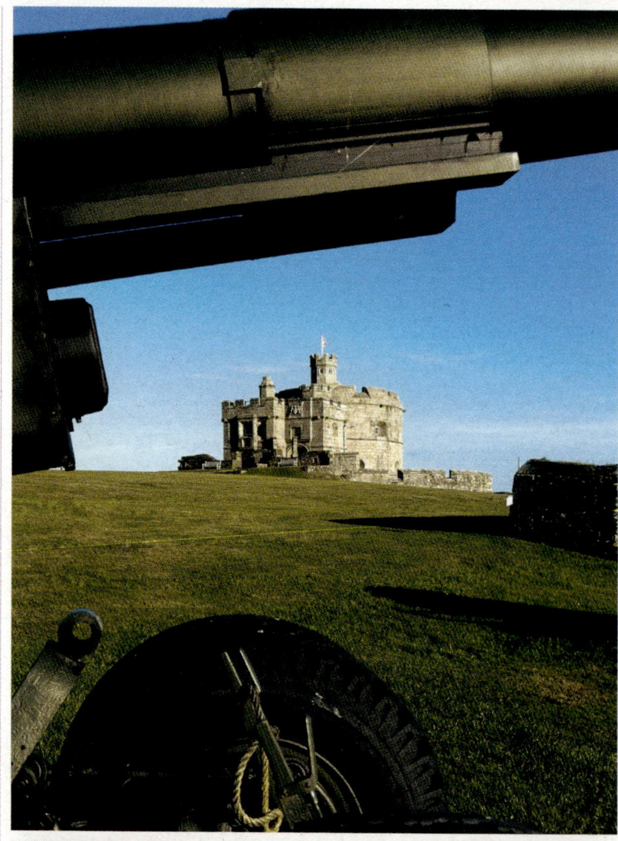

Pendennis Castle is home to a collection of wartime cartoons by George Butterworth. The acclaimed cartoons, which appeared daily throughout World War II, lampooned both Hitler and Mussolini, enraging the Nazi leader so much that the cartoonist was put on his 'hit-list'. During your visit to Pendennis, set aside some time to view the cartoons, generously given to English Heritage by George Butterworth's widow, a neighbour of the castle.

In 1598, during Elizabeth I's reign, a new type of defensive rampart was added around the original fort. The castle was strengthened again prior to the Civil War and played host to the future Charles II in 1646, before he sailed to the Isles of Scilly. It then withstood five months of siege, before becoming the penultimate Royalist garrison on the British mainland to surrender.

Pendennis continued to play a vital role in Cornwall's defences throughout the late 19th and early 20th centuries, and saw significant action during World War II. Evidence of its fascinating history is on show throughout the site and the Guardhouse has been returned to its World War I appearance. You can also visit the Half Moon Battery, including the underground magazine (by guided tour only), as well as the original 16th-century gun tower with its recreated Tudor gun deck.

The refurbished 1901 Royal Artillery Barracks houses an interactive exhibition, tracing the history of the castle, its people, and its links with Falmouth and the trade routes of the British Empire. A key feature is a hands-on scale model of the castle: with the aid of special effects, children can step into the shoes of a soldier on kit parade.

After a busy day exploring, visit the tearoom, situated in the Royal Garrison Artillery Barracks, which serves a delicious selection of refreshments, snacks and light meals made from local Cornish ingredients.

The pre-bookable education suite, with two large child-friendly education rooms and a wet room for creative workshops, can accommodate up to 120 children. The hospitality area is not only a fully-equipped conference centre but also an exceptional wedding venue, with the Fal Estuary as a stunning backdrop.

www.english-heritage.org.uk/pendennis

NON-MEMBERS

Adult	£6.30
Concession	£5.70
Child	£3.80
Family	£16.40

OPENING TIMES

1 Apr-30 Jun, daily	10am-5pm*
1 Jul-31 Aug, daily	10am-6pm*
1-30 Sep, daily	10am-5pm*
1 Oct-31 Mar, daily	10am-4pm
*Closes at 4pm on Saturdays	
The keep will close for 1 hour at lunch on Saturdays if an event is booked	
24-26 Dec and 1 Jan	Closed

HOW TO FIND US

Direction: On Pendennis Headland, 1 mile SE of Falmouth

Train: Falmouth Docks ½ mile

Bus: Western Greyhound service 500; First service 41 also passes nearby

Tel: 01326 316594

Local Tourist Information: 01326 312300

Disabled access (wheelchair access to the grounds, but steep slopes or drops in places. There is also full wheelchair access to the shop, tearoom, Discovery Centre and the Barracks, which contains a virtual tour of the whole site).

Dogs on leads (in grounds only).

Tearoom open daily, Apr-Oct (closes ½ hour before the castle), Nov-Mar 11am-3.30pm.

MAP Page 274 (7C)
OS Map 204, 103/105: SW824318

Available for corporate and private hire

Licensed for civil wedding ceremonies

Holiday cottages available to let

© Richard Pearn

Okehampton Castle
Devon – EX20 1JA

© David Garner

The remains of the largest castle in Devon, in an picturesque setting on a wooded spur above the rushing River Okement. Begun soon after the Norman Conquest as a motte and bailey castle with a stone keep, it was converted into a sumptuous residence in the 14th century by Hugh Courtenay, Earl of Devon, much of whose work survives. After the last Courtenay owner fell foul of Henry VIII in 1538, it declined into an allegedly haunted ruin. Riverside picnic area and woodland walks nearby.

www.english-heritage.org.uk/okehampton

NON-MEMBERS

Adult	£3.70
Concession	£3.30
Child	£2.20

OPENING TIMES

1 Apr-30 Jun, daily	10am-5pm
1 Jul-31 Aug, daily	10am-6pm
1-30 Sep, daily	10am-5pm
1 Oct-31 Mar	Closed

HOW TO FIND US

Direction: Located 1 mile SW of Okehampton town centre (signposted)

Train: Okehampton (summer Sundays only) ½ mile

Bus: First Atlantic Coast Express service X9, Beacon Bus service 118, Western Greyhound service 510 & 599 & Carmel service 318

Tel: 01837 52844

OVP

Audio Guide (also available for the visually impaired).

Woodland Walk Guide available from kiosk.

MAP Page 274 (5E)
OS Map 191, OL28/113: SX583942

Old Sarum
See feature – Page 108

Old Wardour Castle
See feature – Page 109

Over Bridge
Gloucestershire

A single-arch stone bridge spanning the River Severn, built in 1825-30 by the great engineer Thomas Telford.

OPENING TIMES

Any reasonable time

HOW TO FIND US

Direction: 1 mile NW of Gloucester, at junction of A40 (Ross) and A417 (Ledbury)

Train: Gloucester 2 miles

Bus: From Gloucester

P Parking (in lay-by).

MAP Page 275 (1H)
OS Map 162, 179: SO816196

Pendennis Castle
See feature – Page 112

Penhallam Manor
Cornwall

The low and grass-covered but complete ground-plan of a moated 13th-century manor house, in a delightful woodland setting.

OPENING TIMES

Any reasonable time

HOW TO FIND US

Direction: Signposted from Week St Mary, off a minor road off A39 from Treskinnick Cross (10 minute walk from the car park on the forest track)

Bus: Western Greyhound service 595 stops at Treskinnick Cross (2 miles)

P Parking (limited).

MAP Page 274 (5D)
OS Map 190, 111: SX224974

Portland Castle
See feature – Page 111

Restormel Castle
Cornwall – PL22 0EE

The great 13th-century circular shell-keep of Restormel still encloses the principal rooms of the castle in remarkably good condition. It stands on an earlier Norman mound surrounded by a deep dry ditch, atop a high spur beside the River Fowey. Twice visited by the Black Prince, it finally saw action during the Civil War in 1644. It commands fantastic views and is a favourite picnic spot.

www.english-heritage.org.uk/restormel

NON-MEMBERS

Adult	£3.40
Concession	£3.10
Child	£2.00

OPENING TIMES

1 Apr-30 Jun, daily	10am-5pm
1 Jul-31 Aug, daily	10am-6pm
1-30 Sep, daily	10am-5pm
1-31 Oct, daily	10am-4pm
1 Nov-31 Mar	Closed

HOW TO FIND US

Direction: Located 1½ miles N of Lostwithiel, off A390

Train: Lostwithiel 1½ miles

Bus: Western Greyhound 523, Roselyn 293, 296, Gorran Community Bus G4 to Lostwithiel then 1½ mile walk

Tel: 01208 872687

OVP

Access via a stock grazing area, appropriate footwear is advisable. There are steps on the entrance path. Disabled visitors may wish to call the site in advance to arrange alternative access.

MAP Page 274 (6C)
OS Map 200, 107: SX104614

Royal Citadel, Plymouth
Devon

A dramatic 17th-century fortress built to defend the coastline from the Dutch, and keep watch on a recently rebellious town. Still in use by the military today.

ENTRY

Non-member	£5.00
EH members and children	£4.00

OPENING TIMES

By guided tour only, May-Sep:
Tue & Thu only 2.30pm

HOW TO FIND US

Direction: At E end of Plymouth Hoe

Train: Plymouth 1 mile

Bus: Plymouth Citybus 25

Local Tourist Information
Plymouth: 01752 304849

Viewing is only by tours led by Blue Badge Guides – please contact plymouth.citadel.tours@googlemail.com prior to visiting.

MAP Page 274 (6E)
OS Map 201, OL20/108: SX480538

St Breock Downs Monolith
Cornwall

Originally 5 metres (16 feet) high and weighing some 16.75 tonnes, this is Cornwall's largest and heaviest prehistoric monolith. It stands on the summit of St Breock Downs, offering wonderful views.

Managed by the Cornwall Heritage Trust.

OPENING TIMES

Any reasonable time

HOW TO FIND US

Direction: Located on St Breock Downs; 3½ miles SW of Wadebridge off unclassified road to Rosenannon

Train: Roche 5½ miles

Bus: Summercourt Travel 405 (Tue & Fri) to within 2 miles. Western Greyhound 510, 594 then 2½ mile walk

MAP Page 274 (6C)
OS Map 200, 106: SW968683

St Briavels Castle
Gloucestershire

The fine twin-towered gatehouse of this castle, built by Edward I in 1292, once defended a crossbow bolt factory which used local Forest of Dean iron. Once a prison, it is now a youth hostel in wonderful walking country.

OPENING TIMES

Exterior: Any reasonable time

Bailey
1 Apr-30 Sep, daily 1pm-4pm

HOW TO FIND US

Direction: In St Briavels; 7 miles NE of Chepstow off B4228

Train: Chepstow 8 miles

Bus: KWT Coaches 705, Chepstow Classic Bus 707, 708 and Geoff Willetts Coaches 787

Tel: 01594 530272

MAP Page 275 (2H)
OS Map 162, OL14: SO559046

St Catherine's Castle
Cornwall

One of a pair of small artillery forts built by Henry VIII in the 1530s to defend Fowey Harbour, consisting of two storeys with gun ports at ground level.

OPENING TIMES

Any reasonable time

HOW TO FIND US

Direction: 1½ miles SW of Fowey, along a woodland footpath off A3082

Train: Par 4 miles

Bus: First service 25; Western Greyhound 524 & 525 to within ¾ mile walk of the castle

Parking (Ready Money Cove Car Park, Fowey, ¾ mile walk).

MAP Page 274 (6C)
OS Map 200/204, 107: SX119509

St Catherine's Chapel, Abbotsbury: see Abbotsbury, St Catherine's Chapel – Page 97

St Mary's Church, Kempley
Gloucestershire

A delightful Norman church, displaying one of the most outstandingly complete and well-preserved sets of medieval wall-paintings in England, dating from the 12th, 14th and 15th centuries.

Managed by the Friends of Kempley Church.

NEW FOR 2011

New graphic panels in the tower: a free 360-degree virtual tour of the church is now available from the English Heritage website.

OPENING TIMES

1 Mar-31 Oct, daily 10am-6pm

Please call for an appointment in winter

HOW TO FIND US

Direction: 1 mile N of Kempley off B4024; 6 miles NE of Ross-on-Wye

Train: Ledbury 8 miles

Bus: George Youngs Coaches 677 (Tue & Fri)

Tel: 01531 660214

MAP Page 275 (1H)
OS Map 149, 189: SO670313

The Sanctuary: see Avebury – Page 95

Sherborne Old Castle
Dorset – DT9 3SA

Built by Bishop Roger of Salisbury in the 12th century as a strongly-defended palace, Sherborne Old Castle became a powerful Royalist base during the Civil War. Described as 'malicious and mischievous' by Cromwell, it fell in 1645 after a fierce eleven-day siege. Sherborne 'New' Castle is nearby (see p.127).

www.english-heritage.org.uk/sherborne

Sherborne Old Castle

NON-MEMBERS

Adult	£3.40
Concession	£3.10
Child	£2.00

Discount to Sherborne Castle grounds for members: see page 127

OPENING TIMES

1 Apr-30 Jun, daily	10am-5pm
1 Jul-31 Aug, daily	10am-6pm
1-30 Sep, daily	10am-5pm
1-31 Oct, daily	10am-4pm
1 Nov-31 Mar	Closed

HOW TO FIND US

Direction: Located ½ mile E of Sherborne, off B3145

Train: Sherborne ¾ mile

Tel: 01935 812730

OVP

Refreshments available.

Secure cycle parking available. National network route 26.

MAP Page 275 (4H)
OS Map 183, 129: ST648168

Silbury Hill: see Avebury – Page 95

Sir Bevil Grenville's Monument
Bath & NE Somerset

Erected to commemorate the heroism of a Royalist commander and his Cornish pikemen at the Battle of Lansdown, 1643.

OPENING TIMES

Any reasonable time

HOW TO FIND US

Direction: Located 4 miles NW of Bath on the N edge of Lansdown Hill, near the road to Wick

Train: Bath Spa 4½ miles

Bus: Cotswold Green service 620 Bath Spa – Tetbury

P Parking (in lay-by).

MAP Page 275 (3H)
OS Map 172, 155: ST722703

St Mawes Castle Cornwall – TR2 5DE

© Skyscan Balloon Photography

St Mawes Castle is among the best-preserved of Henry VIII's coastal artillery fortresses, and the most elaborately decorated of them all. One of the chain of forts built between 1539 and 1545 to counter an invasion threat from Catholic France and Spain, it guarded the important anchorage of Carrick Roads, sharing the task with Pendennis Castle on the other side of the Fal estuary.

A charming clover-leaf shape surrounded by outer defences, St Mawes was designed to mount heavy 'ship-sinking' guns. But particular care was also taken with its embellishment, and it is still bedecked with carved Latin inscriptions in praise of Henry VIII and his son Edward VI. It owes its fine preservation for modern visitors to the fact that, unlike Pendennis Castle, it was little developed after its completion. Easily falling to landward attack by Civil War Parliamentarian forces in 1646, it remained neglected until partial re-arming during the 19th and early 20th centuries. Other coastal forts built by Henry VIII include Portland, Deal and Walmer Castles.

www.english-heritage.org.uk/stmawes

Available for corporate and private hire

Licensed for civil wedding ceremonies

Holiday cottage available to let

NON-MEMBERS

Adult	£4.30
Concession	£3.90
Child	£2.60

OPENING TIMES

1 Apr-30 Jun, Sun-Fri	10am-5pm*
1 Jul-31 Aug, Sun-Fri	10am-6pm*
1-30 Sep, Sun-Fri	10am-5pm*
1-31 Oct, daily	10am-4pm
1 Nov-31 Mar, Fri-Mon	10am-4pm

*Closed Sat. Property may close at 4pm on Fridays and Sundays and for 1 hour during other days for private events

24-26 Dec and 1 Jan	Closed

HOW TO FIND US

Direction: In St Mawes on A3078

Train: Penmere (Falmouth), 4 miles via Prince of Wales Pier and ferry

Bus: Western Greyhound service 550 ½ mile, but better to catch ferry from Falmouth

Tel: 01326 270526

P OVP

Dogs on leads (grounds only).

MAP Page 274 (7C)
OS Map 204, 105: SW841328

Check www.english-heritage.org.uk for the latest opening times

Stanton Drew Circles and Cove
Bath & NE Somerset

Though the third largest collection of prehistoric standing stones in England, the three circles and three-stone 'cove' of Stanton Drew are surprisingly little-known. Recent surveys have revealed that they were only part of a much more elaborate ritual site.

OPENING TIMES

Cove: any reasonable time.
Two main stone circles: access at the discretion of the landowner, who may levy a charge

HOW TO FIND US

Direction: Cove: in the garden of the Druid's Arms public house. Circles: E of Stanton Drew village

Train: Bristol Temple Meads 7 miles

Bus: Somerbus 640 (Fri) & 754 (Mon), A Bus service 683 (Wed), BANES 752 (Wed), Eurotaxis 834 (Tue)

MAP Page 275 (3H)
OS Map 172/182, 154/155
Cove: ST597631
Circles: ST601633

Stonehenge
See feature – Page 118

Stoney Littleton Long Barrow
Bath & NE Somerset

One of the finest accessible examples of a Neolithic chambered tomb, with its multiple burial chambers open to view.

OPENING TIMES

Any reasonable daylight hours

HOW TO FIND US

Direction: 1 mile S of Wellow off A367

Train: Bath Spa 6 miles

Bus: Somerbus 757 (Wed); First 173, 178 or 184 to Peasedown St John then 2½ mile walk

Parking (limited).

Stoney Littleton Long Barrow

Note: visitors are advised to bring a torch, and that there may be mud on approach and interior floor.

MAP Page 275 (3H)
OS Map 172, 142: ST735572

Temple Church
Bristol

The 'leaning tower' and walls of this large, late medieval church survived bombing during World War II. The graveyard is now a public garden.

OPENING TIMES

Exterior only: any reasonable time

HOW TO FIND US

Direction: Located in Temple St, off Victoria St

Train: Bristol Temple Meads ¼ mile

Bus: From surrounding areas

MAP Page 275 (3H)
OS Map 172, 154/155: ST593727

Tintagel Castle
See feature – Page 122

Totnes Castle
Devon –TQ9 5NU

A classic Norman motte and bailey castle, founded soon after the Conquest to overawe the Saxon town. A later stone shell-keep crowns its steep mound, giving sweeping views across the town rooftops to the River Dart.

www.english-heritage.org.uk/totnes

Totnes Castle

NON-MEMBERS

Adult	£3.40
Concession	£3.10
Child	£2.00

OPENING TIMES

1 Apr-30 Jun, daily	10am-5pm
1 Jul-31 Aug, daily	10am-6pm
1-30 Sep, daily	10am-5pm
1-31 Oct, daily	10am-4pm
1 Nov-31 Mar	Closed

HOW TO FIND US

Direction: In centre of Totnes, at Castle Street, off Station Road opposite railway station. From town centre, turn north off High Street

Train: Totnes ¼ mile

Bus: From surrounding areas

Tel: 01803 864406

OVP

Parking (charged, 64 metres (70 yards); cars only, narrow approach roads).

Keep accessible only via steep steps.

MAP Page 274 (6E)
OS Map 202, OL20/110: SX800605

Tregiffian Burial Chamber
Cornwall

A Neolithic or early Bronze Age chambered tomb with an entrance passage, walled and roofed with stone slabs, leading into the central chamber.

Managed by the Cornwall Heritage Trust.

OPENING TIMES

Any reasonable time

HOW TO FIND US

Direction: Located 2 miles SE of St Buryan, on B3315

Train: Penzance 5½ miles

Bus: Western Greyhound service 504

Parking (in lay-by).

MAP Page 274 (7B)
OS Map 203, 102: SW431244

Stonehenge Wiltshire – SP4 7DE

The great and ancient stone circle of Stonehenge is unique; an exceptional survival from a prehistoric culture now lost to us. The monument was begun around 3000 BC in the late Neolithic period and evolved until around 1600 BC in the middle of the Bronze Age. It is aligned with the rising and setting of the sun at the solstices, but its exact purpose remains a mystery.

Opening times from 20-22 June may be subject to change due to summer solstice. Please call 0870 333 1181 before your visit.

Check www.english-heritage.org.uk for the latest opening times

Over many centuries, there has been intense debate about the significance and uses of Stonehenge. Certainly it became the focal point of a landscape filled with prehistoric ceremonial and burial structures. It also represented an enormous investment of labour and time. A huge effort and great organisation was needed to carry the stones tens – and on occasion hundreds – of miles by land and water, and then to shape and raise them. Only a sophisticated society could have mustered so large a workforce, and produced the design and construction skills necessary to build Stonehenge and its surrounding monuments.

Stonehenge's orientation in relation to the rising and setting sun has always been one of its most remarkable features. Yet it remains uncertain whether this was because its builders came from a sun-worshipping culture or because – as some have asserted – the circle and its banks were part of a huge astronomical calendar.

What cannot be denied is the ingenuity of the builders of Stonehenge. With only very basic tools – such as antler picks and bone 'shovels' – at their disposal, they dug the enclosing ditch and erected the bank, later using similar tools to dig the holes for the stones. Other stone tools were used to shape the mortises and tenons linking the upright stones with the horizontal lintels.

Some of these tools can be seen, together with other artefacts including personal material from graves, on display in the museums at Salisbury and Devizes.

The first monument at Stonehenge (around 3000 BC) consisted of a circular ditch and bank (c. 120m in diameter), possibly with a ring of 56 wooden or stone posts, the pits for which are now called Aubrey Holes. Some 500 years later the first stones arrived: these were bluestones, transported over 240km (150 miles) from the Preseli Hills in Pembrokeshire. Paired bluestones were erected in an arc to the north east of the centre of the monument. Shortly afterwards this was dismantled, and replaced by an arrangement of stones which included the much larger super-hard sarsens, from the Marlborough Downs over 27km (16 miles) to the north. The outer circle was composed of 30 sarsen uprights with a similar number of lintels. This enclosed five sarsen trilithons (pairs of uprights with

A World Heritage Site, Stonehenge and its surrounding prehistoric monuments remain powerful witnesses to the once great civilisations of the Stone and Bronze Ages, between 6000 and 3000 years ago.

a lintel across each), arranged in a horseshoe shape, with the open end towards midsummer sunrise. Bluestones were re-erected within the circle and horseshoe, to mirror the sarsen arrangements. The remains that can be seen today are a remarkable survival of this ancient monument in its final phase.

In the landscape immediately around Stonehenge there are visible remains of many different types of monuments, and many more have been detected. Neolithic monuments include long barrows, the long rectangular earthwork known as the Cursus (once thought to resemble a Roman chariot racecourse) and the henge monuments at Woodhenge (p.121) and Durrington Walls, contemporary with the stone phases at Stonehenge. There are also hundreds of Bronze Age round barrows, which were built during the period after the large sarsens were erected at Stonehenge. Stonehenge is surrounded by 827 hectares of land owned by the National Trust, with excellent walks to some of the monuments mentioned above.

Stonehenge and Avebury became a World Heritage Site in 1986 for their outstanding prehistoric monuments from the Neolithic to the Bronze Age periods.

www.english-heritage.org.uk/stonehenge

NON-MEMBERS

Adult	£7.50
Concession	£6.80
Child	£4.50
Family	£19.50

NT members admitted free

Please note: All education groups must be pre-booked

OPENING TIMES

1 Apr-31 May, daily	9.30am-6pm
1 Jun-31 Aug, daily	9am-7pm
1 Sep-15 Oct, daily	9.30am-6pm
16 Oct-15 Mar, daily	9.30am-4pm
16-31 Mar, daily	9.30am-6pm
26 Dec and 1 Jan	10am-4pm
24-25 Dec	Closed

Stone Circle Access outside normal opening hours by advance booking only. Book during weekday office hours on telephone 01722 343834

Recommended last admission time no later than 30 minutes before the advertised closing time

When weather conditions are bad, access may be restricted and visitors may not be able to use the walkway around the stone circle

Opening times from 20-22 June may be subject to change due to summer solstice. Please call 0870 333 1181 before your visit

HOW TO FIND US

Direction: 2 miles W of Amesbury on junction of A303 and A344/A360

Train: Salisbury 9½ miles, Andover 15½ miles (but taxi links only)

Bus: Wilts & Dorset Stonehenge Tour service
See www.thestonehengetour.info

Tel: 0870 333 1181 (Customer Services)

Local Tourist Information
Amesbury: 01980 622833; and Salisbury: 01722 334956

OVP

Audio tours (complimentary – available in ten languages and hearing loop: subject to availability).

Catering, hot and cold refreshments available throughout the year.

Guidebooks (also available in French, German, Japanese and Spanish; large print and braille guides in English only).

No dogs allowed (except guide and hearing dogs).

Parking (Seasonal parking is charged, refundable on entry).

MAP Page 275 (4J)
OS Map 184, 130: SU122422

Trethevy Quoit
Cornwall

This well-preserved and impressive Neolithic 'dolmen' burial chamber stands 2.7 metres (8.9 ft) high. There are five standing stones, surmounted by a huge capstone.

Managed by the Cornwall Heritage Trust.

OPENING TIMES

Any reasonable time

HOW TO FIND US

Direction: 1 mile NE of St Cleer, near Darite; off B3254

Train: Liskeard 3½ miles

Bus: DAC 79B & Western Greyhound 574

MAP Page 274 (6D)
OS Map 201, 109: SX259688

Uley Long Barrow (Hetty Pegler's Tump)
Gloucestershire

A partly reconstructed Neolithic chambered mound, 37 metres (120 ft) long, atmospherically sited overlooking the Severn Valley. 'Hetty Pegler' was its 17th-century landowner.

Managed by Gloucestershire County Council.

OPENING TIMES

Exterior viewing only

HOW TO FIND US

Direction: Located 3½ miles NE of Dursley, on B4066

Train: Stroud 6 miles

Bus: Stagecoach in the Cotswolds 20 Stroud – Uley (passes close to Stroud); Cotswold Green 281 (Mon, Wed) from Dursley. All to within 1 mile

MAP Page 275 (2H)
OS Map 162, 167/168: SO790000

Upper Plym Valley
Devon

Some 300 Bronze Age and medieval sites, covering 15½ square kilometres (6 square miles) of Dartmoor landscape.

OPENING TIMES

Any reasonable time

HOW TO FIND US

Direction: 4 miles E of Yelverton

MAP Page 274 (6E)
OS Map 202, OL20/OL28: SX580660

West Kennet Avenue: see Avebury – Page 96

West Kennet Long Barrow: see Avebury – Page 96

Windmill Hill: see Avebury, – Page 96

Windmill Tump Long Barrow, Rodmarton
Gloucestershire

A Neolithic chambered tomb with an enigmatic 'false entrance'. Managed by Gloucestershire County Council.

OPENING TIMES

Any reasonable time

HOW TO FIND US

Direction: 1 mile SW of Rodmarton

Train: Kemble 5 miles

Bus: Stagecoach in the Cotswolds 881 from Kemble

Map Page 275 (2J)
OS Map 163, 168: ST933973

Winterbourne Poor Lot Barrows
Dorset

A 'cemetery' of 44 Bronze Age burial mounds of varying types and sizes, straddling the A35 main road.

OPENING TIMES

Any reasonable time

Winterbourne Poor Lot Barrows

HOW TO FIND US

Direction: 2 miles W of Winterbourne Abbas, S of junction of A35 with a minor road to Compton Valence. Access via Wellbottom Lodge – 180 metres (200 yards) E along A35 from junction

Train: Dorchester West or South, both 7 miles

Bus: First 31 Weymouth – Axminster (passes Dorchester South)

No adjacent parking. Warning: cross road with care.

MAP Page 275 (5H)
OS Map 194, OL15/117: SY590907

Woodhenge
Wiltshire

Neolithic monument, dating from about 2300 BC, with concrete markers indicating the location of six concentric rings of timber posts. The timber structure is surrounded by a circular bank and ditch (henge) whose entrance is aligned north-east towards the summer solstice sunrise, like Stonehenge. A small central flint cairn marks the location of a child burial.

Part of the Stonehenge World Heritage Site.

OPENING TIMES

Any reasonable time

Usual facilities may not be available around the summer solstice 20-22 June. Please call 0870 333 1181 before your visit

HOW TO FIND US

Direction: 1½ miles N of Amesbury, off A345, just S of Durrington

Train: Salisbury 9 miles

Bus: Wilts & Dorset 5, 6 & 16

MAP Page 275 (4J)
OS Map 184, 130: SU151434

Yarn Market, Dunster: see Dunster, Yarn Market – Page 100

Tintagel Castle

Cornwall – PL34 0HE

With its spectacular location on one of Britain's most dramatic coastlines, Tintagel is an awe-inspiring and romantic spot, a place of legends.

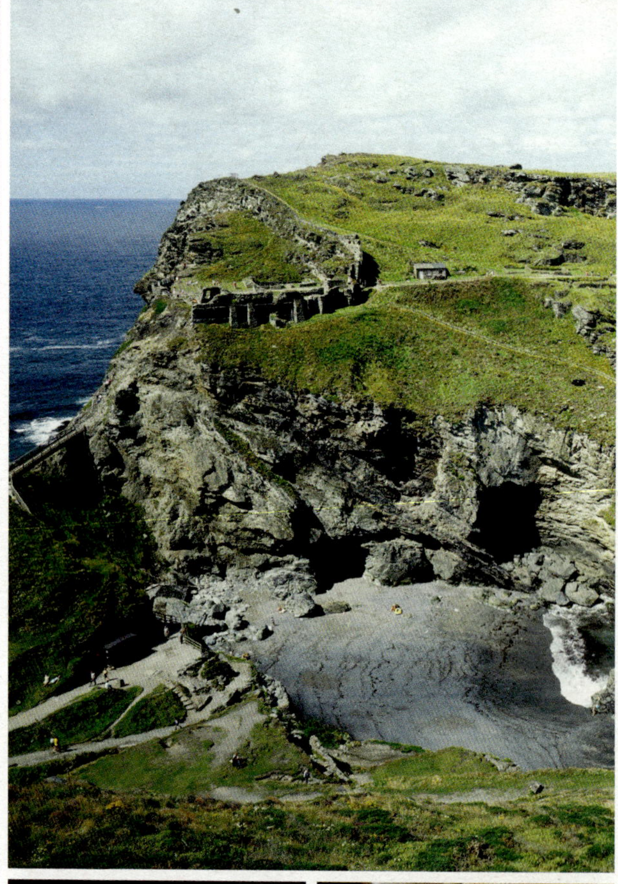

Take time to browse in the superb castle shop which specialises in books, medieval and Arthurian themed gifts and toys, tapestries, jams and chutneys.

Check www.english-heritage.org.uk for the latest opening times

Joined to the mainland by a narrow neck of land, Tintagel Island faces the full force of the Atlantic. On the mainland itself, the gaunt remains of the medieval castle represent only one phase in a long history of occupation. Even before Richard, Earl of Cornwall, built his castle, Tintagel was already associated with the conception of King Arthur. This connection was later renewed by Alfred, Lord Tennyson, in his *Idylls of the King*.

After a period as a Roman settlement and military outpost, Tintagel is thought to have been a trading settlement of Celtic kings during the 5th and 6th centuries. Legend has it that one of these was King Mark, whose nephew Tristan fell in love with Yseult (or Isolde). Their doomed romance is part of Tintagel's story.

The remains of the 13th-century castle are breathtaking. Steep stone steps, stout walls and rugged windswept cliff edges encircle the Great Hall, where Richard, Earl of Cornwall, once feasted.

There are many unanswered questions and legends surrounding Tintagel. The castle has an amazing capacity to surprise us, even after years of investigation.

In 1998, excavations were undertaken under the direction of Professor Chris Morris of the University of Glasgow, on a relatively sheltered and small site on the eastern side of the island, first excavated in the 1930s. Pottery from the 5th and 6th centuries was found, as well as some fine glass fragments believed to be from 6th or 7th-century Málaga in Spain. Even more remarkable was a 1500-year-old piece of slate on which remained two Latin inscriptions. The second inscription reads: 'Artognou, father of a descendant of Coll, has had (this) made'. Who exactly Artognou was continues to be a subject for lively speculation.

Searching for King Arthur, a short audio visual tour through the ages, introduces visitors to the castle, its legends and history.

During the summer you can also enjoy special introductory talks. The site offers a shop and visitor facilities, and the café, set above the beach, serves a delicious selection of hot and cold snacks and light meals – all sourced from the finest local Cornish ingredients.

Access to the castle is difficult for disabled visitors (via over 100 steep steps). There is a Land Rover service from the village which can take visitors to the exhibition and shop (Apr-Oct only). Contact the site for service information.

www.english-heritage.org.uk/tintagel

NON-MEMBERS

Adult	£5.50
Concession	£5.00
Child	£3.30
Family	£14.30

OPENING TIMES

1 Apr-30 Sep, daily	10am-6pm
1-31 Oct, daily	10am-5pm
1 Nov-31 Mar, daily	10am-4pm
24-26 Dec and 1 Jan	Closed

Beach Café open Apr-Oct daily (closes ½ hour before the castle), Nov-Mar 11am-3.30pm

HOW TO FIND US

Direction: On Tintagel Head, 600m (660 yards) along uneven track from Tintagel; no vehicles except Land Rover service, extra charge

Bus: Western Greyhound 594 (with connections available at Wadebridge, Camelford and Boscastle)

Tel: 01840 770328

Local Tourist Information: Tintagel Visitors' Centre: 01840 779084; Camelford (summer only): 01840 212954; Padstow: 01841 533449

P OVP

Disabled access is limited. A Land Rover service to the castle (Apr-Oct) is available at a separate charge. Please call the site for more details.

Parking (600 metres (660 yards) in the village) – not managed by EH.

MAP Page 274 (5C)
OS Map 200, 111: SX049891

The Heritage of Scilly Isles of Scilly

The stunningly beautiful Isles of Scilly hold vast arrays of archaeological riches both above and below sea level. English Heritage recognises the importance of promoting this unique cultural landscape, and provides expert advice and significant funding to regeneration and conservation projects throughout the Isles.

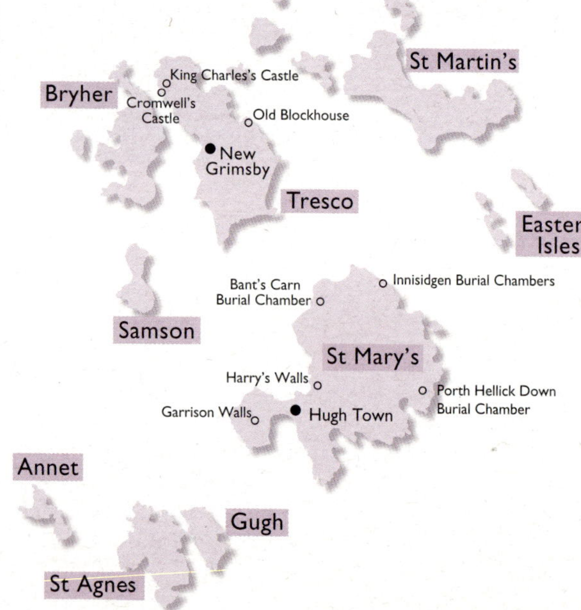

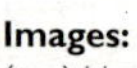

Images:
(top) Harry's Walls
(middle) King Charles's Castle
(bottom) Cromwell's Castle

This compact archipelago of about 100 islands lies around 28 miles to the south-west of Land's End. None of them is any bigger than three miles across and only five are inhabited. Despite their landmass of only 16 square kilometres (6.18 square miles), these islands contain a remarkable number of historic sites. These range from traditional farmhouses and dwellings to ritual burial monuments, cist grave cemeteries and Romano-Celtic shrines. Early settlements provide evidence of a distinctive Scillonian culture which thrived in the island group 2000 years ago. More recently, defensive monuments constructed during the Civil War and World War II stand as testament to the strategic importance of the islands. The Gulf Stream keeps the climate warm, enabling exotic plants and wildlife to thrive.

NEW FOR 2011

New visual displays and downloadable audio tours enable visitors to immerse themselves in the rich histories of these sites. Audio tours and clips, which can be played on iPods, mobile phones or mp3 players, are available from the English Heritage website and allow visitors to listen to experts as they walk around the sites.

OPENING TIMES

All EH properties on the Scillies are open at any reasonable time

HOW TO FIND US

Direction: See individual property entries (opposite) for access details

Bus: Details from St Mary's TIC on 01720 422536

Tel: 0117 9750700 (Regional office)

Bant's Carn Burial Chamber and Halangy Down Ancient Village
St Mary's, Isles of Scilly

The remains of an ancient Iron Age village in a wonderfully scenic location. On the hill above stands a Bronze Age burial mound with entrance passage and inner chamber.

OPENING TIMES

Any reasonable time

HOW TO FIND US

Direction: 1 mile N of Hugh Town

MAP Page 274 (5B)
OS Map 203, 101: SV910123

Cromwell's Castle
Tresco, Isles of Scilly

Standing on a rocky promontory guarding the lovely anchorage between Bryher and Tresco, this round tower is one of the few surviving Cromwellian fortifications in Britain, built after the conquest of the Royalist Scillies in 1651.

OPENING TIMES

Any reasonable time

HOW TO FIND US

Direction: On the shoreline, approach with care, ¾ mile NW of New Grimsby

MAP Page 274 (4A)
OS Map 203, 101: SV882159

Garrison Walls
St Mary's, Isles of Scilly

You can enjoy a two-hour walk alongside the ramparts of these defensive walls and earthworks, dating from the 16th to 18th centuries. Other remains include Elizabethan Star Castle and defences from both World Wars.

OPENING TIMES

Any reasonable time

NEW FOR 2011

There is a new exhibition within the Garrison Walls.

HOW TO FIND US

Direction: Around the headland W of Hugh Town

MAP Page 274 (5A)
OS Map 203, 101: SV898104

Harry's Walls
St Mary's, Isles of Scilly

An unfinished artillery fort, built above St Mary's Pool harbour in 1552-53.

OPENING TIMES

Any reasonable time

HOW TO FIND US

Direction: ¼ mile NE of Hugh Town

MAP Page 274 (5B)
OS Map 203, 101: SV909109

Innisidgen Lower and Upper Burial Chambers
St Mary's, Isles of Scilly

Two Bronze Age communal burial cairns of Scillonian type, with fine views. The upper cairn is the best preserved on the islands.

OPENING TIMES

Any reasonable time

HOW TO FIND US

Direction: 1¾ miles NE of Hugh Town

MAP Page 274 (5B)
OS Map 203, 101: SV922127

King Charles's Castle
Tresco, Isles of Scilly

The ruins of a mid 16th-century coastal artillery fort, later garrisoned – hence the name –

by Civil War Royalists. Reached from New Grimsby by footpath.

OPENING TIMES

Any reasonable time

HOW TO FIND US

Direction: Located ¾ mile NW of New Grimsby. Coastal location, approach with care

MAP Page 274 (4A)
OS Map 203, 101: SV882161

Old Blockhouse
Tresco, Isles of Scilly

Substantial remains of a small 16th-century gun tower protecting Old Grimsby harbour, vigorously defended during the Civil War.

OPENING TIMES

Any reasonable time

HOW TO FIND US

Direction: Located on Blockhouse Point, at the S end of Old Grimsby harbour

MAP Page 274 (4A)
OS Map 203, 101: SV897155

Porth Hellick Down Burial Chamber
St Mary's, Isles of Scilly

A large and imposing Scillonian Bronze Age entrance grave, with kerb, inner passage and burial chamber all clearly visible.

OPENING TIMES

Any reasonable time

HOW TO FIND US

Direction: 1¾ miles E of Hugh Town

MAP Page 274 (5B)
OS Map 203, 101: SV928108

Associated attractions in the South West

These visitor attractions, all independent of EH, offer discounts to our members. Please call before you visit to confirm details. A valid EH membership card must be produced for each member.

The Arthurian Centre
Cornwall PL32 9TT

Walk through newly exposed archaeology to the unique, 1500-year-old 'King Arthur's Stone' on the site of Arthur and Mordred's last battle of 'Camlann'

- Land of Arthur Exhibition
- Great visit for all ages

10 min from Tintagel Castle

Tel: 01840 213947

www.arthur-online.co.uk

20% discount on entry

[#] OVP 6

Bowood House and Gardens
Wiltshire SN11 0LZ

Magnificent family home of the Marquis and Marchioness of Lansdowne, set in beautiful 'Capability' Brown parkland. Families love the amazing Adventure Playground and Soft Play Palace. Rhododendron Walks April–mid-June.

10 miles from J17 of M5

Tel: 01249 812102

www.bowood.org

25% discount on entry

Coldharbour Mill Working Wool Museum
Devon EX15 3EE

This 200-year-old spinning mill still produces knitting yarns and weaves tartan cloth as it tells the story of the once flourishing West Country woollen industry. Restored water wheel and two steam engines also on show.

2 miles from J27 of M5

Tel: 01884 840960

www.coldharbourmill.org.uk

25% discount on entry

Lulworth Castle & Park
Dorset BH20 5QS

Enjoy wide open spaces, historic buildings, stunning landscapes, park and woodland walks. Castle displays, children's activity room and unrivalled Castle Tower views. Pay and display parking. Picnic areas.

50 mins from Portland Castle

Tel: 0845 450 1054

www.lulworth.com

Free entry to the castle

National Maritime Museum Cornwall
Cornwall TR11 3QY

This award-winning museum delivers something for everyone. Family activities every school holiday, changing exhibitions and a host of events. A new generation of museum offering more than you might expect.

1 mile from Pendennis Castle

Tel: 01326 313388

www.nmmc.co.uk

10% discount on entry

Powderham Castle
Devon EX6 8JQ

Take time to enjoy the 600-year-old home of the Earl & Countess of Devon. Fascinating tours, stunning views, deer park safari, play castle, friendly animals, shops, tearoom and special events.

10 miles from J30 of M5

Tel: 01626 890243

www.powderham.co.uk

20% discount on entry

EH Members | OVP OVP Holders | Discounted Child Places Included

Salisbury and South Wiltshire Museum
Wiltshire SP1 2EN

Salisbury Museum is the home of the award-winning Stonehenge Gallery and the famous 'Amesbury Archer'. Displays also reveal the history of medieval Salisbury and Old Sarum.

10 mins from Old Sarum

Tel: 01722 332151

www.salisburymuseum.org.uk

50% discount on standard museum entry ticket 4

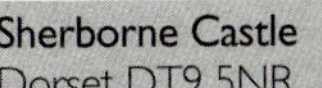

Sherborne Castle
Dorset DT9 5NR

Original house built by Sir Walter Raleigh in 1594. Splendid decorative interiors and collections. 'Capability' Brown lake and landscaped lakeside gardens. Home of the Digby family since 1617. Tearoom and gift shop.

½ mile from Sherborne Old Castle

Tel: 01935 812072

www.sherbornecastle.com

£1.50 off 'Gardens Only' ticket
Castle Interior extra charge. (not valid on special event days) 4

Sudeley Castle
Gloucestershire GL54 5JD

Nestled in the Cotswold Hills, Sudeley is surrounded by 1200 acres of grounds, award-winning gardens and historic ruins. Tours of the Castle apartments on selected weekdays. Former home of Katherine Parr.

10 miles from J9 of M5

Tel: 01242 602308

www.sudeleycastle.co.uk

25% discount on entry

Trevarno Estate & Gardens
Cornwall TR13 0RU

Visit Trevarno, a perfect day out for all the family! Includes the amazing National Museum of Gardening, 35 acres of gardens, shop, Conservatory Tearoom, large play area and real live reindeer.

14 miles from Pendennis Castle

Tel: 01326 574274

www.trevarno.co.uk

10% discount on entry
OVP

Wiltshire Heritage Museum
Wiltshire SN10 1NS

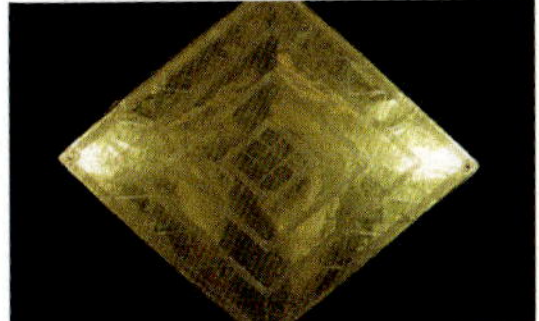

The best Bronze Age archaeology collections in Britain, including objects from Stonehenge and Avebury. The Museum traces the story of Wiltshire, its environment and people over the last 6000 years.

8 miles from Avebury

Tel: 01380 727369

www.wiltshireheritage.org.uk

50% discount on entry

Woodchester Mansion
Gloucestershire GL10 3TS

Abandoned by its builders before completion, Woodchester Mansion has been virtually untouched by time since the mid-1870s. Enjoy a unique opportunity to explore a neo-Gothic building 'frozen' in mid-assembly.

10 mins from J13 of M5

Tel: 01453 861541

www.woodchestermansion.org.uk

£1.00 off admission

Castle Acre Priory: Prior's Chamber ceiling – see page 138

East of England

www.english-heritage.org.uk/eastofengland

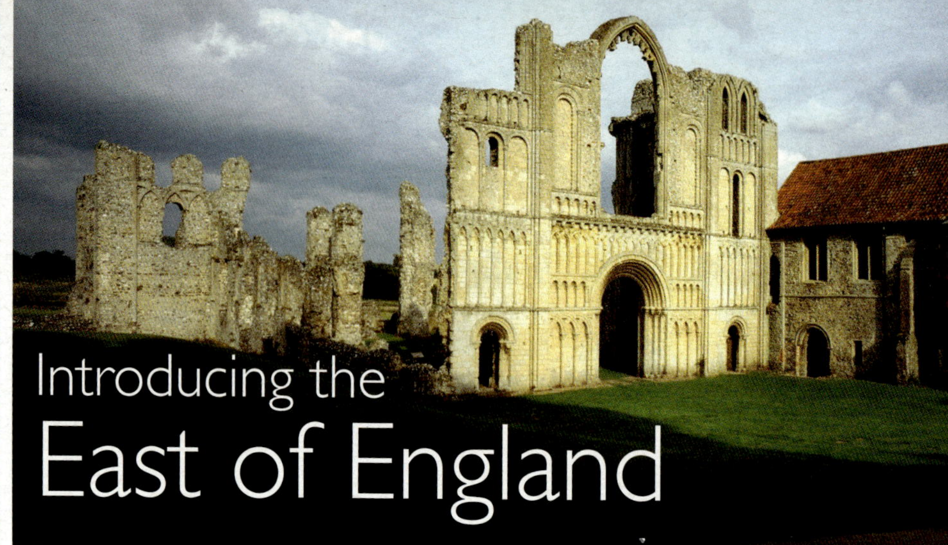

Introducing the East of England

Remember to check opening times before you visit any of our properties.

Details of all bus travel in England are available from Traveline on 0871 200 2233 or visit www.traveline.org.uk

Bedfordshire
- Bushmead Priory
- De Grey Mausoleum, Flitton
- Houghton House
- Wrest Park

Cambridgeshire
- Denny Abbey and the Farmland Museum
- Duxford Chapel
- Isleham Priory Church
- Longthorpe Tower

Essex
- Audley End House and Gardens
- Colchester, St Botolph's Priory
- Colchester, St John's Abbey Gate
- Hadleigh Castle
- Hill Hall
- Lexden Earthworks and Bluebottle Grove
- Mistley Towers
- Prior's Hall Barn, Widdington
- Tilbury Fort
- Waltham Abbey Gatehouse and Bridge

Hertfordshire
- Berkhamsted Castle
- Old Gorhambury House
- Roman Wall, St Albans

Norfolk
- Baconsthorpe Castle
- Berney Arms Windmill
- Binham Market Cross
- Binham Priory
- Blakeney Guildhall
- Burgh Castle
- Caister Roman Fort
- Castle Acre Priory
- Castle Acre Priory, Castle and Bailey Gate
- Castle Rising Castle
- Cow Tower, Norwich
- Creake Abbey
- Great Yarmouth Row Houses & Greyfriars' Cloisters
- Grime's Graves – prehistoric flint mine
- North Elmham Chapel
- St Olave's Priory
- Thetford, Church of the Holy Sepulchre
- Thetford Priory
- Thetford Warren Lodge
- Weeting Castle

Suffolk
- Bury St Edmunds Abbey
- Framlingham Castle
- Landguard Fort
- Leiston Abbey
- Lindsey St James's Chapel
- Moulton Packhorse Bridge
- Orford Castle
- Saxtead Green Post Mill

Norfolk Adventures

Famous for its coast, countryside and nature reserves, north Norfolk is also particularly fortunate in its varied range of English Heritage sites – many of which can be enjoyed with the minimum of driving. The vastly imposing ruins of **Castle Acre Priory**, together with the stupendous castle earthworks and the pretty village which lies between, make a day out in themselves: and not too far away is **Castle Rising Castle**, with its ornately decorated Norman keep.

Along the north Norfolk coast, cars can be dispensed with altogether, in favour (for the energetic) of walking the Norfolk Coast Path from Hunstanton to Cromer, or taking the wonderfully convenient Coast Hopper bus service which allows short sections of the Path to be sampled. This route takes in an array of nature reserves; Holkham Hall with its discounts for English Heritage members; and curious little **Blakeney Guildhall**, near the start point for 'seal viewing' boats. Amid the quiet lanes just inland, footpaths and cycle tracks give access to sites like serene **Creake Abbey**, with a craft centre at hand; impressively complete **Binham Priory** – now with much enhanced facilities, and well worth several hours' visit; and fascinating **Baconsthorpe Castle** with its moat and wildfowl mere, also reachable via a wooded and heathland cross-country path from the attractive market town of Holt. Baconsthorpe church, in the nearby village, displays the monuments of the Heydon owners of the castle. Like nearly all the many ancient village churches hereabouts, it is hospitably open to visitors – yet another reason to explore a region so rich in wildlife, coastal scenery and delightful countryside, as well as English Heritage sites.

Make the most of your membership and keep up to date with upcoming events, the latest news and special offers by subscribing to our e-newsletter. Register online at **www.english-heritage.org.uk/newsletter** and we'll deliver the latest from English Heritage straight to your inbox.

Images:
(left) Castle Acre Priory
(top centre) Binham Priory
(top right) Wrest Park
(bottom centre) Audley End House and Gardens
(bottom right) Baconsthorpe Castle

Audley End House and Gardens

Essex – CB11 4JF

Audley End takes its name from Sir Thomas Audley, Henry VIII's Lord Chancellor, who adapted the extensive buildings of suppressed Walden Abbey as his mansion. His grandson Thomas Howard, first Earl of Suffolk, rebuilt the house on a massive scale between 1603 and 1614. This 'Palace of Audley End' was three times its present size, and one of the largest mansions in England, but in 1618 Suffolk fell from favour and into massive debt, and his great house went into decline.

The Stable Yard, opened in spring 2010, has been a resounding success with visitors.

Children's play area and Cart Yard Café

Charles II bought Audley End in 1668 as a base for attending Newmarket races: his Queen Catherine of Braganza held court here that autumn. Repairs carried out by Sir Christopher Wren proved ruinously costly, and in 1701 William III returned Audley End to the Suffolk family. The witty and accomplished Henrietta Howard lived here, before leaving her 'obstinate, drunken and brutal' husband, the 9th Earl, for a royal lover and her new Thames-side mansion, Marble Hill House (see p.41).

When the Suffolk line died out in 1745, the mansion was bought by the Countess of Portsmouth for her nephew and heir, Sir John Griffin Griffin, later first Baron Braybrooke. He made extensive changes to the house, adding a suite of neo-Classical rooms designed by Robert Adam and a Gothick chapel. Meanwhile, 'Capability' Brown was employed to remodel the grounds.

Today the house's interior largely represents the taste of the third Baron Braybrooke, who, during the 1820s, redecorated many of its rooms in the Jacobean style. He installed his extensive picture collection and filled the rooms with inherited furnishings. The fourth Baron Braybrooke's natural history collection also remains an appealing feature.

The Service Wing

The Victorian Service Wing provides a unique insight into the 'below stairs' working of this great household during the 1880s. Rooms open to the public include the kitchen, dairy, dry larder and laundries. Equipped with original and reproduction Victorian fixtures and fittings, they are also vividly animated with lifelike sights and sounds, film projection and even examples of foods eaten in the era. This creates an atmospheric portrait of daily life for the people who once toiled here – from butler down to dairy maid and lowly houseboy.

Incorporating research into the real lives of the 25 or so indoor servants employed here during the 1880s, the Service Wing presentation illustrates how familiar household tasks were conducted on a near-industrial scale for the Braybrooke family and their retinue. The Service Wing was also at the heart of a largely self-sufficient community, where most food for the household was produced on the estate.

Watch out for special days when visitors can see and hear from costumed interpreters cooking, washing and ironing in traditional ways.

The Gardens

Much has been done to restore Audley End's park and fine Victorian gardens to their former glory. The river Cam was dammed to form an artificial lake which runs through delightful 18th-century parkland. The Classical Temple of Concord, built in 1790 in honour of George III, and the restored 19th-century formal parterre garden dominate the views from the back of the house.

Visitors can also see Robert Adam's ornamental garden buildings, and the Elysian Garden cascade. The walled organic kitchen garden is a memorable part of any visit.

The Stables

The Stable Yard, opened in spring 2010, has been a resounding success with visitors.

This lovely building in the grounds of Audley End House has been hailed as one of the grandest surviving stables of the early 17th century. It originally housed around 30 pampered horses,

Audley End House and Gardens continued

Please note: In some rooms, light levels are reduced to preserve vulnerable textiles and other collections. No photography or stiletto heels allowed in the house.

with the grooms, coaches, and other equipment needed to service the demands of this great country house. Despite some alterations by successive owners, the stable block has changed very little over the years. During World War II it was used for training by the Special Operations Executive, Polish Section.

It is now home to our new multi-media exhibition, which interprets the gardens, parkland and estate, linking them to the working life of the house. Hear about the estate staff who worked here in the 1880s, including the coachman, groom, gamekeepers and gardeners. Horses are in residence throughout the year, and you can talk to our Horse Manager about their life and times, with 'hands-on' fun for the little ones.

The Children's Play area, inspired by the surroundings of Audley End, is next to the Cart Yard Café and provides a welcome break while viewing the Stable Yard and Organic Kitchen Garden nearby.

www.english-heritage.org.uk/audleyend

Holiday cottage available to let

NON-MEMBERS

Full Estate

Adult	£12.50
Concession	£11.30
Child	£7.50
Family	£32.50

Stables, Service Wing & Gardens (not available on event days)

Adult	£8.70
Concession	£7.80
Child	£5.20
Family	£22.60

OPENING TIMES

1 Apr-30 Sep, Wed-Sun & Bank Hols	10am-6pm
House	12pm-5pm
1-31 Oct, Wed-Sun	10am-5pm
House	12pm-4pm
1 Nov-18 Dec, Sat-Sun (Gardens, Stables and Service Wing open, House closed)	10am-4pm
19 Dec-31 Jan	Closed
1-12 Feb, Sat-Sun (Gardens, Stables and Service Wing open, House closed)	10am-4pm
13-29 Feb, Wed-Sun (Gardens, Stables and Service Wing open, House closed)	10am-4pm
1-31 Mar, Wed-Sun (Gardens, Stables and Service Wing open, House closed)	10am-5pm

Guided Tours (House)

1-29 Apr, Wed-Sun (except Easter)

3 May-15 Jul, Wed-Fri (except 1-3 June)

1 Sep-21 Oct, Wed-Sun

Please note that the house opens at 11am on guided tour days. On these days access is by guided tour only. Please note this may be subject to change on event days

HOW TO FIND US

Direction: 1 mile W of Saffron Walden on B1383 (M11 exit 8 or 10)

Train: Audley End 1¼ miles. Note: Footpath is beside busy main road

Bus: C.J.Myall service 101; Hedingham Burtons 59; Excel 5, 301; Four Counties Buses 313; Freedom Travel 18, Renown 11, Viceroy 443, 590 all pass within ¼ mile of entrance

Tel: 01799 522842 (info line)

Local Tourist Information
Saffron Walden: 01799 524002
Cambridge: 01223 464732

E P OVP

Disabled access (grounds, Great Hall, Stable Yard and Service Wing only. Please call for more information).

MAP Page 279 (5F)
OS Map 154, 195: TL525382

Baconsthorpe Castle
Norfolk

Surrounded by a reedy moat and a wildfowl-haunted mere, the evocative ruins of this fortified manor house chronicle the rise and fall of the ambitious Heydon family over two centuries. The wealthy but 'crafty and quarrelsome' John Heydon built the imposing inner gatehouse as a self-contained fortress in the 1450s, during the troubled Wars of the Roses period, and his son Sir Henry extended the gunport-defended mansion. Subsequent generations converted part of the house into a textile factory, and added the turreted Elizabethan outer gatehouse, but the family eventually succumbed to bankruptcy and sold their mansion for salvage.

The castle stands astride walking and cycle trails. A free downloadable audio tour is available from the English Heritage website.

OPENING TIMES

Any reasonable time

HOW TO FIND US

Direction: ¾ mile N of village of Baconsthorpe off unclassified road, 3 miles E of Holt

Train: Sheringham 4½ miles

Bus: Sanders 16,17 serve the village

MAP Page 279 (1H)
OS Map 133, 252: TG121382

Berkhamsted Castle
Hertfordshire

The substantial remains of a strong and important motte and bailey castle dating from the 11th to 15th centuries, with surrounding walls, ditches and earthworks. Lived in by Thomas Becket in the 12th century: Richard Earl of Cornwall added a 13th century palace complex.

Berkhamsted Castle

OPENING TIMES

Summer, daily	10am-6pm
Winter, daily	10am-4pm
25 Dec and 1 Jan	Closed

HOW TO FIND US

Direction: Near ≷ Berkhamsted

Train: Berkhamsted, adjacent

Bus: From surrounding areas

MAP Page 278 (6D)
OS Map 165, 181: SP995082

Berney Arms Windmill
Norfolk

One of Norfolk's best and largest extant marsh mills, built to grind a constituent of cement and in use until 1951, finally pumping water to drain surrounding marshland.

For access information to Berney Arms Windmill please call the Great Yarmouth Row Houses on 01493 857900.

OPENING TIMES

Please ring 01493 857900

HOW TO FIND US

Direction: 3½ miles NE of Reedham on the N bank of River Yare. Accessible by hired boat, or by footpath from Halvergate (3½ miles)

Train: Berney Arms ¼ mile

Tel: 01493 857900

MAP Page 279 (3K)
OS Map 134, OL40: TG465049

Binham Market Cross
Norfolk

The tall shaft of a 15th-century cross, on the site of an annual fair held from the 1100s until the 1950s.

Managed by Binham Parochial Church Council.

OPENING TIMES

Any reasonable time

HOW TO FIND US

Direction: Located on the Binham village green adjacent to the Priory

Bus: Sanders service 46 otherwise nearest service is Norfolk Green 29 to Wighton

MAP Page 279 (1H)
OS Map 132, 251: TF984396

Binham Priory
Norfolk

Among the most impressive monastic sites in East Anglia, Binham Priory retains its nave – now the parish church – virtually complete, with a striking 13th-century west front and triple tiers of late Norman arches within, along with screens revealing medieval saints peeping through later overpainting. The extensive ruins beyond, notably the massive piers of the fallen church tower, emphasise the original size of this Benedictine priory.

Major recent enhancements, carried out by local initiatives with English Heritage support, make a visit even more worthwhile. They include much improved disabled access, a fascinating display of site finds, toilets, and a children's activity area.

Binham Priory

OPENING TIMES

Binham Priory (monastic ruins): Any reasonable time

Priory Church:

Daily (summer)	10am-6pm
Daily (winter)	10am-4pm

HOW TO FIND US

Direction: ¼ mile NW of village of Binham on road off B1388

Bus: Sanders service 46 otherwise nearest service is Norfolk Green 29 to Wighton

Tel: 01328 830362

MAP Page 279 (1H)
OS Map 132, 251: TF982399

Blakeney Guildhall
Norfolk

A relic of Blakeney's medieval prosperity, the remains of a flint 15th-century merchant's house with complete brick-vaulted undercroft. Later the guildhall of the port's fish merchants.

Managed by Blakeney Parish Council.

OPENING TIMES

Any reasonable time

HOW TO FIND US

Direction: In Blakeney off A149

Train: Sheringham 9 miles

Bus: Norfolk Green Coasthopper service (36), Sanders service 46

Tel: 01263 741106

MAP Page 279 (1H)
OS Map 133, 251: TG028441

Burgh Castle
Norfolk

The imposing stone walls, with added towers for catapults, of a Roman 3rd-century 'Saxon Shore' fort. Panoramic views over Breydon Water, into which the fourth wall long since collapsed.

Managed by Norfolk Archaeological Trust.

Burgh Castle

NEW FOR 2011

New graphic panels guide you round the site.

OPENING TIMES

Any reasonable time

HOW TO FIND US

Direction: At far W end of Breydon Water on unclassified road, 3 miles W of Great Yarmouth

Train: Great Yarmouth 5 miles

Bus: First 5 from Great Yarmouth then a short walk

MAP Page 279 (3K)
OS Map 134, OL40: TG475047

Bury St Edmunds Abbey
Suffolk

The extensive remains of the wealthiest and most powerful Benedictine monastery in England, shrine of St Edmund. They include the complete 14th-century Great Gate and Norman Tower, and the impressive ruins and altered west front of the immense church.

Managed by St Edmundsbury Borough Council.

OPENING TIMES

Any reasonable time

HOW TO FIND US

Direction: E end of town centre

Train: Bury St Edmunds 1 mile

Bus: From surrounding areas

Tel: 01284 764667

MAP Page 279 (4G)
OS Map 155, 211: TL857642

Bushmead Priory
Bedfordshire – MK44 2LD

A rare survival of the complete refectory of an Augustinian priory, with fine timber roof and notable 14th-century wall paintings.

Bushmead Priory

NON-MEMBERS

Adult	£5.30
Concession	£4.80
Child	£3.20

OPENING TIMES

1 May-31 Aug, entry by pre-booked guided tours on the first Sat of the month only. Tel: 01525 860000 to book

HOW TO FIND US

Direction: Located off B660, 2 miles S of Bolnhurst

Train: St Neots 6 miles

Bus: Cedar Coaches 153, 154 pass within 1 mile

MAP Page 278 (4E)
OS Map 153, 225: TL115607

Caister Roman Fort
Norfolk – NR30 5JS

The partial excavated remains of a Roman 'Saxon Shore' fort, including wall and ditch sections and building foundations. Built around AD 200 for a unit of the Roman army and navy, and occupied until the end of the 4th century.

Managed by Great Yarmouth Borough Council.

OPENING TIMES

Any reasonable time

HOW TO FIND US

Direction: From Great Yarmouth, follow the A149 northbound and then the A149 Caister Bypass. Follow brown tourist signs for Caister Roman Fort. From other directons follow signs for Great Yarmouth and then brown tourist signs from the Caister Bypass roundabout. Parking and the entrance to the Fort are situated off a lay-by on Norwich Road ¼ mile from the roundabout.

Train: Great Yarmouth 3 miles

Bus: First services 1, 1A, 3, 8 & 8A from Great Yarmouth

MAP Page 279 (2K)
OS Map 134, OL40: TG517123

Castle Acre Priory, Castle and Bailey Gate
Norfolk

The delightful village of Castle Acre boasts an extraordinary wealth of history.

Situated on the Peddar's Way, a major trade and pilgrim route to Thetford, Bromholm Priory and Walsingham, it is a very rare and complete survival of a Norman planned settlement, including a castle, town, fine parish church and associated monastery. All this is the work of a powerful Norman baronial family, the Warennes, mainly during the 11th and 12th centuries.

First came the castle, founded soon after the Conquest by the first William de Warenne, probably as a stone 'country house'. During the first half of the 12th century, however, more disturbed conditions prompted its progressive conversion into a strong keep, further defended by stone walls and an immense system of earthworks. These massive ramparts and ditches are perhaps the finest castle earthworks anywhere in England.

Meanwhile, the 'planned town', deliberately established outside the castle, was also protected by ditched earthwork defences with stone gates. The north or Bailey Gate survives, with the main road into the village still running between its towers.

Visitors to Castle Acre can likewise trace the ancient street layout of this now peaceful village, lined with attractive flint or brick houses, before exploring both the great castle earthworks and the extensive priory remains. A village and castle trail can be downloaded from the Castle Acre Priory page of the English Heritage website.

Castle Acre Castle and Bailey Gate
Norfolk

OPENING TIMES

Any reasonable time

HOW TO FIND US

Direction: Located at the E end of Castle Acre, 5 miles N of Swaffham

Bus: West Norfolk Community Transport (weekdays), Freestone Coaches 32; Peelings 1 (Tue)

(Castle only)

MAP Page 279 (2G)
OS Map 132, 236/238
Bailey Gate: TF819152
Castle: TF819152

Castle Acre Priory
See feature – Page 138

Castle Rising Castle
Norfolk – PE31 6AH

One of the biggest, most complete and most lavishly decorated Norman keeps in England, with an impressive entrance forebuilding, surrounded by stupendous earthworks. Begun in 1138 by William d'Albini for his wife, the widow of Henry I, in the 14th century it became the luxurious prison of Queen Isabella, widow (and alleged murderess) of Edward II. www.castlerising.co.uk

Owned and managed by Lord Howard of Rising.

NON-MEMBERS

Adult	£4.00
Concession	£3.30
Child	£2.50

OPENING TIMES

1 Apr-1 Nov, daily (closes at dusk if earlier in Oct)	10am-6pm
2 Nov-31 Mar, Wed-Sun	10am-4pm
24-26 Dec	Closed

HOW TO FIND US

Direction: Located 4 miles NE of King's Lynn off A149

Train: King's Lynn 4½ miles

Bus: Some journeys on First services 40A & 41A serve the village. Otherwise First 40 or 41 and Norfolk Green 35 to Castle Rising turn and walk (½ mile)

Tel: 01553 631330

Audio tours (charged).

Disabled access (exterior only, toilets).

Dogs on leads (restricted areas).

MAP Page 279 (2G)
OS Map 132, 250: TF666246

Castle Acre Priory Norfolk – PE32 2XD

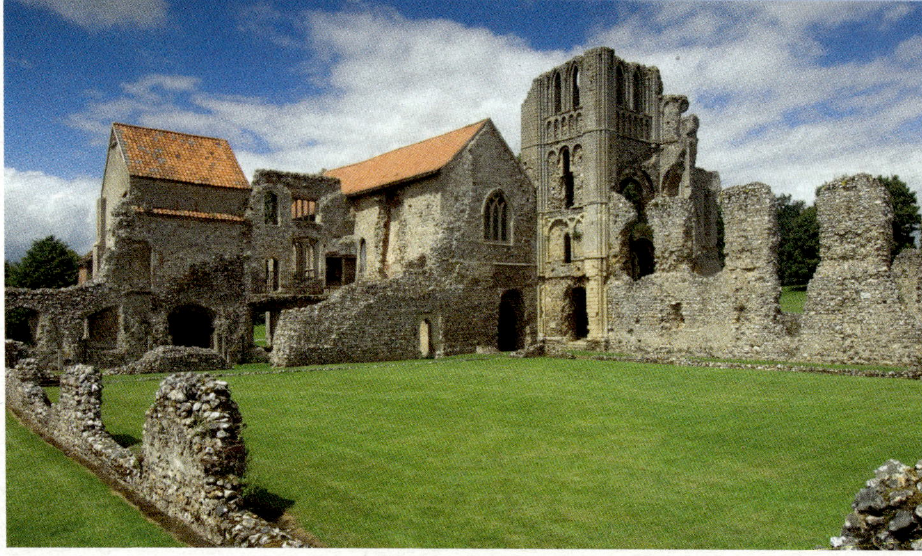

Among the largest and best preserved monastic sites in all England, Castle Acre Priory often surprises new visitors by its immense size and variety. Its foundation in about 1090 by William de Warenne II reflected his family's devotion to the famous French monastery of Cluny: the Cluniac order's love of architectural decoration is displayed in the beautiful west front of the great 12th-century priory church, bedecked with tiers of intersecting round arches. Beyond extend the impressive remains of the cloister and monks' living quarters, including a gigantic two-storey 24-seater toilet block.

Best preserved of all is the west range, virtually complete and fully roofed. Its timber-framed and flint-chequered porch and oriel-windowed prior's lodging form an outstandingly attractive grouping with the church's west front.

A mansion in itself, the lodging includes a chamber sumptuously revamped in early Tudor times for one of the last priors; with decorated fireplace, ceiling painted with Tudor roses, and two massive timber chests still in place. The adjacent prior's chapel was once even more elaborately adorned, with traces of medieval wall paintings still visible.

There is much more to see, including our exhibition and display of archaeological finds, site model and audio tour featuring a 15th-century chant from a Castle Acre song book. The recreated herb garden grows plants the monks would have used for medicinal and culinary purposes. There is also a large activities barn for schools. A priory terrain guide can be downloaded from the Castle Acre Priory page of the English Heritage website.

NON-MEMBERS

Adult	£5.60
Concession	£5.00
Child	£3.40
Family	£14.60

OPENING TIMES

1 Apr-30 Sep, daily	10am-5pm
1 Oct-31 Mar, Thu-Mon	10am-4pm
24-26 Dec and 1 Jan	Closed

HOW TO FIND US

Direction: ¼ mile W of village of Castle Acre, 5 miles N of Swaffham

Bus: West Norfolk Community Transport (weekdays), Freestone Coaches 32; Peelings 1 (Tue)

Tel: 01760 755394

E P OVP

Disabled access (ground floor and grounds only).

Toilets (a short walk. Not accessible for wheelchairs; 50 metres from entrance, with single step for access).

MAP Page 279 (2G)

OS Map 132, 236/238: TF814148

Church of the Holy Sepulchre, Thetford, Norfolk:

see Thetford, Church of the Holy Sepulchre – Page 149

Colchester, St Botolph's Priory

Essex

The remains of one of the first Augustinian priories in England, founded c. 1100. An impressive example of early Norman architecture, built in flint and re-used Roman brick, the church displays massive circular pillars and round arches and an elaborate west front. Later badly damaged by cannon fire during the Civil War siege of 1648.

Managed by Colchester Borough Council.

OPENING TIMES

Any reasonable time

HOW TO FIND US

Direction: Nr Colchester Town station

Train: Colchester Town, adjacent

Bus: Bus services to/from Colchester are provided by Beestons (of Hadleigh), Chambers (of Bures), First Essex, Hedingham Omnibuses and Network Colchester. Priory is 2 minutes walk from the bus station

Tel: 01206 282931

MAP Page 279 (5H)
OS Map 168, 184: TL999249

Colchester, St John's Abbey Gate

Essex

This pinnacled gatehouse, elaborately decorated in East Anglian 'flushwork', is the sole survivor of the wealthy Benedictine abbey of St John. It was built c. 1400 to strengthen the abbey's defences following the Peasants' Revolt. Later part of the mansion of the Royalist Lucas family, the gatehouse was bombarded and stormed by Parliamentarian soldiers during the Civil War siege.

Managed by Colchester Borough Council.

OPENING TIMES

Any reasonable time

HOW TO FIND US

Direction: S side of central Colchester

Train: Colchester Town ¼ mile

Bus: Bus services to/from Colchester are provided by Beestons (of Hadleigh), Chambers (of Bures), First Essex, Hedingham Omnibuses and Network Colchester

Tel: 01206 282931

MAP Page 279 (5H)
OS Map 168, 184: TL998248

Cow Tower, Norwich

Norfolk

One of the earliest purpose-built artillery blockhouses in England, this brick tower was built in c. 1398-9 to command a strategic point in Norwich's city defences External viewing only.

Managed by Norwich City Council.

OPENING TIMES

Any reasonable time

HOW TO FIND US

Direction: In Norwich, near cathedral (approx. 1 mile walk)

Bus: From surrounding areas

Train: Norwich ½ mile

Tel: 01603 213434

MAP Page 279 (2J)
OS Map 134, OL40/237: TG240092

Creake Abbey

Norfolk

Tranquil ruins of an Augustinian abbey church, unusual because visibly reduced in size after a serious fire in the 15th century.

Managed by Mrs A C Scott.

NEW FOR 2011

New graphic panels guide you round the ruins.

OPENING TIMES

Any reasonable time

HOW TO FIND US

Direction: N of North Creake off B1355

Bus: Norfolk Green 27 (weekdays)

MAP Page 279 (1H)
OS Map 132, 251: TF856395

Denny Abbey and the Farmland Museum

Cambridgeshire – CB25 9PQ

Denny Abbey has a unique and fascinating history. Founded in 1159 as a Benedictine monastery, it then became a retirement home for elderly Knights Templars. After the Templars' suppression for alleged heresy in 1308, it next passed to the Countess of Pembroke, who converted part into a house and established in the rest a convent of 'Poor Clare' Franciscan nuns. This in turn was dissolved by Henry VIII in 1539, whereafter the buildings became a farm until the 1960s, with the nuns' great refectory as its barn. Among its tenants was Thomas Hobson, the horsehirer whose refusal to allow customers to select their mounts gave rise to the expression 'Hobson's choice'.

All these changes are still traceable in the building: they are now interpreted for visitors by graphic panels illustrated by local artist Anne Biggs, together with a time-line tracing the site's history from 4000 BC, a viewing platform and displays of site finds. Family-friendly activities include imaginative hands-on interactives about medieval tiles, stained glass and arches.

Denny's later farming story is continued by Walnut Tree Cottage, furnished as a labourer's home of the 1940s. The site's Farmland Museum also features a fenman's hut, blacksmith's and wheelwright's workshops, a village shop display and many other aspects of Cambridgeshire rural life.

Managed by the Farmland Museum Trust.

NON-MEMBERS

Museum and Abbey

Adult	£4.00
Concession	£3.00
Child	£2.00
Family	£10.00

Museum charge

The abbey is free to members but there is a small charge to visit the museum.

Adult	£2.80
Concession	£2.00
Child	£1.00
Family	£6.00

All members (inc. life members) must pay for special events

OPENING TIMES

1 Apr-31 Oct, Mon-Fri	12pm-5pm
Sat-Sun & Bank Hols	10.30am-5pm

HOW TO FIND US

Direction: Located 6 miles N of Cambridge on A10

Train: Waterbeach 3 miles

Bus: Stagecoach in Cambridge 9 & X9 Cambridge – Ely

Tel: 01223 860489/860988

OVP

Disabled access (museum and abbey ground floor only).

Dogs on leads (restricted areas only).

Tearoom/restaurant (weekends only).

MAP Page 279 (4F)
OS Map 154, 226: TL492685

De Grey Mausoleum, Flitton

Bedfordshire

Among the largest sepulchral chapels attached to any English church, this cruciform mausoleum houses a remarkable sequence of 17 sculpted and effigied monuments, spanning nearly three centuries (1615-1859), to the De Grey family of Wrest Park. You can download the audio tour prior to visiting from the English Heritage website.

OPENING TIMES

Weekends only. Contact the keykeeper in advance: Mrs Stimson, 3 Highfield Road, Flitton. Tel: 01525 860094

HOW TO FIND US

Direction: Attached to Flitton church; through Flitton, on an unclassified road 1½ miles W of A6 at Silsoe

Train: Flitwick 2 miles

Bus: A limited service is provided by Flittabus (of Ampthill); Cedar service 146; Centrebus 20, X44; Grant Palmer service 200

MAP Page 278 (5E)
OS Map 153, 193: TL059359

Duxford Chapel

Cambridgeshire

A modest but complete and attractive 14th-century chantry chapel, perhaps originally a hospital.

Managed by South Cambridgeshire District Council.

OPENING TIMES

Any reasonable time

Check www.english-heritage.org.uk for the latest opening times

Duxford Chapel

HOW TO FIND US

Direction: Adjacent to Whittlesford station off A505

Train: Whittlesford, adjacent

Bus: Stagecoach Cambridge Citi7; Myall 101, 132; Stagecoach 139

MAP Page 279 (4F)
OS Map 154, 209: TL485473

Framlingham Castle

See feature – Page 142

Great Yarmouth Row Houses and Greyfriars' Cloisters

Norfolk – NR30 2RG

Living space was very much at a premium in early 17th-century Great Yarmouth, then among the most prosperous fishing port in England. Hence the inhabitants crowded into the town's distinctive 'Rows', a network of narrow alleyways linking Yarmouth's three main thoroughfares. Many 'Row houses' were damaged by World War II bombing or demolished during post-War clearances, but two surviving properties in the care of English Heritage show what these characteristic dwellings looked like at various stages in their history.

Both Row 111 and the Old Merchant's House were originally built in the early 17th century as wealthy merchants'

Great Yarmouth Row Houses and Greyfriars' Cloisters

residences, but later sub-divided into tenements. The Old Merchant's House, which has spectacular Jacobean plaster ceilings in two of its rooms, is presented as it was in about 1870, when the Atkins and Rope families of fishermen – represented by models of family members at work or rest – shared the property. Adjacent Row 111 house is shown as it was in about 1942 (just before it received a direct hit from an incendiary bomb), likewise with figures of the three families which then occupied parts of it. Both houses also display a wonderful collection of fixtures and fittings – including painted panels, elaborate wall-ties and door-knockers – rescued from other now-demolished Row dwellings, a treasure trove for lovers of period decoration.

Nearby stands Greyfriars' Cloisters, the remains of a 13th-century friary of Franciscan 'grey friars', later swallowed up by Row development and converted into a number of dwellings large and small. Traces of their interior features can still be seen on the brick-built walls of parts of the cloister and church, laid bare by wartime bombing. Early 14th-century wall-paintings were discovered here in the 1960s.

NON-MEMBERS

Adult	£4.20
Concession	£3.80
Child	£2.50
Family	£10.90

OPENING TIMES

1 Apr-30 Sep, Mon-Fri 12pm-5pm

Access to Greyfriars' Cloisters is by pre-arrangement only

Great Yarmouth Row Houses and Greyfriars' Cloisters

HOW TO FIND US

Direction: Great Yarmouth, follow signs for Historic Quay. The houses are directly behind the Norfolk Nelson Museum on the Historic South Quay

Train: Great Yarmouth ½ mile

Bus: Bus services to Great Yarmouth are operated by Anglian (of Beccles), Ambassador Travel and First

Tel: 01493 857900

OVP

New guidebook.

MAP Page 279 (2K)
OS Map 134, OL40
Houses: TG525072
Cloisters: TG524073

Grime's Graves

See feature – Page 144

Hadleigh Castle

Essex

The romantic ruins of a royal castle overlooking the Essex marshes. Hadleigh was begun in about 1215 by Hubert de Burgh, but extensively refortified by Edward III during the Hundred Years War, becoming a favourite residence of the ageing king. The barbican and two striking drum towers – one later used by Georgian revenue men looking out for smugglers – are part of his substantial building works during the 1360s.

OPENING TIMES

Any reasonable time

HOW TO FIND US

Direction: ¾ mile S of A13 at Hadleigh

Train: Leigh-on-Sea 1½ miles by footpath

Bus: First, First/Regal and Arriva from surrounding areas to within ½ mile

MAP Page 279 (7G)
OS Map 178, 175: TQ810860

Framlingham Castle Suffolk – IP13 9BP

Framlingham is a magnificent example of a late 12th-century castle. Built by Roger Bigod, Earl of Norfolk, one of the most influential people at the court of the Plantagenet kings, the castle, together with Framlingham Mere, was designed both as a stronghold and a proclamation of power and status. Architecturally, the fortress is notable for its curtain wall with regular mural towers, being an early example of this style.

NEW FOR 2011

A refreshment kiosk selling hot & cold drinks and light refreshments.

The castle fulfilled a number of roles. It was at the centre of the struggle between the Bigod barons and the Crown, and Mary Tudor mustered her supporters here in 1553, before being crowned Queen. At the end of the 16th century it was a prison; later still a Poorhouse was built within the walls. Today the imposing stone walls and crenellated towers with their ornate Tudor chimneys dominate, while the grassy earthworks around the castle are subdued reminders of its outer defences. To the west, the Mere provides a stunning setting.

Visitors can explore over 800 years of life at Framlingham Castle in an introductory exhibition in the Poorhouse, which tells the story of the people who lived in the castle during its long and varied history. The displays illustrate the struggle for power between monarchs and the lords of Framlingham; the tragic stories of family members Anne Boleyn and Catherine Howard, both married to and beheaded by Henry VIII; the accession of Queen Mary Tudor; and the Poorhouse, still in use until 1839.

The Poorhouse Kitchen provides an area where visitors can enjoy a selection of factual and fictional books relating to Framlingham Castle. Entry also includes access to the Lanman Trust's Museum of local history.

Embark on a self-guided journey of discovery around the site with our themed trails and lively audio tour, and explore the Mere, the castle's outer courts and the wall-walk with its spectacular views over the surrounding landscape. Younger audiences can discover more about life in the castle with a variety of themed games and interactives.

www.english-heritage.org.uk/framlinghamcastle

NON-MEMBERS

Adult	£6.30
Concession	£5.70
Child	£3.80
Family	£16.40

OPENING TIMES

1 Apr-30 Jun, daily	10am-5pm
1 Jul-31 Aug, daily	10am-6pm
1 Sep-31 Oct, daily	10am-5pm
1 Nov-31 Mar, Thu-Mon	10am-4pm
24-26 Dec and 1 Jan	Closed

The property may close early if an event is booked, please ring in advance for details

HOW TO FIND US

Direction: In Framlingham on B1116

Train: Wickham Market 6½ miles; Saxmundham 7 miles

Bus: First service 63; Far East Travel 118, 119 & 481

Tel: 01728 724189

Local Tourist Information
Woodbridge: 01394 382240

E P OVP

Disabled access (grounds and ground floor only).

Parking charge, refundable to EH members and paying visitors on admission.

MAP Page 279 (4J)
OS Map 156, 212: TM287637

Grime's Graves – prehistoric flint mine

Norfolk – IP26 5DE

Grime's Graves is the only Neolithic flint mine open to visitors in Britain. A grassy lunar landscape of over 400 shafts, pits, quarries and spoil dumps, they were first named Grim's Graves by the Anglo-Saxons – meaning the pagan god Grim's quarries, or 'the Devil's holes'.

© Skyscan Balloon Photography

What the prehistoric miners sought here was the fine quality, jet-black flint floorstone, which occurs some nine to twelve metres below surface level.

It was not until one of them was excavated by Canon Greenwell in 1870 that they were identified as flint mines dug over 5000 years ago, during the later Neolithic and Early Bronze Ages.

What the prehistoric miners sought here was the fine quality, jet-black flint floorstone, which occurs some nine to twelve metres below surface level. Digging with red-deer antler picks, they sank shafts and dug radiating galleries which followed the seams of flint. Today visitors can descend 9 metres (30 ft) by ladder into one excavated shaft – an unforgettable experience.

Grime's Graves flint was prized for its distinctive colour and easily 'knapped' qualities. Rough-outs of axes and other tools were made on site, but then traded on and finished elsewhere.

Set amid the distinctive Breckland heath landscape, Grime's Graves is also a Site of Special Scientific Interest: the habitat of a variety of rare and distinctive plants and animals. The Breckland flora are especially attractive from April to July.

A small introductory exhibition in the visitor centre includes information about Neolithic mining, a virtual tour of the mines and landscape, and touchable reproduction Neolithic tools. A trail leaflet guides visitors round the multi-period site, explaining features from the earliest times until today.

The family explorer kit will enable you to read vital clues about the site. It includes a recording sheet, crayons, binoculars and plastic gloves for inspecting rabbit and sheep droppings.

See the Neolithic mine, and the plants and creatures which thrive in this unique landscape.

NON-MEMBERS

Adult	£3.30
Concession	£3.00
Child	£2.00
Family	£8.60

No entry to the mines for children under 5 years of age

OPENING TIMES

1-31 Mar, Thu-Mon	10am-5pm
1 Apr-30 Jun, daily	10am-5pm
1 Jul-31 Aug, daily	10am-6pm
1-30 Sep, daily	10am-5pm
1-31 Oct, Thu-Mon	10am-5pm
1 Nov-29 Feb	Closed

HOW TO FIND US

Direction: Located 7 miles NW of Thetford off A134

Train: Brandon 3½ miles

Bus: Coach Services Thetford service 40 to Lynford

Tel: 01842 810656

P OVP

Disabled access (exhibition area only; access track rough).

Dogs on leads (restricted areas).

Visitors intending to descend the shaft should wear flat shoes.

New guidebook.

MAP Page 279 (3G)
OS Map 144, 229: TL817899

Hill Hall
Essex – CM16 7QQ

This fine Elizabethan mansion features some of the earliest external Renaissance architectural detail in the country, and two rare and outstanding sets of 16th-century wall paintings of mythical and Biblical subjects. Hill Hall has now been divided into private houses, but parts remain open to the public by prior arrangement.

NON-MEMBERS

Adult	£5.30
Concession	£4.80
Child	£3.20

OPENING TIMES

1 Apr-30 Sep. Pre-booked guided tours on Wednesdays only

Tel: 01799 522842 to book

HOW TO FIND US

Direction: 3 miles SE of Epping. Entrance ½ mile N of Theydon Mount Church

Bus: Arriva 375 or Blue Triangle 575 to Passingford Bridge (2¾ miles)

Train: Epping or Theydon Bois 2½ miles

MAP Page 279 (6F)
OS Map 167/177, 174: TQ489995

Houghton House
Bedfordshire – MK45 2EZ

The shell of a 17th-century mansion commanding magnificent views, reputedly the inspiration for the 'House Beautiful' in John Bunyan's *Pilgrim's Progress*. Built around 1615 for Mary, Dowager Countess of Pembroke, in a mixture of Jacobean and Classical styles; the ground floors of two Italianate loggias survive, possibly the work of Inigo Jones.

Information panels describe the house, its owners and the surrounding hunting estate. A free downloadable audio tour is available from the English Heritage website.

OPENING TIMES

Any reasonable time

HOW TO FIND US

Direction: 1 mile NE of Ampthill off B530, 8 miles S of Bedford

Train: Flitwick or Stewartby, both 3 miles

Bus: Stagecoach in Northants services J2; Grant Palmer service X42; Flittbus F5, F6B, F8

MAP Page 278 (5E)
OS Map 153, 193: TL039395

Isleham Priory Church
Cambridgeshire

The best example in England of a small, Norman, Benedictine priory church, surviving in a surprisingly unaltered state despite later conversion into a barn.

OPENING TIMES

Any reasonable time. Contact the keykeeper, Mrs R Burton, 18 Festival Road, Isleham – 5 min walk

HOW TO FIND US

Direction: Located in centre of Isleham, 16 miles NE of Cambridge on B1104

Train: Newmarket 8½ miles, Ely 9 miles

Bus: Freedom Travel service 203 (Tues & Sat); Ely & Soham Dial A Ride 204

MAP Page 279 (4G)
OS Map 143, 226: TL642743

Landguard Fort
Suffolk – IP11 3TX

The site of the last opposed seaborne invasion of England in 1667 and the first land battle of the Royal Marines. The current fort was built in the 18th century and modified in the 19th century with substantial additional 19th/20th-century outside batteries.

Guided tours and audio tours of the fort are supplemented by an audio-visual presentation of the site's history, and by guided tours of the outside batteries.

The nearby submarine mining building houses Felixstowe Museum's Collections of local interest.

Managed by Landguard Fort Trust.

NON-MEMBERS

Adult	£3.50
Concession	£2.50
Child	£1.00

Free entry for children under 5 and wheelchair users

OPENING TIMES

2 Apr-31 May, daily	10am-5pm
1 Jun-30 Sep, daily	10am-6pm
1-30 Oct, daily	10am-5pm

Last admission 1 hour before closing

There may be a small premium payable by all visitors, including members, on event days – please check our website for details

Tel: 07749 695523

HOW TO FIND US

Direction: 1 mile S of Felixstowe town centre – follow signs to Landguard Point

Train: Felixstowe 2½ miles

Bus: First service 77 to Felixstowe Dock

Tel: 07749 6955523

MAP Page 279 (5J)
OS Map 169, 197: TM284319

Leiston Abbey
Suffolk

The mainly 14th-century remains of an abbey of Premonstratensian canons. Among Suffolk's most impressive monastic ruins, with some spectacular architectural features.

Managed by Pro Corda Music School.

OPENING TIMES

Any reasonable time

HOW TO FIND US

Direction: N of Leiston off B1069

Bus: Nightingale 196 and Simonds 626 (Tue) pass the site. First services 64; Anglian service 165 & 197 all serve Leiston (1½ mile walk)

Train: Saxmundham 5 miles

MAP Page 279 (4K)
OS Map 156, 212: TM445642

Lexden Earthworks and Bluebottle Grove
Essex

The banks and ditches of a series of late Iron Age defences protecting the western side of Camulodunum – pre-Roman Colchester. There are also many pre-Roman graves hereabouts, including Lexden Tumulus, allegedly the burial place of the British chieftain Cunobelinus.

Managed by Colchester Borough Council.

OPENING TIMES

Any reasonable time

HOW TO FIND US

Direction: 2 miles W of Colchester off A604. Lexden Earthworks are on Lexden Straight Rd. To visit Bluebottle Grove from Lexden, turn left into Heath Rd, left into Church Lane, right into Beech Hill and follow the signs to the site

Train: Colchester or Colchester Town, both 2½ miles

Lexden Earthworks and Bluebottle Grove

Bus: Hedingham 4 and Network Colchester services 5 & 15

Tel: 01206 282931

MAP Page 279 (5H) OS Map 168,184
Lexden Earthworks: TL965246
Bluebottle Grove: TL975245

Lindsey St James's Chapel
Suffolk

A pretty, thatched, 13th-century chapel with lancet windows.

OPENING TIMES

All year, daily	10am-4pm

HOW TO FIND US

Direction: Located on an unclassified road ½ mile E of Rose Green and 8 miles E of Sudbury

Train: Sudbury 8 miles

Bus: Hadleigh Community Transport 'Suffolk Links Cosford' demand responsive bus service telephone 01473 826242 to book

Disabled access (single step).

MAP Page 279 (5H)
OS Map 155, 196: TL9784444

Longthorpe Tower
Cambridgeshire – PE1 1HA

Longthorpe Tower displays one of the most complete and important sets of 14th-century domestic wall paintings in northern Europe. This varied 'spiritual encyclopaedia' of worldly and religious subjects includes the Wheel of Life, the Nativity and King David.

NON-MEMBERS

Adult	£5.30
Concession	£4.80
Child	£3.20

OPENING TIMES

1 Apr-30 Sep. Pre-booked visits with introductory talk on first Sun of the month only

Tel: 01536 203230 during office hours to book

Longthorpe Tower

HOW TO FIND US

Direction: Located 2 miles W of Peterborough on A47

Train: Peterborough 1½ miles

Bus: Short walk from Peterborough Bus Station. Served by Delaine, Judd's, Kimes, Peterborough City Transport and Stagecoach services

Tel: 01536 203230

Parking (not at site).

MAP Page 278 (3E)
OS Map 142, 227/235: TL162984

Mistley Towers
Essex

Two porticoed Classical towers, which stood at each end of a grandiose but highly unconventional Georgian church, designed by Robert Adam in 1776.

Managed by Mistley Thorn Residents' Association.

OPENING TIMES

Key available from Mistley Quay Workshops: 01206 393884

HOW TO FIND US

Direction: Located on B1352, 1½ miles E of A137 at Lawford, 9 miles E of Colchester

Train: Mistley ¼ mile

Bus: Hedingham service 2, 85, Carters 93C, 96; First 102, 103, 104, 193; Hadleigh Community Transport 745

Disabled access (exterior only).

Dogs on leads (restricted areas).

MAP Page 279 (5H)
OS Map 168/169,184/197: TM116320

Moulton Packhorse Bridge
Suffolk

A pretty, four-arched, late medieval bridge spanning the River Kennett on the old route from Cambridge to Bury St Edmunds.

Moulton Packhorse Bridge

OPENING TIMES

Any reasonable time

HOW TO FIND US

Direction: In Moulton off B1085, 4 miles E of Newmarket

Train: Kennett 2 miles

Bus: Freedom Travel 47; Mulley's Motorways services 311, 312, 400 & 401

MAP Page 279 (4G)
OS Map 154, 210/226: TL698645

North Elmham Chapel
Norfolk

A place with an unusual story, illustrated on graphic panels. The small Norman chapel here stands on the site of an earlier timber church, probably the Saxon cathedral of East Anglia. In the 14th century it was converted into a fortified manor house by Henry Despenser, the unpopular Bishop of Norwich who brutally suppressed the Peasants' Revolt of 1381.

Managed by North Elmham Parish Council.

OPENING TIMES

Any reasonable time

HOW TO FIND US

Direction: Located 6 miles N of East Dereham on B1110

Bus: Konectbus service 7, 7A & 18. Carters service 9 (Wed). Also National Express service 497

MAP Page 279 (2H)
OS Map 132, 238: TF988216

Old Gorhambury House
Hertfordshire

The remains of a once immense mansion built in 1563-8 by Sir Nicholas Bacon, Queen Elizabeth's Lord Keeper, and visited by the queen on at least four occasions. Its elaborately-decorated, Classical two-storey porch survives, with parts of the hall, chapel and clock-tower.

OPENING TIMES

By foot
All year 8.30am-5.30pm
except 1 Jun and Sat, 1 Sep-1 Feb

By car
1 May-30 Sep, Thu 2pm-5pm

HOW TO FIND US

Direction: Just off A4147 on western outskirts of St Albans. Walk up 2 mile drive on permissive path. Access by car is limited, see opening times

Train: St Albans Abbey 3 miles, St Albans 3½ miles

Bus: Arriva/Uno services 300, 301 and Tiger Line T5 pass start of drive

MAP Page 278 (6E)
OS Map 166, 182: TL110076

Orford Castle
See feature – Page 150

Prior's Hall Barn, Widdington
Essex

One of the finest surviving medieval barns in eastern England, tree-ring dated to the mid-15th century, with a breathtaking aisled interior and crown-post roof, the product of some 400 oaks.

Prior's Hall Barn, Widdington

OPENING TIMES

1 Apr-30 Sep, Sat-Sun 10am-6pm

HOW TO FIND US

Direction: In Widdington, on unclassified road 2 miles SE of Newport, off B1383

Train: Newport 2 miles

Bus: Excel 301; Regal 322

MAP Page 279 (5F)
OS Map 167, 195: TL537318

Roman Wall, St Albans
Hertfordshire

A section of the two-mile-long wall built between AD 265 and 270 to defend the Roman city of Verulamium, including the foundations of towers and the London Gate.

OPENING TIMES

Any reasonable time

HOW TO FIND US

Direction: Located on the S side of St Albans, ½ mile from the centre, off the A4147

Train: St Albans Abbey ½ mile, St Albans 1¼ miles

Bus: Uno services S8 & S9 operate close to the Roman Wall site

MAP Page 278 (6E)
OS Map 166, 182: TL137066

Saxtead Green Post Mill
Suffolk – IP13 9QQ

This corn mill, whose whole body revolves on its base, was one of many built in Suffolk from the late 13th century. Though milling ceased in 1947, it is still in

Saxtead Green Post Mill

working order. Climb the stairs to various floors, which are full of fascinating mill machinery.

NON-MEMBERS

Adult	£3.50
Concession	£3.20
Child	£2.10

OPENING TIMES

1 Apr-30 Sep, Fri-Sat & Bank Hols	12pm-5pm

HOW TO FIND US

Direction: 2½ miles NW of Framlingham on A1120

Train: Wickham Market 9 miles

Bus: Far East Travel 119; Simonds 100 (Tue, Fri)

Tel: 01728 685789

OVP

MAP Page 279 (4J)
OS Map 156, 212: TM253644

St Botolph's Priory
Essex: see Colchester,
St Botolph's Priory – Page 139

St John's Abbey Gate
Essex: see Colchester,
St John's Abbey Gate – Page 139

St Olave's Priory
Norfolk

The wonderfully complete, 14th-century, brick-vaulted refectory undercroft – later a cottage occupied until 1902 – of a small Augustinian priory.

NEW FOR 2011

New graphic panels describe the site

OPENING TIMES

Any reasonable time

HOW TO FIND US

Direction: Located 5½ miles SW of the town of Great Yarmouth on A143

Train: Haddiscoe 1¼ miles

St Olave's Priory

Bus: Anglian 577, 581

Dogs on leads (restricted areas only).

MAP Page 279 (3K)
OS Map 134, OL40: TM459996

Thetford, Church of the Holy Sepulchre
Norfolk

The only surviving remains in England of a priory of Canons of the Holy Sepulchre, who aided pilgrims to Christ's tomb, the ruined nave of their 14th-century church, later used as a barn.

Managed by Thetford Town Council.

OPENING TIMES

See Thetford Priory

HOW TO FIND US

Direction: Located on the W side of Thetford on A134

Bus: Coach Services of Thetford 25, 40, 84, 190, T1, T1A; Mulleys 200, 201

Train: Thetford ¾ mile

MAP Page 279 (3H)
OS Map 144, 229: TL865831

Thetford Priory
Norfolk

The extensive remains of one of the most important East Anglian monasteries, the Cluniac Priory of Our Lady of Thetford, burial place of the earls and dukes of Norfolk for 400 years. Founded in the early 12th century, it owed much of its prosperity to a miraculous appearance of the Virgin Mary, whose statue here was discovered to conceal relics of saints, and became a magnet for pilgrims. Two of the greatest men in early Tudor England, Thomas Howard, victor of Flodden, and Henry Fitzroy, illegitimate son of Henry VIII, were buried near her shrine. Survivals include the lower walls of the church and cloister, along with the impressive shell of the priors' lodging and, reached by a pathway from the main site, an almost complete 14th-century gatehouse.

Managed by Thetford Town Council.

OPENING TIMES

1 Apr-30 Sep, daily	10am-6pm
1 Oct-31 Mar, daily	10am-4pm
25 Dec	Closed

HOW TO FIND US

Direction: Located on the W side of Thetford, near the station

Train: Thetford ¼ mile

Bus: Coach Services of Thetford 25, 40, 84, 190, T1, T1A; Mulleys 200, 201

MAP Page 279 (3G)
OS Map 144, 229: TL865831

Thetford Warren Lodge
Norfolk

Probably built c. 1400 by the Prior of Thetford, this defensible lodge protected gamekeepers and hunting parties against armed poachers. Much later used by the local 'warreners' who harvested rabbits here.

OPENING TIMES

Any reasonable time

HOW TO FIND US

Direction: Located 2 miles W of Thetford off B1107

Train: Thetford 2½ miles

Bus: Coach Services of Thetford 25, 40, 84, 190, T1, T1A; Mulleys 200, 201

MAP Page 279 (3G)
OS Map 144, 229: TL839984

Orford Castle Suffolk – IP12 2ND

© Skyscan Balloon Photography

The unique polygonal tower keep of Orford Castle stands beside the pretty town and former port, which Henry II also developed here in the 1160s. His aim was to counterbalance the power of turbulent East Anglian barons like Hugh Bigod of Framlingham, and to guard the coast against foreign mercenaries called to their aid.

An 18-sided drum with three square turrets and a forebuilding reinforcing its entrance, the keep was built to a highly innovative design. The progress of its construction between 1165 and 1173 is extensively recorded in royal documents. Both exterior and interior survive almost intact, allowing visitors to explore the basement, with its vital well, and the lower and upper halls – the latter the principal room of the castle. Round these polygonal rooms is a maze of passages leading to the chapel, kitchen and other chambers in the turrets. From the roof there are magnificent views seaward to Orford Ness.

Recent archaeological work has provided a clearer understanding of how the castle worked and a painting by Frank Gardiner shows how the keep and its vanished outer defences looked in their heyday. The upper hall now houses a display by the Orford Museum Trust, including local finds of Roman brooches, medieval seals and coins and some of the borough regalia. Graphic panels display maps, documents, pictures and photographs, illustrating Orford's history up to the 20th century.

NON-MEMBERS

Adult	£5.60
Concession	£5.00
Child	£3.40
Family	£14.60

OPENING TIMES

1 Apr-30 Jun, daily	10am-5pm
1 Jul-31 Aug, daily	10am-6pm
1-30 Sep, daily	10am-5pm
1 Oct-31 Mar, Thu-Mon	10am-4pm
24-26 Dec and 1 Jan	Closed

HOW TO FIND US

Direction: In Orford on B1084, 20 miles NE of Ipswich

Train: Wickham Market 8 miles

Bus: Far East Travel service 71

Tel: 01394 450472

P OVP

MAP Page 279 (4J)
OS Map 169, 212: TM419499

Tilbury Fort
Essex – RM18 7NR

The artillery fort at Tilbury on the Thames estuary protected London's seaward approach from the 16th century through to World War II. Henry VIII built the first fort here, and Queen Elizabeth I, famously rallied her army nearby to face the threat of the Armada. The present fort was begun in 1672 under Charles II: it is much the best example of its type in England, with its complete circuit of moats and bastioned outworks still substantially surviving. The fort mounted powerful artillery to command the river, as well as landward defences. Later, two magazines were constructed to store vast quantities of gunpowder. The east magazine houses an exhibition which traces the role of the fort in the defence of London. Perhaps because of its strength, Tilbury Fort has never been involved in the kind of action for which it was designed. The worst bloodshed within the fort occurred in 1776, when a fight following a Kent-Essex cricket match left a cricketer and the fort's sergeant dead.

Tilbury Fort

Visitors can now enter the north-east bastion. For those with an interest in military history there are displays of guns and gunpowder barrels, and information on advances in military engineering. The audio tour includes Elizabeth I's Armada speech and a description of life at Tilbury by 'Nathan Makepiece', the fort's Master Gunner. The interactive oral history programme provides every visitor with a fascinating insight into Tilbury and also provides 360° views of inaccessible areas.

Sharpe, the TV historical drama set during the Napoleonic Wars.

NON-MEMBERS

Adult	£4.30
Concession	£3.90
Child	£2.60
Family	£11.20

OPENING TIMES

1 Apr-31 Oct, Thu-Mon	10am-5pm
1 Nov-31 Mar, Thu-Mon	10am-4pm
24-26 Dec and 1 Jan	Closed

HOW TO FIND US

Direction: Located ½ mile E of Tilbury off A126, close to the Port of Tilbury

Train: Tilbury Town 1½ miles

Bus: Cintona service 99 connects with trains at Tilbury Town and passes the fort

Ferry: Gravesend – Tilbury Ferry, then ¼ mile

Tel: 01375 858489

Disabled access (exterior, magazines and fort square).

Dogs on leads (restricted areas).

MAP Page 279 (7G)
OS Map 177/178,162/163: TQ651753

Waltham Abbey Gatehouse and Bridge
Essex

A fine 14th-century gatehouse, bridge and other remains of the abbey refounded by Harold, last Saxon King of England.

Managed by Lee Valley Park.

OPENING TIMES

Any reasonable time

HOW TO FIND US

Direction: In Waltham Abbey off A112

Train: Waltham Cross 1¼ miles

Bus: Regal 211, 212, 213 & 240; Regal/Arriva 251; Arriva 250, 505; Centrebus C3; TWH 555

Tel: 01992 702200

Sensory trail guide.

MAP Page 279 (6F) OS Map 166,174
Gatehouse: TL381007
Harold's Bridge: TL382009

Weeting Castle
Norfolk

The ruins of a substantial early, medieval moated manor house, built in local flint.

OPENING TIMES

Any reasonable time

HOW TO FIND US

Direction: Located 2 miles N of Brandon off B1106

Train: Brandon 1¼ miles

Bus: Coach Services 25, 28, 40; Neals Travel (of Isleham) service R1

MAP Page 279 (3G)
OS Map 144, 229: TL778891

Wrest Park
See feature – Page 152

Wrest Park Bedfordshire – MK45 4HR

One of the most magnificent gardens in England, yet among the least well-known. In 2011 this 'Sleeping Beauty' of a garden will be awakened once more by an ambitious English Heritage project to restore the gardens and greatly improve the site's visitor facilities. For the first time the Walled Garden will be opened to visitors and there will be new parking facilities, a new visitor centre, café, and play area.

Don't miss our St George's Day event here, the largest in the country.

Wrest Park was the home of the De Grey family from the 13th century until 1917. The gardens are celebrated for their rare survival of a formal, early 18th-century layout of wooded walks and canals, centred on the architectural highlight of the pavilion designed by Thomas Archer in 1709-11. Subsequent generations refined the layout and added garden buildings, choosing to build on the structure of the established garden rather than sweeping everything away and starting again, as was fashionable with landscapers of the mid to late 18th century. The present French Revival House was completed in 1839, and acts as a stunning backdrop to the more formal gardens, including the Italian Garden and Parterre.

Please note: No photography or stiletto heels in the house.

www.english-heritage.org.uk/wrestpark

Available for corporate and private hire

Licensed for civil wedding ceremonies

NEW FOR 2011

August 2011 sees the opening up of Wrest Park, with longer opening times, more to see and a greater range of events.

Visitors will enter the site through our new Visitor Centre, which houses a brand new café and introductory exhibition. Many of Wrest Park's lost network of paths will be re-instated and these will be served by a free, regular, golf cart shuttle service to help visitors explore the whole landscape. The Italian and Rose Flower Gardens will be completely restored. New exhibitions in the house and garden buildings, a new audio tour and podcasts will help to bring this wonderful landscape to life. Children will enjoy exploring with our specially designed activities, and can let off steam in the new children's play area. Keep in touch with developments via our website or in *Heritage Today*.

NON-MEMBERS

From 1 April to 31 July	
Adult	£5.50
Concession	£4.70
Child	£2.80
Family	£13.80
From 1 August	
Adult	£8.00
Concession	£7.20
Child	£4.80
Family	£20.80

OPENING TIMES

1 Apr-31 Jul, Sat-Sun & Bank Hols	10am-6pm
1 Aug-18 Sep, Thu-Mon	10am-6pm
19 Sep-31 Oct, Thu-Mon	10am-5pm
1-30 Nov, Sat-Sun	10am-4pm
1 Dec-29 Feb	Closed
1-31 Mar, Sat-Sun	10am-4pm

Last entry 1 hour before closing

Walled Garden and Visitor Centre only

1 Aug-18 Sep, Wed-Mon	10am-6pm
19 Sep-31 Oct, Thu-Mon	10am-5pm
1 Nov-31 Mar, Sat-Sun	10am-4pm
24-26 Dec and 1 Jan	Closed

The house may be closed if an event is booked. Entry to the gardens may also be restricted earlier than the usual '1 hour before closing time', although access to the gardens for those who have already arrived will continue until normal closing times. Please call to check

HOW TO FIND US

Direction: ¾ mile E of Silsoe off A6, 10 miles S of Bedford

Train: Flitwick 4 miles

Bus: Stagecoach in Northants S1 Bedford – Luton

Tel: 01525 860000

OVP

Buggies available for disabled visitors.

New guidebook.

MAP Page 278 (5E)

OS Map 153, 193: TL091355

Associated attractions in the East of England

These visitor attractions, all independent of EH, offer discounts to our members. Please call before you visit to confirm details. A valid EH membership card must be produced for each member.

Felixstowe Museum
Suffolk IP11 7JG

Fourteen display rooms of local social, military and aviation history, housed within the 1878-built Submarine Mining Establishment. Large photograph archive, shop and tearoom. New exhibition for 2011 *'Odds and Sods'*.

Next to Landguard Fort

Tel: 01394 674355

www.felixstowe-museum.co.uk

20% discount on entry

Flag Fen Archaeology Park and Bronze Age Centre
Cambridgeshire PE6 7QJ

Discover how our ancestors lived 3000 years ago at Britain's Bronze Age Centre. Explore the recreated Bronze Age fen and roundhouses. Free guided tour, subject to availability. Check website for details.

3 miles from Peterborough

Tel: 01733 313414

www.flagfen.org

20% discount on entry

3

Holkham Hall
Norfolk NR23 1AB

Surrounded by acres of rolling parkland, this grand Palladian Hall is full of stunning architecture and art, original furniture and classical statuary. Visit the 18th-century walled gardens to see restoration work in progress.

2 miles West of Wells-next-the-Sea

Tel: 01328 710227

www.holkham.co.uk

20% discount on entry

Imperial War Museum Duxford
Cambridgeshire CB22 4QR

Discover the history of aviation in times of war and peace in one of the world's finest aviation heritage sites; explore over 200 aircraft including the legendary Spitfire and Concorde.

10 mins from Duxford Chapel

Tel: : 01223 835 000

www.iwm.org.uk/duxford

2 for 1 adult entry

Layer Marney Tower
Essex CO5 9US

England's tallest Tudor gatehouse, built in 1523. Climb the tower to enjoy magnificent views. Children's play areas, gardens, parkland, wildlife walks, gift shop and tearoom serving light lunches and homemade cakes.

6 miles to A12 Kelvedon

Tel: 01206 330784

www.layermarneytower.co.uk

20% discount on entry

OVP

Norwich Castle Museum & Art Gallery
Norfolk NR1 3JQ

One of the city's most famous landmarks, Norwich Castle was built by the Normans as a Royal Palace. Explore the magnificent keep and galleries, with outstanding collections of fine art, archaeology and natural history.

10 mins from centre of Norwich

Tel: 01603 493625/495897

www.museums.norfolk.gov.uk

2 for 1 'Castle Ticket' entry

OVP

EH Members | OVP OVP Holders | Discounted Child Places Included

Somerleyton Hall & Gardens
Suffolk NR32 5QQ

Originally Jacobean, extensively re-modelled in 1844. 12 acres of fabulous landscaped gardens including original ancient yew hedge maze. Guided tours of Hall. Excellent tearoom and gift shop. Offer not valid on Bank Holiday weekends.

10 mins from centre of Lowestoft

Tel: 01502 734901

www.somerleyton.co.uk

3 for 2 on Hall tour and garden
OVP

Time and Tide – Museum of Great Yarmouth Life
Norfolk NR30 3BX

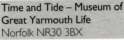

A short walk from the South Quay and Seafront. Housed in a former Victorian herring curing factory which has been beautifully restored, this museum tells the story of Great Yarmouth's rich maritime heritage.

½ mile from Great Yarmouth Row Houses

Tel: 01493 743930

www.museums.norfolk.gov.uk

25% discount on entry

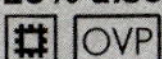

Woburn Abbey and Gardens
Bedfordshire MK17 9WA

Home to the Duke of Bedford and birthplace of Afternoon Tea. Enjoy priceless art and treasures, beautiful gardens all set in 3000 acres of deer park.

10 mins from J13 of M1

Tel: 01525 290333

www.woburn.co.uk/abbey

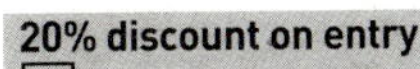

Cambridge Lodge holiday cottage at Audley End House

To stay at one of our holiday cottages, see page 26

The Garden Tower at Ashby de la Zouch Castle – see page 161

East Midlands

www.english-heritage.org.uk/eastmidlands

Introducing the East Midlands

Remember to check opening times before you visit any of our properties.

Details of all bus travel in England are available from Traveline on 0871 200 2233 or visit www.traveline.org.uk

Derbyshire

- Arbor Low Stone Circle and Gib Hill Barrow
- Bolsover Castle
- Bolsover Cundy House
- Hardwick Old Hall
- Hob Hurst's House
- Nine Ladies Stone Circle
- Peveril Castle
- Sutton Scarsdale Hall
- Wingfield Manor

Leicestershire

- Ashby de la Zouch Castle
- Jewry Wall
- Kirby Muxloe Castle

Lincolnshire

- Bolingbroke Castle
- Gainsborough Old Hall
- Lincoln Medieval Bishops' Palace
- Sibsey Trader Windmill
- Tattershall College

Northamptonshire

- Apethorpe Hall
- Chichele College
- Eleanor Cross, Geddington
- Kirby Hall
- Rushton Triangular Lodge

Nottinghamshire

- Mattersey Priory
- Rufford Abbey

Rutland

- Lyddington Bede House

Taking Time to Look

Hurrying along the M1 motorway through Derbyshire, travellers catch glimpses of great mansions to left and right. They are worth far more than a glimpse. **Hardwick Old Hall**, for instance, looks from the road like a gaunt ruin, but you can still ascend through four storeys to the wall-tops, viewing decorative plasterwork on the way, and enjoy wonderful views of the magnificent 'New Hall' nearby. Both are the work of that terrifying Elizabethan 'millionairess' and obsessive mansion-builder, Bess of Hardwick, whose extraordinary story is told in a display here.

Sutton Scarsdale Hall, a little further north, really is a ruined shell, but an immensely spectacular one, whose awe-inspiring Baroque grandeur repays viewing close to. Built regardless of expense in the 1740s, it was ruthlessly unroofed and stripped out in 1919-20, when its grandest rooms were transported bodily to America, one being regularly used as a Hollywood film set. Graphic panels (new this year) tell its story.

Bolsover Castle, grandest of them all, also includes some dramatically ruined buildings. But the dominant 'Little Castle' with its lavishly decorated interior has been magnificently restored: like the wonderful Riding House here, it really must be experienced to be believed. This lavish 17th century 'prodigy house' vividly reflects the personalities of its creators, Bess of Hardwick's son, Sir Charles Cavendish, and the even larger than life William, Duke of Newcastle – tutor to the young Charles II, defeated Royalist general, bad poet and fanatical trainer of 'great horses.' Also worth a closer look is charming **Bolsover Cundy House**, from which water was fed via a 300 metre 'conduit' to power the castle's Venus Fountain.

Make the most of your membership and keep up to date with upcoming events, the latest news and special offers by subscribing to our e-newsletter. Register online at **www.english-heritage.org.uk/newsletter** and we'll deliver the latest from English Heritage straight to your inbox.

Images:
(left) Hardwick Old Hall
(top centre) Bolsover Castle
(top right) Hardwick Old Hall
(bottom centre) Bolsover Castle
(bottom right) Sutton Scarsdale Hall

Apethorpe Hall
Northamptonshire – PE8 5AQ

Among England's finest country houses, big and stately Apethorpe Hall was begun in the late 15th century. It contains one of the country's most complete Jacobean interiors and hosted thirteen royal visits between 1565 and 1636.

While restoration work continues, English Heritage is pleased to offer access to visitors during 2011 on a limited, pre-booked and guided-tour basis only. For further details please visit our website or phone 0870 333 1181.

Please note: Apethorpe is still classed as a building site, and suitable footwear must be worn. There are lots of stairs, and no resting/seating points available. Children under 16 must be accompanied by an adult and we are unable to admit children under 5.

NON-MEMBERS
Please call for details

OPENING TIMES
By pre-booked tour only – please call for details

HOW TO FIND US
Direction: Located off the A43 towards King's Cliffe. If entering Apethorpe via King's Cliffe Road, advance to Laundry Lane, not the High Street. If entering via Bridge St, pass the stone cross and turn left into Laundry Lane

Train: Stamford 11 miles or Peterborough 14 miles

Bus: Stagecoach 23 Peterborough – Oundle (not Sun); Mark Bland Travel 180 Oundle – Stamford (weekdays)

Tel: 0870 333 1181

Access via narrow residential lane – please observe 10mph speed limit at all times.

MAP Page 281 (5H)
OS Map 141, 224/234: TL023954

Arbor Low Stone Circle and Gib Hill Barrow
Derbyshire

The region's most important prehistoric site, Arbor Low is a Neolithic henge monument atmospherically set amid high moorland. Within an earthen bank and ditch, a circle of some 50 white limestone slabs, all now fallen, surrounds a central stone 'cove' – a feature found only in major sacred sites. Nearby is enigmatic Gib Hill, a large burial mound.

Please note: The farmer who owns access to the property will levy a charge for entry.

Managed by Peak District National Park Authority.

OPENING TIMES
Any reasonable time

Access charge of £1 per person to cross private land to the monument

HOW TO FIND US
Direction: ½ mile E of A515, 2 miles S of Monyash

Train: Buxton 10 miles

Bus: TM Travel (Sun) service 181 passes the site; Bowers service 42 and Clowes service 446 both serve Parsley Hay within a 1 mile walk

Tel: 01629 816200

MAP Page 280 (2E)
OS Map 119, OL24: SK160636

Ashby de la Zouch Castle
See feature opposite

Bolingbroke Castle
Lincolnshire

The remains of a 13th-century hexagonal castle, birthplace in 1366 of the future King Henry IV, with adjacent earthworks. Besieged and taken by Cromwell's Parliamentarians in 1643.

Bolingbroke Castle

Managed by Heritage Lincolnshire.

OPENING TIMES
Any reasonable time

HOW TO FIND US
Direction: In Old Bolingbroke, 16 miles N of Boston off A16

Train: Thorpe Culvert 10 miles

Bus: Translinc Spilsby Call Connect 6S. To book telephone 0845 234 3344

Tel: 01529 461499

MAP Page 281 (2J)
OS Map 122, 273: TF349650

Bolsover Castle
See feature – page 162

Bolsover Cundy House
Derbyshire

This charming, cottage-like, 17th-century conduit house, with vaulted stone-slab roof, once supplied water to Bolsover Castle.

Managed by Bolsover Civic Society.

OPENING TIMES
Any reasonable time

HOW TO FIND US
Direction: Off M1 at junction 29A, follow signs for Bolsover Castle. At junction of Craggs Rd and Houghton Rd, Bolsover, 6 miles E of Chesterfield on A362

Train: Chesterfield 6 miles or Langwith – Whaley Thorns 4½ miles

Bus: Stagecoach in Chesterfield service 82 & TM Travel Bolsover town services B2 & B3 actually pass the property. Stagecoach Chesterfield services 53, 53A and TM Travel serice 46 serve Hilltop Avenue a short walk from the Cundy House

Tel: 01246 822844 (Bolsover Castle)

MAP Page 281 (2F)
OS Map 120, 269: SK471709

Ashby de la Zouch Castle Leicestershire – LE65 1BR

© Skyscan Balloon Photography

Ashby Castle forms the backdrop to the famous jousting scenes in Sir Walter Scott's classic novel of 1819, *Ivanhoe*. Now a ruin, the castle began as a manor house in the 12th century. It only achieved castle status in the 15th century, by which time the hall and buttery had been enlarged with a solar to the east and a large integral kitchen added to the west.

Between 1474 and his execution by Richard III in 1483, Edward IV's Chamberlain Lord Hastings added the chapel and the impressive keep-like Hastings Tower – a castle within a castle. Visitors can climb the 24 metre (78 feet) high tower, which offers fine views. Later the castle hosted many royal visitors, including Henry VII, Mary Queen of Scots, James I and Charles I.

A Royalist stronghold during the Civil War, the castle finally fell to Parliament in 1646, and was then made unusable. An underground passage from the kitchen to the tower, probably created during this war, can still be explored today. Archaeologists recently investigated the mysterious castle garden, famous for its elaborately shaped sunken features.

Interpretation boards display family-friendly information, including beautiful illustrations evoking the splendour of Lord Hastings' additions to the castle. The audio guide provides an amusing account of the castle's dramatic history, drawing upon a masque performed here for Alice Spencer, Countess of Derby, in the early 17th century.

www.english-heritage.org.uk/ashbydelazouchcastle

NON-MEMBERS

Adult	£4.30
Concession	£3.90
Child	£2.60
Family	£11.20

OPENING TIMES

1 Apr-30 Jun, Thu-Mon	10am-5pm
1 Jul-31 Aug, daily	10am-5pm
1 Sep-31 Oct, Thu-Mon	10am-5pm
1 Nov-31 Mar, Thu-Mon	12pm-4pm
24-26 Dec and 1 Jan	Closed

HOW TO FIND US

Direction: In Ashby de la Zouch, 12 miles S of Derby on A511. Restricted parking on site, please park in town car park

Train: Burton on Trent 9 miles

Bus: Arriva 3, 9A & 16; Cresswells 7 & 129; Arriva/Midland Classic 9

Local Tourist Information: 01530 411767

Tel: 01530 413343

OVP

Disabled access (grounds only).

Parking (restricted on site, please park in town car park – charge applies).

MAP Page 280 (4E)

OS Map 128, 245: SK361166

Bolsover Castle Derbyshire – S44 6PR

There is nothing else in Britain quite like Bolsover Castle – a unique survival of a 17th-century fantasy mansion intended solely for pleasure and extravagant display.

Following years of restoration by English Heritage, it is easy to imagine Bolsover as the setting for Cavendish's lavish lifestyle.

Fireplace in The Star Chamber

Dominating the countryside from its hilltop like a great ship, Bolsover occupies the site of a medieval castle built by the Peverel family. Sir Charles Cavendish – who already owned several other mansions, including one only a few miles away – bought the old fortress in 1612 and began work on his Little Castle project. Though playfully battlemented and pinnacled, his creation was not designed for defence, but as a fashionable retreat into an imaginary golden age of chivalry, courtly love – and opulent wealth.

His son William – playboy, poet, courtier and later Royalist general and first Duke of Newcastle – inherited the Little Castle in 1617 and set about its completion, assisted by the architect John Smythson. The exquisitely carved fireplaces and richly-coloured murals and panelling of its interiors still take the visitor on an allegorical journey from earthly concerns to heavenly (and erotic) delights.

William also added the immense Terrace Range, now a dramatic roofless shell. To show off his achievement, in 1634 he invited King Charles I and his court to *Love's Welcome to Bolsover*, a masque specially written by Ben Jonson for performance in the Fountain Garden. Finally he constructed the cavernous Riding House, with its magnificent roof: among the finest surviving indoor riding schools in the country and a landmark in British equestrianism. Here he indulged his passion for training great horses in stately dressage.

Following years of restoration by English Heritage, it is easy to imagine Bolsover as the setting for Cavendish's lavish lifestyle, attended by armies of servants from well-born gentleman ushers to the 'necessary woman' who emptied the chamberpots.

The Venus Fountain, with its 23 statues, has been restored to full working order, and the 'Caesar paintings', commissioned by Cavendish and depicting Roman emperors and empresses, can again be seen at Bolsover.

Bolsover Castle regularly hosts living history events and also offers an engaging audio tour. There is also a Discovery Centre in the Stables, with audio-visual displays. Disabled access to some parts of the Riding House and Terrace Range is subject to seasonal changes, please call 01246 822844 in advance of your visit for further details.

www.english-heritage.org.uk/bolsovercastle

Available for corporate and private hire

Licensed for civil wedding ceremonies

NEW FOR 2011

A family-friendly interactive exhibition in the Riding House stables to introduce the site. Discover the remarkable legacy of William Cavendish, his passion for horses and his contribution to the modern sport of dressage. Explore the newly-refurbished model of the Little Castle, and find out about a lavish banquet held there for the king and queen in 1634.

NON-MEMBERS

Adult	£7.80
Concession	£7.00
Child	£4.70
Family	£20.30

OPENING TIMES

1 Apr-31 Oct, daily	10am-5pm
1 Nov-31 Mar, Thu-Mon	10am–4pm
24-26 Dec and 1 Jan	Closed

Part of the castle may close for 1 hour if an event is booked. Please call to check

HOW TO FIND US

Direction: In Bolsover, 6 miles E of Chesterfield on A632. Off M1 at junction 29A (signposted)

Train: Chesterfield 6 miles

Bus: G&J Hallmark service 49; TM Travel B2; Stagecoach in Chesterfield service 83 pass the castle entrance

Tel: 01246 822844

Local Tourist Information (Chesterfield): 01246 345777

Parking (in Castle Car Park, off main gate. Charge payable, refundable to EH members and paying visitors on admission). This is also the coach drop off point.

There is good access to the grounds, but please note that the Little Castle is not accessible to wheelchairs.

MAP Page 281 (2F)
OS Map 120, 269: SK470707

Chichele College
Northamptonshire

The gatehouse, chapel and other remains of a communal residence for priests serving the parish church, founded by locally-born Archbishop Chichele before 1425. Regularly used to display works of art.

OPENING TIMES

Quadrangle – any reasonable time. Contact the keykeeper for the chapel: Mrs D Holyoak, 12 Lancaster St, Higham Ferrers Tel: 01933 314157

HOW TO FIND US

Direction: In Higham Ferrers

Train: Wellingborough 5 miles

Bus: Stagecoach X46, M50; Expresslines 125, H1 & H2

Tel: 01933 655401

Dogs on leads (restricted areas only).

MAP Page 281 (6G)
OS Map 153, 224: SP960687

Eleanor Cross, Geddington
Northamptonshire

In 1290 Eleanor of Castile, the beloved wife of Edward I and mother of his 14 children, died at Harby in Nottinghamshire. The places where her body rested on the journey south to its tomb in Westminster Abbey were marked by stone crosses. The stately triangular Geddington cross, with its canopied statues surmounted by a slender hexagonal pinnacle, is the best-preserved of only three intact survivors. Other crosses stand at Hardingstone near Northampton and Waltham Cross, Hertfordshire.

OPENING TIMES

Any reasonable time

HOW TO FIND US

Direction: Located in the village of Geddington, off A43 between Kettering and Corby

Train: Kettering 4 miles

Bus: Centrebus service 8 Kettering – Corby

MAP Page 281 (5G)
OS Map 141, 224: SP894830

Gainsborough Old Hall
Lincolnshire – DN21 2NB

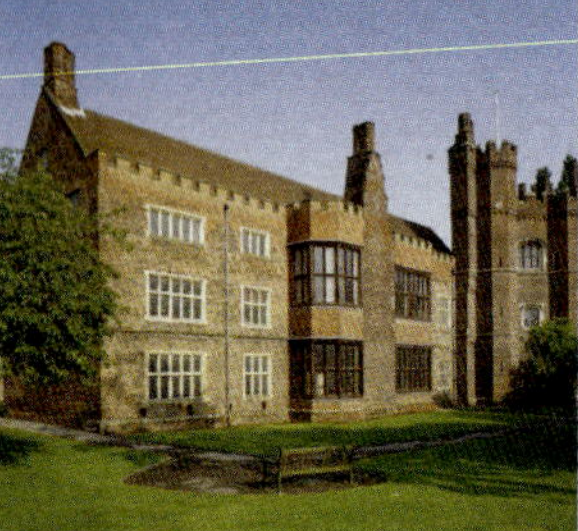

Undeservedly little-known, Gainsborough Old Hall is among the biggest and best-preserved medieval manor houses in England, part timber-framed but mostly brick-built. Later 15th-century with Elizabethan additions, it has an impressive kitchen with an enormous fireplace, a noble great hall, and an imposing lodgings tower. Many rooms are furnished as they may have appeared in the 15th century and there is an exhibition tracing the Hall's later links with the Pilgrim Fathers.

Managed by Lincolnshire County Council.

NON-MEMBERS

Admission charged.
Please contact site for details

OPENING TIMES

1 Mar-31 Oct,	
Mon-Fri	10am-5pm
Sat-Sun	11am-5pm
1 Nov-29 Feb,	
Mon-Fri	10am-4pm
Sat	11am-4pm
Sun	Closed
20 Dec-3 Jan	Closed

HOW TO FIND US

Direction: In Gainsborough, opposite the library

Train: Gainsborough Central ½ mile, Gainsborough Lea Road 1 mile

Bus: Short walk from Gainsborough bus station

Tel: 01522 782040 or 01427 612669

Disabled access (most of ground floor).

MAP Page 281 (1G)
OS Map 112/121, 280: SK813900

Hardwick Old Hall
Derbyshire – S44 5QJ

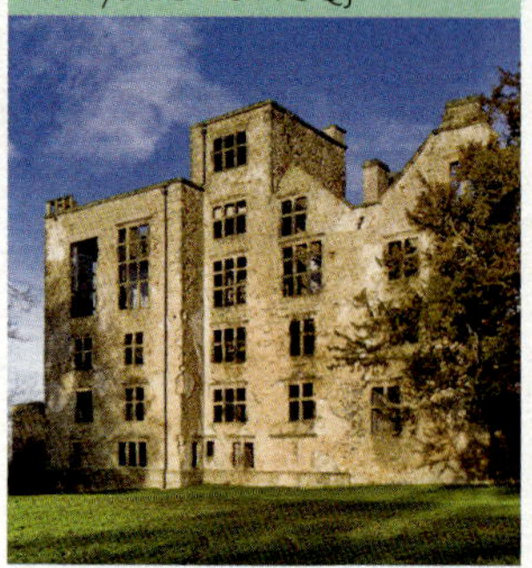

The remodelled family home of Bess of Hardwick, one of the richest and most remarkable women of Elizabethan England, stands beside the New Hall she raised later in the 1590s. Though the Old Hall is now roofless, visitors can still ascend four floors to view surviving decorative plasterwork, as well as the kitchen and service rooms.

Hardwick Old Hall

An exhibition in the West Lodge describes Bess's adventures in architecture and how she transformed her birthplace from a medieval manor house into a luxurious Elizabethan mansion. An audio tour tells Bess's story, and on the ground floor there is a virtual tour of the first floor rooms (which are only accessible via steps).

Managed by English Heritage and owned by the National Trust.

Holiday cottage available to let

NON-MEMBERS

Adult	£4.80
Concession	£4.30
Child	£2.90
Family	£12.50

National Trust members admitted free, but small charge at EH events. Tickets for the New Hall (the National Trust) and joint tickets for both properties available at extra cost

OPENING TIMES

1 Apr-31 Oct, Wed-Sun	10am-5pm
1 Nov-31 Mar	Closed

HOW TO FIND US

Direction: 9½ miles SE of Chesterfield, off A6175, from J29 of M1

Train: Chesterfield 8 miles

Bus: Trent Barton/Stagecoach in Chesterfield 'Pronto' service or G&J Hallmark service 49 (alight Glapwell 'Young Vanish', then 2 mile walk) or Stagecoach Yorkshire/TM Travel serice 96 to Hardstoft and 2 mile walk

Tel: 01246 850431

MAP Page 281 (2F)
OS Map 120, 269: SK462637

Hob Hurst's House
Derbyshire

A square prehistoric burial mound with earthwork ditch and bank amid remote moorland. Named after a local goblin.

Managed by the Peak District National Park Authority.

OPENING TIMES

Any reasonable time

HOW TO FIND US

Direction: On open moorland from unclassified road off B5057, 9 miles W of Chesterfield

Train: Chesterfield 9 miles

Bus: TM Travel services 214, 215 (Sun) & 473 (Sun) to Beeley then 2 mile walk

Tel: 01629 816200

MAP Page 280 (2E)
OS Map 119, OL24: SK287692

Jewry Wall
Leicestershire – LE1 4LB

A length of Roman bath-house wall over 9 metres (30 feet) high, near a museum displaying the archaeology of Leicester and its region. Graphic panels describe the Roman baths.

OPENING TIMES

Feb-Oct, daily	11am-4.30pm
Nov-Jan open for advance bookings only	
Museum Feb-Oct, daily	11am-4.30pm
Nov-Jan open for special events only	

HOW TO FIND US

Direction: In St Nicholas St, W of Church of St Nicholas

Train: Leicester ¾ mile

Bus: First 12, 18, 70; Stagecoach 48; Arriva 15, 50, 50A, 51, 104, 152, 153, 158; Robinson's 13A; Coachcare 162

Tel: 01162 254971 (Jewry Wall Museum)

Jewry Wall

Parking (by museum, within St Nicholas Circle).

MAP Page 281 (4F)
OS Map 140, 233: SK582045

Kirby Hall
See feature – Page 166

Kirby Muxloe Castle
Leicestershire – LE9 2DH

The picturesque moated remains – including the fine gatehouse and a complete corner tower – of this brick-built fortified mansion have recently been extensively conserved by English Heritage. Begun in 1480 by Lord Hastings, the castle was left unfinished after his execution by Richard III in 1483.

NON-MEMBERS

Adult	£3.20
Concession	£2.90
Child	£1.90

OPENING TIMES

1 May-31 Aug, Sat, Sun & Bank Hols	10am-5pm

HOW TO FIND US

Direction: 4 miles W of Leicester off B5380; close to M1 junction 21A, northbound exit only

Train: Leicester 5 miles

Bus: Robinson's service 13A

Tel: 01162 386886

MAP Page 281 (4F)
OS Map 140, 233: SK524046

Lincoln Medieval Bishops' Palace
See feature – Page 167

Kirby Hall Northamptonshire – NN17 3EN

Kirby Hall is one of England's greatest Elizabethan and 17th-century houses. Begun by Sir Humphrey Stafford, it was purchased by Sir Christopher Hatton, one of Queen Elizabeth I's 'comely young men' and later her Lord Chancellor. Hatton hoped in vain to receive the Queen here during one of her annual 'progresses' around the country. Although this vast mansion is partly roofless, most of its walls survive to their full impressive height; as does the prodigious three-tier inner porch, begun following French pattern books and later embellished in the Classical style by the sculptor Nicholas Stone.

Kirby Hall's exceptionally rich decoration proclaims that its successive owners were always in the forefront of new ideas about architecture and design. The Great Hall and state rooms remain roofed and intact, their interiors refitted and redecorated to authentic 17th- and 18th-century specifications.

Sir Christopher Hatton the Fourth added the great gardens (described as 'ye finest garden in England') in the late 17th century. They have been recreated as they may have appeared at that time, with elaborate period style 'cutwork', statues, urns, seating, topiary and other features.

The gardens and ground floor of the mansion are easily accessible by wheelchair users.

An audio tour guides visitors through the house and gardens, accompanied by commentaries from experts in garden history, conservation and country houses.

Jane Austen's *Mansfield Park* (1999) and *Tristram Shandy: A Cock and Bull Story* (2005).

www.english-heritage.org.uk/kirbyhall

Owned by the Earl of Winchilsea and managed by English Heritage.

Holiday cottage available to let

NON-MEMBERS

Adult	£5.60
Concession	£5.00
Child	£3.40
Family	£14.60

OPENING TIMES

1 Apr-31 Oct, Thu-Mon	10am-5pm
1 Nov-31 Mar, Thu-Mon	12pm-4pm
24-26 Dec and 1 Jan	Closed

May close early for private events. Please call to check

HOW TO FIND US

Direction: On an unclassified road off A43, 4 miles NE of Corby

Train: Corby 4 miles

Bus: There are no bus services to the property. The closest is service 9 operated by Centrebus. Alight at Rockingham Raceway then ½ mile

Tel: 01536 203230

P OVP

Disabled access (grounds, gardens and ground floor only).

Dogs on leads (restricted areas).

MAP Page 281 (5G)
OS Map 141, 224: SP926927

Lincoln Medieval Bishops' Palace Lincolnshire – LN2 1PU

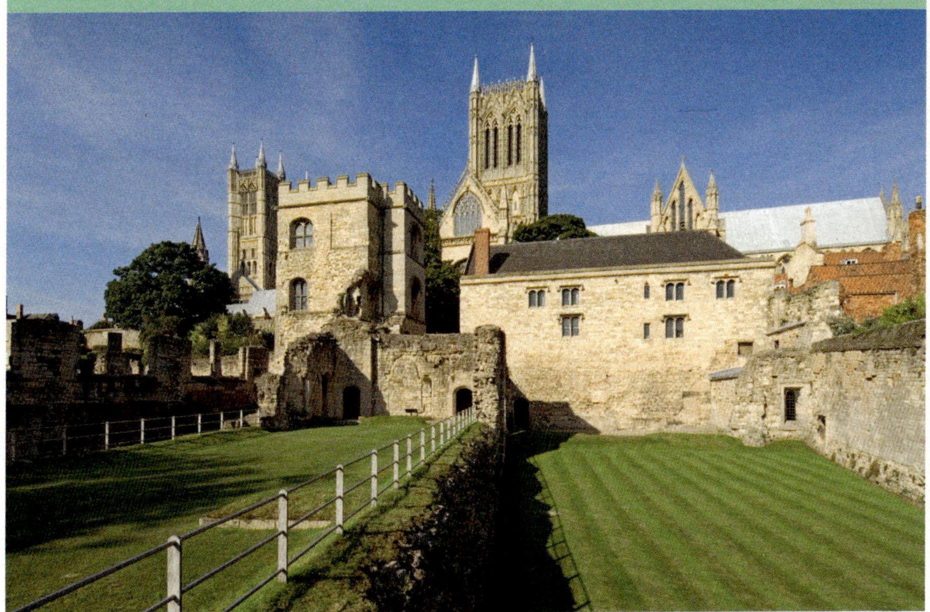

Standing almost in the shadow of Lincoln cathedral, with sweeping views over the ancient city and the countryside beyond, the medieval bishops' palace was once among the most important buildings in the country. The administrative centre of the largest diocese in medieval England, stretching from the Humber to the Thames, its architecture reflected the enormous power and wealth of the bishops as princes of the church.

Begun in the late 12th century, the palace's most impressive feature is the undercrofted West Hall, initiated by Bishop St Hugh and completed in the 1230s. The chapel range and entrance tower were built by Bishop William Alnwick, who modernised the palace in the 1430s. Having hosted visits from Henry VIII and James I, the palace was sacked by Royalist troops during the Civil War.

Built on hillside terraces, the palace also boasts a Contemporary Heritage Garden, designed by Mark Anthony Walker. Its form was inspired by the cathedral's medieval vaulting, with trees shaped to echo spires. Award-winning audio tour.

www.english-heritage.org.uk/lincolnbishops

NON-MEMBERS

Adult	£4.40
Concession	£4.00
Child	£2.60
Family	£11.40

OPENING TIMES

1 Apr-31 Oct, Thu-Mon	10am-5pm
1 Nov-31 Mar, Thu-Mon	10am-4pm
24-26 Dec and 1 Jan	Closed

HOW TO FIND US

Direction: On the south side of Lincoln Cathedral. From the cathedral precinct gate, follow wall to your right to the gateway directly opposite cathedral south porch, then take tunnelled walkway (Chesney Gate). Entrance to the left down the pathway

Train: Lincoln 1 mile

Bus: From surrounding areas

Tel: 01522 527468

OVP

Parking (limited disabled parking on site).

MAP Page 281 (2H)
OS Map 121, 272: SK978717

Lyddington Bede House
Rutland – LE15 9LZ

Set beside the church of a picturesque ironstone village, Lyddington Bede House originated as the medieval wing of a palace belonging to the Bishops of Lincoln. By 1600 it had passed to Sir Thomas Cecil, son of Queen Elizabeth I's chief minister, who converted it into an almshouse for twelve poor 'bedesmen' over 30 years old and two women (over 45), all free of lunacy, leprosy or the French pox. Visitors can wander through the bedesmen's rooms, with their tiny windows and fireplaces, and view the former bishops' Great Chamber with its beautifully carved ceiling cornice.

There is a small herb garden.

NON-MEMBERS

Adult	£4.20
Concession	£3.80
Child	£2.50
Family	£10.90

OPENING TIMES

1 Apr-31 Oct, Thu-Mon 10am-5pm

HOW TO FIND US

Direction: In Lyddington, 6 miles N of Corby; 1 mile E of A6003, next to the church

Train: Oakham 7 miles

Bus: Veolia 'Rutland Flyer' service 1 Corby – Oakham (passes close to Oakham)

Tel: 01572 822438

Disabled access (ground floor only).

MAP Page 281 (5G)
OS Map 141, 234: SP876970

Mattersey Priory
Nottinghamshire

The remains, mainly the 13th-century refectory and kitchen, of a small monastery for just six Gilbertine canons – the only wholly English monastic order.

OPENING TIMES

Any reasonable time

HOW TO FIND US

Direction: ¾ mile down rough drive, 1 mile E of Mattersey off B6045

Train: Retford 7 miles

Bus: Stagecoach East Midlands service 27, 27A, Veolia 83 & 83A to village centre then ½ mile walk

MAP Page 281 (1G)
OS Map 112/120, 280: SK703896

Nine Ladies Stone Circle
Derbyshire

A small, early Bronze Age stone circle traditionally believed to represent nine ladies turned to stone as a penalty for dancing on Sunday. Their fiddler became the nearby King Stone. Part of an extensive complex of prehistoric remains on Stanton Moor.

Managed by Peak District National Park Authority.

OPENING TIMES

Any reasonable time

HOW TO FIND US

Direction: From an unclassified road off A6, 5 miles SE of Bakewell

Train: Matlock 4½ miles

Bus: Hulleys service 172 to Stanton in Peak (within 1 mile)

Tel: 01629 816200

MAP Page 280 (2E)
OS Map 119, OL24: SK249635

Peveril Castle
See feature opposite

Rufford Abbey
Nottinghamshire

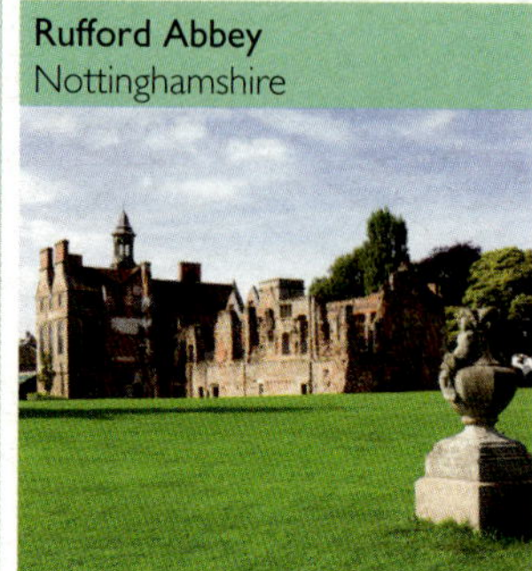

The best-preserved remains of a Cistercian abbey west cloister range in England, dating mainly from c. 1170. Incorporated into part of a 17th-century and later mansion, set in Rufford Country Park. Graphic panels show how the abbey was transformed into a great house.

Managed by Nottinghamshire County Council

OPENING TIMES

All year, daily	10am-5pm
25 Dec	Closed

Call for full details of opening times and other site facilities

HOW TO FIND US

Direction: 2 miles S of Ollerton off A614

Train: Mansfield 8 miles

Bus: 'The Sherwood Arrow' (Stagecoach) Nottingham – Worksop; Travelwright 227 (Wed, Fri)

Tel: 01623 821338

P

Occasional charge for members on event days.

Parking (charge applies – not managed by EH).

Shop – craft centre.

MAP Page 281 (2F)
OS Map 120, 270: SK646648

Peveril Castle Derbyshire – S33 8WQ

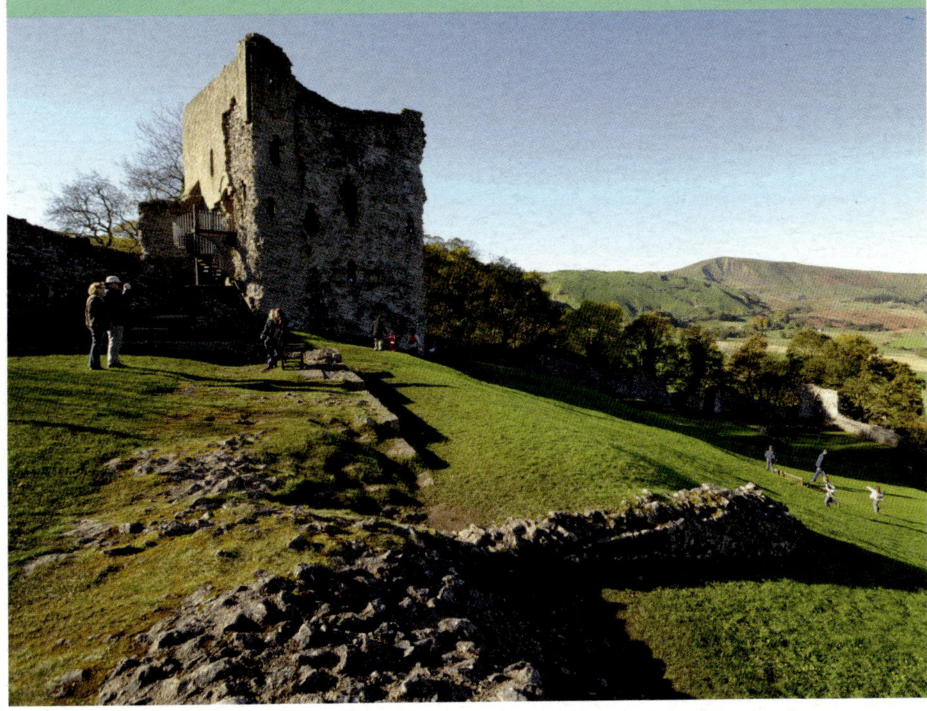

Perched high above the pretty village of Castleton, the castle offers breathtaking views of the Peak District. Founded soon after 1066 by William Peverel, one of William the Conqueror's most trusted knights, it played an important role in guarding the Peak Forest.

Henry II made a number of additions to 'Castle Peak' (as it was known in the Middle Ages). Most notable is the great square keep, with its round-headed windows, built in 1176. Thirteenth-century developments included the great hall and though by 1400 the fortress had ceased to be strategically important, its impregnability guaranteed its continued use as a prison.

Displays in the visitor centre tell the story of Peveril as the focal point of the Royal Forest of the Peak, a royal hunting preserve since the 11th century.

Wheelchair access is available to the visitor centre only.

www.english-heritage.org.uk/peverilcastle

NEW FOR 2011

Introductory guided tours to the highlights of Peveril Castle. Every weekend in June at 11.30am and 2.30pm.

NON-MEMBERS

Adult	£4.30
Concession	£3.90
Child	£2.60
Family	£11.20

OPENING TIMES

1 Apr-31 Oct, daily	10am-5pm
1 Nov-31 Mar, Thu-Mon	10am-4pm
24-26 Dec and 1 Jan	Closed

HOW TO FIND US

Direction: Via the market place in Castleton; 15 miles W of Sheffield on A6187

Train: Hope 2½ miles

Bus: Hulley's 68, 173, 174, 260 (Sun), 276; First 272; TM Travel service 242 & 373 all to Castleton then short walk

Tel: 01433 620613

OVP

Parking (in town).

MAP Page 280 (2E)
OS Map 110, OL1: SK149826

Rushton Triangular Lodge
Northamptonshire – NN14 1RP

This delightful triangular building was designed by Sir Thomas Tresham (father of one of the Gunpowder Plotters) and constructed between 1593 and 1597. It is a testament to Tresham's Roman Catholicism: the number three, symbolising the Holy Trinity, is apparent everywhere. There are three floors, trefoil windows and three triangular gables on each side. On the entrance front is the inscription 'Tres Testimonium Dant' ('there are three that give witness'), a Biblical quotation from St John's Gospel referring to the Trinity. It is also a pun on Tresham's name: his wife called him 'Good Tres' in her letters.

NON-MEMBERS

Adult	£3.20
Concession	£2.90
Child	£1.90

OPENING TIMES

1 Apr-31 Oct, Thu-Mon	11am-4pm

HOW TO FIND US

Direction: 1 mile W of Rushton, on unclassified road; 3 miles from Desborough on A6

Train: Kettering 5 miles

Rushton Triangular Lodge

Bus: Stagecoach in Northants service 18 Market Harborough – Kettering, alight Desborough Cemetery, then 1 mile. Rushden Community Minibus serves the site. Tel: 01536 418970 for details

Tel: 01536 710761

OVP

Dogs on leads (restricted areas only).

Parking (limited parking in nearby lay-by).

MAP Page 281 (5G)
OS Map 141, 224: SP830831

Sibsey Trader Windmill
Lincolnshire – PE22 0SY

Built in 1877, this restored six-storey mill, with complete gear, sails and fantail, still works today. The award-winning tearoom sells produce made from the mill's organic, stone-ground flour.

Managed by Ian Ansell.
Tel: 07718 320449.

NON-MEMBERS

Adult	£2.50
Concession	£2.00
Child	£1.00

OPENING TIMES

1 Mar-30 Apr,	
Sat & Bank Hols	10am-6pm
Sun	11am-6pm
1 May-30 Sep,	
Sat & Bank Hols	10am-6pm
Sun	11am-6pm
Tue	10am-6pm

Sibsey Trader Windmill

1-31 Oct,	
Sat	10am-6pm
Sun	11am-6pm
1 Nov-29 Feb	
Sat	11am-5pm

Group and education visits outside these hours by arrangement

HOW TO FIND US

Direction: ½ mile W of Sibsey off A16, 5 miles N of Boston

Train: Boston 5 miles

Bus: Brylaine 113 and Grayscroft 8 (Wed) to Sibsey, then ½ mile walk

Tel: 01205 460647/07718 320449

OVP

Disabled access (exterior only).

MAP Page 281 (3J)
OS Map 122, 261: TF345510

Sutton Scarsdale Hall
Derbyshire

The imposing shell of a grandiose Georgian mansion built in 1724-9, with an immensely columned exterior. Roofless since 1919, when its interiors were dismantled and some exported to America: but there is still much to discover within, including traces of sumptuous plasterwork. Set amid contemporary garden remains, including a ha-ha ditch and parish church.

NEW FOR 2011

New graphic panels guide you round the site.

Sutton Scarsdale Hall

OPENING TIMES

Summer, daily	10am-6pm
Rest of year, daily	10am-4pm
24-26 Dec and 1 Jan	Closed

HOW TO FIND US

Direction: Between Chesterfield and Bolsover, 1½ miles S of Arkwright Town

Train: Chesterfield 5 miles

Bus: G&J Holmes 'Hallmark' service 48

MAP Page 281 (2F)
OS Map 120, 269: SK442689

Tattershall College
Lincolnshire

Remains of a grammar school for church choristers, founded in the mid-15th century by Ralph, Lord Cromwell, the builder of Wingfield Manor and nearby Tattershall Castle (the National Trust).

The college is managed by Heritage Lincolnshire.

OPENING TIMES

Any reasonable time

HOW TO FIND US

Direction: In Tattershall, 14 miles NE of Sleaford on A153

Train: Ruskington (U) 10 miles

Bus: Brylaine Interconnect service 5 and Translinc Call Connect service 6K

Tel: 01529 461499

MAP Page 281 (2H)
OS Map 122, 261: TF213578

Wingfield Manor
Derbyshire – DE55 7NH

The vast and immensely impressive ruins of a palatial medieval manor house arranged round a pair of courtyards, with a huge undercrofted Great Hall and a defensible High Tower 22 metres (72 feet) tall. This monument to late medieval 'conspicuous consumption' was built in the 1440s for the wealthy Ralph, Lord Cromwell, Treasurer of England.
Later the home of Bess of Hardwick's husband, the Earl of Shrewsbury, who imprisoned Mary Queen of Scots here in 1569, 1584 and 1585.

Please note: Wingfield Manor is part of a working farm and the owner's privacy should be respected at all times.

Wingfield Manor

No access to the public except by pre-booked guided tours.

Zeffirelli's film *Jane Eyre*.

NON-MEMBERS

Adult	£5.30
Concession	£4.80
Child	£3.20

OPENING TIMES

Entry by pre-booked guided tours only, on first Sat of the month Apr-Sep

Please call Customer Services on 0870 333 1183 to book

HOW TO FIND US

Direction: 17 miles N of Derby; 11 miles S of Chesterfield on B5035; ½ mile S of South Wingfield. From M1 junction 28, W on A38, A615 (Matlock Road) at Alfreton, 1½ miles and turn onto B5035

Train: Alfreton 4 miles

Bus: Yourbus 140 & 142; TM Travel service 150

Tel: 0870 333 1183 to book (Customer Services)

Parking (none on site or in gateway).

MAP Page 280 (3E)
OS Map 119, 269: SK374548

Associated attractions in the East Midlands

These visitor attractions, all independent of EH, offer discounts to our members. Please call before you visit to confirm details. A valid EH membership card must be produced for each member.

Althorp
Northamptonshire NN7 4HQ

Enjoy an insight into the personalities of the people who lived here. Plus a fascinating collection of pictures, ceramics and furniture, the result of one family's uninterrupted occupation for 500 years.

30 mins from Rushton Triangular Lodge

Tel: 01604 770107

www.althorp.com

Free entry upstairs rooms

6

Ashby de la Zouch Museum
Leicestershire LE65 1HU

2010 and 2007 Leicestershire Museum of the Year. Models of Ashby Castle and Ivanhoe Baths. Temporary exhibitions, research facilities, archives, talks, workshops and guided walks. Education and Family Historian officers.

5 mins from Ashby de la Zouch Castle

Tel: 01530 560090

www.ashbydelazouchmuseum.org.uk

FREE admission

2

Belvoir Castle
Leicestershire NG32 1PE

Our hilltop setting commands stunning views over the Vale of Belvoir. With glorious gardens and a fascinating magical castle to explore, there's something for everyone at this family home.

50 mins from Jewry Wall

Tel: 01476 871002

www.belvoircastle.com

2 for 1 entry

Bosworth Battlefield
Leicestershire CV13 0AD

Re-live the drama and excitement of the Battle of Bosworth, 1485, at the award-winning Bosworth Battlefield Visitor Centre. Facilities include interactive exhibition, reclaimed medieval Tithe Barn restaurant, gift shop and country park trail.

Tel: 01455 290429

www.bosworthbattlefield.com

50% off exhibition tickets

Burghley House
Lincolnshire PE9 3JY

Burghley was built and designed by William Cecil, Lord High Treasurer to Queen Elizabeth I. England's greatest Elizabethan House.

30 mins from Kirby Hall

Tel: 01780 752451

www.burghley.co.uk

20% discount House & Garden Adult Ticket

Creswell Crags
Nottinghamshire and Derbyshire Border S80 3LH

Creswell Crags is internationally recognised as home to Britain's only known cave art. Featuring some of the most remarkable Ice Age artefacts, the new visitor attraction provides a glimpse of life during the Ice Age.

30 mins from Hardwick Hall

Tel: 01909 720378

www.creswell-crags.org.uk

25% off Ice Age Tour

EH Members | OVP OVP Holders | Discounted Child Places Included

Crich Tramway Village
Derbyshire DE4 5DP

Travel through time on vintage trams along the period street and out into the open countryside. Watch trams being restored and enjoy the woodland walk, with captivating sculptures around every corner.
Not valid on premier events.

Tel: 01773 854321

www.tramway.co.uk

£2 off adult/snr **£1 off** child

78 Derngate: The Charles Rennie Mackintosh House & Galleries
Northamptonshire NN1 1UH

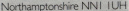

The house at 78 Derngate was remodelled by the world-famous architect, Charles Rennie Mackintosh, in his iconic Modernist style in 1916. Restaurant, gift and craft shop and changing gallery exhibitions. Winner of the Enjoy England small visitor attraction of the year 2009.

Tel: 01604 603407

www.78derngate.org.uk

2 for 1 entry

The Heights of Abraham
Derbyshire S44 3PT

Derbyshire's oldest tourist attraction, first opened to visitors in 1870, now with modern cable car ride to the top. Enjoy cavern tours, a Victorian prospect tower, exhibition, a thatched summer house built in 1801 and take in views across the Peak District.

Tel: 01629 582365

www.heightsofabraham.com

£2 off adult **£1 off** child/snr

OVP

Kelmarsh Hall & Gardens
Northamptonshire NN6 9LY

18th-century James Gibbs house set in beautiful gardens. Once home of Nancy Lancaster, acclaimed for creating the 'English Country House Style'. Plus Croome Court exhibition, showcasing furniture and paintings commissioned by the 6th Earl of Coventry.

15 mins from M1/M6

Tel: 01604 686543

www.kelmarsh.com

2 for 1 entry

Papplewick Pumping Station
Nottinghamshire NG15 9AJ

Britain's finest working Victorian water pumping station, with ornate engine house, cooling pond, landscaped grounds, original twin beam engines and six boilers, woodland play area and miniature railway.

Close to J27 of the M1

Tel: 0115 9632938

www.papplewickpumpingstation.co.uk

25% discount on entry

Rockingham Castle
Leicestershire LE16 8TH

Begun by William the Conqueror. A royal fortress for 450 years, and a much-loved family home for another 450 years. Surrounded by 18 acres of gardens. Eye spy and quiz for children.

8 miles from A14

Tel: 01536 770240

www.rockinghamcastle.com

2 for 1 entry

Witley Court and Gardens
– see page 192

West Midlands

Introducing the West Midlands

Remember to check opening times before you visit any of our properties.

Details of all bus travel in England are available from Traveline on 0871 200 2233 or visit www.traveline.org.uk

Herefordshire

- Arthur's Stone
- Edvin Loach Old Church
- Goodrich Castle
- Longtown Castle
- Mortimer's Cross Water Mill
- Rotherwas Chapel
- Wigmore Castle

Shropshire

- Acton Burnell Castle
- Boscobel House and The Royal Oak
- Buildwas Abbey
- Cantlop Bridge
- Clun Castle
- Haughmond Abbey
- Iron Bridge
- Langley Chapel
- Lilleshall Abbey
- Mitchell's Fold Stone Circle
- Moreton Corbet Castle
- Old Oswestry Hill Fort
- Stokesay Castle
- Wenlock Priory
- White Ladies Priory
- Wroxeter Roman City

Staffordshire

- Croxden Abbey
- Wall Roman Site

West Midlands

- Halesowen Abbey
- J.W. Evans Silver Factory

Warwickshire

- Kenilworth Castle and Elizabethan Garden

Worcestershire

- Leigh Court Barn
- Witley Court and Gardens

Severnside Outings

Shropshire's Ironbridge Gorge is now a serenely picturesque wooded valley, but when the revolutionary **Iron Bridge** itself was erected to span it in 1779, it was the roaring powerhouse of the Industrial Revolution. This is the ideal place to begin a day out among the ten museums of the Gorge, which offer English Heritage members a 20% discount on a museums 'passport'. Some reflect the many industries of the gorge, including Coalport china making, tile making, clay pipes and of course ironworking: you can also visit the homes of the Darby family of ironmasters and – most popular of all – wander the recreated Victorian streets, houses and shops of Blist's Hill.

A short distance upstream along the Severn stands a very different site, **Buildwas Abbey**, originally built 'far from the concourse of men'. Not far enough, however, to avoid a raid by vengeful tenants of its Welsh estates, who pillaged the monastery and kidnapped the abbot and monks in 1350. Today its most striking features are its late Norman church, with serried ranks of characteristic circular columns and round arches, and its beautiful early Gothic chapter house.

Older and further upstream again is **Wroxeter Roman City**, which as 'Viroconium' was once the fourth largest city in Roman Britain, and much later became one of Britain's first 'archaeological visitor attractions' following its rediscovery and partial excavation in 1859. The latest development in its story is the recreation there of a Roman town house, using traditional methods interpreted by seven modern building-trade workers. The associated Channel 4 television programme aired in January 2011 and its product – the town house – are well worth a look.

Make the most of your membership and keep up to date with upcoming events, the latest news and special offers by subscribing to our e-newsletter. Register online at **www.english-heritage.org.uk/newsletter** and we'll deliver the latest from English Heritage straight to your inbox.

Images:
(left) Iron Bridge
(top centre) Buildwas Abbey
(top right) Boscobel House and The Royal Oak
(bottom centre) Haughmond Abbey
(bottom right) Wroxeter Roman City

Check www.english-heritage.org.uk for the latest opening times

Acton Burnell Castle
Shropshire

The impressive red sandstone shell of a battlemented tower house mansion, built c. 1283-92 by Bishop Robert Burnell, Edward I's Lord Chancellor. Parliaments were twice held nearby, in 1283 and 1285.

OPENING TIMES

Open in daylight hours only

HOW TO FIND US

Direction: Located in Acton Burnell, signposted from A49, 8 miles S of Shrewsbury

Train: Shrewsbury or Church Stretton, both 8 miles

Bus: Boultons 540

MAP Page 280 (4B)
OS Map 126, 241: SJ534019

Arthur's Stone
Herefordshire

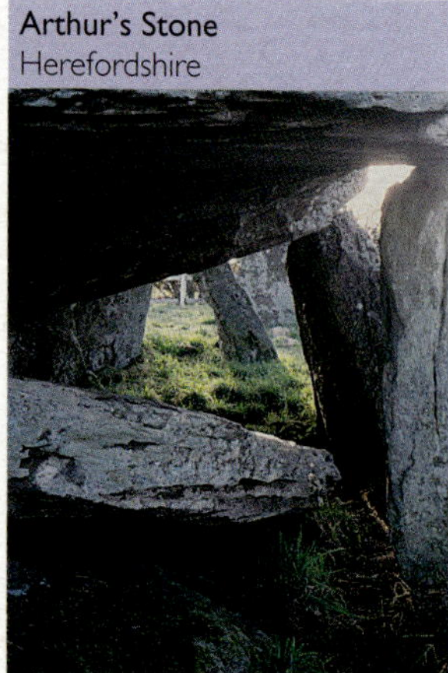

Arthur's Stone

An atmospheric Neolithic burial chamber made of great stone slabs, in the hills above Herefordshire's Golden Valley.

OPENING TIMES

Any reasonable time

HOW TO FIND US

Direction: 7 miles E of Hay-on-Wye off B4348 near Dorstone

Bus: Stagecoach in South Wales service 39; Yeomans Canyon service 39A (Sun) Hereford – Brecon to within ¾ mile

MAP Page 280 (7B)
OS Map 148/161, OL13/201: SO319431

Boscobel House and The Royal Oak
See feature opposite

Buildwas Abbey
Shropshire – TF8 7BW

Impressive ruins of a Cistercian abbey, including its unusually unaltered 12th-century church, beautiful vaulted and tile-floored chapter house and recently re-opened crypt chapel. In a wooded Severn-side setting, not far from the Iron Bridge and Wenlock Priory.

www.english-heritage.org.uk/buildwas

NON-MEMBERS

Adult	£3.40
Concession	£3.10
Child	£2.00

Buildwas Abbey

OPENING TIMES

1 Apr-30 Sep, Wed-Sun & Bank Hols	10am-5pm

HOW TO FIND US

Direction: On S bank of River Severn on A4169, 2 miles W of Ironbridge

Train: Telford Central 6 miles

Bus: Arriva Midlands service 96; M&J 860 (Tue)

Tel: 01952 433274

OVP

Disabled access is limited.

Nature trail (not managed by EH) including site of abbey fishponds.

MAP Page 280 (4C)
OS Map 127, 242: SJ643043

Cantlop Bridge
Shropshire

A single-span, cast-iron road bridge over the Cound Brook. Possibly designed and certainly approved by the great engineer Thomas Telford, who was instrumental in shaping industrial Shropshire and the West Midlands.

OPENING TIMES

Any reasonable time

HOW TO FIND US

Direction: ¾ mile SW of Berrington on an unclassified road off A458

Train: Shrewsbury 5 miles

Bus: Boultons 540

MAP Page 280 (4B)
OS Map 126, 241: SJ517062

Boscobel House and The Royal Oak

Shropshire – ST19 9AR

A pretty timber-framed house that played a brief but important role in English history, Boscobel was converted into a hunting lodge by John Giffard in about 1630. The Giffards were Roman Catholics and tradition holds that its real purpose was to serve as a secret refuge for persecuted Catholics at times of need.

Boscobel was destined for greater fame. Following the execution of King Charles I in 1649, his son made a brave though misguided attempt to regain the throne. Defeated in 1651 at Worcester, the final battle of the Civil War, young Charles fled for his life.

Initially Charles intended to cross the Severn into Wales, but found his way blocked by Cromwell's patrols. He sought refuge instead at Boscobel, hiding first in a tree, known afterwards as 'The Royal Oak', and then in a priest-hole in the house's attic. The future King Charles II then travelled on in disguise via other safe houses before escaping to France.

Boscobel became a much-visited place, although it remained a working farm. Today's visitors can enjoy our audio and visual displays; take a guided tour of the hunting lodge; see the garden and a descendant of the Royal Oak; and find out about Boscobel's past as a working Victorian farm.

There is a permissive path from Boscobel House to White Ladies Priory, another of Charles's hiding places.

www.english-heritage.org.uk/boscobel

NON-MEMBERS

Adult	£5.80
Concession	£5.20
Child	£3.50
Family	£15.10

OPENING TIMES

1 Apr-31 Oct, Wed-Sun & Bank Hols	10am-5pm

House will be closed for 1 hour at 11am and 2pm for guided tours. Guided tours are subject to availability and booking is advisable. Last entry 1 hour before closing

HOW TO FIND US

Direction: On minor road from A41 to A5, 8 miles NW of Wolverhampton. 5 mins drive from M54 J3

Train: Cosford 3 miles

Bus: Arriva/Midland service 3; Coastaliner 17 (Wed); Midland service 880

Tel: 01902 850244

E OVP

Parking (coaches welcome).

New guidebook.

MAP Page 280 (4C)
OS Map 127, 242: SJ838082

Goodrich Castle

Herefordshire – HR9 6HY

Goodrich stands majestically on a wooded hill commanding the passage of the River Wye into the picturesque valley of Symonds Yat.

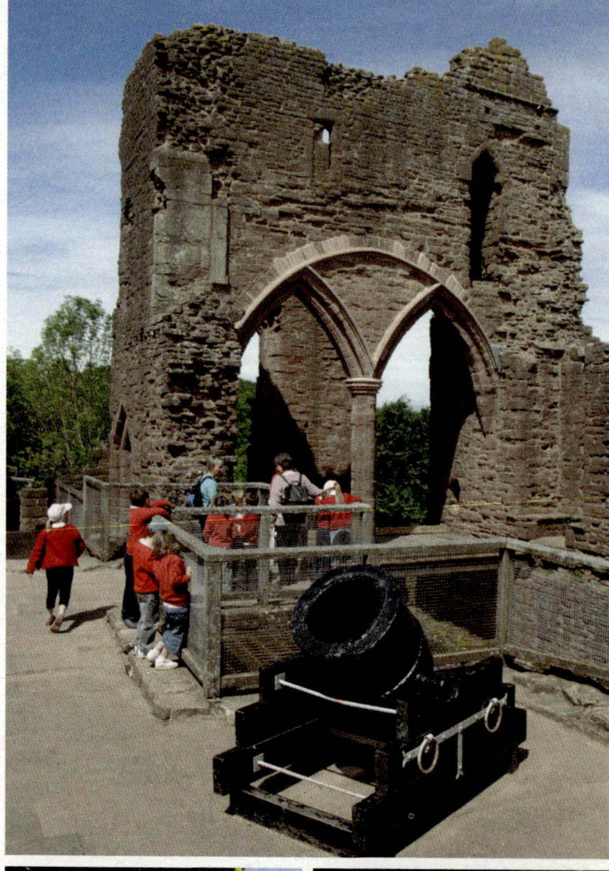

The café has lovely views of the beautiful surroundings and serves a fine selection of light refreshments made from locally-sourced Herefordshire ingredients.

Check www.english-heritage.org.uk for the latest opening times

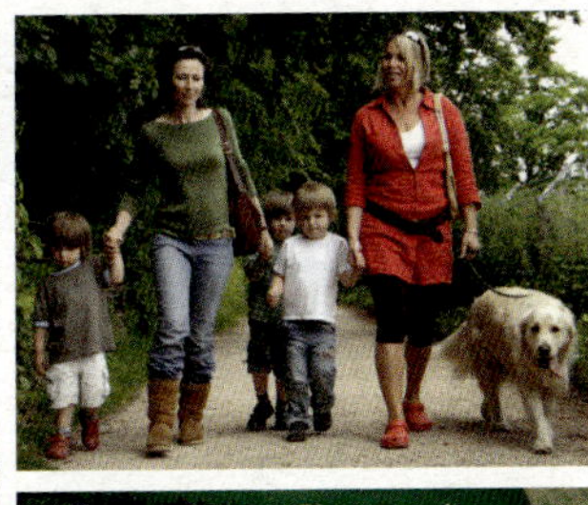

© Skyscan Balloon Photography

The castle was begun in the late 11th century by the English thegn Godric who gave it his name. A generation later the splendidly preserved square keep that still forms its core was added, probably in the time of Richard 'Strongbow' de Clare, Earl of Pembroke and Lord of Goodrich 1148-76.

Under King Richard the Lionheart, Goodrich was granted along with the earldom of Pembroke to the famous William Marshal, a great castle builder who may have initiated work on the inner ward. Each of Marshal's four sons inherited the fortress in turn, the last dying childless at Goodrich in 1245.

Thereafter the fortress and earldom passed to Henry III's half-brother, William de Valence, who rebuilt its defences and living quarters in the most up-to-date style.

Goodrich still boasts one of the most complete sets of medieval domestic buildings surviving in any English castle. William's widow Countess Joan frequently stayed here with an entourage of up to 200, entertaining her relations and friends in the most lavish style.

During the Civil War, Goodrich was held successively by both sides. Sir Henry Lingen's Royalists eventually surrendered in 1646 under threats of undermining and a deadly Parliamentarian mortar. Visitors can see the famous 'Roaring Meg', the only surviving Civil War mortar, which has returned to the castle after over 350 years, and a cache of Civil War cannonballs, found at Goodrich in the 1920s. The visitor centre features an exhibition exploring life at the castle from its late 11th-century origins until its dramatic fall in 1646, including Civil War artefacts.

Goodrich's café has lovely views of the beautiful surroundings and serves a fine selection of light refreshments made from locally-sourced Herefordshire ingredients.

www.english-heritage.org.uk/goodrich

NON-MEMBERS

Adult	£5.80
Concession	£5.20
Child	£3.50
Family	£15.10

OPENING TIMES

1 Apr-30 Jun, daily	10am-5pm
1 Jul-31 Aug, daily	10am-6pm
1 Sep-31 Oct, daily	10am-5pm
1 Nov-29 Feb, Wed-Sun	10am-4pm
1-31 Mar, Wed-Sun	10am-5pm
24-26 Dec and 1 Jan	Closed

HOW TO FIND US

Direction: 5 miles S of Ross-on-Wye off A40

Bus: H&H Coaches service 34 and 411 (Wed) to within ½ mile

Tel: 01600 890538

P OVP

A car parking charge of £2 applies (400 metres from the castle) to ensure that EH members and paying visitors have priority. The charge will be refunded on admission.

Dogs on leads.

Disabled access (limited, please call for details or ask the visitor centre on arrival).

The café will close one hour before the site closes, apart from Wed-Fri between 1 Nov-29 Feb when it will close at 2pm.

MAP Page 280 (7C)
OS Map 162, OL14: SO577200

Clun Castle
Shropshire

The dramatic riverside ruins and extensive earthworks of a Welsh Border castle, its tall 13th-century keep unusually set on the side of its mound.

Information panels tell the story of the castle and the nearby town.

OPENING TIMES
Any reasonable time

HOW TO FIND US
Direction: In Clun, off A488, 18 miles W of Ludlow

Train: Hopton Heath 6½ miles; Knighton 6½ miles

Bus: Minsterley/M&J 745; Shropshire County Council service 782 (Sat, Sun); M&J service 773 & 860 (Tue)

MAP Page 280 (5B)
OS Map 137, 201: SO299809

Croxden Abbey
Staffordshire

The impressive remains of an abbey of Cistercian 'white monks', including towering fragments of its 13th-century church, infirmary and 14th-century abbot's lodging. Information panels tell the story of the abbey's spectacular architecture.

OPENING TIMES
Daily	10am-5pm
24-26 Dec and 1 Jan	Closed

HOW TO FIND US
Direction: 5 miles NW of Uttoxeter off A522

Croxden Abbey

Train: Uttoxeter 6 miles

Bus: Closest service is Phil Smith 184 to Hollington. Otherwise First 32/32A or Alton Towers Transport 30 to Alton then 2½ mile walk

MAP Page 280 (3D)
OS Map 128, 259: SK066397

Edvin Loach Old Church
Herefordshire

The ruins of an 11th-century and later church built within the earthworks of a Norman motte and bailey castle, with a Victorian church nearby.

OPENING TIMES
Any reasonable time

HOW TO FIND US
Direction: Located 4 miles N of Bromyard on an unclassified road off B4203

Bus: Closest bus services are those to Bromyard (3½ miles) operated by First/DRM services 420, 469 and DRM service 482 (Fri only), 672 & 673. Veolia-Astons 405 (Wed only), 472; First 423

MAP Page 280 (6C)
OS Map 149, 202: SO663584

Goodrich Castle
See feature – Page 180

Halesowen Abbey
West Midlands – B62 8RJ

Remains of an abbey founded by King John in the 13th century.

OPENING TIMES
Sat 13 and Sun 14 Aug 11am-4pm

With thanks to the Halesowen Abbey Trust

HOW TO FIND US
Directions: Off A456, ½ mile W of J3, M5

Train: Old Hill 2½ miles

Halesowen Abbey

Please note there are no toilets on site.

MAP Page 280 (5D)
OS Map 139, 219: SO975828

Haughmond Abbey
Shropshire – SY4 4RW

The extensive remains of an Augustinian abbey, including its abbots' quarters, refectory and cloister. The substantially surviving chapter house has a frontage richly bedecked with 12th and 14th-century carving and statuary and a fine timber roof of c. 1500. Pictorial interpretation boards guide the visitor and an introductory exhibition displays archaeological finds. Picnic area and light refreshments available.

www.english-heritage.org.uk/haughmond

NON-MEMBERS
Adult	£3.40
Concession	£3.10
Child	£2.00

OPENING TIMES
1 Apr-30 Sep, Wed-Sun & Bank Hols 10am-5pm

HOW TO FIND US
Direction: Located 3 miles NE of Shrewsbury off B5062

Train: Shrewsbury 3½ miles

Bus: Arriva 519 Shrewsbury – Newport

Tel: 01743 709661

OVP

Disabled access (not easy).

MAP Page 280 (4B)
OS Map 126, 241: SJ542152

Iron Bridge Shropshire

The world's first iron bridge was erected over the River Severn here in 1779. Britain's best-known industrial monument, the bridge gave its name to the spectacular wooded gorge which, though now tranquil, was once an industrial powerhouse and the cradle of the Industrial Revolution. Ironbridge Gorge is now a World Heritage Site.

At the beginning of the 18th century, Abraham Darby I pioneered the process of using coke made from local coal to smelt local iron ore, but industrial expansion was hampered by the lack of a bridge over the Severn, which had to be a single span to allow for barge traffic. An iron bridge was first suggested by the Shrewsbury architect Thomas Pritchard: he designed a single span-bridge 30 metres long, but died as work began. The project was then taken over by Abraham Darby III, who cast the bridge in his Coalbrookdale foundry, using 378 tons of iron. Recent research shows that most parts were individually cast to fit, each being slightly different from the next: and that traditional woodworking-style joints were adapted to assemble them.

Costing over £6000, this proclamation of the achievements of Shropshire ironmasters was formally opened on New Year's Day 1781. It continued in full use by ever-increasing traffic until closed and designated an Ancient Monument in 1934. Massive strengthening works were later undertaken, and in 1999-2000 English Heritage assisted with a full survey of this revolutionary and iconic structure.

The Iron Bridge is the perfect place to begin a tour of the Gorge's many museums and the many other English Heritage sites nearby, including Buildwas Abbey, Wenlock Priory and Wroxeter Roman City.

OPENING TIMES

Any reasonable time

HOW TO FIND US

Direction: Adjacent to A4169

Bus: Arriva 9, 39, 99, 76, 77, 96; Gorge Connect service WH1 (summer Sat, Sun)

MAP Page 280 (4C)
OS Map 127, 242: SJ672034

J. W. Evans Silver Factory

Birmingham – B1 3EA

Established in 1881, J. W. Evans is one of the most complete surviving historic factories in Birmingham's Jewellery Quarter. Behind the frontage of four terraced houses, the workshops retain their original drop stamps and fly presses, They are packed with thousands of dies for the manufacture of silverware, as well as the whole of the working equipment, stock and records of the business. To walk into the factory today is to enter a lost industrial world.

English Heritage stepped in to rescue the factory in 2008. With the completion of the repairs programme, the site will open to the public in summer 2011 on a pre-booked and guided-tour basis only.

www.english-heritage.org.uk/jwevans

OPENING TIMES

By pre-booked tour only – please call for details or visit our website

HOW TO FIND US

Direction: Located ½ mile from Birmingham City Centre. 54-57 Albion Street

Train: Jewellery Quarter 5 minutes, New Street ½ mile

Bus: From surrounding areas

Tel: 0870 333 1181

MAP Page 280 (5D)
OS Map 139, 220: SP062870

Kenilworth Castle and Elizabethan Garden

See feature – Page 186

Langley Chapel
Shropshire

A small chapel tranquilly set all alone in charming countryside. Its atmospheric interior contains a perfect set of 17th-century timber furnishings, including a musicians' pew.

OPENING TIMES

1 Mar-31 Oct, daily	10am-5pm
1 Nov-29 Feb, daily	10am-4pm
24-26 Dec and 1 Jan	Closed

HOW TO FIND US

Direction: 1½ miles S of Acton Burnell, on an unclassified road off A49; 9½ miles S of Shrewsbury

Train: Shrewsbury 9½ miles

Bus: Boultons 540 (then 1¼ mile walk)

MAP Page 280 (5B)
OS Map 126/127/138, 217/241: SJ538001

Leigh Court Barn
Worcestershire

An outstanding display of English medieval carpentry, this mighty timber-framed barn is the largest cruck structure in Britain. Built for Pershore Abbey in 1344, it is 46 metres (150 feet) long, with 18 cruck blades each made from a single oak tree.

OPENING TIMES

1 Apr-30 Sep, Thu-Sun and Bank Hols	10am-5pm

HOW TO FIND US

Direction: 5 miles W of Worcester on an unclassified road off A4103

Train: Worcester Foregate Street 5 miles

Leigh Court Barn

Bus: Veolia-Astons service 417 or First 423 & 425 (Fri) to within 1 mile

MAP Page 280 (6C)
OS Map 150, 204: SO783535

Lilleshall Abbey
Shropshire

Extensive ruins of an Augustinian abbey, later a Civil War stronghold, in a deeply rural setting. Much of the church survives, unusually viewable from gallery level, along with the lavishly sculpted processional door and other cloister buildings. Graphic panels show how the abbey appeared in medieval times.

OPENING TIMES

1 Apr-30 Sep, daily	10am-5pm
1 Oct-31 Mar	Closed

HOW TO FIND US

Direction: On an unclassified road off A518, 4 miles N of Oakengates

Train: Oakengates 4½ miles

Bus: Arriva 481 Telford – Stafford (passes close to ≹ Telford Central and Stafford) to within 1 mile

MAP Page 280 (4C)
OS Map 127, 242: SJ738142

Longtown Castle
Herefordshire

Built within an earlier square earthwork, Longtown Castle is a powerful, thick-walled round keep of c. 1200, characteristic of the Welsh Borders, on a large earthen mound within a stone-walled bailey. Set in the beautiful Olchon valley, with magnificent views of the Black Mountains.

OPENING TIMES

Any reasonable time

HOW TO FIND US

Direction: Located 4 miles WSW of Abbey Dore, off B4347

Longtown Castle

Bus: Abbey Cars service 441 (Wed) & 442 (Tue); Roy Brown Coaches (summer service) B17

MAP Page 280 (7B)
OS Map 161, OL13: SO321291

Mitchell's Fold Stone Circle
Shropshire

A Bronze Age stone circle, the focus of many legends, set in dramatic moorland on Stapeley Hill. It once consisted of some 30 stones, 15 of which are still visible.

OPENING TIMES

Any reasonable time

HOW TO FIND US

Direction: 16 miles SW of Shrewsbury

Train: Welshpool 10 miles

Bus: Minsterley Motors service 553 Shrewsbury – Bishop's Castle (passes close to ≹ Shrewsbury) to within 1 mile

MAP Page 280 (5B)
OS Map 137, 216: SO304984

Moreton Corbet Castle
Shropshire

The ruins of the medieval castle and Tudor manor house of the Corbets are dominated by the theatrical shell of an ambitious Elizabethan mansion wing in Italianate style, which was devastated during the Civil War. Fine Corbet monuments fill the adjacent church.

OPENING TIMES

Open in daylight hours only

Moreton Corbet Castle

HOW TO FIND US

Direction: In Moreton Corbet off B5063 (a turning off A49), 7 miles NE of Shrewsbury

Train: Yorton 4 miles

Bus: Arriva service 64

Guidebook from Buildwas and Haughmond Abbeys.

MAP Page 280 (4C)
OS Map 126, 241: SJ561231

Mortimer's Cross Water Mill
Herefordshire – HR6 9PE

This one-man-operated water mill is remarkable for being so complete and in such good condition. It is owned and managed by Mr C Partington. Special day and evening tours are available by arrangement with the owner. Please call for details.

NON-MEMBERS

Adult	£4.00
Concession	£3.50
Child	£2.50

OPENING TIMES

1 Apr-30 Sep, Sun & Bank Hol Mons	10am-4pm
Other times by arrangement	
Access to the mill is by guided tour only:	11am, 1pm & 3pm

HOW TO FIND US

Direction: Located 7 miles NW of Leominster on B4362

Train: Leominster 7½ miles

Bus: The Little Bus Co 489 (Tue, Fri); Lugg Valley 491 (1st, 3rd & 5th Wed), 494 (Sun), 498 (2nd & 4th Wed), 802 (Sun)

Mortimer's Cross Water Mill

Tel: 01568 708820

Disabled access (exterior and ground floor only).

Warning: there are steep river banks and sluice channels which are hazardous at all times.

MAP Page 280 (6B)
OS Map 137/148/149, 203: SO426637

Old Oswestry Hill Fort
Shropshire

Among the most hugely impressive Iron Age hillforts on the Welsh Borders, covering 40 acres, with formidable multiple ramparts.

Information panels tell you about the hillfort and its inhabitants.

OPENING TIMES

Any reasonable time

HOW TO FIND US

Direction: 1 mile N of Oswestry, off an unclassified road off A483

Train: Gobowen 2 miles

Bus: Arriva service 2 and then a short walk

MAP Page 280 (3B)
OS Map 126, 240/258: SJ295310

Rotherwas Chapel
Herefordshire

The family chapel of the Roman Catholic Bodenham family. The originally simple medieval building has a fine Elizabethan timber roof, a rebuilt 18th-century tower, and striking Victorian interior decoration and furnishings by the Pugins.

OPENING TIMES

Any reasonable time. Key keeper located at nearby filling station

HOW TO FIND US

Direction: 1½ miles SE of Hereford on B4399, left into Chapel Road

Rotherwas Chapel

Train: Hereford 3½ miles

Bus: First service 78, 78A; First/ Yeoman 82 then ½ mile walk

Disabled access via kissing gate only.

MAP Page 280 (7B)
OS Map 149, 189: SO536383

Stokesay Castle
See feature – Page 190

Wall Roman Site (Letocetum)
Staffordshire – WS14 0AW

Wall was an important staging post on Watling Street, the Roman military road to North Wales. It provided overnight accommodation for travelling Roman officials and imperial messengers. The foundations of an inn and bathhouse can be seen and many of the excavated finds are displayed in the on-site museum.

Managed by English Heritage on behalf of the National Trust, with thanks to the Friends of Letocetum.

www.english-heritage.org.uk/wall

OPENING TIMES

Site

1 Mar-31 Oct, daily	10am-5pm
1 Nov-29 Feb, daily	10am-4pm
24-26 Dec and 1 Jan	Closed

Museum

23-25 Apr, 30 Apr, 1 & 2 May, 28-30 May, 25 & 26 Jun, 17, 24, 30 & 31 Jul, 7, 14, 21, 27-29 Aug, 4, 24 & 25 Sep, 29 & 30 Oct	11am-4pm
1 Nov-29 Feb	Closed

HOW TO FIND US

Direction: Off A5 at Wall, near Lichfield

Train: Shenstone 1½ miles

Bus: Heartlands Bus (Invincible Coaches of Tamworth) service 81

MAP Page 280 (4D)
OS Map 139, 244: SK098066

Kenilworth Castle and Elizabethan Garden

Warwickshire – CV8 1NE

A vast medieval fortress which became an Elizabethan palace, Kenilworth Castle is one of Britain's largest and most impressive historic sites. Extensive developments here highlight Kenilworth's famous associations with Queen Elizabeth I and her favourite, Robert Dudley; most spectacularly the re-creation of the fabulous garden, which Dudley commissioned to astound visitors – especially Queen Elizabeth!

The re-created Elizabethan garden features a bejewelled Renaissance aviary, magnificent carved arbours, an 18-foot high marble fountain and a planting scheme abundant in colour, perfume and fruit.

In the impressively-timbered Tudor stables, which now house the castle's tearoom, trebuchet balls from the 1266 siege can be seen in the fascinating interactive display on the castle's history.

Spanning more than five centuries, Kenilworth's varied buildings and architectural styles reflect its long connection with successive English monarchs. Geoffrey de Clinton, Henry I's treasurer, began the massive Norman keep at the core of the fortress in the 1120s, and under Henry II Kenilworth became a royal castle. King John greatly strengthened it between 1210 and 1215, enlarging the surrounding watery 'mere' which effectively made it an island stronghold. Thus it could withstand an epic siege in 1266, when rebellious barons held out against Henry III's siege engines for six months, succumbing only to starvation. In the impressively-timbered Tudor stables, which now house the castle's tearoom, trebuchet balls from the siege can be seen in the fascinating interactive display on the castle's history.

During the late 14th century John of Gaunt, Duke of Lancaster, rebuilt the splendid great hall and staterooms of Kenilworth's inner court, beginning the castle's transition into a palace and favourite residence of the Lancastrian and early Tudor kings. Here Henry V received the insulting French 'gift' of tennis-balls which sparked off the Agincourt campaign, and by Henry VIII's time the castle was already renowned for its 'many fair chambers'. The scene was set for Kenilworth's greatest period of fame.

This began when Queen Elizabeth's favourite, Robert Dudley, Earl of Leicester, took possession of the castle in 1563. He then lavished fortunes on converting it into a great 'prodigy house', designed to receive the Queen and her court on their ceremonial 'progresses' around her realm. Striking evidence of Dudley's transformation can still be seen everywhere at Kenilworth. Not content with remodelling its existing structures, he added the tall, mansion-sized 'Leicester's Building' – complete with a 'dancing chamber' on its top floor – specifically for the Queen's use as well as an imposing new entrance to his quasi-royal palace, 'Leicester's Gatehouse'.

As part of a multi-million pound English Heritage investment in Kenilworth Castle, Leicester's Gatehouse is displayed with the chambers on its lower floors re-created as they might have appeared when the gatehouse was last inhabited in the 1930s, while the top floor houses *'The Queen and the Castle: Robert Dudley's Kenilworth'*. Featuring items both from museums and private collections, this exhibition tells the story of Elizabeth I's relationship with Dudley and her four visits to Kenilworth.

On the last and most famous of these visits, in July 1575, Elizabeth stayed here for 19 days – her longest sojourn in a courtier's house during any of her progresses. Dudley not only entertained her lavishly throughout with music, dancing, hunting and plays; he also created specially for her visit a fabulous garden, the re-creation of which is English Heritage's latest contribution to Kenilworth's long history.

A bejewelled Renaissance aviary; magnificent carved arbours; a planting scheme abundant in colour, perfume and fruit and an 18-foot-high fountain carved from dazzling Carrara marble. These are just some of the glories of Robert Dudley's garden at Kenilworth Castle. In an age famous for its extravagance, it was designed to score off rival aristocratic garden-creators, but principally to astound visitors, including Elizabeth I.

This garden, lost for centuries, has been brought back to life by a pioneering team of historians, archaeologists, plantsmen and plantswomen, designers, craftspeople and gardeners.

Check www.english-heritage.org.uk for the latest opening times

Available for corporate and private hire

Licensed for civil wedding ceremonies

It presents the most complete evocation of an Elizabethan garden anywhere in the world – a garden to seduce and beguile visitors today, just as it did in 1575.

Such an outstandingly comprehensive re-creation of Elizabethan garden architecture, design, statuary and planting has never been attempted on this scale before. It has been made possible by important advances in garden archaeology and the survival of an extraordinary eye-witness description of the Kenilworth garden, written by Robert Langham in 1575. Thus a garden that was once the 'glory of England' can once again be admired at this most romantic of castles. It opens a window on the period's most enduring love story – that of Elizabeth I and her favourite, Robert Dudley.

Though largely unscathed during the Civil War, Kenilworth was afterwards rendered indefensible and gradually fell into dilapidation. Made famous by Walter Scott's romantic novel, *Kenilworth* (1821), it came into state guardianship in 1938.

www.english-heritage.org.uk/kenilworth

NON-MEMBERS

Adult	£8.00
Concession	£7.20
Child	£4.80
Family	£20.80

OPENING TIMES

1 Apr-31 Oct, daily	10am-5pm
1 Nov-29 Feb, daily	10am-4pm
1-31 Mar, daily	10am-5pm
24-26 Dec and 1 Jan	Closed

Note: the gatehouse may close early for private events, please check the website for details

HOW TO FIND US

Direction: In Kenilworth off A46. Clearly signposted from the town centre, off B4103

Train: Warwick or Coventry 5 miles

Bus: Johnsons of Henley 540 & 541 pass the castle site; Travel West Midlands 12; Johnsons 539 & 543 and Stagecoach U2, 16 & X17 all from surrounding area

Tel: 01926 852078

Local Tourist Information
Kenilworth: 01926 748900

Audio tours available (English, French, German and a children's version), except Bank Holiday weekends.

From Nov-Mar tearoom only open Fri, Sat & Sun and for groups by prior arrangement, please phone the site to book.

A car parking charge applies to ensure that EH members and paying visitors have priority. The charge will be refunded on admission, except on Bank Holiday weekends.

MAP Page 280 (5E)
OS Map 140, 221: SP278723

Wenlock Priory
Shropshire – TF13 6HS

The tranquil ruins of Wenlock Priory stand in a picturesque setting on the fringe of beautiful Much Wenlock. An Anglo-Saxon monastery was founded here in about 680 by King Merewalh of Mercia, whose abbess daughter Milburge was hailed as a saint. Her relics were miraculously re-discovered here in 1101, attracting both pilgrims and prosperity to the priory.

By then Wenlock had been re-founded by the Normans as a priory of Cluniac monks. It is the impressive remains of this medieval priory that survive today, everywhere reflecting the Cluniac love of elaborate decoration. Parts of the great 13th-century church still stand high; and in the adjoining cloister garth is a most unusual monks' washing fountain, embellished with 12th-century carvings. Once enclosed in an octagonal building, 16 monks could wash here at once before eating in the nearby refectory.

Perhaps the greatest glory is the extravagantly decorated chapter house of about 1140, its walls bedecked with blind arcading on multiple carved columns.

All this is enhanced by the famous topiary-filled cloister garden and set against the backdrop of the complete infirmary wing, converted into a mansion after the priory's dissolution and still a private residence. Much Wenlock was also the home of Dr William Penny Brookes (1809-95), originator of the still-continuing Wenlock Olympian Games, a major inspiration for the modern International Olympics. The town's connection with the Olympics is the inspiration for 'Wenlock', a London 2012 Olympic mascot.

www.english-heritage.org.uk/wenlockpriory

NON-MEMBERS

Adult	£4.00
Concession	£3.60
Child	£2.40

OPENING TIMES

1-30 Apr, Wed-Sun & Bank Hols	10am-5pm
1 May-31 Aug, daily	10am-5pm
1 Sep-31 Oct, Wed-Sun	10am-5pm
1 Nov-29 Feb, Thu-Sun	10am-4pm
1-31 Mar, Wed-Sun	10am-5pm
24-26 Dec and 1 Jan	Closed

HOW TO FIND US

Direction: In Much Wenlock

Train: Telford Central 9 miles

Bus: Arriva service 39 & 436

Tel: 01952 727466

OVP

MAP Page 280 (5C)
OS Map 127/138, 217/242: SJ625001

White Ladies Priory
Shropshire

Ruins of the late 12th-century church of a small nunnery of 'white ladies' or Augustinian canonesses. Charles II came here in 1651 before seeking refuge at nearby Boscobel House.

Permissive path from Boscobel House to White Ladies Priory.

OPENING TIMES

Open in daylight hours only

HOW TO FIND US

Direction: Located 1 mile SW of Boscobel House off an unclassified road between A41 and A5; 8 miles NW of Wolverhampton

Train: Cosford 2½ miles

Bus: Arriva/Midland service 3; Coastaliner 17 (Wed); Midland service 880 then 1 mile walk

MAP Page 280 (4C)
OS Map 217, 242: SJ826076

Wigmore Castle
Herefordshire

Once the stronghold of the turbulent Mortimer family, Wigmore Castle was later dismantled to prevent its use during the Civil War. Now it is among the most remarkable ruins in England. Largely buried up to first floor level by earth and fallen masonry, yet many of its fortifications survive to full height, including parts of the keep on its towering mound. Graphic panels tell the story of this important medieval castle, now conserved for its wildlife habitats as well as its historic interest.

OPENING TIMES

Any reasonable time

HOW TO FIND US

Direction: Located 8 miles W of Ludlow on A4110. Accessible via footpath ¾ mile from the village on Mortimer Way

Train: Bucknell 6 miles, Ludlow 10 miles

Bus: The Little Bus Co 489 (Tue, Fri); Lugg Valley 490 (Mon), 491 (1st, 3rd & 5th Wed), 498 (2nd & 4th Wed), 802 (Sun); Veolia Cymru X11 (Mon)

Toilets (including disabled) at the Village Hall.

There are steep steps to the summit, which are hazardous in icy conditions. Children must stay under close control and should not climb the walls or banks. Strong footwear is recommended. There is no staff presence.

MAP Page 280 (6B)
OS Map 137/148, 203: SO408693

Stokesay Castle

Shropshire – SY7 9AH

Stokesay Castle is quite simply the finest and best preserved fortified medieval manor house in England. Set in peaceful countryside near the Welsh border, the castle, timber-framed gatehouse and parish church form an unforgettably picturesque group.

An audio tour will help you to imagine Stokesay as the centre of medieval life. Its grounds include cottage-style gardens, a tearoom open from April to October, and a gift shop.

Check www.english-heritage.org.uk for the latest opening times

Lawrence of Ludlow, a wealthy local wool-merchant wishing to set up as a country gentleman, bought the property in 1281, when the long Anglo-Welsh wars were ending. So it was safe to raise here one of the first fortified manor houses in England, 'builded like a castle' for effect but lit by large domestic-style windows.

Extensive recent tree-ring dating confirms that Lawrence had completed virtually the whole of the still-surviving house by 1291, using the same team of carpenters throughout. More remarkably, the dating also revealed that it has scarcely been altered since.

Stokesay's magnificent open-hearthed great hall displays a fine timber roof, shuttered gable windows and a precipitous staircase, its treads cut from whole tree-trunks. It is flanked by the north tower, with an original medieval tiled floor and remains of a wall painting, and a 'solar' or private apartment block and beyond this is the tall south tower – the most castle-like part of the house, self-contained and reached by a defensible stairway.

The solar block contains one of the few post-medieval alterations to the house, a fine panelled chamber. Its dominating feature is a fireplace with a richly carved overmantel, still bearing clear traces of original painting in five colours. This was added in about 1641, at the same time as the truly delightful gatehouse: an outstanding and recently-conserved example of the Marches style of lavishly showy timber-framing, bedecked with charming carvings of Adam and Eve.

A few years later, in 1645, Stokesay experienced its only known military encounter, surrendering without fighting to a Parliamentarian force. So the house remained undamaged and sensitive conservation by Victorian owners and English Heritage have left it the medieval jewel which survives today.

An audio tour helps you to imagine Stokesay as a centre of medieval life. Its grounds include beautiful cottage-style gardens, a tearoom open from April to October, and a gift shop.

www.english-heritage.org.uk/stokesaycastle

NON-MEMBERS

Adult	£5.80
Concession	£5.20
Child	£3.50
Family	£15.10

OPENING TIMES

1 Apr-30 Sep, daily	10am-5pm
1-31 Oct, Wed-Sun	10am-5pm
1 Nov-29 Feb, Thu-Sun	10am-4pm
1-31 Mar, Wed-Sun	10am-5pm
24-26 Dec and 1 Jan	Closed

HOW TO FIND US

Direction: 7 miles NW of Ludlow off A49

Train: Craven Arms 1 mile

Bus: Minsterley Motors (of Stiperstones) 435 to Stokesay turning on the A49 then ½ mile walk

Tel: 01588 672544

Local Tourist Information
Ludlow: 01584 875053

A car parking charge of £2 applies to ensure EH members and paying visitors have priority. The charge will be refunded on admission.

Disabled access (call site for details).

Entrance to the courtyard is through an historic gate. Unsuitable for motorised scooters and unassisted wheelchair users.

Tearoom (Seasonal: 1 Apr-31 Oct).

MAP Page 280 (5B)
OS Map 137/148, 203: SO446787

Check www.english-heritage.org.uk for the latest opening times

Witley Court and Gardens

Worcestershire – WR6 6JT

A hundred years ago, Witley Court was one of England's great country houses, hosting many extravagant parties. Today it is a spectacular ruin, the result of a disastrous fire in 1937. Restoration work to the West Wing has made several new rooms accessible to the public.

The largest of Witley Court's huge stone fountains represents Perseus and Andromeda, which in its day was described as making the 'noise of an express train' when fired.

East Parterre

Major restoration works in the East Parterre garden have recently been completed. Based on two years of archaeological investigation and old photographs of the garden in its prime, a scrollwork of box hedges has been planted, interspersed with areas of coloured gravels and colourful bedding plant displays. Said to resemble embroidery, it is truly beautiful.

The vast and rambling remains of the palatial 19th-century mansion are surrounded by magnificent landscaped gardens, which still contain huge stone fountains. The largest, representing Perseus and Andromeda – now restored – was described as making the 'noise of an express train' when fired.

Before 1846, when William Humble Ward (later first Earl of Dudley) inherited Witley Court, the land surrounding the house was laid out in the 18th-century English landscape style. As part of Ward's transformation of the estate, he called in the leading landscape designer of the time, William Andrews Nesfield, whose skills in designing intricate and elegant parterres were complemented by his great ability as an artist and engineer.

Nesfield started work in 1854, creating the South Parterre with its great Perseus and Andromeda fountain. His scheme involved elegantly designed plantings and parterres of clipped evergreens and shrubs. The East Parterre garden, with its Flora Fountain, was designed in the Parterre de Broderie style, resembling embroidery.

Following the disastrous fire in 1937 the Witley Estate, including its gardens, fell into long decline. English Heritage has now restored the south garden. In addition, Wolfson Foundation funding has assisted with recently-completed major restoration works in the East Parterre garden, based on two years of archaeological investigation and old photographs of the garden in its prime. A scrollwork pattern of box hedges has been planted, interspersed with areas of coloured gravels and colourful bedding plant displays. The showpiece Woodland Walks in the North Park pass many different species of tree and shrub from all over the world.

Close to Witley Court is Great Witley Church (not managed by English Heritage), with its amazing Italianate Baroque interior. The church has a tearoom and Witley Court has a superb gift shop. The restored Perseus and Andromeda fountain, with the original high cascades operating, will be firing between April and October. (Weekdays: 11am, 12pm, 2pm, 3pm and 4pm. Weekends: on the hour every hour from 11am to 4pm.)

Holiday cottage available to let

NON-MEMBERS

Adult	£6.30
Concession	£5.70
Child	£3.80
Family	£16.40

OPENING TIMES

1 Apr-30 Jun, daily	10am-5pm
1 Jul-31 Aug, daily	10am-6pm
1 Sep-31 Oct, daily	10am-5pm
1 Nov-29 Feb, Wed-Sun	10am-4pm
1-31 Mar, Wed-Sun	10am-5pm
24-26 Dec and 1 Jan	Closed

HOW TO FIND US

Direction: 10 miles NW of Worcester on A443

Train: Worcester Foregate St 9½ miles

Bus: Yarranton 758 Worcester – Tenbury Wells (passes close to Worcester Foregate St)

Tel: 01299 896636

Local Tourist Information
Worcester: 01905 726311

P OVP

Disabled access (exterior and grounds only). A terrain guide is available on the website.

Tearooms open daily, Apr-Sep, Sat and Sun in Oct (not managed by EH).

MAP Page 280 (6C)
OS Map 138/150, 204: SO769649

Wroxeter Roman City Shropshire – SY5 6PH

© Paul Highnam

Wroxeter (or 'Viroconium') was the fourth largest city in Roman Britain. It began as a legionary fortress and later developed into a thriving civilian city, populated by retired soldiers and traders. Though much still remains below ground, today the most impressive features are the 2nd-century municipal baths and the remains of the huge wall dividing them from the exercise hall in the heart of the city. The site museum and audio tour reveal how Wroxeter worked in its heyday and the health and beauty practices of its 5000 citizens. Dramatic archaeological discoveries provide a glimpse of the last years of the Roman city and its possible conversion into the headquarters of a 5th century British or Irish warlord.

www.english-heritage.org.uk/wroxeter

NEW FOR 2011

A Roman Town House has been created at Wroxeter, as filmed for Channel 4. Come and see how modern builders have fared constructing this house using historic building methods.

NON-MEMBERS

Adult	£4.80
Concession	£4.30
Child	£2.90
Family	£12.50

OPENING TIMES

1 Apr-31 Oct, daily	10am-5pm
1 Nov-29 Feb, Wed-Sun	10am-4pm
1-31 Mar, daily	10am-5pm
24-26 Dec and 1 Jan	Closed

HOW TO FIND US

Direction: Located at Wroxeter, 5 miles E of Shrewsbury on B4380

Train: Shrewsbury 5½ miles; Wellington Telford West 6 miles

Bus: Arriva 96 Telford – Shrewsbury (passes close to Telford Central)

Tel: 01743 761330

OVP

A car parking charge of £2 applies to ensure EH members and paying visitors have priority. The charge will be refunded on admission.

MAP Page 280 (4B)
OS Map 126, 241: SJ565087

Associated attractions in the West Midlands

These visitor attractions, all independent of EH, offer discounts to our members. Please call before you visit to confirm details. A valid EH membership card must be produced for each member.

Eastnor Castle
Herefordshire HR8 1RL

Eastnor is a dramatic, fairytale castle situated in a 5000-acre estate in the Malvern Hills, within an Area of Outstanding Natural Beauty. The castle is surrounded by a lake, deer park and arboretum, with magnificent views of the rolling Herefordshire countryside.

10 mins from J2 of M50

Tel: 01531 633160

www.eastnorcastle.com

50% discount on entry

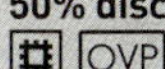 OVP 1

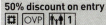

Heritage Motor Centre
Warwickshire CV35 0BJ

The Centre is home to the world's largest collection of historic British cars. Fun for everyone: Museum, Go-Karts, 4x4 Experience, café, shop. Check website for holiday activities and special events.

30 mins to Kenilworth Castle

Tel: 01926 641188

www.heritage-motor-centre.co.uk

2 for 1 museum entry

1

Ironbridge Gorge Museums
Shropshire TF8 7DQ

The ten Ironbridge Gorge Museums offer a remarkable insight into the industrial heritage of the area. Walk around the recreated streets and meet the Victorians at Blists Hill Victorian Town.

2 miles from the Iron Bridge

Tel: 01952 433424

www.ironbridge.org.uk

20% Passport Discount

Stoneleigh Abbey
Warwickshire CV8 2LF

Riverside gardens, stunning state rooms, Queen Victoria's bedroom, medieval Gatehouse, Regency stables, Jane Austen tours with guides in period costume, 'Through the Keyhole' tours of private residences and traditional tea room.

5 mins from Kenilworth Castle

Tel: 01926 858535

www.stoneleighabbey.org

15% discount on entry
to house and gardens

The Wedgwood Museum
Staffordshire ST12 9ER

Home of one of the world's most interesting ceramic collections, the Wedgwood Museum's galleries tell the story of Josiah Wedgwood, his family, and the company he founded two-and-a-half centuries ago.

10 mins from J15 of M6

Tel: 01782 371900

www.wedgwoodmuseum.org.uk

25% discount on entry

OVP

Warwick Castle
Warwickshire CV34 4QU

Immerse yourself in a thousand years of history – come rain or shine. See lavishly decorated state rooms, walk the towers and ramparts, or explore the 60 acres of glorious landscaped grounds and gardens. It could only be Warwick Castle.

Close to Kenilworth Castle

www.warwick-castle.com

50% discount on entry

2

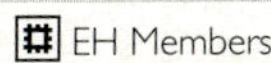 EH Members OVP OVP Holders ? Discounted Child Places Included

Middleham Castle: Statue of Richard III – see page 208

Yorkshire & The Humber

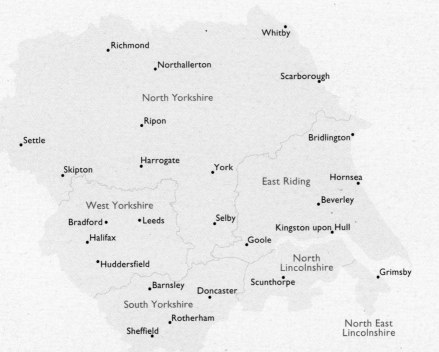

Whitby
Richmond
Northallerton
Scarborough
North Yorkshire
Ripon
Settle
Bridlington
Harrogate
Skipton
York
East Riding
Hornsea
West Yorkshire
Beverley
Bradford
Leeds
Selby
Kingston upon Hull
Halifax
Goole
North Lincolnshire
Huddersfield
Grimsby
Scunthorpe
Barnsley
Doncaster
South Yorkshire
Rotherham
North East Lincolnshire
Sheffield

Introducing
Yorkshire and The Humber

Remember to check opening times before you visit any of our properties.

Details of all bus travel in England are available from Traveline on 0871 200 2233 or visit www.traveline.org.uk

East Riding of Yorkshire

Burton Agnes Manor House
Howden Minster
Skipsea Castle

North Lincolnshire

Gainsthorpe Medieval Village
St Peter's Church, Barton-upon-Humber
Thornton Abbey and Gatehouse

North Yorkshire

Aldborough Roman Site
Byland Abbey
Clifford's Tower
Easby Abbey
Helmsley Castle
Kirkham Priory
Marmion Tower
Middleham Castle
Mount Grace Priory
Pickering Castle
Piercebridge Roman Bridge
Richmond Castle
Rievaulx Abbey
St Mary's Church, Studley Royal
Scarborough Castle
Spofforth Castle
Stanwick Iron Age Fortifications
Steeton Hall Gateway
Wharram Percy Deserted Medieval Village
Wheeldale Roman Road
Whitby Abbey
York Cold War Bunker

South Yorkshire

Brodsworth Hall and Gardens
Conisbrough Castle
Monk Bretton Priory
Roche Abbey

Yorkshire Variety

Yorkshire provides opportunities for many single-centre days out and one of the most varied is based on the Ryedale market town of Helmsley. The star here for many is **Helmsley Castle**, a very short stroll from the impressive market place around which – like so many old North Yorkshire towns – Helmsley is arranged. With its stupendous earthwork ramparts, dominant keep-like east tower and Elizabethan mansion range, as well as a visitor centre and recently-installed hands-on displays, the great castle is also a good place to get an overview of the surrounding landscape. Not far away, and also accessible from the town, is Duncombe Park (with discounted entry for English Heritage members), the mansion which succeeded Helmsley Castle in the early 18th century, and for which indeed the old fortress was preserved as a 'romantic eyecatcher'.

The castle also forms the backdrop to charming Helmsley Walled Garden, which once grew produce for Duncombe Park and has been lovingly restored as a fully working 5-acre Victorian kitchen garden by a local charity, offering a tranquil environment for those in need. Just by its entrance runs the Cleveland Way long-distance footpath, tempting the reasonably fit to the 3½ mile walk to another tranquil place, **Rievaulx Abbey**. The comparatively few 'ups and downs' along the way are more than repaid by the views, and of course by the abbey itself in its unrivalled Rye-side setting. Founded by Walter Espec of Helmsley Castle, this is surely among the most complete and imposing monastic ruins in all Britain. And whether you walk or drive there, Rievaulx also has a tearoom!

Make the most of your membership and keep up to date with upcoming events, the latest news and special offers by subscribing to our e-newsletter. Register online at **www.english-heritage.org.uk/newsletter** and we'll deliver the latest from English Heritage straight to your inbox.

Images:
(left) Helmsley Castle
(top centre) Rievaulx Abbey
(top right) Whitby Abbey
(bottom centre) Brodsworth Hall and Gardens
(bottom right) Rievaulx Abbey

Brodsworth Hall and Gardens

South Yorkshire – DN5 7XJ

Brodsworth Hall is unique. This is no glossily restored showpiece, frozen in manicured grandeur. 'Conserved as found', it is a mansion which has grown comfortably old over 120 years, a country house as it really was: still reflecting its original opulence, but well-worn, gently conserved – and full of surprises.

In contrast to the house, the extensive gardens have been wonderfully restored to their original horticultural splendour as 'a collection of grand gardens in miniature'.

Built in the Italianate style of the 1860s by the fabulously wealthy Charles Thellusson, Brodsworth Hall was occupied by the Thellusson family for over 120 years. The 'grand rooms' on the ground floor recall the house's Victorian heyday, while the family's sporting interests are reflected in paintings of their yachts and race-horses and trophies like the Doncaster Cup won by 'Rataplan' in 1855. This famous horse's desiccated hooves are also on display in the Billiard Room, itself evocatively preserved as a Victorian 'gentlemen's retreat'.

But elsewhere in the house, Brodsworth's gentle decline during the 20th century is much more apparent. The last resident, the indomitable Sylvia Grant-Dalton, fought a losing battle against subsidence and leaking roofs in her latter years. Following her death in 1988, English Heritage took on the house and gardens, boldly deciding to conserve the interiors as they were found, rather than restore them.

Thus the house appears as she used it, making do and mending as funds and numbers of servants dwindled. The Library's original wallpaper and carpets are faded, and Charles Thellusson's woodworking room is crowded with delightful clutter, including a recently identified 'passenger pigeon', a rare stuffed specimen of an American bird hunted to extinction by 1914. Some bedrooms, like the principal guest room with its magnificent 'boat-bed', fell out of use, along with the spartan rooms of the redundant servants' wing. Other rooms were partially modernised over the years, so that in addition to the Victorian furnishings, there are objects from the 1900s to the 1980s, which can be startlingly familiar to many visitors. They may also recognise music from the family's long-accumulated record collection from which samples are played in the South Hall in the summer, ranging from the atmospheric operatic Caruso recordings to hits of the Swinging Sixties.

Downstairs, the cavernous Victorian kitchen with its stupendous cooking range was deserted for a cosier 'Aga kitchen' and scullery. These remain as they were at the end of Brodsworth's active life, with their Tupperware, Formica and Fanny Craddock cookbooks. Beside the Aga rests the once-grand but battered and mended armchair of the house's last cook-housekeeper.

A fascinating exhibition, *Triumph at Sea*, spotlights the finest and most fascinating painting at Brodsworth Hall, whose dining room was specifically designed to display it. Recent research has revealed that the seascape painting, by the famous Dutch 'Golden Age' artist Ludolph Backhuysen (1630-1708), commemorates a notorious English naval disaster (see left). For it depicts in wonderful detail the English flagship the *Royal Charles*, captured during the calamitous Dutch raid on the Medway in 1667, being escorted in triumph towards Amsterdam by the Dutch flagship the *Dolphin*.

Interactive technology – including a computer game for children – allows visitors to 'walk into the painting'. They can step onto the deck of the *Dolphin*, explore the history of the picture and the event it commemorates, and discover the stories hidden within it.

For garden lovers

In contrast to the house, the extensive gardens have been wonderfully restored to their original splendour as 'a collection of grand gardens in miniature'. Work continues to reveal new features, along with vistas last enjoyed before World War I: the original focus of the formal garden, the restored 'Dolphin Fountain', now flows again. The plants in the Victorian Alpine rock garden reflect the Thellussons' love of travel.

The flower garden displays a fine selection of period bedding plants, while romantic views from

Brodsworth Hall and Gardens continued

the restored summerhouse take in both the formal gardens and the pleasure grounds. Stroll through the statue walks; the fern dell grotto, planted with unusual specimens; and the beautiful wild rose dell, currently bidding for national collection status.

The gardens at Brodsworth Hall are a delight at any time, but here are our suggestions for enjoying the best of the collections:

Spring

150,000 Snowdrops, Bluebells and Daffodils put on a fantastic show from February onwards. 12,000 bedding plants make a riot of colour in the formal flower garden in May, when the Alpine beds start to burst into flower.

Summer

The Rose Garden with its hundred varieties is a feast for the senses, especially in June. Bedding plants in the scheme feature sub-tropical species like bananas. Two contrasting herbaceous borders reach their peaks in June and September. The fern dell is full of architectural foliage, displayed in a purpose-built amphitheatre. On summer Sunday afternoons, the best of Yorkshire's brass bands play in the gardens.

Autumn

Brilliant autumn colours in the acer dell contrast with the clipped evergreen foliage of the formal gardens, making this an ideal time to see the garden structure at its best.

Winter

The evergreen structure stands out strongly now, and the collection of Victorian hollies comes into its own.

A family-friendly property

Brodsworth Hall and Gardens are outstandingly user-friendly for visitors of all ages. For children, there is a playroom and a hands-on resources room in the house, and an outdoor play area, featuring a real ex-naval training boat, now known as the 'Thellusson Explorer'. The friendly volunteer room stewards are another unique Brodsworth attraction: many knew the property before English Heritage acquired it.

Mobility around the site

Visitors please note that prams and back carriers for babies are not allowed in the hall. Small padded pushchairs and slings are available instead. For visitors with mobility needs or families with young children, a six-seater electric buggy operates a shuttle service from the car park. Benches throughout the gardens enable visitors to rest along the way, although some steps and steep slopes limit access to parts of the garden. The hall is accessed by ramps and has seats along the route, many handrails and a lift to the first floor.

Available for corporate and private hire

www.english-heritage.org.uk/brodsworthhall

NON-MEMBERS

House and gardens

Adult	£9.00
Concession	£8.10
Child	£5.40

Gardens only

Adult	£5.50
Concession	£5.00
Child	£3.30

OPENING TIMES

House

1 Apr-30 Sep, Tue-Sun & Bank Hols	1pm-5pm
1-31 Oct, Sat-Sun	12pm-4pm

Gardens and tearoom

1 Apr-31 Oct, Tue-Sun & Bank Hols	10am-5.30pm

Gardens, tearoom, shop and servants' wing

1 Nov-31 Mar, Sat-Sun	10am-4pm
24-26 Dec and 1 Jan	Closed

Last admission ½ hour before closing

HOW TO FIND US

Direction: In Brodsworth, 5 miles NW of Doncaster off A635 Barnsley Road; from junction 37 of A1(M)

Train: South Elmsall 4 miles; Moorthorpe 4½ miles; Doncaster 5½ miles; Adwick Le Street 3 miles

Bus: Wilfreda Beehive service 203 Doncaster – Mexborough, alight Pickburn Five Ways, then ⅔ mile

Local Tourist Information
Doncaster: 01302 734309

Tel: 01302 722598

Info-line: 01302 724969

OVP

No cameras (house).

MAP Page 283 (5G)
OS Map 111, 279: SE506070

Check www.english-heritage.org.uk for the latest opening times

Aldborough Roman Site
N. Yorkshire – YO51 9ES

Among the northernmost urban centres in the Roman Empire, Aldborough was the 'capital' of the Romanised Brigantes, the largest tribe in Britain. One corner of the defences is laid out amid a Victorian arboretum, and two mosaic pavements can be viewed in their original positions. The site museum has an outstanding collection of Roman finds.

NON-MEMBERS

Adult	£3.30
Concession	£3.00
Child	£2.00

OPENING TIMES

1 Apr-30 Sep, Sat-Sun & Bank Hols	11am-5pm

HOW TO FIND US

Direction: Located in Aldborough, ¾ mile SE of Boroughbridge on a minor road off B6265; within 1 mile of junction of A1 and A6055

Train: Cattal 7½ miles

Bus: Harrogate Coach Travel service 142, 143; Harrogate & District 57

Tel: 01423 322768

Dogs on leads (restricted areas only).

MAP Page 283 (3G)
OS Map 299, 99: SE405662

Brodsworth Hall and Gardens
See feature – Page 200

Burton Agnes Manor House
East Riding of Yorkshire

A medieval manor house interior, with a rare and well-preserved Norman undercroft and a 15th-century roof, all encased in brick during the 17th and 18th centuries.

OPENING TIMES

1 Apr-31 Oct, daily	11am-5pm

The nearby Burton Agnes Hall and Gardens are privately owned and are not managed by English Heritage

HOW TO FIND US

Direction: In Burton Agnes village, 5 miles SW of Bridlington on A166

Train: Nafferton 5 miles

Bus: East Yorkshire service 121 & 744

Parking (in Hall and Gardens car park, subject to charge).

MAP Page 283 (3J)
OS Map 101, 295: TA102632

Byland Abbey
See feature – Page 204

Clifford's Tower, York
N. Yorkshire – YO1 9SA

In 1068-9, William the Conqueror built two motte and bailey castles in York to strengthen his military hold on the North. Clifford's Tower, an unusual four-lobed keep built in the 13th century atop the mound of William's larger fortress, is now the principal surviving stonework remnant of York's medieval castle. The sweeping views of the city from the tower still show why it played such an important part in controlling northern England.

During the summer holidays family events bring the history of the tower to life.

NON-MEMBERS

Adult	£3.90
Concession	£3.50
Child	£2.30
Family	£10.10

OPENING TIMES

1 Apr-30 Sep, daily	10am-6pm
1-31 Oct, daily	10am-5pm
1 Nov-31 Mar, daily	10am-4pm
24-26 Dec and 1 Jan	Closed

HOW TO FIND US

Direction: Tower St, York

Train: York 1 mile

Bus: From surrounding areas

Tel: 01904 646940

Local Tourist Information
York: 01904 550099

P OVP

Parking (local charge).

Access (via steep steps).

New guidebook.

MAP Page 283 (3G)
OS Map 105, 290: SE605515

Byland Abbey

North Yorkshire – YO61 4BD

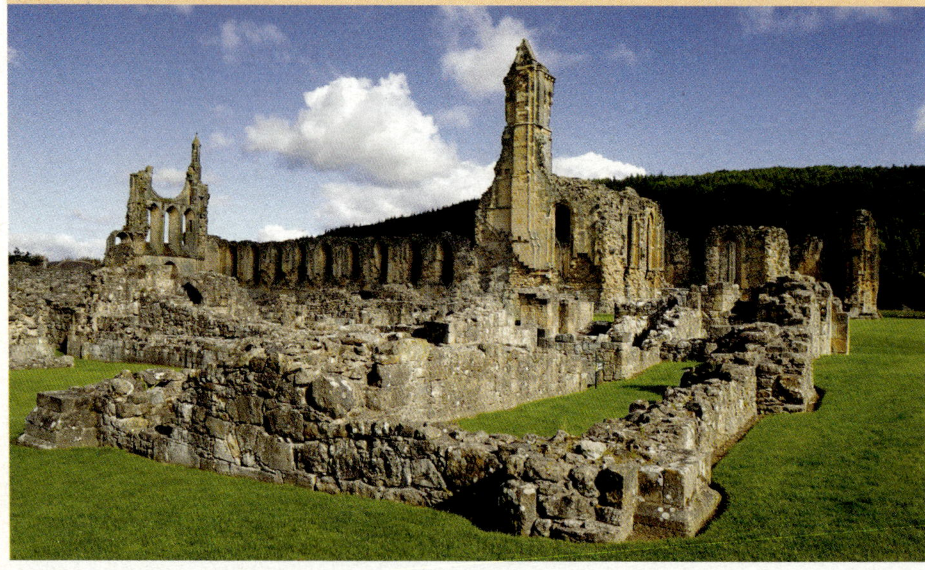

Byland was one of the great Yorkshire Cistercian abbeys, housing at its zenith well over 200 monks and lay brothers. Much of its huge cathedral-sized church survives, including the whole north side and the greater part of the 13th-century west front. The mixture of rounded Romanesque and pointed Gothic arches shows how architectural styles changed, and reveals that Byland was one of the earliest Gothic buildings in the north. Its great circular rose window, now surviving only in part, was probably the model for the rose window of York Minster. New archaeological research by English Heritage is beginning to throw light on the abbey's wider landscape setting and revealing how the monks tamed a very boggy and inhospitable site when building work started in the mid-12th century.

The museum displays colourful interpretation panels together with archaeological finds from the site, giving an insight into monastic life.

Rievaulx Abbey and Helmsley Castle are within reasonable travelling distance.

NON-MEMBERS

Adult	£4.30
Concession	£3.90
Child	£2.60

OPENING TIMES

1 Apr-30 Jun, Wed-Mon	11am-6pm
1 Jul-31 Aug, daily	11am-6pm
1-30 Sep, Wed-Mon	11am-5pm

HOW TO FIND US

Direction: 2 miles S of A170, between Thirsk and Helmsley; near Coxwold village

Train: Thirsk 10 miles

Bus: Stephensons/Hodgsons service 31X; Moorsbus services M11 & M15

Tel: 01347 868614 (Byland Abbey) 01347 868204 (Abbey Inn)

Local Tourist Information
01439 770173

OVP

Parking (adjacent to Abbey Inn).

Toilets at Abbey Inn.

MAP Page 283 (2G)
OS Map 100, OL26/299: SE549789

Conisbrough Castle
S. Yorkshire – DN12 3BU

Conisbrough's spectacular magnesian limestone keep, nearly 100 feet high, is cylindrical with wedge-shaped turret-buttresses, a design unique in Britain. Now with reinstated roof and floors, it was built in the late 12th century for Hamelin Plantagenet, illegitimate half-brother of King Henry II, and subsequently reinforced by turreted curtain walls. Conisbrough was among the inspirations for Sir Walter Scott's classic novel, *Ivanhoe*.

NON-MEMBERS

Adult	£4.50
Concession	£4.10
Child	£2.70
Family	£11.70

OPENING TIMES

1 Apr-30 Jun, Sat-Wed	10am-5pm
1 Jul-31 Aug, daily	10am-5pm
1-30 Sep, Sat-Wed	10am-5pm
1 Oct-31 Mar, Sat-Wed	10am-4pm
24-26 Dec and 1 Jan	Closed
Open Mon-Fri all year for schools	

HOW TO FIND US

Direction: Located NE of Conisbrough town centre off A630; 4½ miles SW of Doncaster

Train: Conisbrough 7 miles or Rotherham 6 miles

Bus: Stagecoach X78, 220, 221 & 222

Tel: 01709 863329

OVP

Conisbrough Castle

Dogs on leads (restricted areas only).

Parking (visitors with disabilities may be dropped off at the visitor centre).

Access (limited to some areas).

MAP Page 283 (5G)
OS Map 111, 279: SK515989

Easby Abbey
N. Yorkshire

The substantial remains of an abbey of Premonstratensian 'white canons', probably most notable for its lavish roof-height refectory of c. 1300 and other monastic buildings. Within the precinct is the still-active parish church, displaying fine 13th-century wall-paintings. In a beautiful setting by the River Swale, Easby can be reached via a pleasant walk from Richmond Castle.

NEW FOR 2011

New graphic panels guide you round the abbey.

OPENING TIMES

1 Apr-30 Sep, daily	10am-6pm
1-31 Oct, daily	10am-5pm
1 Nov-31 Mar, daily	10am-4pm
24-26 Dec and 1 Jan	Closed

HOW TO FIND US

Direction: 1 mile SE of Richmond, off B6271

Easby Abbey

Bus: Town & Country 32, 32A; Dales & District 55; Arriva/ Hodgsons X34

Guidebook (from Richmond Castle).

MAP Page 283 (2F)
OS Map 92, 304: NZ185003

Gainsthorpe Medieval Village
North Lincolnshire

A deserted medieval village, one of the best-preserved examples in England, clearly visible as a complex of grassy humps and bumps. According to legend demolished as a den of thieves, the real reason for its abandonment remains uncertain.

OPENING TIMES

Any reasonable time

HOW TO FIND US

Direction: Located on minor road W of A15 – towards Cleatham; S of Hibaldstow; 5 miles SW of Brigg

Train: Kirton Lindsey 3 miles

Bus: Stagecoach in Lincolnshire service 94

MAP Page 283 (5J)
OS Map 112, 281: SE954011

Helmsley Castle
See feature – Page 206

Helmsley Castle

North Yorkshire – YO62 5AB

Surrounded by spectacular banks and ditches, this great medieval castle's impressive ruins stand beside the attractive market town of Helmsley.

Rievaulx and Byland Abbeys are both nearby. Rievaulx can be reached on foot via the Cleveland Way National Trail. Approx. 1½ hours (3½ miles/ 5.6 km) each way. Strong footwear is required.

Sculptures by Malcolm Brocklesby

The fortress was probably begun after 1120 by Walter Espec – 'Walter the Woodpecker'. Renowned for piety as well as soldiering, this Norman baron of 'gigantic stature' also founded nearby Rievaulx Abbey and Kirkham Priory, both English Heritage properties.

Most of Helmsley's surviving stonework defences were raised during the late 12th and 13th centuries by the crusader Robert de Roos and his descendants. They include a pair of immensely strong 'barbican' entrances and the high, keep-like east tower, unusually D-shaped in plan, which still dominates the town.

But Helmsley is not only a medieval fortress. During the Elizabethan period the Manners family remodelled the castle's chamber block into a luxurious mansion, whose fine plasterwork and panelling still partly survive. The castle's first and last military trial came during the Civil War. Held for King Charles, it endured a three-month siege before being starved into submission in November 1644 by Parliamentarians under Sir Thomas Fairfax, who was seriously wounded in the fighting. Fairfax then dismantled the defences but spared the mansion, subsequently the home of his daughter and her husband, the profligate Duke of Buckingham.

Demoted to a romantic backdrop when later owners moved to nearby Duncombe Park, Helmsley Castle has undergone a thorough makeover by English Heritage, making it more accessible to a wide range of visitors. This includes a visitor centre building with shop and information point, an audio tour and an imaginative hands-on exhibition in the mansion range. Displaying a fascinating array of finds from Civil War cannon balls to early tableware, this exhibition explores the social and domestic, as well as the military, aspects of the fortress. Facilities for disabled visitors include full ground-level ramping, a virtual tour of less accessible areas, and a tactile model with braille text. Enhanced learning resources include family-friendly books and activities.

www.english-heritage.org.uk/helmsleycastle

NON-MEMBERS

Adult	£4.80
Concession	£4.30
Child	£2.90
Family	£12.50

OPENING TIMES

1 Apr-30 Sep, daily	10am-6pm
1-31 Oct, Thu-Mon	10am-5pm
1 Nov-29 Feb, Thu-Mon	10am-4pm
1-31 Mar, Thu-Mon	10am-5pm
24-26 Dec and 1 Jan	Closed

HOW TO FIND US

Direction: Near the town centre

Bus: Stephenson's/Hodgsons 31, 31X, 195, 196; Scarborough & District 128; Hodgson 199 (Fri); Moorsbus HB1, HB2, HB3, M2, M3, M9, M11, M13, M15

Tourist Information Centre
Tel: 01439 770173
Email: helmsley.tic@english-heritage.org.uk

Tel: 01439 770442

Audio tours.

Parking (large car park adjacent to castle; charge payable).

Toilets (in car park and town centre).

MAP Page 283 (2G)
OS Map 100, OL26: SE611836

Check www.english-heritage.org.uk for the latest opening times

Howden Minster
East Yorkshire – DN14 7BL

The elaborately decorated ruins of a 14th-century chancel and chapter house (viewable only from the outside), attached to the still operational cathedral-like minster church.

OPENING TIMES

Any reasonable time	
24-26 Dec and 1 Jan	Closed

HOW TO FIND US

Direction: In Howden; 23 miles W of Kingston Upon Hull, 25 miles SE of York, near the junction of A63 and A614

Train: Howden 1½ miles

Bus: East Yorkshire services 155, 156, 160 (Wed, Sun), 358 (Tue)

Parking (on-street parking nearby – pay and display).

MAP Page 283 (4H)
OS Map 105/106, 291: SE748283

Kirkham Priory
N. Yorkshire – YO60 7JS

The riverside ruins of an Augustinian priory, picturesquely set in the beautiful Derwent valley. Features include a gatehouse bedecked with heraldry, including that of the De Roos family, Barons of Helmsley Castle; handsome monastic washbasins; and interpretation of the property's surprising role in World War II.

Kirkham Priory

NON-MEMBERS

Adult	£3.30
Concession	£3.00
Child	£2.00

OPENING TIMES

1 Apr-31 Jul, Thu-Mon	10am-5pm
1-31 Aug, daily	10am-5pm
1-30 Sep, Thu-Mon	10am-5pm

HOW TO FIND US

Direction: 5 miles SW of Malton, on a minor road off A64

Train: Malton 6 miles

Bus: Yorkshire Coastliner X40/840/3/5 (pass York and Malton) to Whitwell on the Hill and then ¾ mile walk; W.P.Hutchinson 184/185 serve Kirkham village on (Tue, Fri, Sat)

Tel: 01653 618768

Local Tourist Information
01653 600048

OVP

MAP Page 283 (3H)
OS Map 100, 300: SE736658

Marmion Tower
N. Yorkshire

The fine 15th-century gatehouse of a vanished riverside manor house, with a beautiful oriel window. The monuments of the manor's Marmion family owners grace the adjacent church.

OPENING TIMES

1 Apr-30 Sep, daily	10am-6pm
1-31 Oct, daily	10am-5pm
1 Nov-31 Mar, daily	10am-4pm
24-26 Dec and 1 Jan	Closed

HOW TO FIND US

Direction: On A6108 in West Tanfield

Train: Thirsk 10 miles

Bus: Dales & District 159; Vintage Omnibus 127 (summer only)

MAP Page 283 (3F)
OS Map 99, 298: SE268787

Middleham Castle
N. Yorkshire – DL8 4QG

The childhood and favourite home of Richard III, Middleham Castle was a fortress of the mighty Neville family, Earls of Westmoreland and of Warwick. Around the massive 12th-century central keep, they progressively constructed three ranges of luxurious chambers and lodgings, turning the castle into a fortified palace by the mid-15th century. Though roofless, many of these buildings survive, making Middleham a fascinating castle to explore. Here Richard spent part of his youth, in the guardianship of 'Warwick the Kingmaker'.

An exhibition about notable personalities from the castle's past includes a replica of the beautiful Middleham Jewel, a 15th-century pendant decorated with a large sapphire found near the castle. Family-friendly books and activities.

NON-MEMBERS

Adult	£4.30
Concession	£3.90
Child	£2.60

OPENING TIMES

1 Apr-30 Sep, daily	10am-6pm
1 Oct-31 Mar, Sat-Wed	10am-4pm
24-26 Dec and 1 Jan	Closed

HOW TO FIND US

Direction: Located at Middleham; 2 miles S of Leyburn on A6108

Train: Leyburn (Wensleydale Railway) 2 miles

Bus: Dales & District service 159 also Vintage Omnibus Service 127 (summer only)

Middleham Castle

Tel: 01969 623899

Local Tourist Information
Leyburn: 01969 623069

Disabled access (except keep).

MAP Page 283 (2F)
OS Map 99, OL30: SE127876

Monk Bretton Priory
S. Yorkshire

The substantial ruins of a Cluniac monastery, with an unusually well-marked ground plan, an almost complete west range and a 15th-century gatehouse.

NON-MEMBERS

Charge may apply on event days

OPENING TIMES

1 Apr-31 Mar, daily (managed by a keykeeper)	10am-3pm
24-26 Dec and 1 Jan	Closed

HOW TO FIND US

Direction: Located 1 mile E of Barnsley town centre, off A633

Train: Barnsley 2½ miles

Bus: Stagecoach 32, 35, 35A, 36, 46 and 47

MAP Page 283 (5G)
OS Map 110.111, 278: SE373065

Mount Grace Priory
N. Yorkshire – DL6 3JG

Set amid the North York Moors, Mount Grace was once the home of Carthusian monks, who lived as hermits in cottage-like cells. A reconstructed and furnished monk's cell and a recently revamped herb plot offer a glimpse into the lives of the medieval residents. Two additional rooms in the guest house are now open following refurbishment. The gardens are a haven for wildlife, including the famous 'Priory Stoats'. There are also children's activities during school holidays.

Owned by the National Trust, maintained and managed by English Heritage.

Holiday cottage available to let

Available for corporate and private hire

NON-MEMBERS

Adult	£5.00
Concession	£4.50
Child	£3.00
Family	£13.00

National Trust members admitted free, except on event days

OPENING TIMES

1 Apr-30 Sep, Thu-Mon	10am-6pm
1 Oct-31 Mar, Thu-Sun	10am-4pm
24-26 Dec and 1 Jan	Closed

Please note: on days when there are summer evening theatre events, the site will open at 12 noon

HOW TO FIND US

Direction: 12 miles N of Thirsk; 6 miles NE of Northallerton, on A19

Train: Northallerton 6 miles

Bus: Arriva service 27; Abbott services 80, 89; Moorsbus M10 alight Priory Road End, ½ mile

Tel: 01609 883494

Local Tourist Information
Thirsk: 01845 522755

MAP Page 283 (2G)
OS Map 99, OL26: SE449985

Pickering Castle
N. Yorkshire – YO18 7AX

A fine early Norman castle set in an attractive moors-edge market town, with spectacular views from the motte–top. Pickering is a classic and well-preserved example of an early earthwork castle refortified in stone during the 13th and 14th centuries. There is an exhibition in the chapel and family-friendly books and activities.

NON-MEMBERS

Adult	£3.80
Concession	£3.40
Child	£2.30
Family	£9.90

OPENING TIMES

1 Apr-30 Jun, Thu-Mon	10am-5pm
1 Jul-31 Aug, daily	10am-5pm
1-30 Sep, Thu-Mon	10am-5pm

HOW TO FIND US

Direction: In Pickering; 15 miles SW of Scarborough

Train: Malton (9m) or Pickering (North Yorkshire Moors Rly) ¼ mile

Bus: Scarborough & District 128; W.P.Hutchinson 173, 174, 175; Yorkshire Coastliner 840; Moorsbus M5, M6, M7, M14

Tel: 01751 474989

Local Tourist Information
Pickering: 01751 473791

Disabled access (except motte).

MAP Page 283 (2H)
OS Map 100, OL27: SE799845

Rievaulx Abbey

North Yorkshire – YO62 5LB

'Everywhere peace, everywhere serenity, and a marvellous freedom from the tumult of the world.' Written over eight centuries ago by the monastery's third abbot, St Aelred, these words still describe Rievaulx today.

Set in a beautiful and tranquil valley, Rievaulx is among the most atmospheric and complete of all the ruined abbeys in the North.

The tearoom has an indoor and outdoor seating area and serves a delicious variety of locally-sourced food, including ingredients grown in the Rievaulx Abbey garden.

Words are not the only link to Rievaulx's medieval monks. Over the past few years, the site has become something of an archaeological treasure, with unexpected discoveries shedding new light on the lives of the monks and the extensive renewal and rebuilding of their abbey church in the Early English Gothic style. Archaeologists continue to study the landscape around Rievaulx, revealing the remarkable extent of the abbey's influence and industry. Their discoveries are showcased within the on-site museum.

The abbey was founded by St Bernard of Clairvaux, as part of the missionary effort to reform Christianity in western Europe. Twelve Clairvaux monks came to Rievaulx in 1132. From these modest beginnings grew one of the wealthiest monasteries of medieval England and the first northern Cistercian monastery. Rievaulx also enjoyed the protection of Walter Espec of nearby Helmsley Castle, who provided much of the abbey's land. The monks of neighbouring Byland Abbey initially disputed land ownership with Rievaulx, but subsequently moved to their present location and relinquished the disputed land, thus allowing the major expansion of Rievaulx Abbey. You can still see traces of the channels dug by the Rievaulx monks.

A steady flow of monks came to Rievaulx, attracted by the prestige of Abbot Aelred, author and preacher, who was regarded then and later as a wise and saintly man. Following his death in 1167, the monks of Rievaulx sought canonisation for their former leader, and in the 1220s they rebuilt the east part of their church in a much more elaborate style to house his tomb. Most of this 13th-century 'presbytery' still stands to virtually its full impressive height, a reminder of Rievaulx's original splendour.

Rievaulx was still a vibrant community when Henry VIII dissolved it in 1538. Its new owner, Thomas Manners, first Earl of Rutland, swiftly instigated the systematic destruction of the buildings, yet the substantial remains constitute one of the most eloquent of all monastic sites, free 'from the tumult of the world'. Schoolchildren from the local area have helped to create a Sensory Garden full of scented and flavoured herbs, amid tile motifs based on medieval designs.

Don't miss the exciting indoor exhibition, *The Work of God and Man*, which explores the agricultural, industrial, spiritual and commercial aspects of Rievaulx's history, employing a variety of lively and interactive displays. There are family-friendly events, books and activities during school holidays.

Holiday cottage available to let

www.english-heritage.org.uk/rievaulxabbey

NON-MEMBERS

Adult	£5.60
Concession	£5.00
Child	£3.40

OPENING TIMES

1 Apr-30 Sep, daily	10am-6pm
1-31Oct, Thu-Mon	10am-5pm
1 Nov-31 Mar, Thu-Mon	10am-4pm
24-26 Dec and 1 Jan	Closed

HOW TO FIND US

Direction: In Rievaulx; 2¼ miles N of Helmsley, on minor road off B1257

Bus: Moorsbus M8 from Helmsley (connections on Scarborough & District service 128 from Scarborough) Tue & Thu all year, Mon-Sat June-Sep, Sundays, Apr-Oct. Hutchinson service 199 and Moorsbus M2 & M9 pass within ½ mile

Tel: 01439 798228

Local Tourist Information
Helmsley: 01439 770173

Audio tours (also available for the visually impaired, those with learning difficulties and in French and German).

Parking: Pay and display parking, refundable to EH members and paying visitors upon admission.

MAP Page 283 (2G)
OS Map 100, OL26: SE577850

Richmond Castle

North Yorkshire – DL10 4QW

Impressive Richmond Castle is breathtakingly sited on a rocky promontory above the River Swale, overlooking an outstandingly picturesque market town at the foot of beautiful Swaledale. Among the oldest Norman stone fortresses in Britain, it was begun in about 1071 by William the Conqueror's Breton supporter Alan the Red. The towering keep, added a century later during the reign of Henry II, stands over 100 feet (30m) high, with walls up to 11 feet (3.35m) thick. It is remarkably complete within, and visitors can climb to the top for panoramic views over the castle's great courtyard, the cobbled market place of Richmond and the Yorkshire Dales beyond.

Graffiti by conscientious objector.

According to legend, King Arthur and his knights lie sleeping in a cavern beneath the keep, and the drumbeats of a drummer-boy lost in a secret passage can still be heard.

More certainly, two medieval kings of Scotland were imprisoned here after defeat in battle, as more recently were conscientious objectors – including many Dales Quakers – who refused to fight in World War I. Their story is told in an interactive display exploring the castle's nine centuries of history, which is also woven into the contemporary Cockpit Garden overlooking the Swale. Family-friendly books and activities.

NON-MEMBERS

Adult	£4.60
Concession	£4.10
Child	£2.80

OPENING TIMES

1 Apr-30 Sep, daily	10am-6pm
1 Oct-31 Mar, Thu-Mon	10am-4pm
24-26 Dec and 1 Jan	Closed

HOW TO FIND US

Direction: In Richmond just off the market place

Bus: Arriva X26, 27, X27, 29, 34, X59; Harrogate & District Community Transport 30; Town & Country 32, 32A; Hodgsons X34, 79; Dales & District 54, 55, 73, 159; Hurworth Taxis 79A

Tel: 01748 822493

Parking (2 hrs free in market place – not managed by EH; disabled parking at Castle).

MAP Page 283 (2F)

OS Map 92, 304: NZ172007

Piercebridge Roman Bridge
N. Yorkshire

Stonework foundations of a bridge, now marooned in a field, which once led to Piercebridge Roman Fort.

OPENING TIMES
Any reasonable time

HOW TO FIND US
Direction: At Piercebridge; 4 miles W of Darlington, on B6275

Train: Darlington 5 miles

Bus: Arriva 75/6 Darlington – Barnard Castle (passes close to Darlington)

MAP Page 283 (1F)
OS Map 93, 304: NZ214155

Rievaulx Abbey
See feature – Page 215

Richmond Castle
See feature opposite

Roche Abbey
S. Yorkshire – S66 8NW

Beautifully set in a valley landscaped by 'Capability' Brown in the 18th century, the most striking feature of this Cistercian abbey is the eastern end of its church, built in the new Gothic style c. 1170. It has one of the most complete ground plans of any English Cistercian monastery, laid out as excavated foundations. The story of the pillaging of Roche, recorded by the son of an eye-witness, is among the most vivid documents of the Dissolution of the Monasteries.

NON-MEMBERS
Adult	£3.30
Concession	£3.00
Child	£2.00

Roche Abbey

OPENING TIMES
1 Apr-30 Sep,
Thu-Sun & Bank Hols 11am-4pm

HOW TO FIND US
Direction: 1½ miles S of Maltby, off A634

Train: Conisbrough 7 miles

Bus: First services 1, 2 & 10; Veolia Transport service 10A, 20 & 122; Powell's Bus service X7, 18 & 18A to Maltby then 1½ miles walk

Tel: 01709 812739

OVP

MAP Page 283 (6G)
OS Map 111/120, 279: SK544898

St Mary's Church, Studley Royal
N. Yorkshire – HG4 3DY

This magnificent High Victorian Anglican church was designed in the 1870s by the flamboyant architect William Burges and has been called his 'ecclesiastical masterpiece'. The extravagantly decorated interior displays coloured marble, stained glass, a splendid organ and painted and gilded figures in all their original glory.

Owned by English Heritage and managed by the National Trust as part of the Fountains Abbey and Studley Royal Estate (see p.220).

OPENING TIMES
2 Apr-30 Sep, daily 12pm-4pm

HOW TO FIND US
Direction: Located 2½ miles W of Ripon, off B6265; in the grounds of the Studley Royal Estate

Bus: Dales & District 139

Tel: 01765 608888

Parking (at visitor centre or Studley Royal).

MAP Page 283 (3F)
OS Map 99, 298/299: SE275693

St Peter's Church, Barton-upon-Humber
North Lincolnshire – DN18 5EX

This famous Anglo-Saxon and medieval church is an archaeological as well as an architectural treasure-trove and Britain's largest resource for historic bone analysis. The *Buried Lives* exhibition offers greater understanding of the church begun in c. 970, and the archaeological revelations it has produced. The analysis of 2800 burials here, ranging from Anglo-Saxon to Victorian times, has yielded unprecedented insights into medieval disease and diet, and medical and burial practices. Thornton Abbey and Gatehouse (see p.215) is nearby.

NON-MEMBERS
Adult	£3.50
Concession	£3.20
Child	£2.10

OPENING TIMES
1 Apr-30 Sep,
Sat-Sun & Bank Hols 11am-3pm

HOW TO FIND US
Direction: In Barton-upon-Humber

Train: Barton-upon-Humber ½ mile

Bus: Stagecoach Lincolnshire 450 passes the site; Stagecoach Lincolnshire 45, 360; J.L. Johnson 252, 253; North Lincs Council Villager 260; Stagecoach/East Yorkshire Humber Fast Cat 350 all pass close by

Tel: 01652 632516/01302 722598

E OVP

MAP Page 283 (5J)
OS Map 107, 112, 281: TA035219

Scarborough Castle North Yorkshire – YO11 1HY

Scarborough Castle defends a prominent headland between two bays, with sheer drops to the sea and only a narrow landward approach. Specially constructed viewing platforms on the battlements offer panoramic views. Long before the castle was built, this natural fortress was favoured by prehistoric settlers and later housed a defended Roman signal station.

Henry II's towering 12th-century keep, dominating the approach, is the centrepiece of fortifications developed over later centuries in response to repeated sieges – notably by rebel barons in 1312 and twice during the Civil War. Though again strengthened with barracks and gun-batteries against Jacobite threats in 1745, the castle failed to defend the harbour against the American sea-raider John Paul Jones in 1779, and was itself damaged by German naval bombardment in 1914. During World War II it played the more covert role of hosting a secret listening post.

The site's 3000 year history is explored in interactive displays in the restored Master Gunner's House, accompanied by artefacts from each period of Scarborough's past. Less mobile visitors can enjoy a ground-floor, touch-screen virtual tour of the displays, as well as virtual views reproducing those from the raised platforms.

Timelined graphic panels around the castle focus on characters from the past and there are free activity sheets, an audio tour, and an investigative story box to help younger visitors visualise and understand the history of the castle.

www.english-heritage.org.uk/scarboroughcastle

NON-MEMBERS

Adult	£4.80
Concession	£4.30
Child	£2.90
Family	£12.50

OPENING TIMES

1 Apr-30 Sep, daily	10am-6pm
1 Oct-31 Mar, Thu-Mon	10am-4pm
24-26 Dec and 1 Jan	Closed

HOW TO FIND US

Direction: Castle Road, E of the town centre

Train: Scarborough 1 mile

Bus: From surrounding areas

Tel: 01723 372451

Local Tourist Information
Helmsley: 01723 383636

E OVP

Parking (pre-booked parking only for disabled visitors, otherwise located in town centre).

Tearoom open summer only.

MAP Page 283 (2J)
OS Map 101, 301: TA050892

Check www.english-heritage.org.uk for the latest opening times

Thornton Abbey & Gatehouse North Lincolnshire – DN39 6TU

The enormous and ornate fortified gatehouse of Thornton Abbey is the largest and among the finest of all English monastic gatehouses. An early example of brick building in England, it proclaimed the wool trade-based prosperity of one of the wealthiest English Augustinian monasteries, for centuries a focus of spiritual and economic influence. Begun in the 1360s, the gatehouse was enlarged and fortified with battlements after the Peasants' Revolt of 1381, presumably as insurance against further trouble. Standing some 21 metres (69 feet) high and resembling a castle keep gatehouse, it may have protected the abbey's treasures as well as providing spacious lodgings for the abbot and his guests.

Within the grounds stand the ruins of the monastic buildings, notably the elegantly decorated octagonal chapter house of 1282-1308. These buildings were plundered for stone to build a 'most stately' Jacobean manor house which, mysteriously, 'fell quite down to the bare ground without any visible cause' (Abraham de la Pryme). The remains of its formal gardens have recently been rediscovered.

An exterior oak staircase gives visitors access to the restored gatehouse's atmospheric interior. The gatehouse is open daily, and includes features revealed following restoration work. An exhibition and graphic panels offer an insight into the abbey's history, including its career as the focus of huge Victorian Temperance rallies.

St Peter's Church, Barton-upon-Humber (see p.213) is nearby.

NON-MEMBERS

Adult	£4.30
Concession	£3.90
Child	£2.60

OPENING TIMES

1 Apr-30 Jun, Wed-Sun & Bank Hols	10am-5pm
1 Jul-31 Aug, daily	10am-5pm
1 Sep-31 Mar, Fri-Sun	10am-4pm
24-26 Dec and 1 Jan	Closed

HOW TO FIND US

Direction: 18 miles NE of Scunthorpe, on a road N of A160; 7 miles SE of the Humber Bridge, on a road E of A1077

Train: Thornton Abbey ¼ mile

Bus: Stagecoach service 360 and North Lincs Council 'The Villager' 260 pass the site

Tel: 01469 541445

E P OVP

Disabled access (except gatehouse interior and part of chapter ruins).

Dogs on leads (restricted areas only).

MAP Page 283 (5J)
OS Map 113, 284: TA118189

Scarborough Castle

See feature – Page 214

Skipsea Castle
East Riding of Yorkshire

An impressive Norman motte and bailey castle, dating from before 1086 and among the first raised in Yorkshire, with the earthworks of an attendant fortified 'borough'.

OPENING TIMES

Any reasonable time

HOW TO FIND US

Direction: Located 8 miles S of Bridlington; W of Skipsea village

Train: Bridlington 9 miles

Bus: East Yorkshire services 130

Dogs on leads (restricted areas only).

Waterproof footwear recommended.

MAP Page 283 (3J)
OS Map 107, 295: TA162551

Spofforth Castle
N. Yorkshire

The ruined hall and chamber of a fortified manor house of the powerful Percy family, begun in the 13th and rebuilt in the 15th century. Its undercroft is cut into a rocky outcrop.

NEW FOR 2011

New graphic panels guide you round the house.

Managed by Spofforth-with-Stockeld Parish Council.

OPENING TIMES

1 Apr-30 Sep, daily	10am-6pm
1 Oct-31 Mar, daily (managed by a keykeeper)	10am-4pm
24-26 Dec and 1 Jan	Closed

Spofforth Castle

HOW TO FIND US

Direction: 3½ miles SE of Harrogate; off A661 at Spofforth

Train: Pannal 4 miles

Bus: Harrogate & District services 770

Dogs on leads (restricted areas only).

MAP Page 283 (4G)
OS Map 104, 289: SE360511

Stanwick Iron Age Fortifications
N. Yorkshire

An excavated section, part cut into rock, of the ramparts of the huge Iron Age trading and power-centre of the Brigantes, the most important tribe in pre-Roman northern Britain. Some 4 miles (6½ kilometres) long, the defences enclosed an area of 766 acres (310 hectares). Following Roman conquest, the Brigantian centre moved to Aldborough Roman Site (see p.203).

OPENING TIMES

Any reasonable time

HOW TO FIND US

Direction: Located on a minor road off A6274, at Forcett Village

Train: Darlington 10 miles

Bus: Arriva service 29; Hodgsons 78A (Wed); Hurworth Taxis 79A (Thu)

Dogs on leads (restricted areas only).

MAP Page 283 (1F)
OS Map 92, 304: NZ179124

Steeton Hall Gateway
N. Yorkshire LS25 5PD

A fine example of a small, well-preserved manorial gatehouse dating from the 14th century.

OPENING TIMES

Daily (exterior only)	10am-5pm

HOW TO FIND US

Direction: Located 4 miles NE of Castleford, on a minor road off A162 at South Milford

Train: South Milford 1 mile

Bus: Arriva services Yorkshire services 492 & 493

Dogs on leads (restricted areas only).

MAP Page 283 (4G)
OS Map 105, 290: SE484314

Thornton Abbey & Gatehouse

See feature – Page 215

Wharram Percy Deserted Medieval Village
N. Yorkshire

The most famous and intensively studied of Britain's 3000 or so deserted medieval villages, Wharram Percy occupies a remote but attractive site in a beautiful Wolds valley. Above the substantial ruins of the church and a recreated fishpond, the outlines of many lost houses are traceable on a grassy plateau. First settled in prehistoric times, Wharram flourished as a village between the 12th and 14th centuries, before final abandonment in c. 1500. Graphic interpretation panels tell its story and recreate the original appearance of the buildings. A free downloadable audio tour is available from the English Heritage website.

Wharram Percy Deserted Medieval Village

OPENING TIMES

Any reasonable time

HOW TO FIND US

Direction: 6 miles SE of Malton, on minor road from B1248; ½ mile S of Wharram-le-Street. Park in car park, then ¾ mile walk via uneven track, steep in places. Site also accessible on foot via Wolds Way ramblers' path. Sturdy and waterproof footwear required. Parts of site slope steeply, and farm livestock likely to be present on site and access path

Train: Malton 8 miles

Bus: Moorsbus M14; Royal Mail Malton – Foxholes postbus to Wharram Le Street then ½ mile walk

Please note: site is hazardous in snowy conditions.

MAP Page 283 (3H)
OS Map 100, 300: SE859644

Wheeldale Roman Road
N. Yorkshire

A mile-long stretch of enigmatic ancient road – probably Roman but possibly later or earlier – still with its hard core and drainage ditches. Amid wild and beautiful moorland. Managed by North York Moors National Park.

OPENING TIMES

Any reasonable time

HOW TO FIND US

Direction: S of Goathland; W of A169; 7 miles S of Whitby

Train: Goathland (North Yorkshire Moors Rly) (4 miles) or Newtondale Halt (then 3 mile forest walk)

Bus: Yorkshire Coastliner service 840 to Goathland then 4 mile walk

Local Tourist Information
Pickering: 01751 473791

MAP Page 283 (2H)
OS Map 94/100, OL27: SE806977

Whitby Abbey
See feature – Page 218

York Cold War Bunker

N. Yorkshire – YO24 4HT

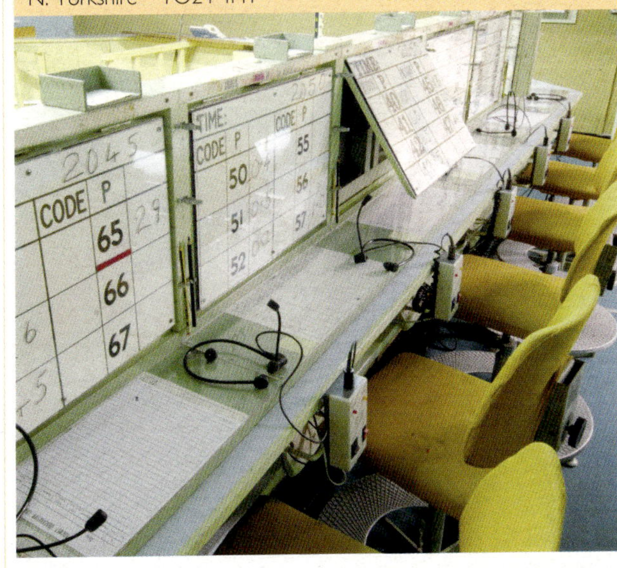

English Heritage's most modern, most unusual and perhaps most spine-chilling site, 'No. 20 Group Royal Observer Corps HQ' is the semi-subterranean bunker which would have monitored nuclear explosions and fallout in the Yorkshire region. In service between 1961 and 1991, the Bunker's control rooms display 'colour-psychology décor' together with original monitoring and communications equipment. Decontamination rooms with air filters and special sewage ejectors were intended to seal off the 60-strong workforce from the devastated outside world. A guided tour, enhanced by a striking 10-minute film (PG rated) and interpretation, tells the story of the Cold War's 'Mutually Assured Destruction.'

NON-MEMBERS

Adult	£6.00
Concession	£5.40
Child	£3.60

OPENING TIMES

1 Apr-31 Mar Sun & Bank Hols	10am-4pm

By tours only, tours every ½ hour. Tours last approx 1 hour. No need to book. Last tour 3pm

Weekdays: Admission for schools and groups only. Booking 14 days in advance, minimum fee applies

HOW TO FIND US

Direction: Monument Close, off Acomb Road, near the Carlton Tavern, approx. 2 miles from York city centre

Train: York 2 miles

Bus: First in York service 1; Arriva 412 & 413

Tel: 01904 646940 (Clifford's Tower)

Local Tourist Information
York: 01904 550099

Parking (limited to 3 spaces).

New guidebook.

MAP Page 283 (3G)
OS Map 105, 290: SE580515

Check www.english-heritage.org.uk for the latest opening times

Whitby Abbey North Yorkshire – YO22 4JT

Dominating the picturesque seaside town of Whitby, the dramatic ruins of the abbey stand on a headland rich in over thirteen centuries of history.

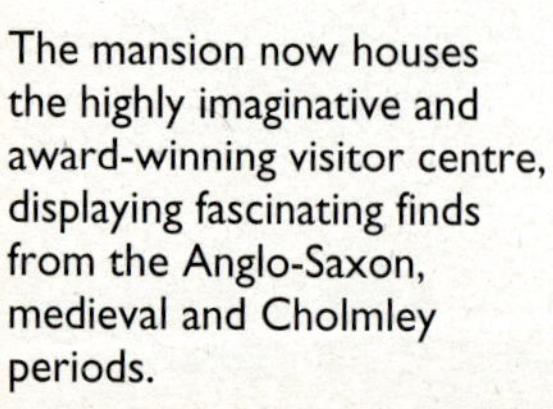

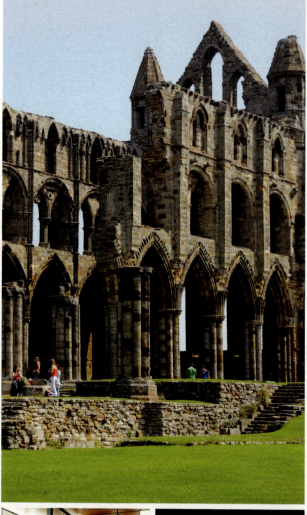

The mansion now houses the highly imaginative and award-winning visitor centre, displaying fascinating finds from the Anglo-Saxon, medieval and Cholmley periods.

Check www.english-heritage.org.uk for the latest opening times

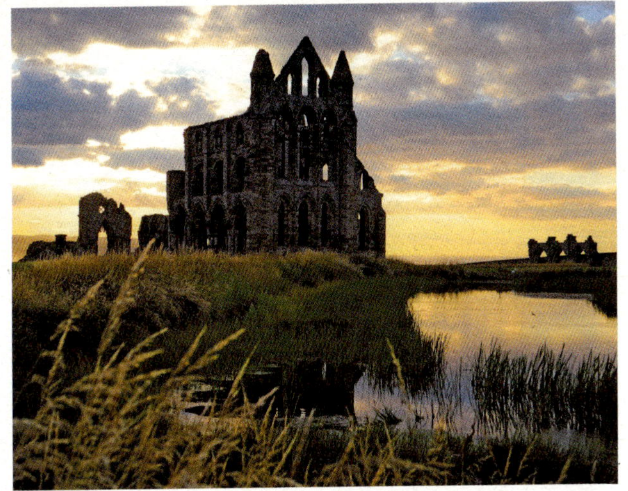

The first monastery here was founded in AD 657 by King Oswy of Northumbria. An Anglo-Saxon style 'double monastery' for men and women, its first ruler was the formidable royal princess Abbess Hild; here Caedmon the cowherd was miraculously transformed into an inspired poet; here the future of the English church was decided in 664; and here the relics of Northumbrian kings and saints were enshrined.

Though many intriguing excavated finds from it are displayed in the visitor centre, nothing survives above ground of this Anglo-Saxon monastery. The imposing ruins belong to the church of the Benedictine abbey refounded on its site by the Normans. Begun in about 1220 in the Early English style of Gothic, the pinnacled east end and north transept still stand high, richly carved with characteristic 'dog's tooth' embellishment. Time, war and nature have left their marks. Parts of the church collapsed during storms, its west front was hit by German naval shelling in 1914 and centuries of wind and rain have added their own etched and pitted decoration.

These supremely romantic ruins enjoy panoramic views, and literary renown as the backdrop to Bram Stoker's *Dracula*, the Victorian novel which has made Whitby the 'Goth' capital of Britain. More recently the site has inspired *Shadowmancer* and other best-selling children's novels by ex-vicar, ex-policeman and exorcist, GP Taylor.

The ruins share the headland with the Cholmley family mansion, begun after Henry VIII's suppression of the abbey. Its impressive Classical façade of 1672 is fronted by a restoration of the 'hard garden' courtyard rediscovered during English Heritage excavations. The courtyard's centrepiece is a specially-commissioned bronze copy of the famous 'Borghese Gladiator' statue. The Roman marble original of this spectacular life-sized statue, now in the Paris Louvre, dates from the 1st century BC: it was found in 1611 in Italy and bronze casts were made for King Charles I. Copies graced many great English houses and gardens including the Cholmleys' Whitby mansion, recalling the family's Civil War support for the Royalist cause.

The mansion now houses the highly imaginative and award-winning visitor centre. Displaying fascinating finds from the Anglo-Saxon, medieval and Cholmley periods, this is packed with computer-generated images and entertaining interactives: touch-screens allow visitors to question Whitby personalities, from Abbess Hild via a medieval monk to Bram Stoker.

Please note: from the Whitby harbour area, the abbey can only be directly reached on foot via the 199 'abbey steps'. Alternatively, a well-signposted road leads from the town outskirts to the cliff-top abbey.

www.english-heritage.org.uk/whitbyabbey

NON-MEMBERS

Adult	£6.00
Concession	£5.40
Child	£3.60
Family	£15.60

OPENING TIMES

1 Apr-30 Sep, daily	10am-6pm
1 Oct-31 Mar, Thu-Mon	10am-4pm
Open October Half Term	
24-26 Dec and 1 Jan	Closed

HOW TO FIND US

Direction: On cliff top, E of Whitby

Train: Whitby ½ mile

Bus: Esk Valley service 8A, 27; Arriva 5, 5A, X93, 93, 95; Hodgson service 26; MDM service 99; Yorkshire Coastliner 840

Tel: 01947 603568

Local Tourist Information
Whitby: 01947 602674

P OVP

Disabled access (south entrance parking, charged).

Dogs on leads (restricted areas only).

Parking not managed by English Heritage (charge payable).

Tearoom (managed by Youth Hostel Association).

MAP Page 283 (1J)
OS Map 94, OL27: NZ903112

Associated attractions in Yorkshire

These visitor attractions, all independent of EH, offer discounts to our members. Please call before you visit to confirm details. A valid EH membership card must be produced for each member.

Barley Hall
North Yorkshire YO1 8AR

Discover the town house of a medieval Lord Mayor of York. Rediscovered under a relatively modern façade, this stunning building has beautiful exposed timber frames and high roofs.

10 mins from Clifford's Tower

Tel: 01904 615 505

www.barleyhall.org.uk

15% discount on entry

OVP 6

Castle Howard
North Yorkshire YO60 7DA

Magnificent 18th century house in 1000 acres of breathtaking parkland and gardens. Attractions include exhibitions, events, adventure playground, boat trips, shops and cafés.

15 miles north east of York

Tel: 01653 648333

www.castlehoward.co.uk

Discounted house & garden ticket

6

DIG
An Archaeological Adventure
North Yorkshire YO1 8NN

DIG offers you a unique adventure to get you on your way to becoming a real archaeologist. Come and dig in our Roman, Viking, medieval and Victorian pits.

10 mins from Clifford's Tower

Tel: 01904 615 505

www.digyork.com

15% discount on entry

OVP 6

Duncombe Park
North Yorkshire YO62 5EB

A masterpiece of landscape gardening with long sweeping terraces, towering veteran trees, classical temples and breathtaking views over the Rye valley. Visitors will also discover woodland walks, ornamental parterres and a 'secret garden' at the Conservatory.

1 mile from Helmsley Castle

Tel: 01439 770213

www.duncombepark.com

10% off garden and parkland ticket

2

Fountains Abbey & Studley Royal
North Yorkshire HG4 3DY

Spectacular World Heritage Site set in 800 acres of naturally beautiful countryside. Stunning 12th-century abbey ruins, Georgian water garden, deer park and monastic mill with interactive exhibition.

11 miles from Aldborough

Tel: 01765 608888

www.fountainsabbey.org.uk

FREE admission

Harewood House
North/West Yorkshire Border LS17 9LG

A great day out for all the family, with award-winning gardens adventure playground, and bird garden. Sumptuous state rooms with Adam interiors, Chippendale furniture and Renaissance art. Exciting events and exhibitions.

7 miles north of Leeds

Tel: 0113 218 1010

www.harewood.org

25% off adult Freedom tickets from 1 Apr-30 Oct

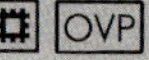

EH Members | OVP OVP Holders | ? Discounted Child Places Included

JORVIK Viking Centre
North Yorkshire YO1 9WT

Take hold of the past and explore the excavations which first unearthed the Viking-age city of Jorvik in our new exhibitions.

2 mins from Clifford's Tower

Tel: 01904 615 505

www.jorvik-viking-centre.co.uk

15% discount on entry

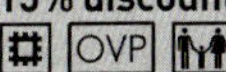

Merchant Adventurers' Hall
North Yorkshire YO1 9XD

One of the world's finest medieval guild halls, dating from 1357, featuring the great hall, undercroft, chapel, gardens, unique collections and interactive exhibits. Fully accessible from Fossgate.

Close to Clifford's Tower

Tel: 01904 654818

www.theyorkcompany.co.uk

50% discount on entry

6

Micklegate Bar Museum
North Yorkshire YO1 6JX

Mickegate Bar has stood sentinel to the city for over 800 years. Visit the ancient gateway to explore the pageantry and barbaric history that has unfolded within these walls.

15 mins from Clifford's Tower

Tel: 01904 615505

www.micklegatebar.com

15% discount on entry

OVP 6

National Media Museum
Bradford BD1 1NQ

Three cinemas including Yorkshire's only IMAX Cinema, with a screen the height of four double-decker buses (charges apply). Devoted to film, photography, television, radio and the web. FREE entry to the Museum.

Tel: 0844 856 3797

www.nationalmediamuseum.org.uk

20% off IMAX tickets

North Yorkshire Moors Railway
North Yorkshire YO18 7AJ

Enjoy a great day out with this popular heritage steam railway, linking moors and coast and running through the North York Moors National Park. Stations at Pickering, Levisham, Goathland and Grosmont, and services to/from Whitby.

Tel: 01751 472508

www.nymr.co.uk

Adults travel at the 'senior' rate on Fri with valid EH card

York Minster
North Yorkshire YO1 7JF

York Minster is one of the great cathedrals of the world. Enjoy its vast spaces and music and witness the human imagination at work on glass, stone and other fabrics.

10 mins from Clifford's Tower

Tel: 0844 939 0016

www.yorkminster.org

50% discount on entry
Separate charge for entry to the tower

OVP 6

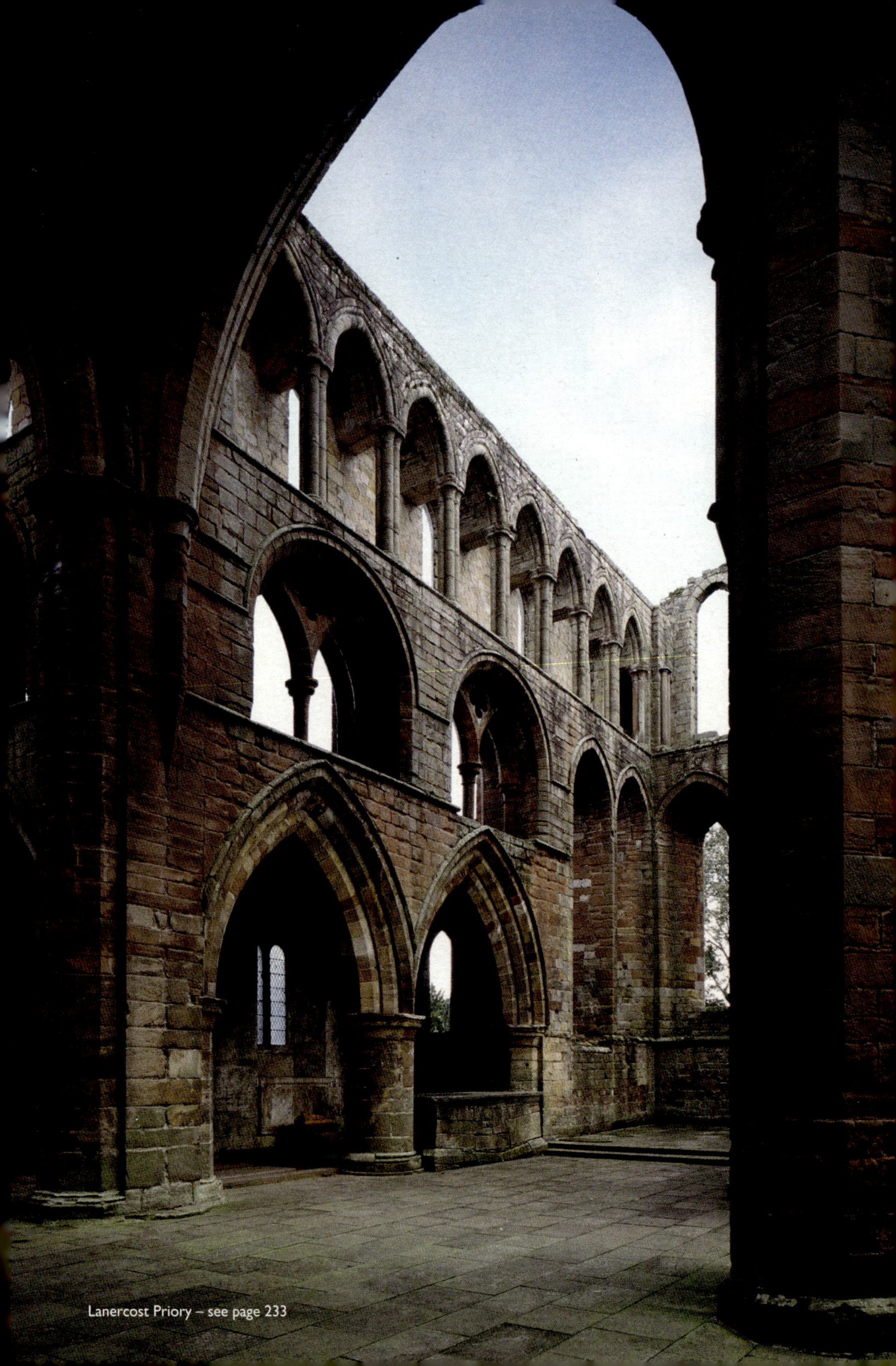

Lanercost Priory – see page 233

North West

www.english-heritage.org.uk/northwest

Introducing the North West

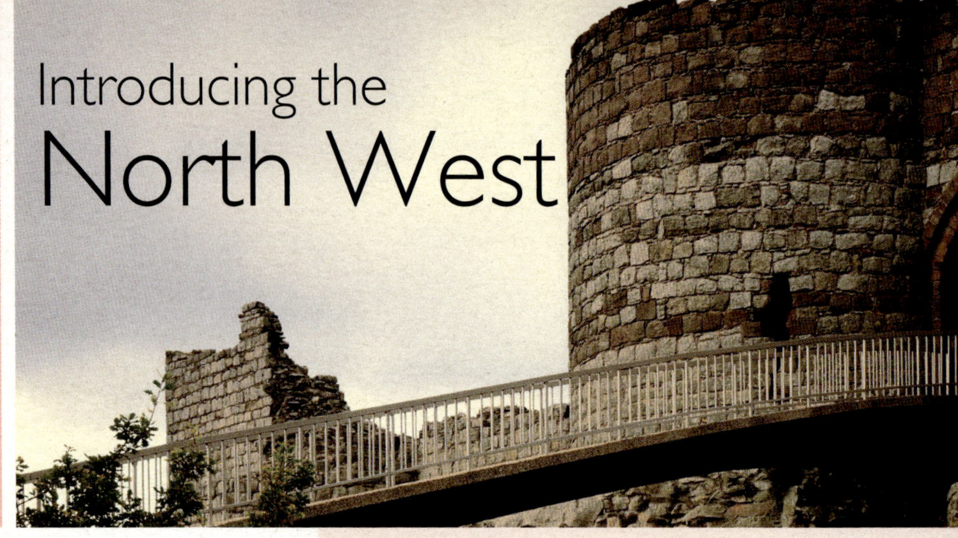

Remember to check opening times before you visit any of our properties.

Details of all bus travel in England are available from Traveline on 0871 200 2233 or visit www.traveline.org.uk

Cheshire

- Beeston Castle and Woodland Park
- Chester Castle: Agricola Tower and Castle Walls
- Chester Roman Amphitheatre
- Sandbach Crosses

Cumbria

- Ambleside Roman Fort
- Bow Bridge
- Brough Castle
- Brougham Castle
- Carlisle Castle
- Castlerigg Stone Circle
- Clifton Hall
- Countess Pillar
- Furness Abbey
- Hadrian's Wall (see page 237)
- Hardknott Roman Fort
- King Arthur's Round Table
- Lanercost Priory
- Mayburgh Henge
- Penrith Castle
- Piel Castle
- Ravenglass Roman Bath House
- Shap Abbey
- Stott Park Bobbin Mill
- Wetheral Priory Gatehouse

Lancashire

- Goodshaw Chapel
- Sawley Abbey
- Warton Old Rectory
- Whalley Abbey Gatehouse

Regional Excursions

Stretching from the Welsh to the Scottish borders, the North West is one of English Heritage's biggest and most varied regions, with many opportunities for 'single-base' excursions. In the south, **Beeston Castle and Woodland Park** make a day out in themselves, with nearby **Chester Castle** and its historic city as a possible addition. In the north, Carlisle, defender of the turbulent 'north-west frontier' for many centuries, is hard to beat. **Carlisle Castle**, with its long and often bloody history, will easily provide fascination for half a day: apart from the fortress itself, the excellent military museum and Roman dig display it contains are well worth visiting. Nearby – for Carlisle is not a large city – is charming red-sandstone Carlisle Cathedral, among the smallest of England's ancient cathedrals, yet boasting a spectacular east window and an array of extremely unusual medieval panel paintings. Close by too is Tullie House Museum and Art Gallery (which offers two for one entry to English Heritage members). Based in a lovely 17th-century house, this outstandingly family-friendly museum hosts very varied collections and frequent special events.

A comparatively short drive from Carlisle, moreover, stands **Lanercost Priory**, astride the line of **Hadrian's Wall**. Among the most beautiful, impressive and complete of all English Heritage's monastic sites (yet less often visited than it deserves due to its remote setting), Lanercost combines an active church, priory ruins and Tudor hall, set beside a working farm and fortified vicarage. It will repay a leisurely exploration not only by its noble architecture and varied contents, but also by its little-changed surroundings in the picturesque Irthing valley.

Make the most of your membership and keep up to date with upcoming events, the latest news and special offers by subscribing to our e-newsletter. Register online at **www.english-heritage.org.uk/newsletter** and we'll deliver the latest from English Heritage straight to your inbox.

Images:
(left) Beeston Castle
(top centre) Chester Roman Amphitheatre
(top right) Lanercost Priory
(bottom centre) Carlisle Castle
(bottom right) Beeston Castle

Beeston Castle and Woodland Park

Cheshire – CW6 9TX

Spectacularly crowning a sandstone crag towering above the Cheshire Plain, Beeston Castle is among the most dramatically-sited fortresses in England. Its extensive wooded surroundings, rich in wildlife, are now even more fascinating to explore. Visitors can experience some of the best views in Cheshire from the top of the castle mound.

© Skyscan Balloon Photography

Beeston Castle is a paradise for walkers, nature-lovers and adventurous children.

Check www.english-heritage.org.uk for the latest opening times

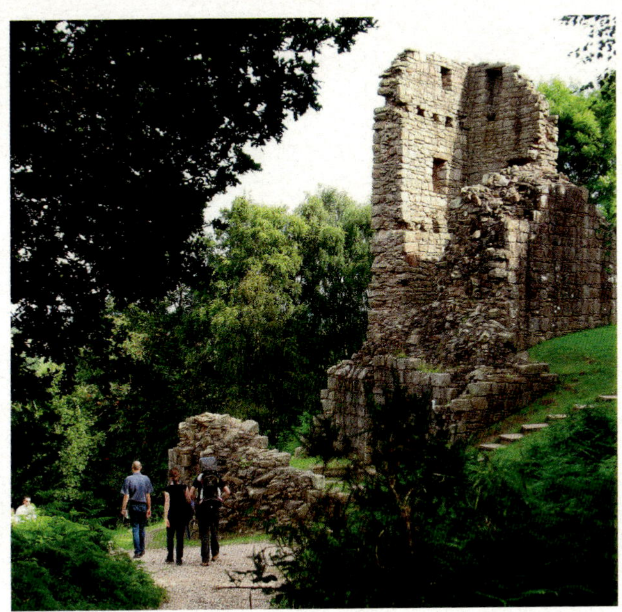

Naturally defended by steep cliffs on three sides, Beeston's crag attracted prehistoric settlers. It became an important Bronze Age metal-working site and later an immense Iron Age hillfort, whose earthwork defences were adapted by medieval castle-builders.

The 'Castle of the Rock' – its medieval title – was begun in the 1220s by Ranulf, Earl of Chester, one of the greatest barons of Henry III's England. A defence against aristocratic rivals and a proclamation of Ranulf's power, his fortress is approached via a ruined gatehouse in a multi-towered outer wall, defining a huge outer bailey climbing steadily up the hill.

At its summit is the crowning glory of Beeston, the inner bailey, defended by a deep rock-cut ditch and a mighty double-towered gatehouse. The best-preserved part of the castle, the inner bailey commands astounding views across eight counties, from the Welsh Mountains to the west, to the Pennines in the east. It also contains the famous castle well, over 100 metres deep and traditionally the hiding place of Richard II's treasure.

Beeston Castle experienced a final blaze of glory as an important English Civil War stronghold, which finally surrendered to Parliament in November 1645 after a long and eventful siege. Thereafter it became the romantic ruin which caught the attention of wealthy Victorian John Tollemache, who promoted Beeston as a tourist attraction, even stocking its grounds with kangaroos.

English Heritage landscape development now helps visitors to explore more of the castle's surroundings – a paradise for walkers, nature-lovers and adventurous children. A circular Woodland Walk leads fairly gently downhill from near the outer bailey gate. Winding around the base of the crag through wildlife-thronged woods, the path provides glimpses of the castle above, before reaching another of Beeston's attractions, the sandstone caves, one of which appeared as 'Robin Hood's Cave' in a 1992 film. The caves can also be reached via a shorter walk from the Visitor Centre, where the *Castle of the Rock* display vividly recounts Beeston's 4000 years of history.

NON-MEMBERS

Adult	£5.50
Concession	£5.00
Child	£3.30

OPENING TIMES

1 Apr-30 Sep, daily	10am-6pm
1 Oct-31 Mar, Thu-Mon	10am-4pm
24-26 Dec and 1 Jan	Closed

HOW TO FIND US

Direction: Located 11 miles SE of Chester, on minor road off A49

Train: Chester 10 miles

Bus: GHA service 83 (Tue) is the only bus service to Beeston; Otherwise Arriva service 84 to Tarporley (2½ miles)

Tel: 01829 260464

Local Tourist Information
Chester: 01244 402111

Please note: Steep climb (no disabled access to the top of the hill). Boots or stout footwear recommended for Woodland Walk.

Parking: please note the car park has increased from £2 to £2.50 per day.

MAP Page 282 (7D)
OS Map 117, 257/258: SJ537593

Check www.english-heritage.org.uk for the latest opening times

Ambleside Roman Fort
Cumbria

The well-marked remains of a 2nd-century fort with large granaries, probably built under Hadrian's rule to guard the Roman road from Brougham to Ravenglass and act as a supply base.

Managed by the National Trust.

OPENING TIMES
Any reasonable time

HOW TO FIND US
Direction: 182 metres W of Waterhead car park, Ambleside

Train: Windermere 5 miles

Bus: Stagecoach Cumbria X8, 505, 516, 555, 599; Traveller's Choice 618

MAP Page 284 (6D)
OS Map 90, OL7: NY372034

Beeston Castle and Woodland Park
See feature – Page 226

Bow Bridge
Cumbria

This narrow, 15th-century stone bridge across Mill Beck carried an old packhorse route to nearby Furness Abbey (see p.232).

OPENING TIMES
Any reasonable time

HOW TO FIND US
Direction: Located ½ mile N of Barrow-in-Furness, on minor road off A590; near Furness Abbey

Train: Barrow-in-Furness 1½ miles

Bus: Stagecoach in Cumbria service 6/6A, X35; Travellers Choice 618 to within ¾ mile

MAP Page 284 (7D)
OS Map 96, OL6: SD224715

Brough Castle
Cumbria

Starkly impressive Brough Castle stands on a ridge commanding strategic Stainmore Pass, on the site of a Roman fort. Frequently the target of Scots raids, its towering keep dates from c. 1200 and more comfortable living quarters were later added by the Clifford family, only to be accidentally burnt following a 'great Christmas' party in 1521. Like so many other castles hereabouts, Brough was restored in the 17th century by Lady Anne Clifford, traces of whose additions can still be seen.

St Michael's Parish Church, in pretty Church Brough near the castle, displays an exhibition about the region. This living church is open 10am-4pm daily (not English Heritage).

NEW FOR 2011
New graphic panels guide you round the castle.

OPENING TIMES
1 Apr-30 Sep, daily	10am-5pm
1 Oct-31 Mar, daily	10am-4pm
24-26 Dec and 1 Jan	Closed

HOW TO FIND US
Direction: 8 miles SE of Appleby S of A66

Train: Kirkby Stephen 6 miles

Bus: Classic service 352; Grand Prix service 563, 571; Cumbria Classic Bus 572; Kirby Lonsdale Coaches/Woofs 564

Please note: approach may be muddy, stout footwear recommended .

Guidebook available at Brougham Castle.

MAP Page 285 (6F)
OS Map 91, OL19: NY791141

Brougham Castle
Cumbria – CA10 2AA

In a picturesque setting beside the crossing of the River Eamont, Brougham Castle was founded in the early 13th century by King John's agent Robert de Vieuxpont. His great keep largely survives amid many later buildings – including the unusual double gatehouse and impressive 'Tower of League' – added by the powerful Clifford family, Wardens of the Marches. Both a formidable barrier against Scots invaders and a prestigious residence, their castle welcomed Edward I in 1300.

A complex of passages and spiral stairways makes Brougham a fascinating castle to explore, as well as an ideal picnic setting: the keep top provides panoramic views over the Eden Valley and the earthworks of the adjacent Roman fort of Brocavum. Having fallen into decay after James I's visit in 1617, the castle was restored by the indomitable Lady Anne Clifford (see also Brough Castle and Countess Pillar). She often visited with her travelling 'court', and died here in 1676.
An exhibition highlights her remarkable life and includes carvings from the Roman fort. There is good wheelchair access to most of the site (excluding the keep).

NON-MEMBERS
Adult	£3.80
Concession	£3.40
Child	£2.30
Family	£9.90

OPENING TIMES
1 Apr-30 Sep, daily	10am-5pm

HOW TO FIND US
Direction: 1½ miles SE of Penrith, off A66.

Train: Penrith 2 miles

Local Tourist information
Penrith: 01768 867466;
Rheged: 01768 860034

Brougham Castle

Tel: 01768 862488

OVP

Please note: Car parking limited: in 'no through road' opposite castle entrance.

MAP Page 284 (5E)
OS Map 90, OL5: NY537290

Carlisle Castle

See feature – Page 230

Castlerigg Stone Circle
Cumbria

Dramatically sited with the mountains of Helvellyn and High Seat as a backdrop, Castlerigg is among the earliest British circles, raised in about 2500 BC during the Neolithic period.

Visitor interpretation panels installed by the National Trust.

Managed by the National Trust.

OPENING TIMES

Any reasonable time

HOW TO FIND US

Direction: 1½ miles E of Keswick

Train: Penrith 16 miles

Bus: Stagecoach Caldbeck Rambler services 73/73A pass the site. Otherwise Stagecoach 555 passes within 1 mile of the site

MAP Page 284 (5D)
OS Map 89/90, OL4: NY291236

Chester Castle: Agricola Tower and Castle Walls
Cheshire

The original gateway to Chester Castle, this 12th-century tower houses a chapel with exceptionally fine wall-paintings of c. 1220, rediscovered in the 1980s. An access stair to the castle's wall-walk is nearby.

Managed by Chester City Council.

Chester Castle: Agricola Tower and Castle Walls

OPENING TIMES

Castle only open for guided tours. Please call 01829 260464 for details

HOW TO FIND US

Direction: Access via Assizes Court car park on Grosvenor St

Train: Chester 1¼ miles

Bus: From surrounding areas

Disabled access (certain parts only).

MAP Page 282 (7C)
OS Map 117, 266: SJ405657

Chester Roman Amphitheatre
Cheshire

The largest Roman amphitheatre in Britain, used for entertainment and military training by the 20th Legion, based at the fortress of 'Deva' (Chester). Excavations by English Heritage and Chester City Council in 2004-5 revealed two successive stone-built amphitheatres with wooden seating. The first included access to the upper tiers of seats via stairs on the rear wall, as at Pompeii, and had a small shrine next to its north entrance. The second provided seat access via vaulted stairways. The two buildings differed both from each other and from all other British amphitheatres, underlining the importance of Roman Chester.

Managed by Chester City Council.

OPENING TIMES

Any reasonable time

HOW TO FIND US

Direction: On Vicars Lane, beyond Newgate, Chester

Train: Chester ¾ mile

Bus: From surrounding areas

Disabled access (no access to amphitheatre floor).

Chester Roman Amphitheatre

MAP Page 282 (7C)
OS Map 117, 266: SJ408662

Clifton Hall
Cumbria

This 15th-century tower, sole surviving part of the manor house of the Wybergh family, was plundered by Jacobites in 1745 before the Battle of Clifton Moor, the last battle fought on English soil.

OPENING TIMES

Any reasonable time

24-26 Dec and 1 Jan — Closed

HOW TO FIND US

Direction: Next to Clifton Hall Farm; 2 miles S of Penrith, on A6

Train: Penrith 2½ miles

MAP Page 284 (5E)
OS Map 90, OL5: NY530271

Countess Pillar, Brougham
Cumbria

A monument erected in 1656 by Lady Anne Clifford of nearby Brougham Castle, to commemorate her final parting here from her mother. On the low stone beside it, money was given to the poor each anniversary of their parting.

OPENING TIMES

Any reasonable time

HOW TO FIND US

Direction: ¼ mile E of Brougham. A new access route has also been created, which runs from the B6262 (to Brougham) and starts near the junction with the A66

Train: Penrith 2½ miles

Warning: site on a very busy main road. Parking on B6262, close to the junction with A66. Safe access by footpath.

MAP Page 284 (5E)
OS Map 90, OL5: NY546289

Carlisle Castle Cumbria – CA3 8UR

A mighty presence in the city it has dominated for nine centuries, Carlisle Castle was a constantly updated working fortress until well within living memory. Now its rich and varied visitor attractions reflect its long and eventful history.

The castle remained the headquarters of the Border Regiment until 1959.

Check www.english-heritage.org.uk for the latest opening times

Even before the medieval castle was begun, this site was an important Roman fortress. Today, the castle still plays a prominent role as one of Cumbria's best loved landmarks.

The commanding keep, begun during the 12th century by King Henry I of England and completed by King David I of Scotland, is both the oldest part of the castle and a reminder that Carlisle was a disputed frontier fortress, long commanding the especially turbulent western end of the Anglo-Scottish border. The keep houses displays about the castle's history, from medieval assaults via the exploits of Elizabethan Border Reivers to the Civil War siege and Bonnie Prince Charlie's Jacobite Rising of 1745-6.

Carlisle was then the very last English fortress ever to suffer a siege: overwhelmed by the Duke of Cumberland's Hanoverian army, its Jacobite garrison were imprisoned in the keep's dank basement, where visitors can see the legendary 'licking stones',which they supposedly licked for life-giving moisture. Equally famous are the strange and fantastic carvings on the keep's second floor, cut in about 1480. The Warden's Apartments in the castle's outer gatehouse have been furnished as they appeared at about this date.

By the time Mary Queen of Scots was imprisoned here in 1567-8, Henry VIII's updating for heavy artillery had left its mark on Carlisle, including the keep's rounded 'shot-deflecting' battlements and the Half Moon Battery defending the Captain's Tower gateway. The castle's military history did not end after the Jacobite Rising: fear of a radical revolution made it a permanently occupied garrison from the 1820s, when the barrack blocks lining the outer ward were begun. Indeed, the castle remained the headquarters of the Border Regiment until 1959 and the 300-year history of this famous local infantry regiment is vividly told here in Cumbria's Military Museum (entry included in the castle admission charge, tel 01228 532774).

www.english-heritage.org.uk/carlislecastle

NON-MEMBERS

Adult	£5.00
Concession	£4.50
Child	£3.00

OPENING TIMES

1 Apr-30 Sep, daily	9.30am-5pm
1 Oct-31 Mar, daily	10am-4pm
24-26 Dec and 1 Jan	Closed

HOW TO FIND US

Direction: In Carlisle city centre

Train: Carlisle ½ mile

Bus: Stagecoach 38, 60, 60A, 61, 61A, 67, 68, 93, 300, 554, 600. Also Reay's Coaches service 39 (Tue, Fri) at Stacey's 71

Tel: 01228 591922

Local Tourist Information: 01228 625600

Disabled access (limited).

Dogs on leads (restricted areas only).

Guided tours (available at peak times at a small extra charge; groups please pre-book).

Parking (disabled only, but signposted city centre car parks nearby).

MAP Page 284 (4D)
OS Map 85, 315: NY396562

Furness Abbey
Cumbria – LA13 0PJ

The impressive remains of an abbey founded by Stephen, later King of England, including much of the east end and west tower of the church, the ornately decorated chapter house and the cloister buildings. Originally of the Savigniac order, it passed to the Cistercians in 1147 and despite damage by Scottish raiders, became (after Fountains Abbey) the second most prosperous Cistercian abbey in all England. Set in the 'vale of nightshade', the romantic ruins were celebrated by Wordsworth in his *Prelude* of 1805.

An exhibition on the history of the abbey, with a display of elaborately carved stones, can be seen in the visitor centre. (See also Bow Bridge, p.228)

NON-MEMBERS

Adult	£3.80
Concession	£3.40
Child	£2.30

OPENING TIMES

1 Apr-30 Sep, Thu-Mon	10am-5pm
1 Oct-31 Mar, Sat-Sun	10am-4pm
24-26 Dec and 1 Jan	Closed

HOW TO FIND US

Direction: Located 1½ miles N of Barrow-in-Furness, off A590

Train: Barrow-in-Furness 2 miles

Bus: Stagecoach in Cumbria service 6/6A, X35; Travellers Choice 618 to within ¾ mile

Tel: 01229 823420

Furness Abbey

Dogs on leads (restricted areas only).

MAP Page 284 (7D)
OS Map 96, OL6: SD218717

Goodshaw Chapel
Lancashire

English Heritage's only Nonconformist place of worship, this atmospheric Baptist chapel displays a complete set of box-pews, galleries and pulpit dating from c. 1742 to 1809. A festival of hymns and sermons is held on the first Sunday in July.

OPENING TIMES

Please call the keykeeper for details. Tel: 01706 227333

HOW TO FIND US

Direction: In Crawshawbooth, 2 miles N of Rawtenstall via A682 (in Goodshaw Ave – turning off A682 opp. Jester public house). Chapel approx. 1½ miles from main road

Train: Burnley Manchester Road 4½ miles

Bus: Transdev Burnley & Pendle 'Witch Way' services X43/4

MAP Page 282 (4E)
OS Map 103, OL21: SD814261

Hadrian's Wall
See page 237

Hardknott Roman Fort
Cumbria

This remote and dramatically-sited fort was founded under Hadrian's rule in the 2nd century. Well-marked remains include the headquarters building, commandant's house and bath house. The site of the parade ground survives beside the fort and the road which Hardknott guarded can be traced for some distance as an earthwork.

Managed by the National Trust.

OPENING TIMES

Any reasonable time

HOW TO FIND US

Direction: 9 miles NE of Ravenglass; at W end of Hardknott Pass

Train: Dalegarth (Ravenglass & Eskdale) 3 miles or Ravenglass 10 miles

Warning: access may be hazardous during the winter months.

MAP Page 284 (6C)
OS Map 89/90, OL6: NY218015

King Arthur's Round Table
Cumbria

A Neolithic earthwork henge, dating from c. 2000 BC, but much later believed to be King Arthur's jousting arena. Mayburgh Henge is adjacent.

OPENING TIMES

Any reasonable time

HOW TO FIND US

Direction: Located at Eamont Bridge, 1 mile S of Penrith. Mayburgh Henge is nearby

Train: Penrith 1½ miles

Bus: Stagecoach 108; Appolo 8 Travel/Grand Prix/Stagecoach/ Services 106 & 107

MAP Page 284 (5E)
OS Map 90, OL5: NY523284

Lanercost Priory
Cumbria – CA8 2HQ

The beautiful and now tranquil setting of Augustinian Lanercost Priory belies an often troubled history. Standing close to Hadrian's Wall, it suffered frequent attacks during the long Anglo-Scottish wars, once by Robert Bruce in person. The mortally sick King Edward I rested here for five months in 1306-7, shortly before his death on his final campaign.

Yet there is still much to see in this best–preserved of Cumbrian monasteries. The east end of the noble 13th-century church survives to its full height, housing within its dramatic triple tier of arches some fine monuments, including the exquisite effigy of four-month-old Elizabeth Dacre Howard. The nave, with its soaring west front, is still in full use as the parish church.

Lanercost's cloisters include a beautiful vaulted 13th-century refectory undercroft. They partly owe their preservation to their conversion, after the priory's suppression, into the Tudor mansion of the Dacre family. The cloister west range includes the Dacre Hall, still displaying fragments of 16th-century wall-painting, as well as the four-storey Dacre Tower, adapted from the monastic kitchen.

Set beside a still-active farm, vicarage, and 'vicar's pele tower' (viewable only from outside), Lanercost Priory's extensive remains make an unforgettable ensemble. Information panels tell you about the priory and its later conversion into a grand mansion.

The parish church and Dacre Hall are not managed by English Heritage.

NON-MEMBERS

Adult	£3.30
Concession	£3.00
Child	£2.00

OPENING TIMES

1 Apr-30 Sep, daily	10am-5pm
1-31 Oct, Thu-Mon	10am-4pm

HOW TO FIND US

Direction: Off a minor road S of Lanercost; 2 miles NE of Brampton

Train: Brampton 3 miles

Bus: Alba/Classic Hadrian's Wall bus AD122 April-November. Otherwise Stagecoach/Arriva service 685 to within 2½ miles

Tel: 01697 73030

OVP

Lanercost tearoom and farm shop is open every day except 25, 26 Dec and 1 Jan. www.lanercost.co.uk Tel: 016977 41267 (not managed by English Heritage).

MAP Page 284 (4E)
OS Map 86, 315: NY556637

Mayburgh Henge
Cumbria

A large and impressive Neolithic henge, much better preserved than neighbouring King Arthur's Round Table. Its banks stand up to 3 metres (10 feet) high and unusually are constructed of pebbles collected from the nearby river. Near the centre is a single standing stone: old drawings suggest that it was one of a group of four here, four more having been removed from the entranceway.

Mayburgh Henge

OPENING TIMES

Any reasonable time

HOW TO FIND US

Direction: 1 mile S of Penrith off A6

Train: Penrith 1½ miles

Bus: Stagecoach 108. Also Appolo 8 Travel/Grand Prix/Stagecoach/ Services 106 & 107 stop nearby

MAP Page 284 (5E)
OS Map 90, OL5: NY519284

Penrith Castle
Cumbria

Penrith Castle was begun at the end of the 14th century by Ralph Neville, who played a key role in defending this area against the Scots. It was later transformed into a luxurious residence by Richard, Duke of Gloucester (subsequently Richard III). Surviving to their full height, the castle walls stand in a public park. Graphic panels tell the story of the castle.

OPENING TIMES

Park:

Summer	7.30am-9pm
Winter	7.30am-4.30pm

HOW TO FIND US

Direction: Opposite Penrith railway station

Train: Penrith (adjacent)

Bus: From surrounding areas

MAP Page 284 (5E)
OS Map 90, OL5: NY513299

Piel Castle
Cumbria

The impressive ruins of a 14th-century castle with a massive keep, inner and outer baileys and towered curtain walls still standing. It was built by the Abbot of Furness on the south-eastern point of Piel Island, to guard the deep-water harbour of Barrow-in-Furness against pirates and Scots raiders.

OPENING TIMES

Any reasonable time. Access by ferry boat not managed by EH

HOW TO FIND US

Direction: Piel Island, 3¼ miles SE of Barrow-in-Furness

By small boat: Two ferries operate services to Piel Island (subject to tides and weather). Call Steve Chattaway on 07516 453784 or Alan Cleasby on 07798 794550. There is a small charge for this service

Train: Barrow-in-Furness 4 miles

Bus: Stagecoach in Cumbria 11 Barrow-in Furness – Ulverston

MAP Page 284 (7D)
OS Map 96, OL6: SD233636

Ravenglass Roman Bath House
Cumbria

The remains of the bath house of Ravenglass Roman fort, established in AD 130, are among the tallest Roman structures surviving in northern Britain: the walls stand almost 4 metres (13 feet) high. The fort at Ravenglass (whose earthworks can be seen near the bath house) guarded what was probably a useful harbour, and there is evidence that soldiers stationed here served in Hadrian's fleet.

OPENING TIMES

Any reasonable time

HOW TO FIND US

Direction: ¼ mile E of Ravenglass, off minor road leading to A595

Train: Ravenglass (adjacent)

Bus: 3D Travel service 6 or AA Travel service X6

MAP Page 284 (6C)
OS Map 96, OL6: SD088959

Sandbach Crosses
Cheshire

The two massive Saxon stone crosses, elaborately carved with animals and Biblical scenes including the Nativity of Christ and the Crucifixion, dominate the cobbled market square of Sandbach. Probably dating from the 9th century and originally painted as well as carved, they are among the finest surviving examples of Anglo-Saxon high crosses.

OPENING TIMES

Any reasonable time

HOW TO FIND US

Direction: Market Sq, Sandbach

Train: Sandbach 1½ miles

Bus: From surrounding areas

MAP Page 282 (7D)
OS Map 118, 268: SJ759608

Sawley Abbey
Lancashire

The remains of a Cistercian abbey founded in 1148, set on the banks of the Ribble against a backdrop of dramatic hills. After its dissolution in 1536, the monks were briefly returned to the abbey during the Pilgrimage of Grace. They remained in possession until the insurrection's collapse and the execution of their abbot.

Managed by the Heritage Trust for the North West.

OPENING TIMES

1 Apr-30 Sep, daily	10am-6pm
1 Oct-31 Mar, daily	10am-4pm
24-26 Dec and 1 Jan	Closed

HOW TO FIND US

Direction: Located at Sawley; 3½ miles N of Clitheroe, off A59

Train: Clitheroe 4 miles

MAP Page 282 (4D)
OS Map 103, OL41: SD777464

Shap Abbey
Cumbria

The impressive full-height 15th-century tower and other remains of a remote abbey of Premonstratensian 'white canons'.

Information panels guide you round the abbey and illustrate daily monastic life.

OPENING TIMES

Any reasonable time

HOW TO FIND US

Direction: 1½ miles W of Shap, on the bank of the River Lowther

Train: Penrith 10 miles

Bus: Stagecoach in Cumbria/ Apollo 8/Grand Prix service 106 Penrith – Kendal within 1½ miles

P

Disabled access (limited views from outside the site).

Steep access road is unsuitable in wintry weather.

MAP Page 284 (6E)
OS Map 90, OL5: NY548152

Stott Park Bobbin Mill
Cumbria – LA12 8AX

This extensive working mill was begun in 1835 to produce the wooden bobbins vital to the Lancashire spinning and weaving industries. Although small compared to other mills, some 250 men and boys (some drafted in from workhouses) worked here over the years in often arduous conditions to produce a quarter of a million bobbins a week. Guided tours are included in the admission charge: the last tour begins ½ hour before closing.

NON-MEMBERS

Adult	£6.00
Concession	£5.40
Child	£3.60
Family	£15.60

OPENING TIMES

1 Apr-31 Oct, Mon-Fri	11am-5pm

Please call for details of steam days

HOW TO FIND US

Direction: Located 1½ miles N of Newby Bridge, off A590

Train: Grange-over-Sands 8 miles; Lakeside Station (Lakeside & Haverthwaite railway) ¾ mile

Bus: Lecks 538 (Thu). Alternatively Stagecoach service X35 or 618 to Newby Bridge and 1½ mile walk

Ferry: Windermere ferry from Ambleside or Bowness to Lakeside, then 1 mile

Tel: 01539 531087

Local Tourist Information
Hawkshead: 01539 436525

Stott Park Bobbin Mill

Disabled access (ground floor only. Specific interpretation for visually impaired visitors).

Parking (lower car park).

Dogs welcome (restricted areas only).

MAP Page 284 (6D)
OS Map 96/97, OL7: SD372881

Warton Old Rectory
Lancashire

A rare survival of a large, 14th-century stone house with great hall and chambers. It served as a residence and courthouse for the wealthy and powerful rectors of Warton.

Managed by the Heritage Trust for the North West.

OPENING TIMES

1 Apr-30 Sep, daily	10am-6pm
1 Oct-31 Mar, daily	10am-4pm
24-26 Dec and 1 Jan	Closed

HOW TO FIND US

Direction: At Warton; 1 mile N of Carnforth, on minor road off A6

Train: Carnforth 1 mile

Bus: Stagecoach in Lancashire service 55; Kirby Lonsdale Minibuses L1, 430 & 435

MAP Page 282 (3D)
OS Map 97, OL7: SD499723

Wetheral Priory Gatehouse
Cumbria

Well-preserved 15th-century gatehouse, the sole survivor of a small Benedictine priory. A miniature 'pele-tower' containing two storeys of comfortable rooms, it later became a fortified vicarage, a defence against border raiders.

Wetheral Priory Gatehouse

OPENING TIMES

1 Apr-30 Sep, daily	10am-6pm
1 Oct-31 Mar, daily	10am-4pm
24-26 Dec and 1 Jan	Closed

HOW TO FIND US

Direction: Near Wetheral village; 6 miles E of Carlisle, on B6263

Train: Wetheral ½ mile

Bus: Reay's/Stagecoach in Cumbria services 75 to Wetheral then short walk

MAP Page 284 (4E)
OS Map 86, 315: NY468541

Whalley Abbey Gatehouse
Lancashire

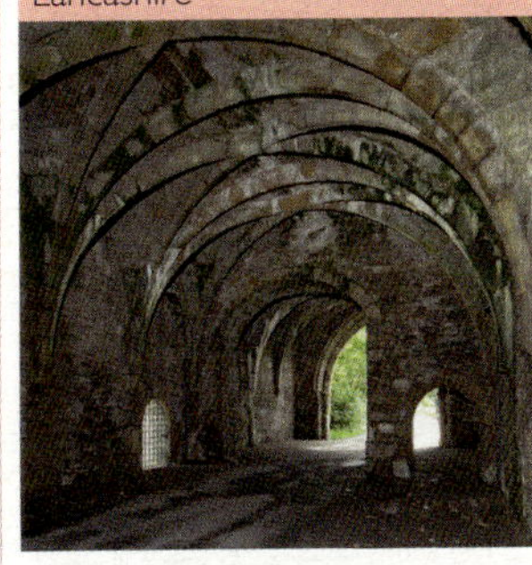

The 14th-century gatehouse of the nearby Cistercian abbey, the second wealthiest monastery in Lancashire, beside the River Calder. The first floor was probably a chapel.

OPENING TIMES

Any reasonable time

HOW TO FIND US

Direction: In Whalley; 6 miles NE of Blackburn, on minor road off A59

Train: Whalley ¼ mile

Bus: From surrounding area

MAP Page 282 (4D)
OS Map 103, 287: SD729362

Associated attractions in the North West

These visitor attractions, all independent of EH, offer discounts to our members. Please call before you visit to confirm details. A valid EH membership card must be produced for each member.

Muncaster Castle
Cumbria CA18 1RQ

Historic haunted castle: extensive gardens, World Owl Centre with daily bird show and Heron Happy Hour. Indoor Meadow Vole Maze. Gift shops, café, playground. B&B available. Special events all year.

1hr approx from J36/M6

Tel: 01229 717614

www.muncaster.co.uk

Group rate discount on entry

Norton Priory Museum & Gardens
Cheshire WA7 1SX

Discover the ruins and grounds of this 12th-century Augustinian priory, set in 40 acres of beautiful gardens. Lovely Georgian Walled Garden, café, plant sales and children's play area

3 miles from J11 of M56

Tel: 01928 569895

www.nortonpriory.org

£2 off adult ticket price

Pendle Heritage Centre
Lancashire BB9 6JQ

Historic farmhouse, restored using traditional building skills. Exhibitions, 18th-century walled garden, shop and café.

Close to J13 of M65

Tel: 01282 677151

www.htnw.co.uk

50% discount on entry 6

Smithills Hall
Greater Manchester BL1 7NP

Set in over 2,200 acres of woodland, on the edge of the West Pennine Moors, Smithills Hall is one of the oldest and best preserved manor houses in the North West.

1 mile to Moss Bank Way A58

Tel: 01204 332377

www.boltonmuseums.org.uk

20% discount on entry

Stretton Watermill
Cheshire SY14 7HS

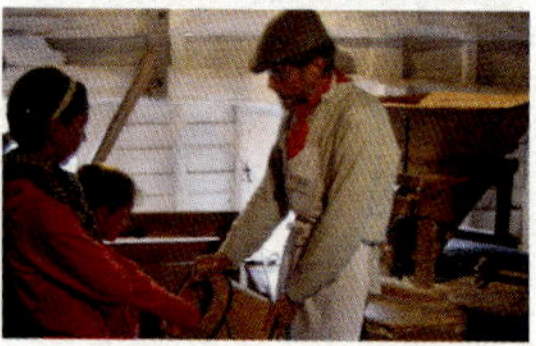

Step back in time and visit a working mill in beautiful rural Cheshire. See one of the country's best preserved demonstration water-powered corn mills.

Close to Beeston Castle

Tel: 01606 271640

www.strettonwatermill.org.uk

2 for 1 entry

Weaver Hall Museum and Workhouse
Cheshire CW9 8AB

Weaver Hall Museum is the new name for the Salt Museum, Northwich. You will discover the fascinating history of Cheshire and explore the workhouse history of the imposing Victorian building.

Close to Beeston Castle

Tel: 01606 271640

www.cheshirewestandchester.gov/museums

2 for 1 entry

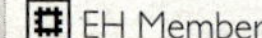 EH Members

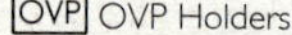 OVP Holders

Discounted Child Places Included

Hadrian's Wall

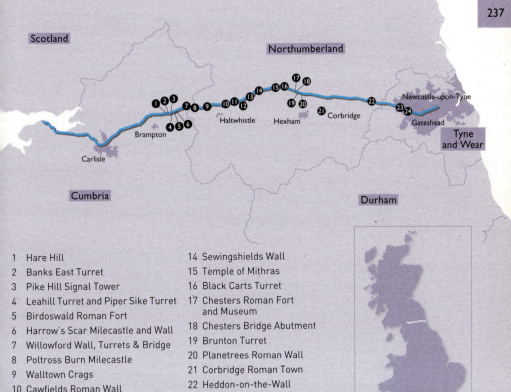

1 Hare Hill
2 Banks East Turret
3 Pike Hill Signal Tower
4 Leahill Turret and Piper Sike Turret
5 Birdoswald Roman Fort
6 Harrow's Scar Milecastle and Wall
7 Willowford Wall, Turrets & Bridge
8 Poltross Burn Milecastle
9 Walltown Crags
10 Cawfields Roman Wall
11 Winshields Wall
12 Roman Vindolanda
13 Housesteads Roman Fort
14 Sewingshields Wall
15 Temple of Mithras
16 Black Carts Turret
17 Chesters Roman Fort and Museum
18 Chesters Bridge Abutment
19 Brunton Turret
20 Planetrees Roman Wall
21 Corbridge Roman Town
22 Heddon-on-the-Wall
23 Denton Hall Turret
24 Benwell Roman Temple and Vallum Crossing

www.english-heritage.org.uk/hadrianswall

Introducing Hadrian's Wall

The Hadrian's Wall Bus (AD122) runs throughout the spring and summer months between Newcastle, Hexham and Carlisle, and is an excellent way to see the stunning scenery in this part of England. It stops at Corbridge, Chesters, Housesteads, Vindolanda and Birdoswald Roman Sites – as well as main railway stations, market places, towns and villages along the way.

Taking it Easier

It is of course possible to see the principal forts of Hadrian's Wall by car in a single very long day, or to walk the whole Wall in a strenuous week or so. But a day out less demanding of stamina or petrol might begin at riverside **Chesters Roman Fort**. This most pastorally-set of the major Wall forts has the added bonus of a unique site museum housing a fabulous array of Roman finds collected from many Wall sites by the Victorian, John Clayton, and now restored to its 'traditional museum' appearance.

Just over five miles away, as a change from the Romans, stands Hexham with its magnificent medieval priory church: Hexham Old Gaol, the oldest purpose-built prison in England, offers 'two for one' entry for English Heritage members. Not far away again is excavated **Corbridge Roman Town**, long a much-needed rest and recreation centre for off-duty Wall soldiers: here you can enjoy the unusual experience of walking along a Roman 'high street' and also visit perhaps the best modern museum in the Wall region, with 'Grricola the Roman Lion' on hand to guide children. From the Roman site, the later (though far from modern) town of Corbridge is clearly visible, including the Saxon tower of St Andrew's church, partly built with recycled Roman masonry, as was the medieval fortified 'Vicar's Pele Tower' in its churchyard. A refuge from possible present-day 'Wall fatigue', Corbridge is now notable for its boutiques and food shops.

Banks East Turret
Cumbria

Imposing and well-preserved turret with adjoining stretches of Hadrian's Wall.

HOW TO FIND US

Direction: On minor road E of Banks village; 3½ miles NE of Brampton

Train: Brampton for Banks East Turret

Bus: Alba/Classic service AD122 Carlisle – Hexham (April-Oct). Otherwise nearest bus service is Stagecoach 95 to Brampton and Greenhead or Stacey's 185 to Greenhead & Housesteads

OS Map 86, 315: NY575647

Benwell Roman Temple
Tyne and Wear

The remains of a small temple to the native god 'Antenociticus', in the 'vicus' (civilian settlement) which stood outside Benwell fort.

HOW TO FIND US

Direction: Temple located immediately S of A69, at Benwell in Broomridge Ave; Vallum Crossing in Denhill Park

Train: Newcastle 2 miles

Bus: Stagecoach 10, 11, 38, 39, 40, X82; Go North East 684; Arriva/ Stagecoach Cumberland 685

OS Map 88, 316: NZ217647

Benwell Vallum Crossing
Tyne and Wear

A stone-built causeway, where the road from the south crossed the Vallum earthwork on its way to Benwell fort.

HOW TO FIND US

Direction: Temple located immediately S of A69, at Benwell in Broomridge Ave; Vallum Crossing in Denhill Park

Train: Newcastle 2 miles

Bus: Frequent from centre of Newcastle

OS Map 88, 136: NZ216646

Birdoswald Roman Fort
See feature – Page 240

Black Carts Turret
Northumberland

A 460-metre (1509 feet) length of Hadrian's Wall including one turret.

Please note: It is not possible for visitors to park here.

HOW TO FIND US

Direction: 2 miles W of Chollerford on B6318

Train: Hexham 7 miles

Bus: Alba/Classic service AD122 Carlisle – Hexham (Apr-Oct)

OS Map 87, OL43: NY884713

Brunton Turret
Northumberland

Wall section and a surviving piece of turret 2½ metres (8.2 feet) high, built by men of the Twentieth Legion.

HOW TO FIND US

Direction: ¼ mile S of Low Brunton, off A6079

Train: Hexham 4½ miles

Bus: Alba/Classic service AD122 Carlisle – Hexham (Apr-Oct); also Tyne Valley/Snaith service 880 from Hexham

OS Map 87, OL43: NY922698

Cawfields Roman Wall
Northumberland

© Skyscan Balloon Photography

A fine stretch of Hadrian's Wall on a steep slope, with turrets and an impressive milecastle, probably built by the Second Legion.

HOW TO FIND US

Direction: 1¼ miles N of Haltwhistle, off B6318

Train: Haltwhistle 2 miles

Bus: Alba/Classic service AD122 Carlisle – Hexham (April-Oct); also Telford service 185

Parking not operated by EH. Parking charge applies (payable to Northumberland National Park).

OS Map 86/87, OL43: NY716667

Chesters Bridge Abutment
Northumberland

Close to Chesters Roman Fort are the remains of a bridge which carried Hadrian's Wall across the North Tyne. Visible on both river banks, they are most impressive on the eastern side.

HOW TO FIND US

Direction: ½ mile S of Low Brunton, on A6079

Train: Hexham 4½ miles

Bus: Alba/Classic service AD122 Carlisle – Hexham (Apr-Oct); also Tyne Valley/Snaith service 880 from Hexham

OS Map 87, 43: NY914701

Chesters Roman Fort
See feature – Page 242

Birdoswald Roman Fort

Cumbria – CA8 7DD

For those who want an introduction to Hadrian's Wall in Cumbria, or an overview of its history and appearance at one single site, Birdoswald is the place to visit.

If you would like to stay at a real Roman fort while walking the Wall as part of a residential or educational trip, there is a 36-bed farmhouse here, which is suitable for groups.

Not only can a Roman fort, turret and milecastle all be seen here, but also, to the east, the longest continuous stretch of Wall visible today. The Visitor Centre has interesting displays and reconstructions, tracing the history of the Wall via audiovisuals, strikingly life-like figures and excavated artefacts: these also tell the intriguing story of Birdoswald and its people over the past 2000 years.

Birdoswald likewise has the best preserved defences of any of the 16 major forts which supported Hadrian's frontier system. Known to the Romans as 'Banna', from the early 3rd century its garrison was a thousand-strong infantry unit originating in Dacia (modern Romania). Three main gates of their fortress are still traceable, along with perimeter walls, angle towers, granaries and an unusual drill hall.

Overlaying these, and another distinctive feature of Birdoswald, are the remains of the successive buildings raised here after the Roman withdrawal. First, in the 5th century, a large timber hall – now marked out by posts – was built, perhaps for a local British chieftain. Later a medieval fortified tower rose here, replaced by an Elizabethan 'bastle house', a defence against the notorious 'Border Reivers'. Finally the present, attractively turreted, farmhouse was built. Adjacent buildings now house a cosy tearoom, a well-stocked shop for souvenirs and the displays. The fort stands on the line of the Hadrian's Wall Path National Trail, and is the perfect resting place for walkers. Guided tours for groups are available at a small additional fee. Please contact the site for details and bookings.

Accommodation

If you would like to stay within the walls of the fort, there is a 36-bed farmhouse, which can be booked for groups. A great base for exploring this and other sites on the Wall, it is also an excellent educational visits resource.

To find out more about staying at Birdoswald, please call 016977 47602 or email birdoswald.accommodation@english-heritage.org.uk

NON-MEMBERS

Adult	£5.00
Concession	£4.50
Child	£3.00

There are free education visits and Discovery Visits which incur a charge

OPENING TIMES

1 Apr-30 Sep, daily	10am-5.30pm (last admission 5pm)
1-31 Oct, daily	10am-4pm

HOW TO FIND US

Direction: 4 miles west of Greenhead off B6318. Signposted from A69 Carlisle-Hexham road at Brampton roundabout

Train: Brampton 8 miles, Haltwhistle 7 miles

Bus: Alba/Classic service AD122 Carlisle – Hexham (Apr-Oct)

Tel: 016977 47602

Haltwhistle Tourist Information
01434 322022

Parking: Pay and display parking refunded to all visitors and members who visit the site.

Disabled access (to visitor centre, toilets, shop, tearoom and part of site. Disabled parking on site).

MAP Page 284 (4E)
OS Map 86, OL43: NY615663

Chesters Roman Fort and Museum Northumberland – NE46 4EU

Picturesquely set in the beautiful valley of the River North Tyne, Chesters is the best-preserved example of a Roman cavalry fort in Britain. The site also features a museum containing an amazing collection of archaeological discoveries.

Known as 'Cilurnum', Chesters was one of the series of permanent forts added during the construction of the Wall. It housed a garrison of some 500 troops, by the 3rd century a cavalry regiment from Asturias in northern Spain. There is much still to see, including remains of all four principal gates; the headquarters building with courtyard, hall and regimental shrine; and the elaborate and luxurious commandant's house.

Even better preserved, between the fort and the river, is the garrison's bath house. This still displays the complex of rooms which offered soldiers hot, cold or steam baths, as well as a changing-room cum club house with niches for statues of gods.

Hundreds of Roman finds from the central section of the Wall – retrieved by the Victorian antiquarian, John Clayton – are crowded into Chester's highly distinctive museum, which has been restored to its Victorian glory with its original colour-scheme and 'traditional' museum layout. Recent additions include a portrait of John Clayton, a tactile model of the site, ramped access to the museum and a viewing platform overlooking the river.

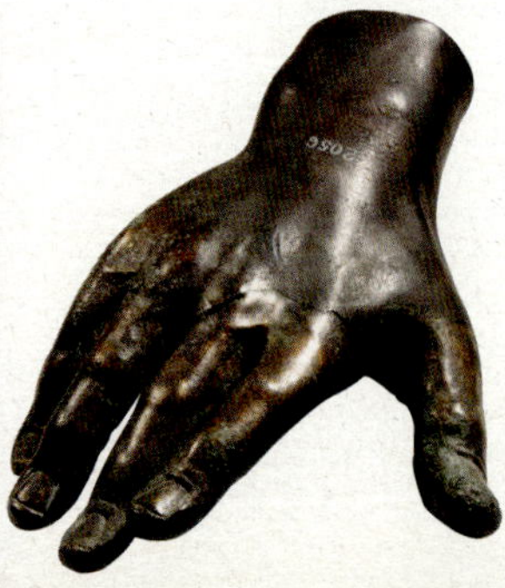

NON-MEMBERS

Adult	£5.00
Concession	£4.50
Child	£3.00

OPENING TIMES

1 Apr-30 Sep, daily	10am-6pm
1 Oct-31 Mar, daily	10am-4pm
24-26 Dec and 1 Jan	Closed

HOW TO FIND US

Direction: ¼ mile W of Chollerford, on B6318

Train: Hexham 5½ miles

Bus: Alba/Classic service AD122 Carlisle – Hexham (Apr-Oct); also Tyne Valley/Snaith service 880 from Hexham

Tel: 01434 681379

Local Tourist Information
Hexham: 01434 652220

P OVP

Disabled access (companion recommended. Disabled parking and toilets).

Dogs on leads (restricted areas only).

Tearoom (summer only; not managed by English Heritage).

Parking (pay and display. Charge refundable upon admission).

New guidebook.

MAP Page 285 (4F)
OS Map 87, OL43: NY912702

Corbridge Roman Town
Northumberland – NE45 5NT

Visitors to Corbridge can walk along the main street of this Roman garrison town, flanked by the remains of granaries, a fountain house, markets, workshops and temples.

Astride the intersection of Roman Dere Street and Stanegate, Corbridge was initially the site of a series of important forts, but after Hadrian's Wall was fully commissioned it developed into a prosperous town, a tempting leave-centre for off-duty Wall garrisons. Abandoned after the collapse of Roman rule in Britain, the town centre has been systematically excavated, producing the fascinating array of finds now most attractively displayed in the site museum.

Covering every aspect of Roman life, the artefacts here include the tombstone of little Ertola, who 'lived most happily four years and sixty days', shown still playing with her ball; and the famous Corbridge lion carving, the recognised symbol of the site. His counterpart, Grricola the Roman lion, takes younger visitors on a trail around the museum, finding his favourite items.

NON-MEMBERS

Adult	£5.00
Concession	£4.50
Child	£3.00

OPENING TIMES

1 Apr-30 Sep, daily	10am-5.30pm (last admission 5pm)
1-31 Oct, daily	10am-4pm
1 Nov-31 Mar, Sat-Sun	10am-4pm
24-26 Dec and 1 Jan	Closed

HOW TO FIND US

Direction: ½ mile NW of Corbridge, on minor road, then signposted

Train: Corbridge 1¼ miles

Bus: Alba/Classic AD122 (April-October); Go North East 10, 687; Arriva/Stagecoach in Cumbria services 685; Wrights service 888

Tel: 01434 632349

Local Tourist Information
01434 652220

Dogs on leads (restricted areas only).

Disabled access (parking, toilet, audio tour, access to the museum and perimeter of site).

MAP Page 285 (4F)
OS Map 87, OL43: NY982648

Denton Hall Turret
Tyne and Wear

The foundations of a turret and a 65-metre (213 feet) length of Wall.

HOW TO FIND US

Direction: 4 miles W of Newcastle-upon-Tyne city centre, on A69

Train: Blaydon 2 miles

Bus: Stagecoach 10, 39, 40, 685, X82; Go North East 684; Veolia service 50

OS Map 88, 316: NZ198655

Hare Hill
Cumbria

A short length of Wall, still standing 2.7 metres (8.8 feet) high.

HOW TO FIND US

Direction: ¾ mile NE of Lanercost

Train: Brampton 4 miles

Bus: Alba/Classic service AD122 (April-Oct). Otherwise nearest bus service is Reay's service 95 to Brampton and Greenhead or Telford 185 to Greenhead & Housesteads

OS Map 86, 43: NY564646

Housesteads Roman Fort Northumberland – NE47 6NN

Housesteads is the most complete example of a Roman fort anywhere in Britain and among the most popular sites on the Wall. It stands high on the wild Whin Sill escarpment, flanked by dramatic stretches of the Wall.

The permanent fort of Housesteads was known as 'Vercovicium', 'the place of effective fighters'. It was garrisoned by around 1000 infantry (generally Tungrians from what is now Belgium), later reinforced by Germanic cavalry.

Entry is via a small museum, containing a fine model of the fort and locally excavated carvings, including images of the mysterious 'hooded gods'. Displaying the imposing remains of four gateways and a turreted curtain wall, the fort itself is crowded with clearly traceable buildings, including the head-quarters, commandant's house, barracks, hospital – and the renowned communal latrines.

The fort lies uphill from the car park (via a fairly strenuous 10-minute walk, which also gives access to Hadrian's Wall Path National Trail). The education room has extensive handling collections of real and replica Roman objects for pre-booked school parties. Owned by the National Trust, the fort is managed by English Heritage.

NON-MEMBERS

Adult	£5.00
Concession	£4.50
Child	£3.00

Free to National Trust members

OPENING TIMES

1 Apr-30 Sep, daily	10am-6pm
1 Oct-31 Mar, daily	10am-4pm
24-26 Dec and 1 Jan	Closed

HOW TO FIND US

Direction: Bardon Mill 4 miles

Bus: Alba/Classic service AD122 (Apr-Oct); otherwise Telford service 185 or Wright Bros service 681

Tel: 01434 344363

Local Tourist Information
Hexham: 01434 652220

OVP

Disabled access (companion recommended). Limited access to site. 750-metre walk up a steep gradient. Disabled parking available at the top of the hill. Please enquire at the information centre in the bottom car park to arrange disabled parking.

Car park not operated by English Heritage (charge payable to Northumberland National Park).

MAP Page 285 (4F)
OS Map 86/87, OL43: NY790688

Harrow's Scar Milecastle and Wall
Cumbria

A mile-long section of the Wall, rebuilt in stone later in Hadrian's reign. It is linked to Birdoswald Roman Fort (see p.240).

HOW TO FIND US

Direction: ¼ mile E of Birdoswald, on minor road off B6318

Train: Brampton 4 miles

Bus: Alba/Classic service AD122 (April-Oct). Otherwise nearest bus services are Reay's service 95; Arriva/Stagecoach 685 to Brampton and Greenhead or Telford service 185 to Greenhead & Housesteads

Parking at Birdoswald Roman Fort

OS Map 86, OL43: NY620664

Heddon-on-the-Wall
Northumberland

A consolidated stretch of Wall, up to 2 metres (6½ feet) thick in places.

HOW TO FIND US

Direction: Immediately E of Heddon village; S of A69

Train: Wylam 3 miles

Bus: Go North East service 684; Arriva/Stagecoach service 685 from Newcastle-upon-Tyne

MAP OS Map 88, 316: NZ137669

Housesteads Roman Fort
See feature on opposite page

Leahill Turret and Piper Sike Turret
Cumbria

Turrets west of Birdoswald: Piper Sike has a cooking-hearth.

HOW TO FIND US

Direction: On minor road 2 miles W of Birdoswald Fort

Train: Brampton 5 miles

Bus: Alba/Classic service AD122 (April-Oct). Otherwise nearest bus services are Reay's service 95; Stagecoach/Arriva 685 to Brampton and Greenhead or Telford's 185 to Greenhead & Housesteads

OS Map 86, OL43/315: NY586652

Pike Hill Signal Tower
Cumbria

The remains of one of a network of signal towers predating Hadrian's Wall, Pike Hill was later joined to the Wall at an angle of 45 degrees.

HOW TO FIND US

Direction: On minor road E of Banks village

Bus: Alba/Classic service AD122 (April-Oct). Otherwise nearest bus services are Reay's service 95; Stagecoach/Arriva 685 to Brampton and Greenhead or Telford's 185 to Greenhead & Housesteads

OS Map 86, 315: NY577648

Planetrees Roman Wall
Northumberland

A 15-metre (49 feet) length of narrow Wall on broad foundations, reflecting a change of policy concerning the thickness of the Wall during construction.

HOW TO FIND US

Direction: 1 mile SE of Chollerford on B6318

Train: Hexham 5½ miles

Bus: Alba/Classic service AD122 (Apr-Oct); also Tyne Valley service 880 or Snaith's 882 from Hexham

OS Map 87, OL43: NY929696

Poltross Burn Milecastle
Cumbria

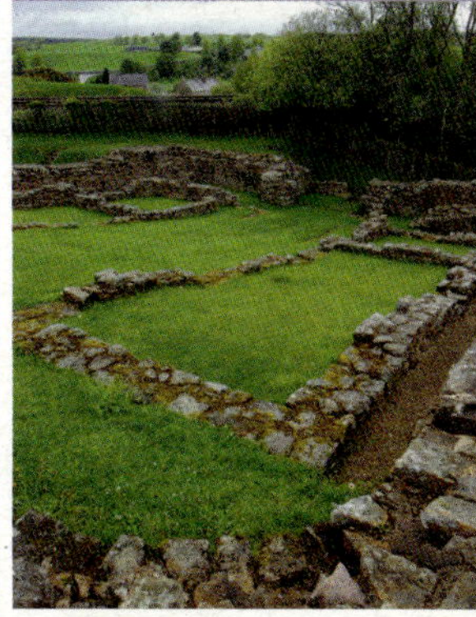

One of the best-preserved milecastles on Hadrian's Wall, Poltross includes an oven, a stair to the rampart walk, and the remains of its north gateway.

HOW TO FIND US

Direction: On minor road E of Banks village. Immediately SW of Gilsland village, by old railway station

Train: Haltwhistle 1 mile

Bus: Reay's service 95; Stagecoach/Arriva 685; Telford service 185; also Alba/Classic service AD122 (April-Oct)

Parking (near the Station Hotel).

OS Map 86, OL43: NY634662

Sewingshields Wall
Northumberland

A length of Wall with milecastle remains, impressively sited along the Whin Sill, commanding fine views of many prehistoric and later earthworks to the north.

HOW TO FIND US

Direction: N of B6318; 1½ miles E of Housesteads Fort

Train: Haydon Bridge 4 miles

Bus: Alba/Classic service AD122 (April-Oct); also Telford's service 185

OS Map 86/87, OL43: NY805702

Temple of Mithras, Carrawburgh
Northumberland

Near Carrawburgh fort stands a fascinating temple to the eastern god Mithras, with facsimiles of altars found during excavation. Sited like many Mithraic temples near a military base, it was founded in the 3rd century and eventually desecrated, probably by Christians. Nearby, but no longer visible, was the shrine of the water nymph Coventina.

HOW TO FIND US

Direction: 3¾ miles W of Chollerford, on B6318

Temple of Mithras

Train: Hexham 7 miles

Bus: Alba/Classic service AD122 (April-Oct)

P

Parking charge payable to Northumberland National Park.

OS Map 87, 43: NY859711

Walltown Crags
Northumberland

One of the best places of all to see the Wall, dramatically snaking and diving along the crags of the Whin Sill.

HOW TO FIND US

Direction: 1 mile NE of Greenhead, off B6318

Train: Haltwhistle 3½ miles

Bus: Alba/Classic service AD122 (April-Oct); also Telford's service 185

OS Map 86/87, 43: NY674663

Willowford Wall, Turrets and Bridge
Cumbria

Willowford Wall, Turrets and Bridge

A fine 914 metre (2999 feet) stretch of Wall, including two turrets and impressive bridge remains beside the River Irthing. Linked by a bridge to Birdoswald Roman Fort (see p.240).

HOW TO FIND US

Direction: W of minor road, ¾ mile W of Gilsland

Train: Brampton 5 miles

Bus: Alba/Classic service AD122 (April-Oct). Otherwise nearest bus services are Reay's 95 or Stagecoach/Arriva 685 to Brampton and Greenhead or Telford's 185 to Greenhead & Housesteads

OS Map 86, OL43: NY627664

Winshields Wall
Northumberland

The highest point on the Wall, in rugged country with spectacular views.

HOW TO FIND US

Direction: W of Steel Rigg car park; on minor road off B6318

Train: Bardon Mill 2 miles, Haltwhistle 4½ miles

Bus: Alba/Classic service AD122 (April-Oct), also Telford's service 185 and Wright Bros service 681

OS Map 86/87, 43: NY742676

Don't forget to check our website for details of opening times and the latest property information.

www.english-heritage.org.uk

Associated attractions at Hadrian's Wall

These visitor attractions, all independent of EH, offer discounts to our members. Please call before you visit to confirm details. A valid EH membership card must be produced for each member.

Hexham Old Gaol
Northumberland NE46 1XD

Built 1330-3, this is the earliest recorded purpose-built prison in England. This fully-accessible building introduces visitors to the history of the prisoners, and to the Border Reivers, warring Borders families of the 1500s.

3 miles to Corbridge Roman Town

Tel: 01434 652349

www.northumberland.gov.uk

2 for 1 entry
[EH Members]

Roman Vindolanda
Northumberland NE47 7JN

Extensive Roman fort and settlement in the central section of Hadrian's Wall. Active archaeological programme and superb museum, plus open air museum set in charming gardens.

2 miles west of Housesteads

Tel: 01434 344277

www.vindolanda.com

10% discount on entry
[EH Members]

Segedunum Roman Fort, Bath House and Museum
Tyne and Wear NE28 6HR

Segedunum is once again the gateway to Hadrian's Wall. It is the most excavated fort along the Wall, with a large interactive museum and a 35m high viewing tower, providing outstanding views across this World Heritage Site.

3 miles from A19

www.twmuseums.org.uk/segedunum

10% discount on entry
[EH Members]

Tullie House Museum and Art Gallery
Cumbria CA3 8TP

Tullie House Museum and Art Gallery is an excellent choice for a great day out for all the family. It is recognised for its first class customer service and a varied and exciting events and exhibitions programme.

Close to Carlisle Castle

Tel: 01228 618718

www.tulliehouse.co.uk

2 for 1 entry
[EH Members] [OVP]

The Hadrian's Wall Bus (AD122)

runs throughout spring and summer between Newcastle, Hexham and Carlisle

[EH Members] EH Members   OVP OVP Holders   Discounted Child Places Included

Tynemounth Priory and Castle – see page 263.

North East

Berwick-upon-Tweed
Alnwick
Northumberland
Morpeth
Blyth
Newcastle upon Tyne
Tynemouth
Hadrian's Wall
Hexham
Gateshead
Sunderland
Tyne and Wear
Consett
Durham
Peterlee
Durham
Hartlepool
Bishop Auckland
Billingham
Middlesbrough
Barnard Castle
Darlington
Tees Valley

www.english-heritage.org.uk/northeast

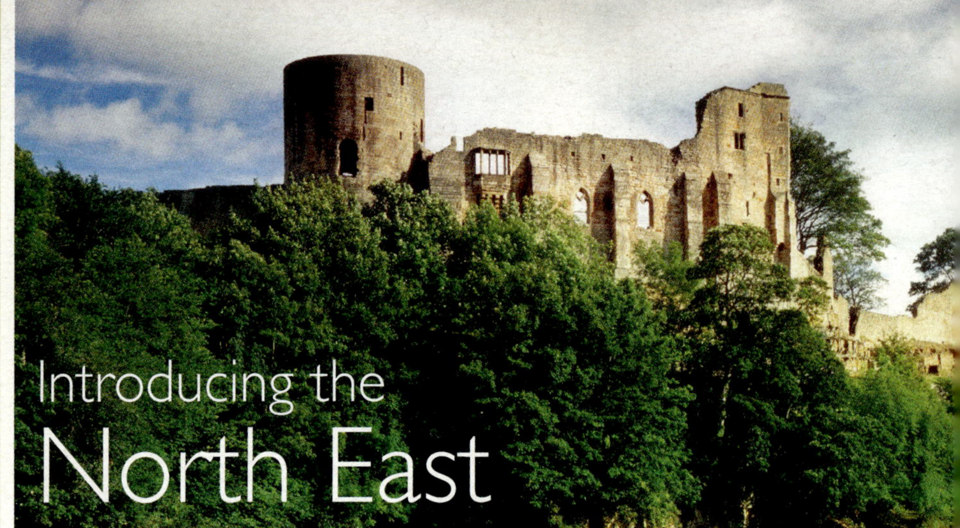

Introducing the North East

Remember to check opening times before you visit any of our properties.

Details of all bus travel in England are available from Traveline on 0871 200 2233 or visit www.traveline.org.uk

Durham

- Auckland Castle Deer House
- Barnard Castle
- Bowes Castle
- Derwentcote Steel Furnace
- Egglestone Abbey
- Finchale Priory

Northumberland

- Aydon Castle
- Belsay Hall, Castle and Gardens
- Berwick-upon-Tweed Barracks
- Berwick-upon-Tweed Castle
- Berwick-upon-Tweed Main Guard
- Berwick-upon-Tweed Ramparts
- Black Middens Bastle House
- Brinkburn Priory
- Dunstanburgh Castle
- Edlingham Castle
- Etal Castle
- Lindisfarne Priory
- Norham Castle
- Prudhoe Castle
- Warkworth Castle and Hermitage

Redcar and Cleveland

- Gisborough Priory

Tyne and Wear

- Bessie Surtees House
- Hylton Castle
- St Paul's Monastery, Jarrow
- Tynemouth Priory and Castle

Hadrian's Wall

See page 237

Tees Trip

The interesting and attractive market town of Barnard Castle makes an excellent centre for memorable days out in a beautiful but comparatively little-visited part of England. It takes its name from the mighty fortress of 'Bernard's Castle' or **Barnard Castle**, one of the largest castles in northern England, dramatically sited above the strategic crossing of the River Tees it was built to control. Reached from the town via a huge outer ward now graced by a 'sensory garden', it commands spectacular views of the river in its wooded gorge far below, particularly from an oriel window seemingly added by Richard III and still adorned with his carved 'white boar' badge. The energetic can enjoy some fine walks along the Tees banks, through woods to the north, or south to **Egglestone Abbey** just over a mile away.

Beautifully positioned but never large or wealthy, this little monastery of white-robed Premonstratensian canons enjoyed the patronage of the dominant local Bowes family, who twice unsuccessfully defended Barnard Castle against Tudor rebels and became the ancestors of Elizabeth Bowes-Lyon, afterwards Queen Elizabeth the Queen Mother. Another remarkable family member was responsible for the most amazing building in Barnard Castle (or indeed anywhere in the region) – the Bowes Museum. This immense French-chateau style extravaganza – the first building in England to be designed to metric specifications – was purpose-built by the Victorian plutocrat, John Bowes, and his Parisian actress wife, Josephine, to house their vast and wide-ranging art collections, notably a famous life-sized mechanical silver swan. A delight in bad weather or good, it offers reduced-price entry to English Heritage members.

Images:
(left) Barnard Castle
(top centre) Belsay Hall, Castle and Gardens
(top right) Egglestone Abbey
(bottom centre) Egglestone Abbey
(bottom right) Barnard Castle

Check www.english-heritage.org.uk for the latest opening times

Auckland Castle Deer House

Durham

A charming Gothic Revival 'eyecatcher' built in 1760 in the park of the Bishops of Durham. It provided deer with shelter and food, and had grounds for picnics and rooms for enjoying the view.

Managed by the Church Commissioners for England.

OPENING TIMES

Park

1 Apr-30 Sep, daily	10am-6pm
1 Oct-31 Mar, daily	10am-4pm
24-26 Dec and 1 Jan	Closed

HOW TO FIND US

Direction: Located in Auckland Park, Bishop Auckland; N of town centre on A68

Train: Bishop Auckland 1 mile

Bus: Arriva services 2A, 3, 3B, 5, 5A, 56, 69, X24; Go Ahead Angel 21, X23; Scarlet Band 104

MAP Page 285 (5G)
OS Map 93, 305: NZ216304

Aydon Castle

Northumberland – NE45 5PJ

One of the finest and most unaltered examples of a 13th-century English manor house, Aydon Castle stands in a secluded woodland setting.

It was originally built as an undefended residence, but almost immediately fortified on the outbreak of Anglo-Scottish warfare. Nevertheless, it was pillaged and burnt by the Scots in 1315, seized by English rebels two years later and again occupied by Scots in 1346.
In the 18th century Aydon became a farmhouse, remaining so until 1966.

NON-MEMBERS

Adult	£3.80
Concession	£3.40
Child	£2.30

OPENING TIMES

1 Apr-30 Sep, Thu-Mon	10am-5pm

HOW TO FIND US

Direction: 1 mile NE of Corbridge, on minor road off B6321 or A68

Train: Corbridge 4 miles – approach via bridle path from W side of Aydon Road, immediately N of Corbridge bypass

Bus: Classic service AD122 April – November. Otherwise closest is Corbridge served by Go North East 10, 602, 684, 687 Arriva X85, Stagecoach/Arriva 685 and Wrights 888

Tel: 01434 632450

P OVP

Disabled access (ground floor only).

Dogs on leads (restricted areas only).

MAP Page 285 (4F)
OS Map 87, 316: NZ001663

Barnard Castle

Durham – DL12 8PR

© Skyscan Balloon Photography

Barnard Castle is spectacularly set on a high rock above the River Tees, on the fringe of an attractive market town. Taking its name from its 12th-century founder, Bernard de Balliol, this huge and imposing fortress was later developed by the Beauchamp family and Richard III. Richard's boar emblem is carved above a window in the inner ward, the castle's chief strength: here loyalist forces were besieged during the 1569 Northern Rising against Queen Elizabeth I, before surrendering to 5000 rebels. There are fine views over the Tees Gorge, and a 'sensory garden' of scented plants and tactile objects.

NON-MEMBERS

Adult	£4.30
Concession	£3.90
Child	£2.60

OPENING TIMES

1 Apr-30 Sep, daily	10am-6pm
1 Oct-31 Mar, Sat-Sun	10am-4pm
24-26 Dec and 1 Jan	Closed

HOW TO FIND US

Direction: In Barnard Castle town

Bus: Arriva services 8, 75/6, 88, 95, 96; Classic service 352; Central service 71A, 72; Alston Road service 73; Compass Royston service 70; Hodgson services 78A, 79 & 79X; Cumbria Classic 572

Tel: 01833 638212

OVP

MAP Page 285 (6G)
OS Map 92, OL31: NZ049165

Belsay Hall, Castle and Gardens

See feature – Page 254

Check www.english-heritage.org.uk for the latest opening times

Berwick-upon-Tweed Barracks and Main Guard

Northumberland – TD15 1DF

Berwick Barracks, among the first in England to be purpose-built, were begun in 1717 to the design of the distinguished architect Nicholas Hawksmoor. Today the Barracks host a number of attractions, including *By Beat of Drum* – an exhibition on the life of the British infantryman. While there, visit the King's Own Scottish Borderers Museum, the Berwick Gymnasium Art Gallery and the Berwick Borough Museum.

The Main Guard is a Georgian Guard House near the quay: it displays *The Story of a Border Garrison Town* exhibition.

The Main Guard is managed by Berwick Civic Society.

NON-MEMBERS

Barracks

Adult	£3.80
Concession	£3.40
Child	£2.30

OPENING TIMES

Barracks

1 Apr-30 Sep, Mon-Fri 10am-5pm

Main Guard

Please call for details

HOW TO FIND US

Direction: On the Parade, off Church St in town centre

Berwick-upon-Tweed Barracks and Main Guard

Train: Berwick-upon-Tweed ¼ mile

Bus: From surrounding areas

Tel: 01289 304493

OVP

Disabled access (Main Guard).

Dogs on leads (restricted areas only).

Parking (in town).

New guidebook.

MAP Page 285 (1F) OS Map 75, 346
Barracks: NU001531
Main Guard: NU000525

Berwick-upon-Tweed Castle and Ramparts

Northumberland – TD15 1DF

The remains of a medieval castle crucial to Anglo-Scottish warfare, superseded by the most complete and breathtakingly impressive bastioned town defences in England, mainly Elizabethan but updated in the 17th and 18th centuries. Surrounding the whole historic town, their entire circuit can be walked, guided by interpretation panels.

OPENING TIMES

Any reasonable time

HOW TO FIND US

Direction: The castle is adjacent to Berwick-upon-Tweed railway station. The ramparts surround the town (accessed at various points)

Train: Berwick-upon-Tweed, adjacent

Bus: From surrounding areas

Disabled access (Ramparts).
Parking (in town).

Note: Steep hidden drops. Dangerous after dark.

MAP Page 285 (1F)
OS Map 75, 346 Castle: NT993534
Ramparts: NU003530

Bessie Surtees House

Tyne and Wear – NE1 3JF

These two five-storey, 16th- and 17th-century merchants' houses – which now also house English Heritage's regional office – are fine examples of Jacobean domestic architecture, with some splendid period interiors. The Surtees house is best known as the scene of the elopement of Bessie with John Scott, later Lord Chancellor of England. An exhibition illustrating the history of the houses is on the first floor.

OPENING TIMES

All year round, Mon-Fri	10am-4pm
Bank Hols & 24 Dec-7 Jan	Closed

HOW TO FIND US

Direction: 41-44 Sandhill, Newcastle-upon-Tyne

Train: Newcastle ½ mile

Metro: Central ½ mile

Bus: From surrounding areas

Tel: 0191 269 1200

MAP Page 285 (4G)
OS Map 88, 316: NZ256338

Bishop Auckland Deer House

See Auckland Castle Deer House – Page 252

Belsay Hall, Castle and Gardens

Northumberland – NE20 0DX

Belsay has something for everyone. A fine medieval castle, enlarged into a Jacobean mansion; the imposing Greek Revival villa that succeeded it; and the outstanding plant-rich gardens linking the two buildings.

Level paths and short grass make the gardens suitable for wheelchairs and there are plenty of seats. The tearoom, in the original Victorian kitchens, provides a perfect setting for a break during your visit.

Check www.english-heritage.org.uk for the latest opening times

The whole ensemble is the creation of the Middleton family over more than seven centuries. First came the castle, still dominated by its massive 14th-century defensive 'pele tower'. Built as a refuge at a time of Anglo-Scottish warfare, it was also designed to impress: it still displays rare traces of elaborate medieval wall-paintings. In more peaceful times a Jacobean mansion wing was added: here the family lived until Christmas Day 1817, when they moved into Belsay Hall.

Belsay Hall is an elegantly Classical Greek Revival villa, now displayed without furnishings to reveal the fine craftsmanship of its construction. Begun in 1807, it was designed by Sir Charles Monck (formerly Middleton), a man inspired by Ancient Greece and the buildings he had seen on his honeymoon in Athens. Despite its austere façade, it had a comfortable interior, arranged round its amazing central 'Pillar Hall.'

The vast gardens which provide a magnificent setting for the castle and hall are also largely Sir Charles's work. His romantic Quarry Garden, created where stone was cut for his hall, has ravines and sheer rock faces inspired by Sicilian quarries. His grandson Sir Arthur Middleton, likewise a pioneering plantsman, further embellished the Quarry with the exotic species which thrive in its micro-climate and added the Winter Garden, Yew Garden, and Magnolia Terrace. Pre-booked tours of the garden are now available, led by the Head Gardener. At whatever time of the year you visit, there is always something in flower.

Spring

A white carpet of thousands of Snowdrops, followed by a riot of colour from Daffodils, Spring Snowflakes and Dog's Tooth Violets. Rhododendrons and large Magnolias.

Summer

Rhododendrons (May & June). Giant Himalayan Lilies up to nine feet tall, and other species of lilies. A NCCPG National Collection of Iris can be seen, as well as the Pocket Handkerchief Tree.

Autumn

Amazing autumn colours of red, yellow and orange foliage. The fallen leaves of Cercidiphyllum Japonicum smell of burnt sugar!

Winter

Spectacular Rhododendrons flower, and frosted spiders' webs frame the topiary in the Yew Garden. Scented Viburnums and Jasmines and the appropriately titled Christmas Box (Sarcococca) can be found in the Winter Garden.

www.english-heritage.org.uk/belsayhall

NON-MEMBERS

Adult	£7.50
Concession	£6.80
Child	£4.50
Family	£19.50

OPENING TIMES

1 Apr-30 Sep, daily	10am-5pm
1-31 Oct, Thurs-Mon	10am-4pm
1 Nov-31 Mar, Thu-Mon	10am-4pm
24-26 Dec and 1 Jan	Closed

HOW TO FIND US

Direction: In Belsay; 14 miles NW of Newcastle, on A696

Train: Morpeth 10 miles

Bus: Arriva 508 from Newcastle Sun and Bank Hols only, (May-Oct); Arriva Sun and Bank Hol service 714 Belsay village; Snaith's 808 from Newcastle and Munro's 131 Newcastle – Jedburgh

Tel: 01661 881636

Local Tourist Information
Morpeth: 01670 500700

Disabled access (grounds, tearoom and ground floor only; toilets).

Dogs on leads (restricted areas only).

Tearoom (open daily Apr-Oct, Sat-Sun in Mar).

MAP Page 285 (3G)
OS Map 88, 316: NZ086785

Check www.english-heritage.org.uk for the latest opening times

Black Middens Bastle House
Northumberland

A fortified farmhouse with thick stone walls, of a type distinctive to the troubled 16th-century Anglo-Scottish borders. The living quarters were only accessible at first floor level. Set in splendid walking country, on the Reivers Route cycle trail.

OPENING TIMES
Any reasonable time

HOW TO FIND US
Direction: 180 metres N of minor road, 7 miles NW of Bellingham; or along a minor road from A68

Bus: Arriva service 714 (summer Sun) serves Lanehead (3 miles)

MAP Page 285 (3F)
OS Map 80, OL42: NY773900

Bowes Castle
Durham

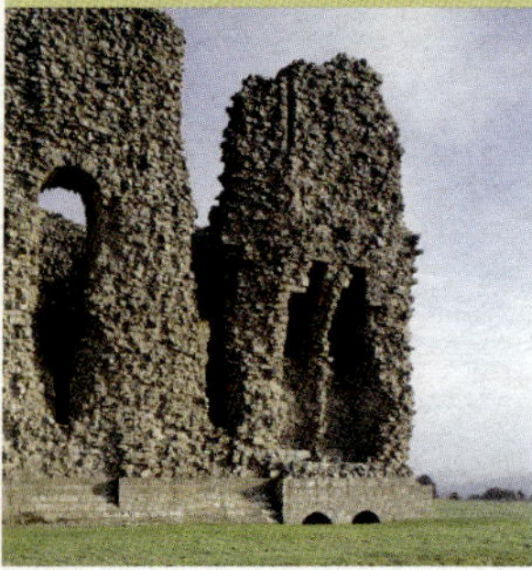

The impressive ruins of Henry II's 12th-century keep, on the site of a Roman fort guarding the approach to strategic Stainmore Pass over the Pennines.

OPENING TIMES
Any reasonable time

HOW TO FIND US
Direction: In Bowes Village off A66; 4 miles W of Barnard Castle town

Bus: Central 72; Hodgsons 79X; Cumbria Classic 572; Classic services 352 & 355

MAP Page 285 (6F)
OS Map 92, OL30/31: NY992135

Brinkburn Priory
Northumberland – NE65 8AR

The beautiful 12th-century church of the Augustinian priory of Brinkburn survives completely roofed and restored. Picturesquely set by a bend in the River Coquet, it is reached by a scenic 10-minute walk from the car park. Parts of the monastic buildings are incorporated into the elegant adjacent manor house.

NON-MEMBERS

Adult	£3.30
Concession	£3.00
Child	£2.00

OPENING TIMES

1 Apr-30 Sep, Thu-Mon	11am-4pm

HOW TO FIND US
Direction: 4½ miles SE of Rothbury, off B6344

Train: Acklington 10 miles

Bus: Arriva service 144 Morpeth – Thropton (passing ⇌ Morpeth)

Tel: 01665 570628

Picnic area (⅓ mile).

MAP Page 285 (3G)
OS Map 92, 325: NZ116983

Derwentcote Steel Furnace
Durham

Built in the 1720s, Derwentcote is the earliest and most complete steel-making furnace in Britain. It produced high-grade steel for springs and cutting tools.

OPENING TIMES
Any reasonable time (Grounds only – no access to Furnace)
Except 24-26 Dec and 1 Jan

HOW TO FIND US
Direction: 10 miles SW of Newcastle, on A694; between Rowland's Gill and Hamsterley

Train: Metro Centre, Gateshead, 7 miles

Bus: Go North East Red Kite services 45/6 Newcastle-upon-Tyne – Consett

Tel: 0191 269 1200 (Mon-Fri)

Dogs on leads (restricted areas only).

Parking across main road from site.

MAP Page 285 (4G)
OS Map 88, 307: NZ130566

Dunstanburgh Castle
Northumberland – NE66 3TT

© Skyscan Balloon Photography

Dunstanburgh Castle

Dramatic Dunstanburgh Castle was built at a time when relations between King Edward II and his most powerful baron, Earl Thomas of Lancaster, had become openly hostile. Lancaster began the fortress in 1313 and the latest archaeological research carried out by English Heritage indicates that he built it on a far grander scale than was hitherto recognised, perhaps more as a symbol of his opposition to the king than as a military stronghold. The innovative gatehouse, for instance, competed with the new royal castles in Wales.

The earl failed to reach Dunstanburgh when his rebellion was defeated, and was taken and executed in 1322. Thereafter the castle passed eventually to John of Gaunt, who strengthened it against the Scots by converting the great twin towered gatehouse into a keep. The focus of fierce fighting during the Wars of the Roses, it was twice besieged and captured by Yorkist forces, but subsequently fell into decay. Its impressive ruins now watch over a headland famous for seabirds.

Owned by the National Trust, maintained and managed by English Heritage.

NON-MEMBERS

Adult	£4.00
Concession	£3.60
Child	£2.40

Free to National Trust members

Dunstanburgh Castle

OPENING TIMES

1 Apr-30 Sep, daily	10am-5pm
1-31 Oct, daily	10am-4pm
1 Nov-31 Mar, Thu-Mon	10am-4pm
24-26 Dec and 1 Jan	Closed

HOW TO FIND US

Direction: 8 miles NE of Alnwick; on footpaths from Craster or Embleton – 1½ miles rugged coastal walk

Train: Chathill (U), not Sun, 5 miles from Embleton, 7 miles from Castle; Alnmouth, 7 miles from Craster, 8¼ miles from Castle

Bus: Arriva service 501 and Travelsure services 401 (Sun) and 411. Alight Craster and take coast walk, 1½ miles

Tel: 01665 576231

Local Tourist Information
Craster: 01665 576007

OVP

Parking (in Craster village; approx 1½ miles walk. A charge is payable).

Nearest toilets located at car park in Craster Village.

MAP Page 285 (2G)
OS Map 75, 332: NU257219

Edlingham Castle
Northumberland

The riverside ruins, principally the solar tower, of a manor house progressively fortified against the Scots during the 14th century.

Managed by the Parochial Church Council of St John the Baptist, Edlingham, with Bolton Chapel.

Edlingham Castle

OPENING TIMES

Any reasonable time

HOW TO FIND US

Direction: At E end of Edlingham village, on minor road off B6341; 6 miles SW of Alnwick

Train: Alnmouth 9 miles

Bus: Travelsure 473 to Banktop then 2 mile walk

Note: waterproof footwear is recommended.

MAP Page 285 (2G)
OS Map 81, 332: NU116092

Egglestone Abbey
Durham

The charming ruins of a small monastery of Premonstratensian 'white canons', picturesquely set above a bend in the River Tees near Barnard Castle (see p.252). Remains include much of the 13th-century church and a range of living quarters, with traces of their ingenious toilet drainage system.

OPENING TIMES

Daily	10am-6pm

HOW TO FIND US

Direction: 1 mile S of Barnard Castle, on a minor road off B6277

Bus: Hodgsons service 78A, 79, 79X then short (½ mile) walk

MAP Page 285 (6G)
OS Map 92, OL31: NZ062151

Etal Castle
Northumberland – TD12 4TN

Etal was built in the mid-14th century by Robert Manners as a defence against Scots raiders, in a strategic position by a ford over the River Till. It fell to James IV's invading Scots army in 1513, immediately before their catastrophic defeat at nearby Flodden. An award-winning exhibition tells the story of Flodden and the Anglo-Scottish border warfare which ended with the accession of James I in 1603.

NON-MEMBERS

Adult	£3.80
Concession	£3.40
Child	£2.30
Family	£9.90

OPENING TIMES

1 Apr-30 Sep, daily	11am-4.30pm

HOW TO FIND US

Direction: In Etal village, 10 miles SW of Berwick

Train: Berwick-upon-Tweed 10½ miles

Bus: Glen Valley 267 Berwick-upon-Tweed – Wooler

Tel: 01890 820332

E P OVP

Dogs on leads (restricted areas only).

Toilets (in village).

MAP Page 285 (1F)
OS Map 74/75, 339: NT925393

Finchale Priory
Durham – DH1 5SH

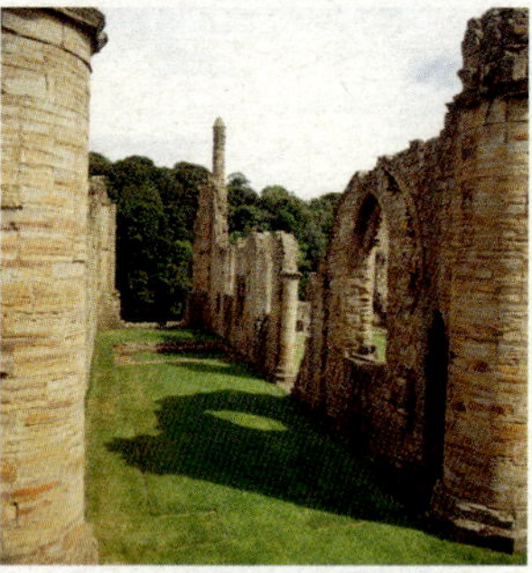

The very extensive remains of a 13th-century priory, founded on the site of the retired pirate St Godric's hermitage. Part of it later served as a holiday retreat for the monks of Durham Cathedral. Beautifully sited by the River Wear, with delightful riverside walks nearby.

OPENING TIMES

Daily	10am-5pm
24-26 Dec and 1 Jan	Closed

HOW TO FIND US

Direction: 3 miles NE of Durham; on minor road off A167

Train: Durham 5 miles

P OVP

Parking (fee applies; not managed by EH).

Tearoom (not managed by EH).

MAP Page 285 (4G)
OS Map 88, 308: NZ296471

Gisborough Priory
Redcar and Cleveland

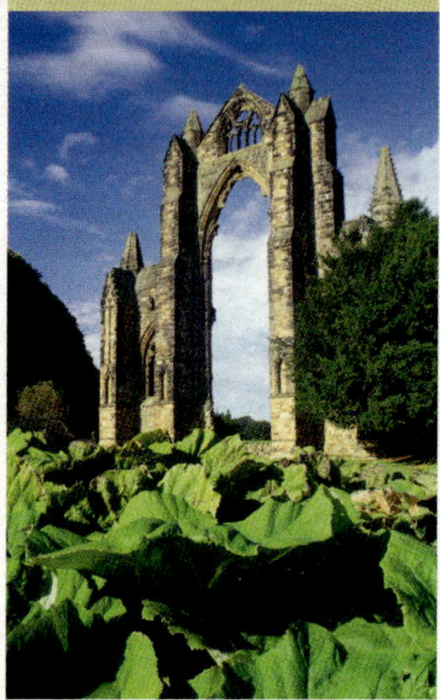

The ruins of an Augustinian priory founded by the Bruce family, afterwards Kings of Scotland. They are dominated by the dramatic skeleton of the 14th-century church's east end.

Managed by Redcar and Cleveland Borough Council.

NON-MEMBERS

Adult	£1.80
Concession	90p
Child	90p
Family	£3.60

OPENING TIMES

6 Apr-4 Oct, Wed-Sun	10am-4pm
5 Oct-31 Mar, Wed-Sun	10am-3pm
24 Dec-1 Jan	Closed

HOW TO FIND US

Direction: In Guisborough town, next to the parish church

Train: Marske 4½ miles

Bus: Arriva services 5A, X5, 26, 28, 81, 93, X93 & 781; Moorsbus M1, M2, M4, M10, M12, M16

Tel: 01287 633801

P

Toilets and parking (in town).

MAP Page 285 (6H)
OS Map 94, OL26/306: NZ617160

Hadrian's Wall

See page 237

Hylton Castle

Tyne and Wear

The distinctive and highly decorative gatehouse-tower of a castle built by the wealthy Sir William Hylton shortly before 1400. Originally containing four floors of self-contained family accommodation, its entrance front displays royal and family heraldry, including Richard II's white hart badge.

OPENING TIMES

Grounds only – no access to Castle	10am-5pm
24-26 Dec and 1 Jan	Closed

HOW TO FIND US

Direction: 3¾ miles W of Sunderland

Hylton Castle

Train: Seaburn Metro (2½ miles) then bus 99; Pallion Metro then bus 29, 29A, 39 or 39A

Bus: Stagecoach services 3, 13; Go North East services 26, 56, X88

Disabled access (grounds only).

MAP Page 285 (4H)
OS Map 88, 308: NZ358588

Lindisfarne Priory

See feature – Page 260

Norham Castle

Northumberland – TD15 2JY

Commanding a vital ford over the River Tweed, Norham was one of the strongest of the border castles and the most often attacked by the Scots. Besieged at least 13 times – once for nearly a year by Robert Bruce – it was called 'the most dangerous and adventurous place in the country'. But even its powerful 12th-century keep and massive towered bailey walls could not resist James IV's heavy cannon, and it fell to him in 1513, shortly before his defeat at Flodden. The extensive 16th-century rebuilding which

Norham Castle

followed, adapting the fortress for its own artillery, is still clearly traceable.

OPENING TIMES

1 Apr-30 Sep, daily	10am-5pm
Winter	Closed

HOW TO FIND US

Direction: In Norham village; 6 miles SW of Berwick-upon-Tweed, on minor road off B6470 (from A698)

Train: Berwick-upon-Tweed 7½ miles

Bus: Perryman's 67 Berwick-upon-Tweed – Galashiels

Disabled access (excluding keep).

MAP Page 285 (1F)
OS Map 74/75, 339: NT906476

Members can take up to six children to any of our properties at no extra charge. See page 6 for details.

Lindisfarne Priory

Northumberland – TD15 2RX

Still a place of pilgrimage today, Lindisfarne Priory on Holy Island was one of the most important centres of early Christianity in Anglo-Saxon England. The dramatic approach to the island across the causeway only emphasises the serene appeal of this atmospheric site.

© Skyscan Balloon Photography

St Aidan founded the monastery in AD 635, but St Cuthbert, Prior of Lindisfarne, is the most celebrated of the priory's holy men. After many missionary journeys and ten years seeking peace as a hermit on lonely Inner Farne Island, he reluctantly became Bishop before retiring to die on Inner Farne in 687. Buried in the priory, his remains were transferred to a pilgrim shrine there after eleven years and found still undecayed – a sure sign of sanctity.

From the end of the 8th century, the isolated island with its rich monastery was easy prey for Viking raiders. In 875 the monks left, carrying Cuthbert's remains, which after long wanderings were enshrined in Durham Cathedral in 1104, where they still rest. Only after that time did Durham monks re-establish a priory on Lindisfarne. The evocative ruins of the richly decorated priory church they built in c. 1150 still stand, with their famous 'rainbow arch' – a vault-rib of the now-vanished crossing tower. The small community lived quietly on Holy Island until the suppression of the monastery in 1537.

The fascinating museum offers a clear and dynamic interpretation of the story of St Cuthbert and the 1300 year history of Lindisfarne Priory, among the most tranquil of all English Heritage sites.

Visitors are welcome to bring a picnic to enjoy in the grounds.

www.english-heritage.org.uk/lindisfarnepriory

NON-MEMBERS	
Adult	£4.80
Concession	£4.30
Child	£2.90

OPENING TIMES	
1 Apr-30 Sep, daily	9.30am-5pm
1-31 Oct, daily	9.30am-4pm
1 Nov-31 Jan, Sat-Mon	10am-2pm
1 Feb-31 Mar, daily	10am-4pm
24-26 Dec and 1 Jan	Closed

The causeway floods at high tide, so it is very important to check the tide times before crossing.

HOW TO FIND US

Direction: On Holy Island, only reached at low tide across causeway; tide tables at each end, or from Tourist Information Centre

Train: Berwick-upon-Tweed 14 miles, via causeway

Bus: Travelsure 477 passes Berwick-upon-Tweed close to ⇄ Berwick-upon-Tweed. Bus times vary with tides

Tel: 01289 389200

Tourist Information Centre
01289 330733

OVP

Dogs on leads (restricted areas only).

Parking and toilets in the village. Parking pay and display operated by Berwick Borough Council.

MAP Page 285 (1G)
OS Map 75, 340: NU126417

Prudhoe Castle Northumberland – NE42 6NA

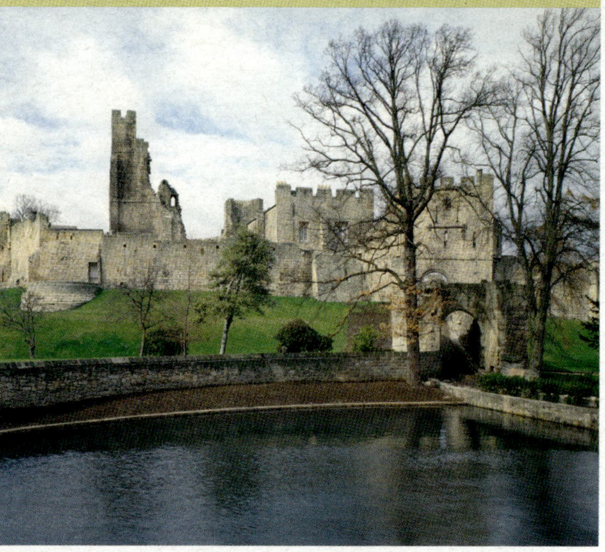

Begun between 1100 and 1120 to defend a strategic crossing of the River Tyne against Scottish invaders, Prudhoe Castle has been continuously occupied for over nine centuries. After two sieges during the 1170s – the Scots attackers reportedly declaring 'as long as Prudhoe stands, we shall never have peace' – the mighty stone keep and a great hall were added, followed in about 1300 by two strong towers. Passing from its original Umfraville owners to the powerful Percies in 1398, it was again updated with a fashionable new great hall.

Even after its last military action against the Scots in 1640, Prudhoe's importance as the centre of a great landed estate continued. Early in the 19th century the Percies restored it, building a fine new manor house within its walls. All these developments are now vividly interpreted in a family-friendly exhibition including site finds, helping visitors to explore and understand the extensive remains of this formidable and long-lived fortress.

NON-MEMBERS

Adult	£4.30
Concession	£3.90
Child	£2.60

OPENING TIMES

1 Apr-30 Sep, Thu-Mon	10am-5pm

HOW TO FIND US

Direction: In Prudhoe, on minor road off A695

Train: Prudhoe ¼ mile

Bus: Go North East 10, 604, 673, 686

Tel: 01661 833459

OVP

Dogs on leads (restricted areas only).

MAP Page 285 (4G)
OS Map 88, 316: NZ091634

St Paul's Monastery, Jarrow
Tyne and Wear

The home of the Venerable Bede, chronicler of the beginnings of English Christianity, Jarrow has become one of the best-understood Anglo-Saxon monastic sites. The Anglo-Saxon church – with the oldest dedication stone in the country, dated AD 685 – partly survives as the chancel of the parish church. A free downloadable audio tour is available from the English Heritage website.

Managed by Bede's World.

OPENING TIMES

Monastery ruins any reasonable time

HOW TO FIND US

Direction: In Jarrow, on minor road N of A185; follow signs for Bede's World

Metro: Bede ¾ miles

Bus: Go North East 16 and The Crusader services 27

Tel: 0191 489 7052

MAP Page 285 (4H)
OS Map 88, 316: NZ339652

Check www.english-heritage.org.uk for the latest opening times

Tynemouth Priory and Castle Tyne and Wear – NE30 4BZ

© John Critchley

Set in an almost impregnable position on a steep headland between the river and the North Sea, Tynemouth has always been as much a fortress as a religious site.

Here stood a 7th-century Anglian monastery, burial place of Oswin, sainted King of Northumbria. After its destruction by Danish raiders, the present Benedictine priory was founded on its site in c. 1090.

The towering east end of the priory church, built in c. 1200 with slender lancet windows and soaring arches, still survives almost to its full height, dominating the headland. Beyond it stands a small but complete and exceptionally well-preserved chapel, with a rose window and an ornately sculpted roof vault. This was built in the mid-15th century as a chantry for the souls of the powerful Percy family, Earls of Northumberland.

Enclosing both headland and monastery, and still surviving in part, were the strong medieval walls which once made Tynemouth among the largest fortified areas in England, and an important bastion against the Scots.

When the priory's 19 monks surrendered Tynemouth to Henry VIII in 1539, it was immediately adopted as a royal castle. Thereafter the fortress headland continued to play its centuries-old part in coastal defence, both against Napoleon and during the two World Wars.

The interactive *Life in the Stronghold* exhibition takes visitors on a journey from Tynemouth's beginnings as an Anglo-Saxon settlement, via its medieval monastery and Tudor fortification, right up to its importance as a Second World War coastal gun battery.

Significant conservation works have been carried out on the gun battery and magazine, restored to look as it they did during World War I. Replica uniforms hang on the walls, alongside the special magazine clothes which soldiers changed into before handling explosive material. Visitors can explore the space in which soldiers worked to prepare ammunition for the guns.

www.english-heritage.org.uk/tynemouthpriory

Available for corporate and private hire

NON-MEMBERS

Adult	£4.50
Concession	£4.10
Child	£2.70
Family	£11.70

OPENING TIMES

1 Apr-30 Sep, daily	10am-5pm
1 Oct-31 Mar, Thu-Mon	10am-4pm
24-26 Dec and 1 Jan	Closed

Gun Battery: Access limited, please ask site staff for details

HOW TO FIND US

Direction: In Tynemouth, near North Pier

Metro: Tynemouth ½ mile

Bus: Arriva 306, 356

Tel: 0191 257 1090

OVP

Disabled access (priory only).
Toilets with disabled access on site.
Limited disabled parking avaiable.

MAP Page 285 (4H)
OS Map 88, 316: NZ373694

Warkworth Castle and Hermitage

Northumberland – NE65 0UJ

The magnificent cross-shaped keep of Warkworth, crowning a hilltop rising steeply above the River Coquet, dominates one of the largest, strongest and most impressive fortresses in northern England. The castle's most famous owners were the Percy family, whose lion badge can be seen carved on many parts of their stronghold. Wielding almost kingly power in the North, their influence reached its apogee under the first Percy Earl of Northumberland and his son 'Harry Hotspur', hero of many Border ballads as the bane of Scots raiders and a dominant character in Shakespeare's *Henry IV*. Having helped to depose Richard II, these turbulent 'kingmakers' both fell victim to Henry IV: the next three Percy earls likewise died violent deaths.

Still roofed and almost complete, the uniquely-planned keep dates mainly from the end of the 14th century. It presides over the extensive remains of a great hall, chapel, fine gatehouse and a virtually intact circuit of towered walls.

Half a mile from the castle, tucked away by the Coquet and accessible only by boat, stands a much more peaceful building: the late medieval cave Hermitage and chapel of a solitary holy man.

The Duke's Rooms in the castle keep are open on Wed, Sun and Bank Holidays from 1 April to 30 September.

www.english-heritage.org.uk/warkworthcastle

NON-MEMBERS

Castle:

Adult	£4.80
Concession	£4.30
Child	£2.90
Family	£12.50

Hermitage:

Adult	£3.20
Concession	£2.90
Child	£1.90

OPENING TIMES

Castle:

1 Apr-30 Sep, daily	10am-5pm
1-31 Oct, daily	10am-4pm
1 Nov-31 Mar, Sat-Mon	10am-4pm
24-26 Dec and 1 Jan	Closed

Hermitage:

1 Apr-30 Sep, Wed, Sun & Bank Hols	11am-5pm

HOW TO FIND US

Direction: In Warkworth; 7½ miles S of Alnwick, on A1068

Train: Alnmouth 3½ miles

Bus: Arriva 518 Newcastle – Alnwick

Tel: 01665 711423

Local Tourist Information
Amble: 01665 712313

Audio tours (also available for the visually impaired and those with learning difficulties).

Disabled access (limited access).

Dogs on leads (restricted areas only).

Parking (Charge payable, which is refundable on admission).

MAP Page 285 (2G)
OS Map 81, 332: NU247058

Associated attractions in the North East

These visitor attractions, all independent of EH, offer discounts to our members. Please call before you visit to confirm details. A valid EH membership card must be produced for each member.

Bamburgh Castle
Northumberland NE69 7DF

Home to the Kings of Northumbria, with fourteen public rooms and over 2000 artefacts, including arms, furniture, paintings and china. Armstrong and Aviation Artefacts Museum.

Tel: 01668 214515

www.bamburghcastle.com

20% discount on entry
EH OVP 6

The Bowes Museum
County Durham DL12 8NP

Has undergone a major transformation to create a stunning 21st Century attraction in beautiful grounds. An inspirational day out for all the family, with fascinating collections, romantic history, fine dining and shopping.

Near Barnard Castle

Open daily **10am–5pm**

Tel: 01833 690606

www.thebowesmuseum.org.uk

£1 off admission
EH 4 OVP

Killhope – The North of England Lead Mining Museum
Durham DL13 1AR

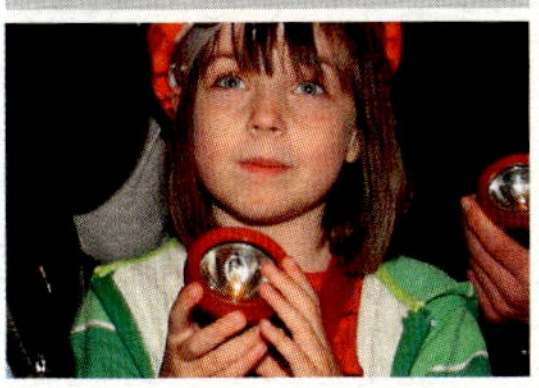

A multi-award winning Victorian Mining Museum, and a grand day out. Accompany a guide on a mine tour. Our enthusiastic team will ensure you have a day to remember.

Open Apr–Oct **10.30am–5pm**

Tel: 01388 537505

www.killhope.org.uk

25% off ticket
EH OVP

Tanfield Railway
County Durham NE16 5ET

The world's oldest railway. Take a 6 mile return trip behind locally built steam engines hauling vintage carriages. 18th-century Causey Arch adjacent. Operates Sundays & Bank Holiday Mondays.

15 mins from J63 A1M

Tel: 0845 4634938

www.tanfield-railway.co.uk

2 for 1 train ticket only
EH OVP 2

Why not give the gift of membership?

English Heritage Gift of Membership makes the ideal present – a whole year of fantastic days out at over 400 properties including historic houses, castles and gardens – all for free.

Call 0870 333 1181 or visit **www.english-heritage.org.uk/gift** for more details.

EH Members | OVP OVP Holders | ? Discounted Child Places Included

Associated Attractions:

Wales, the Isle of Man and Scotland

A
B
C
D
E
Created by Arka Cartographics Ltd. for English Heritage. © 10/10
Scotland
SCOTLAND
The Black House, Arnol
Kisimul Castle
Elgin Cathedral
Spynie Palace
Duff House
Kinnaird Head Castle Lighthouse & Museum
Fort George
Dallas Dhu Historic Distillery
Huntly Castle
Tolquhon Castle
Urquhart Castle
Balvenie Castle
Kildrummy Castle
Corgarff Castle
Elcho Castle
Stanley Mills
Meigle Sculptured Stone Museum
Edzell Castle & Garden
Bonawe Historic Iron Furnace
Huntingtower Castle
Dunfermline Abbey & Palace
St Serf's Church & Dupplin Cross
Dunstaffnage Castle
Iona Abbey & Nunnery
St Vigeans Sculptured Stones
Arbroath Abbey
Loch Leven Castle
St Andrews Castle
St Andrews Cathedral
Aberdour Castle & Garden
Inchcolm Abbey
Castle Campbell
Dunblane Cathedral
Doune Castle
Inchmahome Priory
Argyll's Lodging
Dirleton Castle & Gardens
Tantallon Castle
Seton Collegiate Church
Newark Castle
Stirling Castle
Rothesay Castle
Edinburgh Castle
Dumbarton Castle
Glasgow Cathedral
Bothwell Castle
Crichton Castle
Smailholm Tower
Dundonald Castle
Craignethan Castle
Cairnpapple Hill
Melrose Abbey
Dryburgh Abbey
Linlithgow Palace
Crossraguel Abbey
Jedburgh Abbey & Visitor Centre
Blackness Castle
Craigmillar Castle
Hermitage Castle
Threave Castle
Sweetheart Abbey
Cardoness Castle
Caerlaverock Castle
Glenluce Abbey
New Abbey Corn Mill
Dundrennan Abbey
MacLellan's Castle
Shetland Islands
Jarlshof Prehistoric & Norse Settlement
Orkney Islands
Brough of Birsay
Broch of Gurness
Skara Brae & Skaill House
Bishop's & Earl's Palaces
Maeshowe Chambered Cairn
Hackness Martello Tower & Battery
Wales
WALES
Beaumaris Castle
Conwy Castle
Rhuddlan Castle
Plas Mawr
Caernarfon Castle
Rug Chapel & Llangar Church
Dolwyddelan Castle
Valle Crucis Abbey
Criccieth Castle
Harlech Castle
Strata Florida Abbey
White Castle
Cilgerran Castle
Tretower Court & Castle
Raglan Castle
St Davids Bishop's Palace
Carreg Cennen Castle
Laugharne Castle
Kidwelly Castle
Tintern Abbey
Blaenavon Ironworks
Weobley Castle
Oxwich Castle
Caerphilly Castle
Chepstow Castle
Castell Coch
Caerleon Roman Fortress
Isle of Man
Peel Castle
The Grove Museum of Victorian Life
House of Manannan
Laxey Wheel & Mines Trail
Niarbyl Restaurant & Visitor Centre
Manx Museum
Rushen Abbey & Abbey Restaurant
Old House of Keys
The National Folk Museum
Castle Rushen
Sound Visitor Centre
Nautical Museum & Old Grammar School
1
2
3
4
5
6
7

Cadw

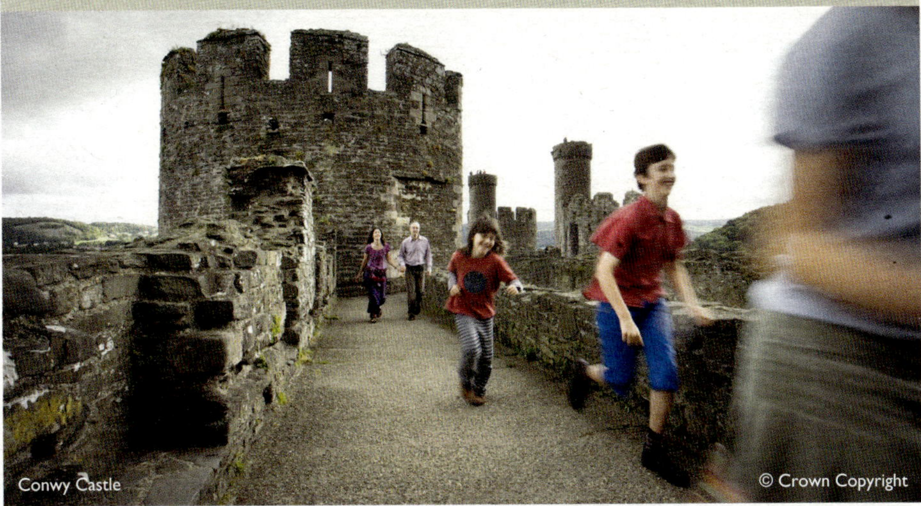
Conwy Castle © Crown Copyright

English Heritage members can gain half-price admission to Cadw attractions during the first year of membership and free entry in subsequent years.

Beaumaris Castle, Anglesey
LL58 8AP
Tel: 01248 810361

Blaenavon Ironworks,
Nr Pontypool, Torfaen NP4 9RN
Tel: 01495 792615

Caerleon Roman Fortress,
Caerleon, Newport NP18 1AE
Tel: 01633 422518

Caernarfon Castle, Caernarfon,
Gwynedd LL55 2AY
Tel: 01286 677617

Caerphilly Castle, Caerphilly
CF83 1JD
Tel: 029 2088 3143

Carreg Cennen Castle, Nr Trapp,
Carmarthenshire SA19 6TS
Tel: 01558 822291

Castell Coch, Cardiff CF15 7JS
Tel: 029 2081 0101

Chepstow Castle, Chepstow,
Monmouthshire NP16 5EY
Tel: 01291 624065

Cilgerran Castle, Nr Cardigan,
Ceredigion SA43 2SF
Tel: 01239 621339

Conwy Castle, Conwy LL32 8AY
Tel: 01492 592358

Criccieth Castle, Criccieth,
Gwynedd LL52 0DP
Tel: 01766 522227

Dolwyddelan Castle, Dolwyddelan,
Gwynedd LL25 0JD
Tel: 01690 750366

Harlech Castle, Harlech,
Gwynedd LL46 2YH
Tel: 01766 780552

Kidwelly Castle, Kidwelly,
Carmarthenshire SA17 5BQ
Tel: 01554 890104

Laugharne Castle, Laugharne,
Carmarthenshire SA33 4SA
Tel: 01994 427906

Oxwich Castle, Oxwich,
Swansea SA3 1NG
Tel: 01792 390359

Plas Mawr, Conwy LL32 8DE
Tel: 01492 580167

Raglan Castle, Raglan,
Monmouthshire NP15 2BT
Tel: 01291 690228

Rhuddlan Castle, Rhuddlan,
Denbighshire LL18 5AD
Tel: 01745 590777

Rug Chapel and Llangar Church,
Corwen, Denbighshire LL21 9BT
Tel: 01490 412025

St Davids Bishop's Palace,
St Davids, Pembrokeshire
SA62 6PE
Tel: 01437 720517

Strata Florida Abbey,
Pontrhydfendigaid, Ceredigion
SY25 6ES
Tel: 01974 831261

Tintern Abbey, Tintern,
Monmouthshire NP16 6SE
Tel: 01291 689251

Tretower Court and Castle,
Tretower, Powys NP8 1RD
Tel: 01874 730279

Valle Crucis Abbey, Nr Llangollen,
Denbighshire LL20 8DD
Tel: 01978 860326

Weobley Castle, Nr Llanrhidian,
Swansea SA3 1HB
Tel: 01792 390012

White Castle, Nr Abergavenny,
Monmouthshire NP7 8UD
Tel: 01600 780380

For more details about Cadw, write to: Plas Carew, Unit 5/7 Cefn Coed, Parc Nantgarw, Cardiff CF15 7QQ Please call 01443 336000 or visit the Cadw website at cadw.wales.gov.uk

Manx National Heritage

Rushen Abbey

English Heritage members can gain half price admission to Manx National Heritage attractions during their first year of membership and free entry in subsequent years. Members must present a valid membership card on admission (Manx National Heritage permit free admission to the member only and children aged 4 years and under). Admission charges apply for special events. Travel connections between the Isle of Man's heritage sites are available through the Victorian Steam Railway, Manx Electric Railway, Horse Tram and Bus Vannin. **To book travel visit www.visitisleofman.com**

Isle of Man

- Castle Rushen – Castletown
- The National Folk Museum – Cregneash
- The Grove – Museum of Victorian Life – Ramsey
- House of Manannan – Peel
- Laxey Wheel and Mines Trail – Laxey
- Manx Museum – Douglas
- Nautical Museum – Castletown
- Niarbyl Restaurant & Visitor Centre – Dalby
- Old Grammar School – Castletown
- Old House of Keys – Castletown
- Peel Castle – Peel
- Rushen Abbey & Abbey Restaurant – Ballasalla
- The Sound Café and Visitor Centre – near Cregneash

For more details, please contact: Manx National Heritage, Kingswood Grove, Douglas, Isle of Man IM1 3LY.

Please call 01624 648000 or visit the Manx National Heritage website at www.storyofmann.com

Portcullis at Castle Rushen

Laxey Wheel

Historic Scotland

Edzell Castle and Garden

English Heritage members can gain half-price admission to Historic Scotland attractions during the first year of membership and free entry in subsequent years.

Aberdour Castle and Garden, Aberdour, Fife
Tel: 01383 860519

Arbroath Abbey, Angus
Tel: 01241 878756

Argyll's Lodging, Stirling, Central
Tel: 01786 450000

Balvenie Castle, Dufftown, Grampian
Tel: 01340 820121

Bishop's and Earl's Palaces, Kirkwall, Orkney
Tel: 01856 871918

The Black House, Arnol, Lewis, Western Isles
Tel: 01851 710395

Blackness Castle, Firth of Forth, Edinburgh and Lothians
Tel: 01506 834807

Bonawe Historic Iron Furnace, Taynuilt, Argyll
Tel: 01866 822432

Bothwell Castle, Bothwell, Greater Glasgow
Tel: 01698 816894

Broch of Gurness, Aikerness, Orkney
Tel: 01856 751414

Brough of Birsay, NW of Kirkwall, Orkney
Tel: 01856 841 815

Caerlaverock Castle, Nr Dumfries, Dumfries and Galloway
Tel: 01387 770244

Cairnpapple Hill, Torphichen, Edinburgh and Lothians
Tel: 01506 634622

Cardoness Castle, Nr Gatehouse of Fleet Dumfries and Galloway
Tel: 01557 814427

Castle Campbell, Dollar Glen, Central
Tel: 01259 742408

Corgarff Castle, Nr Strathdon, Grampian
Tel: 01975 651460

Craigmillar Castle, Edinburgh and Lothians
Tel: 0131 661 4445

Craignethan Castle, Lanark, Greater Glasgow
Tel: 01555 860364

Crichton Castle, Nr Pathhead, Edinburgh and Lothians
Tel: 01875 320017

Crossraguel Abbey, Nr Maybole, Greater Glasgow
Tel: 01655 883113

Dallas Dhu Historic Distillery, Nr Forres, Grampian
Tel: 01309 676548

Dirleton Castle and Gardens, Dirleton, East Lothian
Tel: 01620 850330

Doune Castle, Doune, Central
Tel: 01786 841742

Dryburgh Abbey, Nr Melrose, Borders
Tel: 01835 822381

Duff House, Banff, Grampian
Tel: 01261 818 181

Dumbarton Castle, Dumbarton, Greater Glasgow
Tel: 01389 732167

Dunblane Cathedral, Dunblane, Central
Tel: 01786 823 388

Dundonald Castle, Dundonald, Greater Glasgow
Tel: 01563 851489

Dundrennan Abbey, Nr Kirkcudbright, Dumfries and Galloway
Tel: 01557 500262

Dunfermline Palace and Abbey, Dunfermline, Fife
Tel: 01383 739026

Dunstaffnage Castle, Nr Oban, Argyll
Tel: 01631 562465

Edinburgh Castle, Edinburgh and Lothians
Tel: 0131 225 9846

Edzell Castle and Garden, Edzell, Angus
Tel: 01356 648631

Elcho Castle, Nr Bridge of Earn, Perthshire
Tel: 01738 639998

Elgin Cathedral, Elgin, Highlands
Tel: 01343 547171

Fort George, Nr Ardersier village, Highlands
Tel: 01667 460232

Glasgow Cathedral, Glasgow
Tel: 0141 552 6891

Glenluce Abbey, Nr Glenluce, Dumfries and Galloway
Tel: 01581 300541

Hackness Martello Tower and Battery, Hoy, Orkney
Tel: 01856 701727

Hermitage Castle, Nr Newcastleton, Borders
Tel: 01387 376222

Historic Scotland

1. Urquhart Castle, **2.** Skara Brae, **3.** Kinnaird Head Lighthouse, **4.** Fort George, **5.** Stirling Castle. All images © Historic Scotland

Huntingtower Castle, Nr Perth, Perthshire
Tel: 01738 627231

Huntly Castle, Huntly, Grampian
Tel: 01466 793191

Inchcolm Abbey, Firth of Forth, Fife
Tel: 01383 823332

Inchmahome Priory, Lake of Menteith, Central
Tel: 01877 385294

Iona Abbey and Nunnery, Island of Iona, Argyll
Tel: 01681 700512

Jarlshof Prehistoric and Norse Settlement, Sumburgh Head, Shetland
Tel: 01950 460112

Jedburgh Abbey and Visitor Centre, Jedburgh, Borders
Tel: 01835 863925

Kildrummy Castle, Nr Alford, Grampian
Tel: 01975 571331

Kinnaird Head Castle, Lighthouse and Museum, Fraserburgh, Grampian
Tel: 01346 511022

Kisimul Castle, Isle of Barra, Western Isles
Tel: 01871 810313

Linlithgow Palace, Linlithgow, West Lothian
Tel: 01506 842896

Loch Leven Castle, Lochleven, Perthshire
Tel: 01577 862670

MacLellan's Castle, Kirkcudbright, Dumfries and Galloway
Tel: 01557 331856

Maeshowe Chambered Cairn, Nr Kirkwall, Orkney
Tel: 01856 761606

Meigle Sculptured Stone Museum, Meigle, Angus
Tel: 01828 640612

Melrose Abbey, Melrose, Borders
Tel: 01896 822562

New Abbey Corn Mill, New Abbey, Dumfries and Galloway
Tel: 01387 850260

Newark Castle, Port Glasgow, Greater Glasgow
Tel: 01475 741858

Rothesay Castle, Rothesay, Isle of Bute
Tel: 01700 502691

St Andrews Castle, St Andrews, Fife
Tel: 01334 477196

St Andrews Cathedral, St Andrews, Fife
Tel: 01334 472563

St Serf's Church and Dupplin Cross, Dunning, Perthshire
Tel: 01764 684497

St Vigeans Sculptured Stones, Nr Arbroath, Angus
Tel: 01241 433739

Seton Collegiate Church, Nr Cockenzie, East Lothian
Tel: 01875 813334

Skara Brae and Skaill House, Nr Kirkwall, Orkney
Tel: 01856 841815

Smailholm Tower, Near Smailholm, Borders
Tel: 01573 460365

Spynie Palace, Nr Elgin, Grampian
Tel: 01343 546358

Stanley Mills, North of Perth
Tel: 01738 828268

Stirling Castle, Stirling, Central
Tel: 01786 450000

Sweetheart Abbey, New Abbey, Dumfries and Galloway
Tel: 01387 850397

Tantallon Castle, Nr North Berwick, East Lothian
Tel: 01620 892727

Threave Castle, Nr Castle Douglas, Dumfries and Galloway
Tel: 07711 223101

Tolquhon Castle, Nr Aberdeen, Grampian
Tel: 01651 851286

Urquhart Castle, Drumnadrochit, Highlands
Tel: 01456 450551

For more details on Historic Scotland, write to: Longmore House, Salisbury Place, Edinburgh EH9 1SH

Please call 0131 668 8999, email: hs.members@scotland.gsi.gov.uk or visit the Historic Scotland website at www.historic-scotland.gov.uk

The Friends of Friendless Churches

Wickham Bishops (photo by David Stanford)

The Friends own redundant but beautiful places of worship that would otherwise have been demolished or left to ruin.

Founded by proud Welshman Ivor Bulmer-Thomas in 1957, we now own 40 Grade II* and Grade I buildings in England and Wales. We have recently completed repair campaigns at Boveney (Bucks), Mundon (Essex) and Llancillo (Herefordshire), the first two with help from English Heritage. Pictured above is Wickham Bishops (Essex), once the target for vandals and now in use as a workshop for stained glass artist Benjamin Finn.

We are a small, voluntary organisation that works in partnership, sharing an office and staff with the Ancient Monuments Society, a statutory consultee on listed building consent in England and Wales.

We warmly welcome visitors to our churches, but do not claim sophistication in terms of parking, toilets, attendants or shops, and access may require approach to a key-holder. Our churches are places for quiet study and contemplation, preserved for posterity as beautiful historic buildings.

FRIENDS OF FRIENDLESS CHURCHES

THE FRIENDS OF FRIENDLESS CHURCHES

St Ann's Vestry Hall, 2 Church Entry, London EC4V 5HB

Tel: 020 7236 3934
Email: office@friendsoffriendlesschurches.org.uk

www.friendsoffriendlesschurches.org.uk

Registered charity no: 1113097

Below left to right: Matlock Bath Chapel (photo by Simon Harpur) and Ayshford Chapel, Devon (photo by Apex Photo Agency).

The Churches Conservation Trust

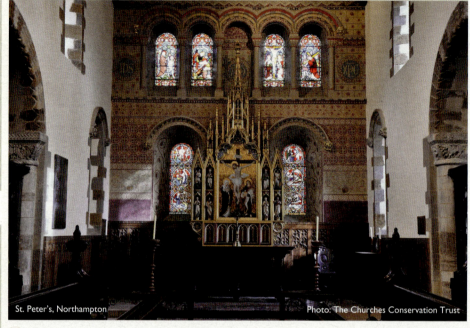

St. Peter's, Northampton

Photo: The Churches Conservation Trust

Explore the beauty and history of some of the most wonderful churches imaginable

The Churches Conservation Trust (CCT) is the national charity protecting historic churches at risk. We've saved over 340 beautiful buildings, which attract more than 1.5 million visitors a year. With our help and with your support they are kept open and in use – living once again at the heart of their communities.

We protect and interpret one of the greatest collections of ecclesiastical architecture and art in the world. Trust churches are scattered throughout the length and breadth of England, in town and country, ranging from ancient, rustic buildings to others of great richness and splendour. Each has been saved because it represents something remarkable.

Our work both in conservation and new uses of churches wins national and international awards. Over 3000 cultural and community events take place in Trust churches across England each year.

We warmly welcome visitors and entry is free. A thousand years of English history awaits you within their walls.

To discover more about this great heritage go to **www.visitchurches.org.uk** where you will find descriptions, directions, photos and much else of interest about the historic churches in the CCT's care.

THE CHURCHES CONSERVATION TRUST

1 West Smithfield
London EC1A 9EE

Tel: 020 7213 0660
Fax: 020 7213 0678
Email: central@tcct.org.uk
www.visitchurches.org.uk

Registered charity no: 258612

The Historic Chapels Trust

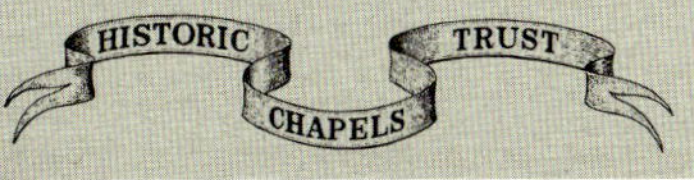

Bethesda Methodist Chapel Photo: The Historic Chapels Trust

Preserving places of worship in England

The Trust was established to take into ownership redundant chapels and other places of worship in England that are of outstanding architectural and historic interest. Our mission is to secure for public benefit their preservation, repair and regeneration.

To the right are 20 of the chapels in our care that you can visit. Please call the keyholder before visiting.

London

The Dissenters' Chapel, Kensal Green Cemetery, London
Tel: 020 7602 0173

St George's German Lutheran Church, Tower Hamlets, London
Tel: 020 7481 0533

South East

Cote Baptist Chapel, Oxfordshire
Tel: 01993 851219

South West

Penrose Methodist Chapel, St Ervan, Cornwall
Tel: 01841 540737

Salem Chapel, East Budleigh, Devon
Tel: 01395 445236/446189

Strict Baptist Chapel, Grittleton, Wiltshire
Tel: 020 7481 0533

East of England

Chantry Chapel, Thorndon Park, Nr Brentwood, Essex
Tel: 020 7481 0533

Walpole Old Chapel, Suffolk
Tel: 01986 798308

West Midlands

Bethesda Methodist Chapel, Stoke-on-Trent, Staffordshire
Tel: 01782 856810

Umberslade Baptist Church, Tanworth-in-Arden, Warwickshire
Tel: 0121 704 2694

Longworth RC Chapel, Bartestree, Herefordshire
Tel: 01432 853200

Yorkshire

Farfield Friends Meeting House, West Yorkshire
Tel: 01756 710587

Todmorden Unitarian Church, West Yorkshire
Tel: 01706 815407

Wainsgate Baptist Church, West Yorkshire
Tel: 01422 843315

North West

Shrine of Our Lady of Lourdes, Blackpool, Lancashire
Tel: 01253 302373

St Benet's Chapel, Netherton, Merseyside
Tel: 0151 520 2600

Wallasey Unitarian Church, Merseyside
Tel: 0151 639 9707

North East

Biddestone RC Chapel, Northumberland
Tel: 01665 574420/01669 630270/01669 620230

Coanwood Friends Meeting House, Northumberland
Tel: 01434 321316

Westgate Methodist Chapel, Co.Durham
Tel: 020 7481 0533

For further information please visit our website www.hct.org.uk or telephone 020 7481 0533.

SOUTH WEST

Bristol
Cornwall
Devon
Dorset
Gloucestershire
Isles of Scilly
Somerset
Wiltshire

English Heritage Sites
Associated Attractions

Isles of Scilly

King Charles's Castle
Cromwell's Castle
Old Blockhouse
Bant's Carn Burial Chamber & Halangy Down Ancient Village
Innisidgen Burial Chambers
Porth Hellick Down Burial Chamber
Garrison Walls
Harry's Walls

Cardigan
Cilgerran Castle
Lampeter
Fishguard
Newport (Pembs.)
Newcastle Emlyn
Talley Abbey
Llandovery
Carreg Cennen Castle
Carmarthen
Llandeilo
Haverfordwest
St. Clears
Laugharne Castle
Kidwelly Castle
Kidwelly
Pont Abraham
Milford Haven
Kilgetty
Saundersfoot
Tenby
Pembroke
Llanelli
Carmarthen Bay
Weobley Castle
Rhossili
Oxwich Castle
Port Talbot
The Mumbles

Lundy Island
Ilfracombe
Combe Martin
Lynmouth
Woolacombe
Croyde
Braunton
Hartland Point
Barnstaple
Bideford
South Molton
Great Torrington
DEVON
Bude
Holsworthy
Hatherleigh
Okehampton
Penhallam Manor
Okehampton Castle
Tintagel Castle
Boscastle
Lydford Castle & Saxon Town
Launceston Castle
Launceston
Tintagel
Grimspound
The Arthurian Centre
CORNWALL
Hound Tor
Camelford
Hurlers Stone Circles
Padstow
Wadebridge
Tavistock
Merrivale Prehistoric Settlement
St Breock Downs Monolith
King Doniert's Stone
Dupath Well
Ashburton
Bodmin
Trethevy Quoit
Upper Plym Valley
Restormel Castle
Liskeard
Totnes Castle
Newquay
Perranporth
St. Austell
PLYMOUTH
Ivybridge
Fowey
Royal Citadel
Looe
St Catherine's Castle
Talland Bay
Modbury
Truro
Kingsbridge
St Ives
St Mawes Castle
Salcombe
Chysauster Ancient Village
Redruth
St. Mawes
Start Point
Ballowall Barrow
St. Just
Trevarno
Falmouth
National Maritime Museum Cornwall
Carn Euny Ancient Village
Penzance
Pendennis Castle
Helston
Land's End
Tregiffian Burial Chamber
Halliggye Fogou
Lizard
Lizard Point

HEREFORDSHIRE
GLOUCESTERSHIRE
S. GLOUCESTERSHIRE
OXFORDSHIRE
BRISTOL
N. SOMERSET
BATH & N.E. SOMERSET
WILTSHIRE
HAMPSHIRE
SOMERSET
DORSET
ISLE OF WIGHT
Bristol Channel
Bill of Portland
Arthur's Stone
Rotherwas Chapel
Longtown Castle
Eastnor Castle
St Mary's Church Kempley
Odda's Chapel
Belas Knap Long Barrow
Hailes Abbey
Sudeley Castle
Rollright Stones
Deddington Castle
Tretower Court & Castle
White Castle
Goodrich Castle
Over Bridge
Notgrove Long Barrow
Minster Lovell Hall & Dovecote
North Leigh Roman Villa
Raglan Castle
Blaenavon Ironworks
Tintern Abbey
St Briavel's Castle
Blackfriars & Greyfriars
Great Witcombe Roman Villa
North Hinksey Conduit House
Offa's Dyke
Nympsfield Long Barrow
Woodchester Mansion
Cirencester Amphitheatre
Abingdon County Hall
Caerphilly Castle
Kingswood Abbey Gatehouse
Uley Long Barrow
Windmill Tump Long Barrow
Caerleon Roman Fortress
Chepstow Castle
Wayland's Smithy
Uffington Castle, White Horse & Dragon Hill
Castell Coch
NMR
Sir Bevil Grenville's Monument
Avebury Stone Circles & Alexander Keiller Museum
Windmill Hill
Silbury Hill
Donnington Castle
Temple Church
Bowood House
West Kennet Avenue & Long Barrow
The Sanctuary
Chisbury Chapel
Stanton Drew Circles & Cove
Bradford-on-Avon Tithe Barn
Hatfield Earthworks (Marden Henge)
Stoney Littleton Long Barrow
Farleigh Hungerford Castle
Wiltshire Heritage Museum
Ludgershall Castle & Cross
Nunney Castle
Bratton Camp & White Horse
Netheravon Dovecote
Woodhenge
Stonehenge
Meare Fish House
Glastonbury Tribunal
Gallox Bridge
Cleeve Abbey
Flowerdown Barrows
Old Sarum
Old Wardour Castle
Wolvesey Castle
Muchelney Abbey
Sherborne Old Castle
Salisbury & South Wilts Museum
Sherborne Castle
Fiddleford Manor
Medieval Merchant's House
Coldharbour Mill Museum
Knowlton Church & Earthworks
Netley Abbey
Calshot Castle
Christchurch Castle & Norman House
Yarmouth Castle
The Nine Stones
Winterbourne Poor Lot Barrows
Maiden Castle
Blackbury Camp
Kingston Russell Stone Circle
Jordan Hill Roman Temple
Hurst Castle
Carisbrooke Castle
Lulworth Castle
Powderham Castle
St Catherine's Chapel
Abbotsbury Abbey Remains
Portland Castle
St Catherine's Oratory
Kirkham House
Bayard's Cove Fort
Dartmouth Castle
Berry Pomeroy Castle
Dunster Butter Cross
Queenswood
Hay-on-Wye
Hereford
Ledbury
Great Malvern
Pershore
Evesham
Upton-upon-Severn
Tewkesbury
Broadway
Moreton-in-Marsh
Banbury
Chipping Norton
Brecon
Tretower
Crickhowell
Ross-on-Wye
Newent
Winchcombe
CHELTENHAM
Stow-on-the-Wold
GLOUCESTER
Woodstock
Abergavenny
Monmouth
Northleach
Burford
Witney
Pont Nedd Fechan
Merthyr Tydfil
Coleford
Aberdare
Blaenafon
Stroud
Cirencester
Lechlade
Faringdon
Abingdon
Chepstow
Caerleon
Tetbury
Wantage
Pontypridd
Caerphilly
Magor
Malmesbury
SWINDON
Chipping Sodbury
Bridgend
Avonmouth
Chippenham
Avebury
Marlborough
Hungerford
Penarth
Barry Island
WESTON-SUPER-MARE
BATH
Newbury
Devizes
Trowbridge
Cheddar
Burnham-on-Sea
Wells
Westbury
Frome
Minehead
Andover
Warminster
Amesbury
Bridgwater
Glastonbury
Stockbridge
Mere
Salisbury
Winchester
Taunton
Podimore
Shaftesbury
EASTLEIGH
Bampton
Wellington
Ilchester
Romsey
Sherborne
SOUTHAMPTON
Yeovil
Fordingbridge
Ilminster
Tiverton
Chard
Blandford Forum
Lyndhurst
Ringwood
Wimborne Minster
Honiton
Ottery St Mary
Axminster
Lymington
Cowes
Christchurch
Bridport
Dorchester
POOLE
EXETER
Seaton
Lyme Regis
Abbotsbury
Wareham
BOURNEMOUTH
Yarmouth
Sidmouth
Exmouth
Budleigh Salterton
Weymouth
Swanage
Dawlish
Teignmouth
TORQUAY
Paignton
Brixham
Dartmouth
0Kms 10 20 30
0Miles 10 20
Created by Arka Cartographics Ltd. for English Heritage. © 10/10

WARWICKSHIRE
Warwick
Warwick Castle
Royal Leamington Spa
Daventry
Althorp
NORTHAMPTON
78, Derngate
Bushmead Priory
St. Neots
BEDFORDSHIRE
Sandy
BEDFORD
Biggleswade
Houghton House
Stratford-upon-Avon
Heritage Motor Museum
Towcester
Newport Pagnell
MILTON KEYNES
Pershore
Evesham
Banbury
Brackley
Buckingham
Bletchley
De Grey Mausoleum
Wrest Park
Woburn Abbey
Letchworth
Broadway
Moreton-in-Marsh
Rollright Stones
Belas Knap Long Barrow
Hailes Abbey
Winchcombe
Sudeley Castle
Chipping Norton
Deddington Castle
BUCKINGHAMSHIRE
Dunstable
Stevenage
CHELTENHAM
Notgrove Long Barrow
Stow-on-the-Wold
Bicester
LUTON
HERTS
Woodstock
Old Gorhambury House
Northleach
Minster Lovell Hall & Dovecote
North Leigh Roman Villa
Aylesbury
Berkhamsted Castle
Tring
Great Witcombe Roman Villa
Burford
Rycote Chapel
Roman Wall
GLOUCESTERSHIRE
Witney
Wendover
Berkhamsted
HEMEL HEMPSTEAD
St. Albans
Cirencester
North Hinksey Conduit House
OXFORD
Thame
Cirencester Amphitheatre
Lechlade
Amersham
London Transport Museum
Windmill Tump Long Barrow
Faringdon
Abingdon County Hall
Abingdon
HIGH WYCOMBE
OXFORDSHIRE
Kensal Green Cemetery
Kenwood
Wayland's Smithy
Malmesbury
SWINDON
NMR
Wantage
Didcot
Wallingford
Marlow
Churchill Museum & Cabinet Rooms
Uffington Castle, White Horse & Dragon Hill
Maidenhead
Henley-on-Thames
SLOUGH
Apsley House
Windmill Hill
Avebury Stone Circles & Alexander Keiller Museum
Chiswick House
Donnington Castle
READING
Windsor
Bowood House
Silbury Hill
Marble Hill House
Avebury
Marlborough
Coombe Conduit
Bracknell
West Kennet Avenue & Long Barrow
The Sanctuary
Hungerford
Newbury
BERKSHIRE
Albert Memorial
Wellington Arch
Chisbury Chapel
Aldermaston
Silchester Roman City Walls & Amphitheatre
Devizes
Wiltshire Heritage Museum
Hatfield Earthworks
WOKING
CAMBERLEY
Fleet
Leatherhead
WILTSHIRE
Ludgershall Castle & Cross
BASINGSTOKE
Aldershot
Reigate
Bratton Camp & White Horse
Netheravon Dovecote
Farnham Castle Keep
GUILDFORD
Dorking
Farnham
Waverley Abbey
Andover
Stonehenge
Woodhenge
SURREY
Amesbury
HAMPSHIRE
Alton
Old Sarum
Stockbridge
Flowerdown Barrows
The Grange at Northington
CRAWLEY
Old Wardour Castle
Salisbury
Winchester
Haslemere
Horsham
Salisbury & South Wilts Museum
Wolvesey Castle
WEST SUSSEX
Bishop's Waltham Palace
Petersfield
Midhurst
Petworth
EASTLEIGH
Romsey
Bramber Castle
Goodwood House
Fordingbridge
SOUTHAMPTON
Medieval Merchant's House
Southwick Priory
Boxgrove Priory
Arundel Castle
Knowlton Church & Earthworks
Titchfield Abbey
Fishbourne Roman Palace
Netley Abbey
Fontwell
Lyndhurst
FAREHAM
Portchester Castle
Arundel
Hove
Ringwood
CHICHESTER
WORTHING
Wimborne Minster
Christchurch Castle & Norman House
Calshot Castle
PORTSMOUTH
Royal Garrison Church
Marlipins Museum
Lymington
Cowes
Fort Cumberland
Bognor Regis
Hayling Island
Christchurch
Hurst Castle
Carisbrooke Castle
Ryde
Selsey
POOLE
Yarmouth
Newport
King James's & Landport Gates
BOURNEMOUTH
Yarmouth Castle
Newport Roman Villa
Fort Brockhurst
Wareham
Sandown
Royal Osborne
Shanklin
ISLE OF WIGHT
St Catherine's Oratory
Swanage
Ventnor
Appuldurcombe House

LONDON AND SOUTH EAST
Berkshire
Buckinghamshire
East Sussex
Hampshire
Isle of Wight
Kent
Oxfordshire
Surrey
West Sussex
English Heritage Sites
Associated Attractions
F
G
H
I
J
K
2
3
4
5
6
7
Newmarket
Bury St Edmunds
Moulton Packhorse Bridge
Bury St Edmunds Abbey
Stowmarket
CAMBRIDGE
Duxford Chapel
Imperial War Museum Duxford
Haverhill
Lavenham
Sudbury
Lindsey/St James's Chapel
Audley End House & Gardens
Saffron Walden
Mistley Towers
Halstead
St Botolph's Priory
Prior's Hall Barn
ESSEX
Flatford
Lexden Earthworks & Bluebottle Grove
St John's Abbey Gate
Braintree
COLCHESTER
Bishop's Stortford
Layer Marney Tower
HERTS
Birchanger Green
Tiptree
Hertford
Witham
West Mersea
HARLOW
CHELMSFORD
Maldon
Waltham Abbey Gatehouse & Bridge
Epping
Hill Hall
London Canal Museum
Southminster
Winchester Palace
HMS Belfast
Brentwood
Ranger's House
The Wernher Collection
Hadleigh Castle
London Wall
BASILDON
SOUTHEND-ON-SEA
Eltham Palace & Gardens
Canvey Island
Tilbury Fort
Rochester Castle
Danson House
Fort Amherst
Sheerness
Milton Chantry
Upnor Castle
Faversham Stone Chapel
Bexley
Reculver Towers & Roman Fort
Herne Bay
MARGATE
Dulwich Picture Gallery
Eynsford Castle
Temple Manor
The Historic Dockyard
Broadstairs
Whitstable
Ramsgate
GILLINGHAM
St Augustine's Cross
Lullingstone Roman Villa
Kit's Coty House
Sittingbourne
Faversham
Richborough Roman Fort & Amphitheatre
Canterbury
Home of Charles Darwin
Sevenoaks
St Leonard's Tower
Maison Dieu
Sandwich
MAIDSTONE
St Augustine's Abbey & Conduit House
Deal Castle
Leeds Castle
Deal
Lullingstone Castle
Old Soar Manor
KENT
Walmer Castle & Gardens
Edenbridge
Tonbridge
Sutton Valence Castle
Western Heights
Ashford
St John's Commandery
Dover Castle
East Grinstead
Penshurst Place
Dover
Royal Tunbridge Wells
Westenhanger Castle
Cranbrook
Dover Museum
Folkestone
The Priest House
Bayham Old Abbey
Tenterden
Hythe
Knights Templar Church
EAST SUSSEX
Horne's Place Chapel
Dymchurch
Haywards Heath
Dymchurch Martello Tower
1066 Battle of Hastings Abbey & Battlefield
Rye
New Romney
Uckfield
Lydd
Camber Castle
Lewes Castle & Barbican House Museum
Battle
Boship
Hailsham
Lewes
Anne of Cleves House
Michelham Priory
HASTINGS
Bexhill
Pevensey
Newhaven
Pevensey Castle
Seaford
EASTBOURNE
Kms 10 20 30
Miles 10 20
Created by Arka Cartographics Ltd. for English Heritage. © 10/10

EAST OF ENGLAND

Bedfordshire
Cambridgeshire
Essex
Hertfordshire
Norfolk
Suffolk

English Heritage Sites
Associated Attractions

NOTTINGHAMSHIRE
Mansfield
Rufford Abbey
Papplewick Pumping Station
NOTTINGHAM
West Bridgford
Newark-on-Trent
Woodhall Spa
Coningsby
Tattershall College
Sleaford
Grantham
Belvoir Castle
Melton Mowbray
Loughborough
Spalding
LEICESTERSHIRE
RUTLAND
Kirby Muxloe Castle
LEICESTER
Oakham
Rutland Water
Stamford
Burghley House
Jewry Wall
Lyddington Bede House
Longthorpe Tower
PETERBOROUGH
Flag F Bronze A Cen
Apethorpe Hall
Rockingham Castle
Kirby Hall
Corby
Oundle
CAMBS.
Market Harborough
Rushton Triangular Lodge
Eleanor Cross
Kelmarsh Hall
Kettering
Huntingdon
TAMWORTH
WOLVERHAMPTON
WALSALL
WEST MIDLANDS
Bosworth Battlefield
Hinckley
NUNEATON
DUDLEY
JW Evans Silver Factory
Merry Hill
BIRMINGHAM
SOLIHULL
COVENTRY
Lutterworth
Halesowen Abbey
RUGBY
NORTHAMPTONSHIRE
Bromsgrove
Kenilworth
Kenilworth Castle & Elizabethan Garden
Stoneleigh Abbey
Royal Leamington Spa
WORCS.
Warwick
Warwick Castle
Daventry
Althorp
Wellingborough
Chichele College
Droitwich Spa
78, Derngate
NORTHAMPTON
Bushmead Priory
St. Neo
WARWICKSHIRE
Stratford-upon-Avon
Heritage Motor Centre
BEDFORDSHIRE
Sandy
BEDFORD
Pershore
Evesham
Towcester
Newport Pagnell
MILTON KEYNES
Biggleswade
Houghton House
Broadway
Banbury
Brackley
De Grey Mausoleum
Wrest Park
Belas Knap Long Barrow
Moreton-in-Marsh
Rollright Stones
Buckingham
Bletchley
Woburn Abbey
Letchworth
Hailes Abbey
Winchcombe
Sudeley Castle
Chipping Norton
Deddington Castle
BUCKINGHAMSHIRE
Stevenage
CHELTENHAM
Stow-on-the-Wold
Bicester
Dunstable
LUTON
Notgrove Long Barrow
Minster Lovell Hall & Dovecote
Woodstock
Old Gorhambury House
HERTS
Great Witcombe Roman Villa
Northleach
North Leigh Roman Villa
Aylesbury
Berkhamsted Castle
Tring
Roman Wall
GLOUS.
Burford
Witney
Rycote Chapel
Wendover
Berkhamsted
HEMEL HEMPSTEAD
St.Albans
Cirencester
Cirencester Amphitheatre
North Hinksey Conduit House
OXFORD
Thame
Lechlade
Lond Transp Museu
Windmill Tump Long Barrow
Faringdon
Abingdon County Hall
Abingdon
Amersham
HIGH WYCOMBE
OXFORDSHIRE
Kensal Green Cemetery
Kenwood
Wayland's Smithy
Malmesbury
SWINDON
NMR
Wantage
Didcot
Wallingford
Marlow
Churchill Museum & Cabinet Rooms
Uffington Castle, White Horse & Dragon Hill
Maidenhead
SLOUGH
Apsley House
Windmill Hill
Avebury Stone Circles & Alexander Keiller Museum
Henley-on-Thames
Chiswick House
Bowood House
Donnington Castle
READING
Windsor
Silbury Hill
Marble Hill House
Avebury
Hungerford
Coombe Conduit
West Kennet Avenue & Long Barrow
Marlborough
The Sanctuary
Chisbury Chapel
Newbury
Aldermaston
BERKSHIRE
Bracknell
Albert Memorial
Wellington Arch

Created by Arka Cartographics Ltd. for English Heritage. © 10/10

F
G
H
J
K
0 Kms 10 20 30
0 Miles 10 20
Sibsey Trader Windmill
Boston
The Wash
Hunstanton
Holkham Hall
Wells-next-the-Sea
Blakeney Guildhall
Sheringham
Cromer
Creake Abbey
Holt
Baconsthorpe Castle
Binham Priory
Binham Market Cross
Mundesley
Castle Rising Castle
Fakenham
Aylsham
North Walsham
Long Sutton
King's Lynn
Castle Acre Bailey Gate
Castle Acre Castle
North Elmham Chapel
Hoveton
Hemsby
Castle Acre Priory
East Dereham
Cow Tower
NORWICH
Great Yarmouth Row Houses & Greyfriars' Cloisters
Caister Roman Site
Great Yarmouth
Wisbech
Downham Market
Swaffham
Norwich Castle
Berney Arms Windmill
Time & Tide Museum
NORFOLK
Wymondham
Loddon
Burgh Castle
March
Somerleyton Hall & Gardens
Grime's Graves
Attleborough
St Olave's Priory
LOWESTOFT
Thetford Warren Lodge
Weeting Castle
Thetford Priory
Bungay
Beccles
CAMBRIDGESHIRE
Brandon
Thetford
Kessingland
Chatteris
Isleham Priory Church
Church of the Holy Sepulchre
Diss
Ely
Halesworth
Southwold
SUFFOLK
Denny Abbey & the Farmland Museum
Bury St Edmunds Abbey
Framlingham Castle
Saxtead Green Post Mill
Newmarket
Bury St Edmunds
Leiston Abbey
Moulton Packhorse Bridge
Stowmarket
CAMBRIDGE
Aldeburgh
Woodbridge
Duxford Chapel
Lavenham
Lindsey/ St James's Chapel
Orford Castle
Orford
Imperial War Museum Duxford
Haverhill
IPSWICH
Sudbury
Saffron Walden
Audley End House & Gardens
Mistley Towers
Felixstowe
Felixstowe Museum
Landguard Fort
Halstead
St Botolph's Priory
Prior's Hall Barn
ESSEX
Flatford
Harwich
Lexden Earthworks & Bluebottle Grove
St John's Abbey Gate
Bishop's Stortford
Braintree
COLCHESTER
Walton-on-the-Naze
HERTS.
Layer Marney Tower
Frinton-on-Sea
Birchanger Green
Tiptree
Witham
Clacton-on-Sea
West Mersea
HARLOW
CHELMSFORD
Maldon
Waltham Abbey Gatehouse & Bridge
Epping
Hill Hall
Southminster
Winchester Palace
Brentwood
Ranger's House
Hadleigh Castle
The Wernher Collection
BASILDON
SOUTHEND-ON-SEA
London Wall
Eltham Palace & Gardens
Canvey Island
Tilbury Fort
Rochester Castle
Danson House
Fort Amherst
Sheerness
Milton Chantry
Upnor Castle
Faversham Stone Chapel
Reculver Towers & Roman Fort
MARGATE
Herne Bay
Broadstairs
Dulwich Picture Gallery
Temple Manor
The Historic Dockyard
Ramsgate
Whitstable
Eynsford Castle
St Augustine's Cross

279

WEST MIDLANDS

Herefordshire
Shropshire
Staffordshire
Warwickshire
West Midlands
Worcestershire

⌗ English Heritage Sites
▲ Associated Attractions

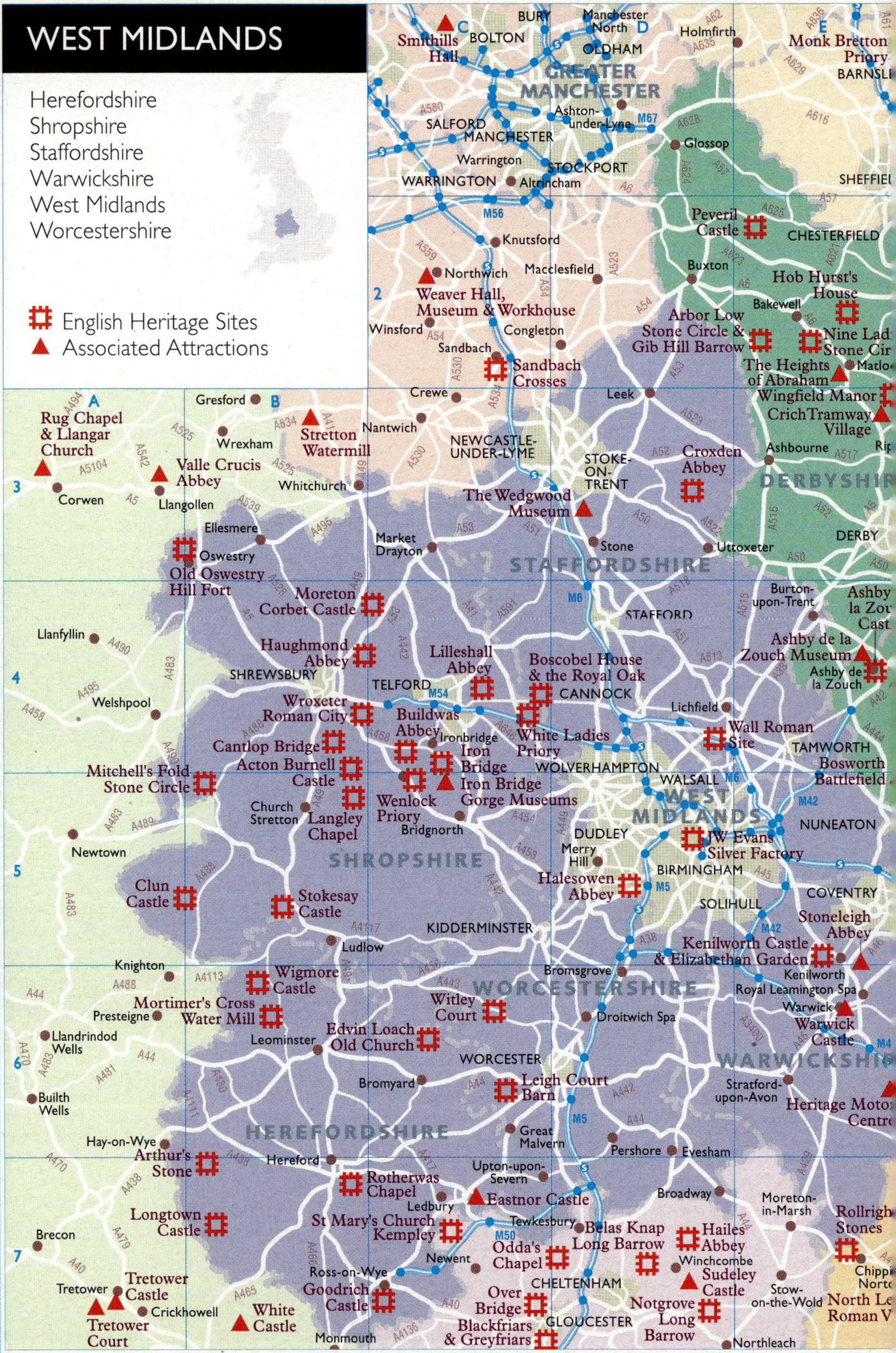

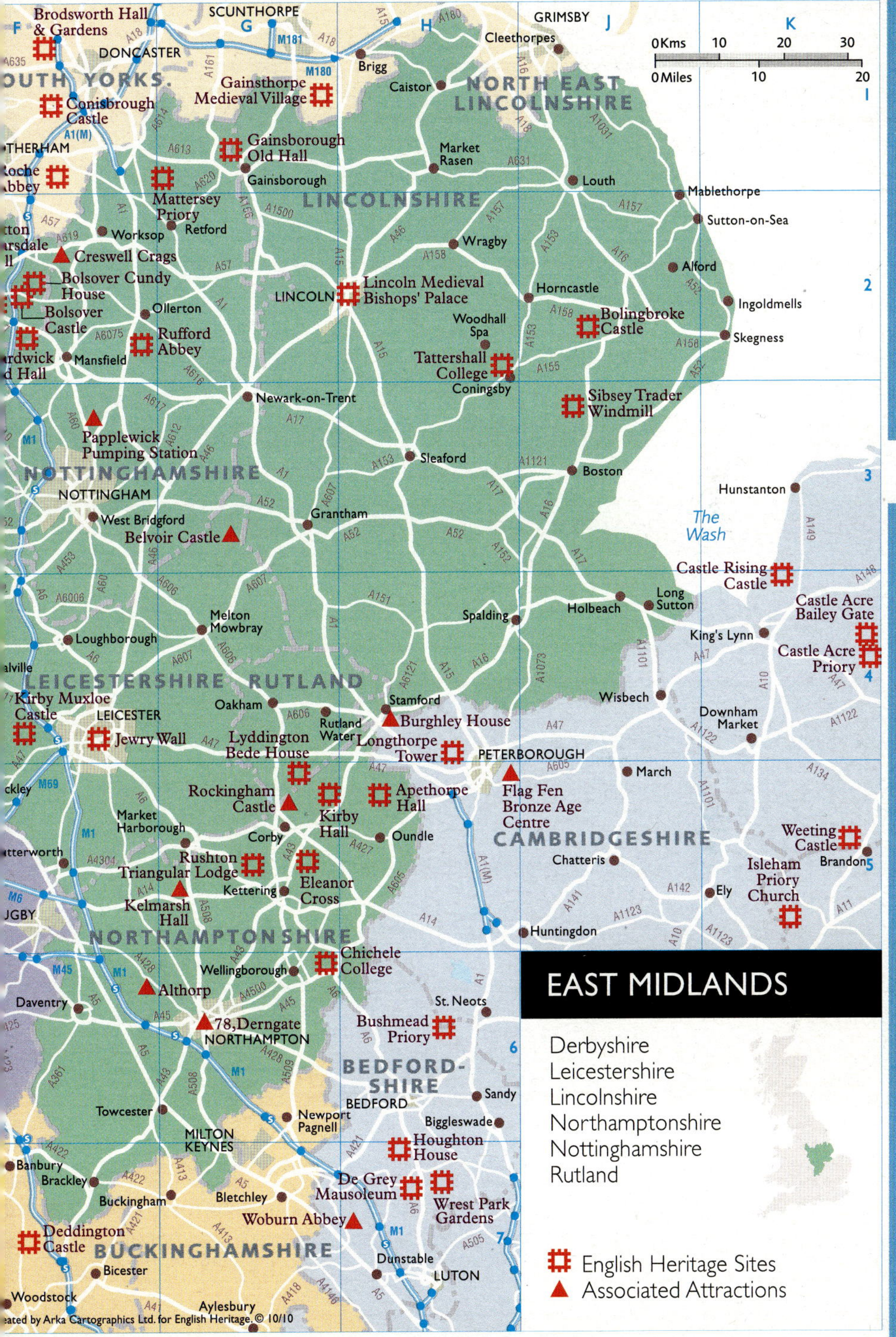
Brodsworth Hall & Gardens
SCUNTHORPE
GRIMSBY
Cleethorpes
DONCASTER
Brigg
Caistor
SOUTH YORKS.
Gainsthorpe Medieval Village
NORTH EAST LINCOLNSHIRE
Conisbrough Castle
Gainsborough Old Hall
Market Rasen
Gainsborough
Louth
Mablethorpe
Mattersey Priory
LINCOLNSHIRE
Sutton-on-Sea
Worksop
Retford
Wragby
Creswell Crags
Alford
Bolsover Cundy House
LINCOLN
Lincoln Medieval Bishops' Palace
Horncastle
Ingoldmells
Bolsover Castle
Ollerton
Woodhall Spa
Bolingbroke Castle
Skegness
Rufford Abbey
Mansfield
Tattershall College
Coningsby
Newark-on-Trent
Sibsey Trader Windmill
Papplewick Pumping Station
Sleaford
NOTTINGHAMSHIRE
Boston
Hunstanton
NOTTINGHAM
The Wash
West Bridgford
Grantham
Belvoir Castle
Castle Rising Castle
Long Sutton
Holbeach
Castle Acre Bailey Gate
Melton Mowbray
Spalding
King's Lynn
Loughborough
Castle Acre Priory
LEICESTERSHIRE
RUTLAND
Kirby Muxloe Castle
Oakham
Stamford
Wisbech
LEICESTER
Rutland Water
Burghley House
Downham Market
Jewry Wall
Lyddington Bede House
Longthorpe Tower
PETERBOROUGH
Rockingham Castle
Apethorpe Hall
Flag Fen Bronze Age Centre
March
Market Harborough
Kirby Hall
Oundle
Weeting Castle
Corby
CAMBRIDGESHIRE
Rushton Triangular Lodge
Eleanor Cross
Chatteris
Isleham Priory Church
Brandon
Kettering
Ely
Kelmarsh Hall
NORTHAMPTONSHIRE
Huntingdon
Chichele College
Wellingborough
Daventry
Althorp
St. Neots
78,Derngate
NORTHAMPTON
Bushmead Priory
BEDFORDSHIRE
Sandy
BEDFORD
Towcester
Newport Pagnell
Biggleswade
MILTON KEYNES
Houghton House
Banbury
Brackley
De Grey Mausoleum
Wrest Park Gardens
Buckingham
Bletchley
Woburn Abbey
Deddington Castle
BUCKINGHAMSHIRE
Dunstable
LUTON
Bicester
Woodstock
Aylesbury
0 Kms 10 20 30
0 Miles 10 20
EAST MIDLANDS
Derbyshire
Leicestershire
Lincolnshire
Northamptonshire
Nottinghamshire
Rutland
English Heritage Sites
Associated Attractions

NORTH WEST (South)
Cheshire
Greater Manchester
Lancashire
Merseyside
English Heritage Sites
Associated Attractions
0Kms 10 20 30
0 Miles 10 20
A
B
C
D
E
1
2
3
4
5
6
7
CUMBRIA
LANCASHIRE
MERSEYSIDE
GREATER MANCHESTER
CHESHIRE
Maryport
Cockermouth
Workington
WHITEHAVEN
Egremont
Penrith Castle
Mayburgh Henge
PENRITH
Brougham Castle
Castlerigg Stone Circle
Clifton Hall
Countess Pillar
Keswick
King Arthur's Round Table
Appleby-in-Westmorland
Ullswater
Shap Abbey
Brough Castle
Brough
Bowes Castle
Seatoller Barn
Grasmere
Ambleside
Hardknott Roman Fort
Ambleside Roman Fort
Waterhead
Kirkby Stephen
Tebay
Sellafield
Windermere
Ravenglass
Muncaster Castle
Hawkshead
Coniston
Kendal
Sedbergh
Ravenglass Roman Bath House
Broughton-in-Furness
Stott Park Bobbin Mill
Hawes
Aysgarth Falls
Bootle
Millom
Ulverston
Grange-over-Sands
Kirkby Lonsdale
Horton-in-Ribblesdale
Furness Abbey
Warton Old Rectory
Ingleton
Bow Bridge
BARROW-IN-FURNESS
Carnforth
Clapham
Morecambe
High Bentham
Settle
Grassington
Piel Castle
Lancaster
Malham
Piel Island
Morecambe Bay
Skipton
Fleetwood
Sawley Abbey
Barnoldswick
Garstang
Cleveleys
Clitheroe
Pendle Heritage Centre
Whalley Abbey Gatehouse
BLACKPOOL
BURNLEY
Accrington
Hebden Bridge
Lytham St. Anne's
PRESTON
BLACKBURN
Goodshaw Chapel
Oswaldtwistle
Rawtenstall
SOUTHPORT
Chorley
Smithills Hall
ROCHDALE
Ormskirk
BURY
Manchester North
Formby
BOLTON
OLDHAM
BOOTLE
KIRKBY
ST. HELENS
St Helens
SALFORD
Ashton-under-Lyne
MANCHESTER
Glossop
LIVERPOOL
Warrington
STOCKPORT
BIRKENHEAD
Runcorn
WIDNES
WARRINGTON
Altrincham
Norton Priory Museum & Gardens
RUNCORN
Knutsford
ELLESMERE PORT
Neston
Northwich
Macclesfield
Flint
Weaver Hall, Museum & Workhouse
CHESTER
Winsford
Mold
Chester Castle
Sandbach
Congleton
Chester Roman Amphitheatre
Beeston Castle & Woodland Park
Sandbach Crosses
Crewe
Leek
Gresford
Wrexham
Stretton Watermill
Nantwich
NEWCASTLE-UNDER-LYME
STOKE-ON-TRENT
Whitchurch
Llandudno
Rhos-on-Sea
Rhyl
Prestatyn
Conwy
Colwyn Bay
Conwy Castle
Plas Mawr
Rhuddlan Castle
Denbigh
Ruthin
Betws-y-Coed
Dolwyddelan Castle
Rug Chapel & Llangar Church
Valle Crucis Abbey
Blaenau Ffestiniog
Corwen
Llangollen
Created by Arka Cartographics Ltd. for English Heritage. © 10/10

YORKSHIRE
East Riding of Yorkshire
North East Lincolnshire
North Lincolnshire
North Yorkshire
South Yorkshire
West Yorkshire
English Heritage Sites
Associated Attractions
Auckland Castle Deer House
Piercebridge Roman Bridge
Stanwick Iron Age Fortifications
Easby Abbey
Middleham Castle
Marmion Tower
St Mary's Church, Studley Royal
Fountains Abbey
Mount Grace Priory
Gisborough Priory
Whitby Abbey
Wheeldale Roman Road
Scarborough Castle
Rievaulx Abbey
Helmsley Castle
Byland Abbey & the Abbey Inn
Duncombe Park
Pickering Castle
North York Moors Railway
Aldborough Roman Site
Castle Howard
Kirkham Priory
Wharram Percy Deserted Medieval Village
Burton Agnes Manor House
Skipsea Castle
Clifford's Tower
Merchant Adventurers' Hall
York Cold War Bunker
DIG
Barley Hall
Micklegate Bar Museum
York Minster
Jorvik Viking Centre
Spofforth Castle
Harewood House
National Media Centre
Steeton Hall Gateway
Howden Minster
St Peter's Church
Thornton Abbey & Gatehouse
Monk Bretton Priory
Brodsworth Hall & Gardens
Conisbrough Castle
Gainsthorpe Medieval Village
Gainsborough Old Hall
Roche Abbey
Mattersey Priory
Creswell Crags
Sutton Scarsdale Hall
Bolsover Cundy House
Bolsover Castle
Hob Hurst's House
Nine Ladies Stone Circle
Hardwick Old Hall
Rufford Abbey
The Heights of Abraham
Wingfield Manor
Crich Tramway Village
Papplewick Pumping Station
Croxden Abbey
HARTLEPOOL
TEES VALLEY
STOCKTON-ON-TEES
MIDDLESBROUGH
DARLINGTON
DURHAM
NORTH YORKSHIRE
SCARBOROUGH
EAST RIDING OF YORKSHIRE
KINGSTON UPON HULL
WEST YORKSHIRE
LEEDS
BRADFORD
HARROGATE
YORK
WAKEFIELD
HUDDERSFIELD
NORTH LINCOLNSHIRE
SCUNTHORPE
GRIMSBY
NORTH EAST LINCOLNSHIRE
SOUTH YORKSHIRE
BARNSLEY
DONCASTER
ROTHERHAM
SHEFFIELD
CHESTERFIELD
DERBYSHIRE
NOTTINGHAMSHIRE
NOTTINGHAM

NORTH WEST (North)

Cumbria

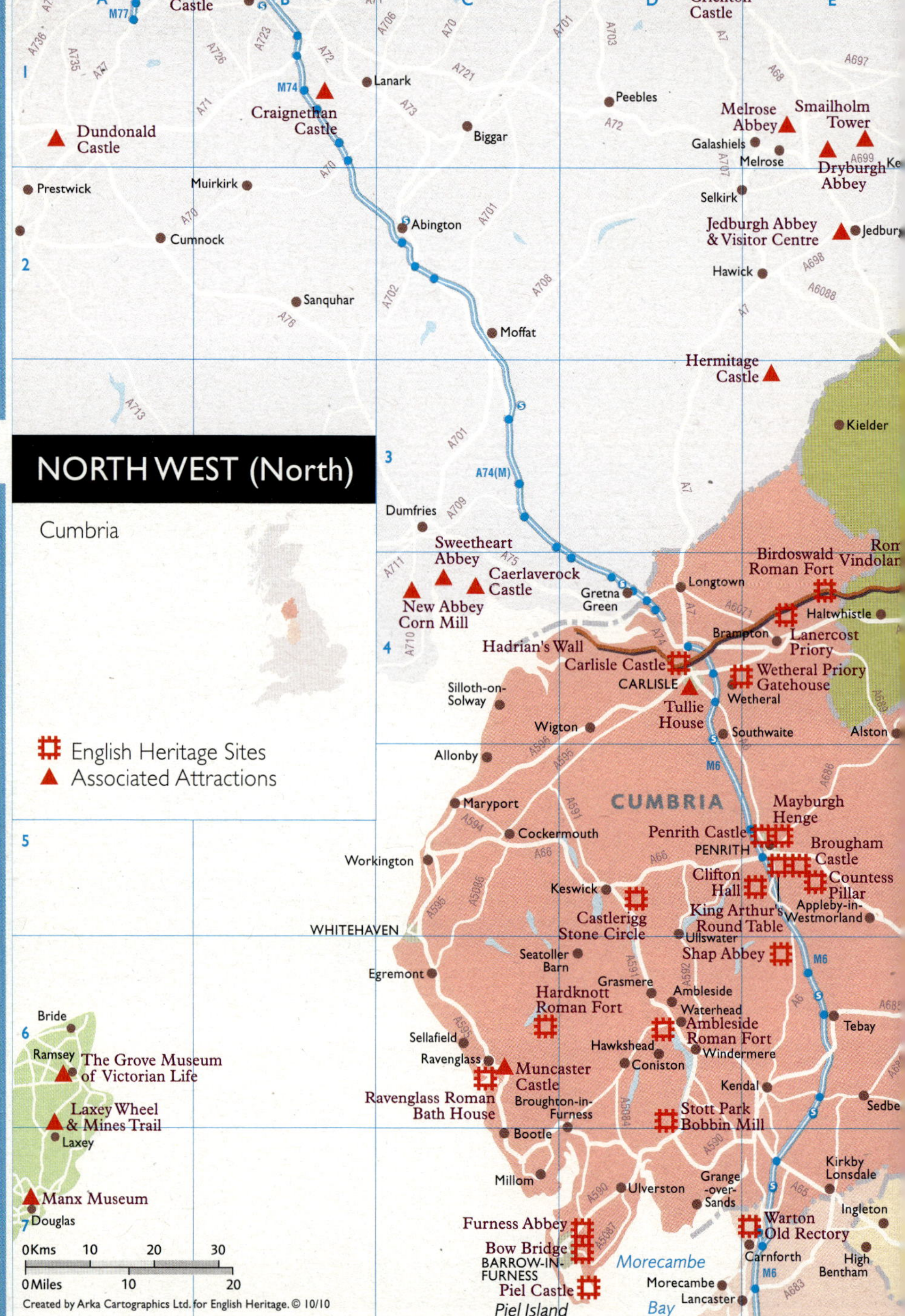

NORTH EAST

County Durham
Northumberland
Tyne & Wear
Tees Valley

English Heritage Sites
Associated Attractions

English Heritage Members' & Visitors' Handbook 2011/12

For English Heritage: Kate Linnell, Kathryn Steele-Childe, Tersia Boorer, Charles Kightly, Emma Simms, Amanda Smyth.

Design and Publishing: Ledgard Jepson Ltd

For Ledgard Jepson Ltd: David Exley, Bev Turbitt, Andrea Rollinson.

Print: Pindar plc

Transport Information: John Burch, CPT.